GW00854178

WORK OUT
BUSINESS STUDIES A-LEVEL

The titles in this series

For GCSE examinations

Accounting
Biology
Business Studies
Chemistry
Computer Studies
Economics
English
French
Geography
German

Graphic Communication
Human Biology
Maths
Modern World History
Numeracy
Physics
Social and Economic history
Spanish
Statistics

For 'A' Level examinations

Accounting
Applied Maths
Biology
Business Studies
Chemistry
Economics
English

English Literature
French (tape and pack available)
Physics
Pure Maths
Sociology
Statistics

College Work Outs for degree and professional students

Dynamics
Electric Circuits
Electromagnetic Fields
Electronics
Elements of Banking
Engineering Materials
Engineering Thermodynamics
Fluid Mechanics

Mathematics for Economists
Molecular Genetics
Operational Research
Organic Chemistry
Physical Chemistry
Structural Mechanics
Waves and Optics

MACMILLAN WORK OUT SERIES

WORK OUT
BUSINESS STUDIES A-LEVEL

Gerry Gorman

MACMILLAN

First published 1992 by
THE MACMILLAN PRESS LTD
Houndmills, Basingstoke, Hampshire RG21 2XS
and London
Companies and representatives
throughout the world

ISBN 0–333–53698–3

A catalogue record for this book is
available from the British Library.

Filmset by Wearside Tradespools,
Boldon, Tyne and Wear
Printed in China

10   9   8   7   6   5   4   3
01 00 99 98 97 96 95 94

CONTENTS

Acknowledgements   vii

1 Introduction to Business   1

The scope of business   1
Business aims and objectives   2
The size of business   4
Small firms   7
Growth   7
Worked examples   10
Self-test questions   13

2 Types of Business Organisation   15

Types of business   15
Principles of business organisation   15
Sole trader   16
Partnership   16
Private limited company   17
Public limited company   18
Registration of joint-stock companies   19
Co-operatives   19
Public corporations   21
Privatisation   22
Worked examples   22
Self-test questions   27

3 Information and Decision-making   28

Business information   28
Presentation of information   29
Decision trees   33
Networks   35
Worked examples   38
Self-test questions   47

4 Finance   52

The need for finance   52
Internal finance   52
External finance   54
The Stock Exchange   56
Worked examples   59
Self-test questions   61

5 Accounting   63

The need for financial records   63
Costs, revenues and profits   63
The balance sheet   65
The funds flow statement   66
The profit and loss account   67
Working capital   68

Stock turnover   69
Ratio analysis   69
Worked examples   71
Self-test questions   77

6 Production   82

The production function   82
Methods of production   82
Division of labour   84
Production planning and control   85
Production activities   85
Location of industry   87
Information technology   88
Worked examples   91
Self-test questions   96

7 Marketing   98

What is marketing?   98
The marketing process   98
Consumer and industrial markets   99
Market demand, supply and price   100
Market demand   101
Market supply   103
Market price   104
Elasticities of demand   105
Market research   107
Worked examples   111
Self-test questions   114

8 The Marketing Mix   116

The marketing mix   116
Product   116
Price   124
Promotion   126
Place   132
Worked examples   137
Self-test questions   142

9 Internal Organisation   146

Functions of management   146
Organisation charts   147
Principles of internal organisation   147
Communication   152
Methods of communication   153
Worked examples   154
Self-test questions   156

10　*Personnel Management*　157

Functions of personnel management　157
Motivation　159
Payment systems　160
Manpower planning　161
Recruitment　162
Selection　164
Induction　165
Training　165
Performance appraisal　167
Worked examples　167
Self-test questions　169

11　*Industrial Relations*　172

What is industrial relations?　172
Trade unions and employers' associations　173
Collective bargaining　174
Worked examples　175
Self-test questions　177

12　*The Economic Framework*　178

Scarcity and choice　178
The free market economy　179
The planned economy　179
The mixed economy　180
Specialisation and exchange　180
External costs and benefits　181
Industrial structure　181
Government economic policy　182

International trade　186
Protectionism　187
The balance of Payments　188
Exchange rates　188
Difficulties of exporting　190
The European Community (EC)　191
Worked examples　191
Self-test questions　194

13　*The External Environment of Business*　196

External influences on business　196
Government assistance to business　196
Government regulation of business　201
Consumer organisations　203
Pressure groups　208
Business and change　208
Worked examples　209
Self-test questions　211

14　*Coursework*　212

Why do coursework?　212
Coursework requirements　212
Getting ideas for coursework　212
Choosing a title　214
What information is needed?　215
Sources of information　215
Writing the assignment　216

Index　217

ACKNOWLEDGEMENTS

The author and publishers wish to thank the following for permission to use copyright material: The Association of Consumer Research, Avon Cosmetics Ltd, British Nuclear Fuels plc, British Steel (Industry) Ltd, Computerland Europe, Co-operative Wholesale Society Ltd, Dalgety PLC, Goodyear Great Britain Ltd, Greenpeace Ltd, Hampshire Development Association, Lombard NatWest Commercial Services Ltd, Nurdin & Peacock PLC, Peugeot Talbot, Singapore Economic Development Board, Survey Research Associates and Laranjo & Associates, Taunton Cider Co. Ltd, TI Group plc for advertising material; Abbey National plc, Kleinwort Benson and Slaughter & May for material from the Abbey National Prospectus; The Advertising Standards Authority Ltd for extracts from the British Code of Advertising Practice and publicity material; Philip Allan Publishers Ltd for a graph from *Economic Review Data Supplement 1989*; The Associated Examining Board and University of Cambridge Local Examinations Syndicate for past examination questions; Barratt Developments PLC for extracts from their Parent Company Balance Sheet; British Gas plc for extracts from 'Aims of British Gas'; British Railways Board for extracts from their Annual Report and Accounts 1987/89; Business Magazine for a graph from *Business*, August 1990; Central Transport Consultative Committee for extracts from a TUCC Southern England leaflet; The Controller of Her Majesty's Stationery Office for Crown copyright material; Patrick Donavan for 'British Coal under fire from MMC', *Guardian*, 26.1.89; The Economist for extracts from various issues of *The Economist* and a *Business Eastern Europe* advertisement; Eurotunnel for material from a

Link supplement; Etam Plc for the Company's Group Profit and Loss account, 1988/89; Financial Times for extracts from *Financial Times*, 31.10.89; The General Electric Company plc for their statement of source and application of funds from the GEC 1989 Report and Accounts; GKN plc for material from their 1988 Annual Report; Glaxo Holdings plc for data and extracts from publicity material; Granada Group plc for their 1988 Organisation Chart; Guardian News Service Ltd for extracts from 20.3.90, 2.3.88 and 20.3.91 issues of the *Guardian*; The International Stock Exchange, London, for SEAQ information 'on screen'; Kirklees Metropolitan Council for extracts from their West Yorkshire Trading Standards Service leaflet; Alfred A. Knopf, Inc. for figure from *Thriving on Chaos*, Tom Peters. Copyright © 1987 by Excel, a California Limited Partnership; Kogan Page Ltd for extracts from *A Handbook of Personnel Management Practice*, 3rd edition, M. Armstrong, 1988, and *Successful Marketing for the Small Business*, D. Patten; The Observer for illustration from 'Shoppers balk at debit cards', *Observer*, 22.9.85; Polaroid (UK) Ltd, for their customer survey questionnaire; The Post Office for material included in exam question and graph from 1989–90 Report and Accounts; Redland PLC for an extract from published accounts, 1985; Today Newspaper for extracts from their 29.11.89 issue of *Today*.

Every effort has been made to trace all the copyright holders, but if any have been inadvertently overlooked the publishers will be pleased to make the necessary arrangement at the first opportunity.

INTRODUCTION TO BUSINESS

The Scope of Business

What is business?

The term 'business' includes many different types of organisation, from a part-time window-cleaner to a multinational company such as General Motors, employing thousands of people in many different countries. Businesses are not just commercial or privately-owned firms – nationalised industries and Government agencies also act according to business principles, producing and supplying goods and services.

Whatever their size or function, however, all organisations share common characteristics:

1. They have *aims* and *objectives* such as making profits or producing a service for the public.
2. They use resources such as capital, labour and materials.
3. They have mechanisms for controlling and making decisions about the running of the business.
4. They are *accountable* to various groups such as owners, workers, customers and Government bodies.
5. They are subject to *external constraints* such as the demand for their products, legislation and pressure groups.

The functions of business

The functions of a business, whether large or small, can be divided into four basic types, as shown in Figure 1.2.

1. *Production* involves the manufacture of goods or the provision of services. Materials, components and other supplies have to be purchased and converted into finished products for the firm's customers.
2. *Personnel* functions are concerned with obtaining the best possible types of workers and creating the conditions in which they can work most effectively by providing appropriate pay, training and working arrangements.
3. *Finance* is essential in any business in order to pay for supplies and invest in new equipment, buildings and other assets. It must be accounted for accurately to measure and improve profitability and provide records for lenders, tax authorities and other agencies.
4. *Marketing* functions range right across the business, including researching the market, designing the product, pricing and advertising goods and services, and ensuring that customer requirements are met.

The management of any organisation involves co-ordinating these functions, which overlap and affect each other. For example a high-quality product can only be produced profitably if employees are adequately skilled, finance is available to purchase supplies and it is marketed correctly to the appropriate final customers.

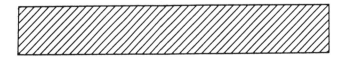

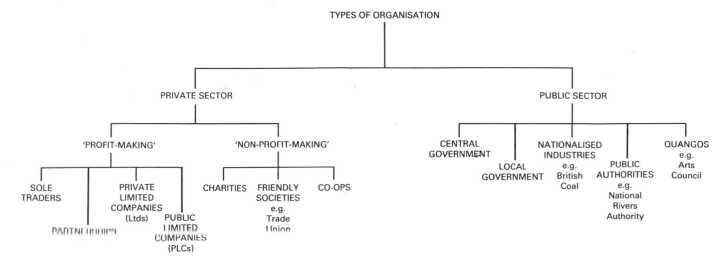

Figure 1.1 Types of organisation

Business Aims and Objectives

Aims

Aims and *objectives* are the principles by which an organisation is run. They may not be written down or expressed in more than the most general terms, but they are implicit in the minds of all managers.

Aims are broad statements of intent, usually expressed in vague terms such as British Gas's 'Principles' in Figure 1.3. Typically, aims do not contain a time-scale or any precise targets. For example Principle 1 does not give any idea of how much profit British Gas hopes to make.

In many cases an aim may not even be measurable, for example British Gas's Principle 6 'foster good relations . . .' says very little in practical terms.

Examples of commonly expressed aims include:

1. Maximising profits

Maximising profit means making the highest possible profit. It is the main aim of a privately-owned business, although some may follow other objectives such as those described below.

Profit is important:

- to allow the business to survive;
- to provide a financial reward to the owners of the business for putting their money into it;
- as a source of finance for future investment.

2. Maximising sales

The firm may attempt to obtain the highest possible sales, even if unprofitable business is taken on. This policy will often be based upon increasing the firm's *market share*, which is its proportion of the sales of the industry as a whole.

3. Maximising share price

This applies to public limited companies (PLCs), whose

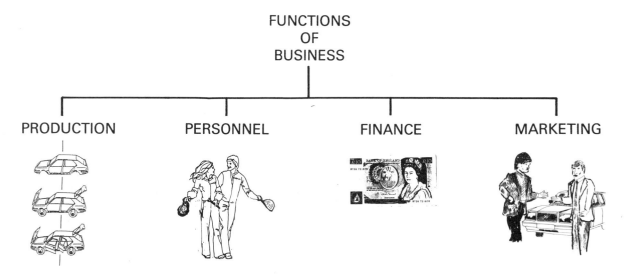

Figure 1.2 Functions of business

■ PRINCIPLE 1

To

Enhance the long term profitability and net worth of the whole of the Company's undertaking in the best interests of its shareholders.

■ PRINCIPLE 2

To

Perform the duties of a public gas supplier in a manner consistent with its responsibilities under the regulatory arrangements; to fulfil its duties to shareholders, customers and employees, and its other legal obligations.

■ PRINCIPLE 3

To

Provide a gas supply that is safe, secure, reliable, economical and supported by the high standards of service which are obtainable with an integrated gas business.

■ PRINCIPLE 4

To

Manage the business in the most effective manner with clear policy direction coming from the Board of Directors and operational authority appropriately delegated to secure commitment and efficiency.

■ PRINCIPLE 5

To

Manage the supporting activities of appliance selling, installation and contracting, and exploration and production, so that each makes the best contribution to the Company's profitability.

■ PRINCIPLE 6

To

Foster good relations with shareholders, customers, employees, suppliers and the communities with which the Company trades or which its operations affect.

Figure 1.3 Aims of British Gas

directors may wish to maintain a high share price. This pleases shareholders and puts off potential takeover bids. However, some PLCs have recently converted back to private limited company status in order to avoid this pressure.

4. Providing a service

All firms have to provide an efficient service to stay in business. For private firms this is essential to keep customers and be profitable. Organisations such as public corporations may have other objectives which are not profitable, such as maintaining a nationwide postal service or transport to remote country areas. These services may be provided at less than their cost.

5. Maximising employee welfare

A firm may be managed in a way which seeks to make its employees content, for example managers may decline to move a business from one area or country to another for personal reasons or tradition, even though this might be more profitable. Some businesses, particularly *co-operatives* (see Chapter 2) are set up to be run by and for their workers.

6. Survival

In many cases, a business's financial position may be so bad that its managers are only interested in keeping it alive. For example, the majority of professional football clubs lose money but survive because of local loyalty.

7. Personal satisfaction

Many small businesses, and even some very large ones, are run for the owner's personal satisfaction or prestige.

8. Social and community aims

Businesses often have general social aims, such as Sainsbury's promotion of the arts or Shell's donations to environmental projects. Social aims may be a key promotional aim, as for Body Shop, or the reason for establishing a business, for example Oxfam shops or the Co-operative movement.

The aims of any business may include some or all of the above, and the different aims are often complementary to each other, for example maximising market share may lead to high profitability and a rising share price.

There may however be conflicts between objectives, and it is often argued that firms do not specify particular objectives and achieve the best result possible. For example there is some research evidence to suggest that most firms are not profit-maximisers, but that managers tend to *satisfice*, that is set minimum levels for profitability, sales, etc., and are satisfied if these targets are met.

Strategic objectives

Objectives are usually expressed in more specific terms. They may be loosely classified into *strategic* and *tactical* objectives.

Strategic objectives state in broad terms what the firm would like to do in the long-run, typically over the next few years. They tend to be more measurable than aims, although still only vaguely expressed. Some writers argue that there is no real difference between aims and strategic objectives.

Examples of strategic objectives might include:

- 'increase annual profits by 10 per cent for the next 5 years';

3

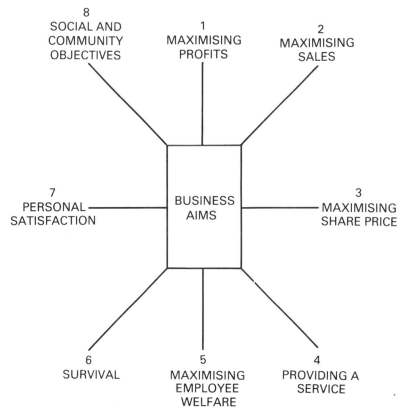

Figure 1.4 Business aims

- 'be the market leader by 1995';
- 'increase sales per employee by 10 per cent in the next year'.

Even broader social objectives can be set in specific terms. For example 3M has an objective of halving the hazardous waste produced by its plants between 1990 and 2000.

Tactical objectives

Tactical objectives are designed to ensure that the strategic objectives are reached. They are more detailed and generally short-term, typically set for the year ahead. For example an area manager of a retail chain might be given the strategic target of increasing annual profits by 10 per cent. This would then be broken down into more detailed tactical objectives, for example a shop manager might be told to 'cut labour costs by 5 per cent' or 'increase sales of product X by 20 per cent'.

These objectives are *quantitative*, that is they can be measured mathematically. Even at the tactical level, however, some objectives may be *qualitative* and difficult to measure exactly, such as 'where possible promote internally' or 'ensure that all branch managers understand grievance procedures'.

Management by objectives

Management by objectives (MBO) involves setting systematic targets for individual employees, usually managers, although the system is sometimes extended to all employees. In simple terms it involves measuring the employee's performance against previously agreed standards. The purpose is to break down the company's strategic objectives into achievable tactical objectives for individual managers. It is usually linked with a system of employee *appraisal* (see Chapter 10).

MBO often uses monetary targets for costs, sales or profits, but can also use targets such as 'reduce labour turnover by 5 per cent' or 'arrange training sessions in customer relations for all staff'.

The main problem of MBO is the difficulty of setting targets which are realistically achievable but which also motivate staff to perform better. An unachievable target may demotivate an employee and unfairly suggest poor performance, but an unambitious target may be easily achieved and encourage the employee to relax effort. MBO is also difficult and time-consuming to establish and administer.

The Size of Business

Measuring size

There is no simple method of assessing the size of a business. Several different methods are used, as shown below, but none can be automatically regarded as the 'best'. Some of the most commonly used measures include.

1. Annual sales (turnover)

This is the most commonly used method, being used in publications such as the *Times 1000*. It is easy to measure and understand, and gives a good idea of a firm's ability to buy in bulk, raise finance and undertake large-scale marketing.

4

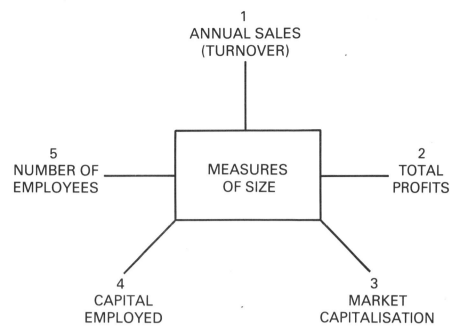

Figure 1.5 Measures of company size

The disadvantages of this measure are that it gives no indication of market share or profitability. Since typical profit margins vary significantly between industries, firms with similar turnovers can have significantly different profits. For example in 1989 BAT Industries and Siemens AG both had annual sales of approximately $32 million, but BAT's profits were $2.58 million compared with Siemens' $1.62.

2. Total profits

This is used by sources such as ELC International. It can be argued that since profit maximisation is the main purpose of private business, total profits is the best indicator of success. As expressed in the earnings per share ratio, profitability is important to current and prospective shareholders.

Against this it can be argued that profits can vary significantly from year to year, and should be used as a measure of success rather than size.

3. Market capitalisation

This is the value of the firm on the Stock Exchange, measured by the equation

Market capitalisation = no. of issued shares × market price

It can be argued that this is the only relevant measure of the firm's value, since it represents what people are prepared to pay for it. It is also an up-to-date assessment of the firm's current performance and future prospects.

The main problem of using this measure is that it can vary dramatically from day to day, with the share value often being influenced by rumours, fashions and many other factors. Often these will have only limited relevance to the real worth or profitability of the business. Also, since less than 1 per cent of UK firms have a Stock Exchange listing, this measure cannot be applied to the majority of businesses.

4. Amount of capital employed

This should show the value of assets employed in the business, although it is important to compare the figure with firms in the same industry. It is sometimes expressed as a ratio of capital employed per employee.

It is however difficult to measure capital employed, especially since the value of assets such as property may be assessed differently by different valuers.

Capital employed may also depend upon many other factors. For example a restaurant or shop in south-east England will nearly always have a higher capital employed than a similar restaurant in northern England, but will not necessarily be more profitable.

5. Number of employees

This can give a general idea of size, but is difficult to use when comparing firms in different industries. It will tend to be higher in service companies than in manufacturing firms. For example in 1989 British Telecom employed almost twice as many workers as BP, but its sales were only a third of BP's. The two companies made virtually identical profits.

Economies of scale

Mass production means producing goods and services in large quantities. The main advantage of mass production is that it can lead to cheaper production because of *economies of large-scale production* or *economies of scale* for short.

Economies of scale are the benefits of increasing output by a firm or industry. They may be *internal* or *external*.

Internal economies of scale occur as the result of a firm growing larger. They can be divided into five categories:

1. *Technical* economies occur because of the *division of labour* and better use of capital equipment. The more a

5

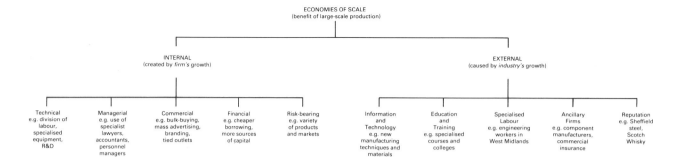

Figure 1.6 Economies of scale

machine or building is used, the lower the *average cost* of each good or service.

For example, if the *fixed costs* of running a factory are £1000 a week and the firm produces 500 units, the firm will have to pay costs of £2 per unit to pay for the factory. If output is 1000 per week, each unit will only take £1 in fixed costs.

Larger firms can also make use of specialised equipment such as machines or vehicles designed for a particular purpose, for example the Post Office uses machines which can automatically read typed addresses. These can only be afforded if the costs can be spread over a large output.

Research and development of new products are vital in industries such as chemicals, drugs and car manufacture. For example in the USA a new medical drug costs at least $100 million to develop before even one unit can be sold. Only the very largest firms can afford to risk such large sums of money.

2. *Managerial* economies occur when a large firm can afford specialist staff such as lawyers, accountants and personnel managers. This allows them to apply division of labour to management.

3. *Commercial* economies can be obtained by large firms when they buy or sell. By buying in bulk they may receive discounts or better terms such as longer credit or goods made to their own standard.

Large firms also have advantages when selling goods and services. It is cheaper to sell and distribute products in large quantities. More can be spent on advertising and marketing products, and many large firms have their own retail outlets, for example breweries own pubs, petrol companies own garages. Some firms such as car manufacturers can offer cheap credit to their customers.

4. *Financial* economies are available to large firms, who can usually borrow money at lower interest rates than small businesses. Public limited companies can obtain capital from sources such as international banks and the Stock Exchange.

5. *Risk-bearing* economies occur when a firm is large enough to withstand business risks such as loss of orders or unpaid debts. Small firms often depend heavily upon a few customers or products. As they grow larger they usually aim to spread the risks by *diversifying* into new products or markets. The largest firms are *conglomerates* (producing many different

products) and usually *multinational* (producing in countries all over the world). Figure 1.7 gives an example of a multinational firm.

External economies of scale occur as the result of an industry growing. They are especially likely to be found where an industry is *localised* in a particular area. In this case they are called *economies of concentration*.

The benefits of external economies are available to all firms within an industry, whatever their size. For example, even the smallest engineering firm can benefit from specialist courses at schools and colleges.

1. Information and technology

Firms may benefit from research and publication of information relevant to their industry such as new materials or manufacturing techniques.

2. Education and training

Educational institutions such as colleges and universities run courses for many industries. If an industry is concentrated in a particular area the local college may run specialist courses, for example Leicester colleges have departments which teach textile technology.

3. Specialised labour

Because of training and experience, many areas have workers who are skilled in particular industries or processes, such as cutlery-makers in Sheffield or engineering workers in the West Midlands.

4. Ancillary firms

Most large industries have firms which specialise in supplying or servicing them. For example the car industry can buy components from firms such as Dunlop, Lucas and Girling. As well as supplies of parts and materials, ancillary firms may supply specialised services such as banking, marketing and insurance.

5. Reputation

When an industry has been in an area for many years, all firms in the region may benefit from its good reputation.

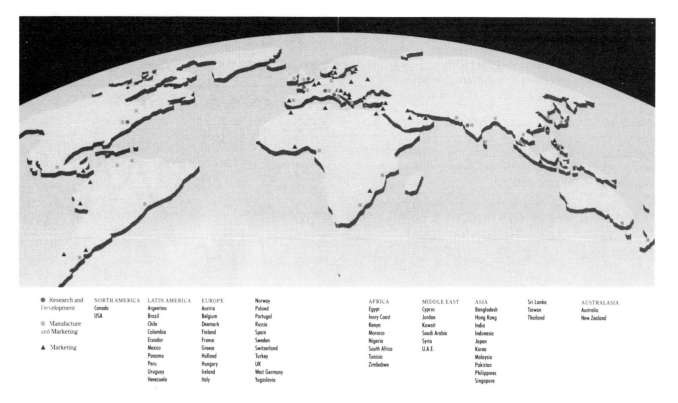

	NORTH AMERICA	LATIN AMERICA	EUROPE	Norway		AFRICA	MIDDLE EAST	ASIA	Sri Lanka	AUSTRALASIA
● Research and Development	Canada	Argentina	Austria	Poland		Egypt	Cyprus	Bangladesh	Taiwan	Australia
	USA	Brazil	Belgium	Portugal		Ivory Coast	Jordan	Hong Kong	Thailand	New Zealand
▩ Manufacture and Marketing		Chile	Denmark	Russia		Kenya	Kuwait	India		
		Colombia	Finland	Spain		Morocco	Saudi Arabia	Indonesia		
		Ecuador	France	Sweden		Nigeria	Syria	Japan		
▲ Marketing		Mexico	Greece	Switzerland		South Africa	U.A.E.	Korea		
		Panama	Holland	Turkey		Tunisia		Malaysia		
		Peru	Hungary	UK		Zimbabwe		Pakistan		
		Uruguay	Ireland	West Germany				Philippines		
		Venezuela	Italy	Yugoslavia				Singapore		

Figure 1.7 Glaxo – a multinational firm

For example Scotch whisky and Sheffield steel have the advantage of a good name for quality.

Diseconomies of scale

It is possible for a firm's average costs to rise as it grows bigger because of *diseconomies of scale*. These are the disadvantages of growing large.

1. Large firms may have very high overheads and waste time and effort with excessive paperwork as communications within the business become more complicated.
2. In large firms, labour problems such as strikes and absenteeism tend to occur more often. The firm is likely to spend more on personnel functions.
3. Public limited companies have many different shareholders and are always vulnerable to being taken over by another firm. This may not always lead to efficient production.
4. *External diseconomies of scale* may occur through the concentration of industry. These problems are often seen in urban areas such as London and other major cities. External diseconomies include pollution, slow transport and shortages of labour and land. These increase firms' costs, such as wages and rent.

Small Firms

Despite the advantages of large firms, many small businesses are very successful. There are a number of reasons for this:

1. Small firms do particularly well in industries where specialised labour and personal service are important, such as in garages, hairdressing and accountancy.
2. The production of many goods and services can be managed without large investment of capital in buildings or equipment.
3. Small firms are often suppliers of goods or services to larger firms.
4. Some goods and services are too specialised for large firms, but can be quite profitable for a small business, such as hand-made jewellery and classic car restoration.
5. Many people who wish to become their own boss by starting a business are happy to run a small concern without the effort and worry involved in growing larger.
6. A small business depends heavily upon its owners, who may not have the business skills needed to make the firm grow.
7. The Government has special schemes to assist small firms (see Chapter 13).

Growth

Internal growth

Internal growth refers to the expansion of a firm by increasing sales 'organically', that is without taking over or merging with other firms. It is sometimes regarded as a more effective method of growth because the firm avoids the problems of mergers and grows by developing its own products according to market conditions. It is argued that mergers are a lazy and less efficient means of achieving growth.

Against this, it may be argued that internal growth is

often slow and may be difficult in mature markets where larger competitors have significant cost or marketing advantages. Although many mergers are unsuccessful, companies such as Hanson and BTR have grown rapidly and successfully by taking over other companies.

Integration

Integration occurs when a business merges with or takes over another business. It can be divided into *horizontal*, *lateral* and *vertical* integration:

1. *Horizontal* integration occurs when two firms producing the same product merge, such as one car firm taking over another. This will usually take place in order to increase a firm's market share by making it larger.
2. *Lateral* or *conglomerate* integration is the merger or takeover of a firm producing a different product, such as a car firm taking over a building company. In some cases the two firms will produce similar products, such as a brewery taking over a chain of restaurants. However, a *conglomerate* such as Lonrho or Hanson may own many completely different types of firms.
3. *Vertical* integration means taking over a supplier or customer. It is *backward vertical* integration if a supplier is taken over, such as a car firm buying a steel mill. *Forward vertical* integration means buying an outlet for the firm's product, such as a car manufacturer buying car showrooms.

Reasons for mergers

There are several different motives for a firm taking over or merging with another company:

1. *Increased market share.* Sometimes it may be difficult to expand market share without merging, for example in mature markets or where there are 'tied' retail outlets such as brewery-owned pubs.
2. *Economies of scale.* This is the main economic justifica-

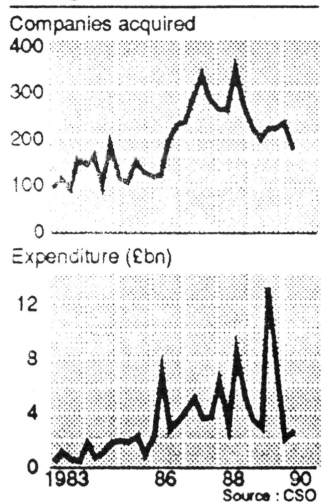

Figure 1.9   Uk mergers 1983–89

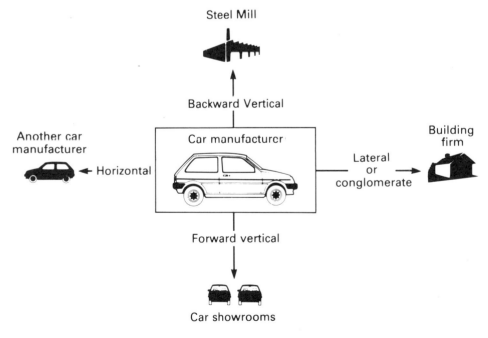

Figure 1.8   Integration by a car manufacturer

tion for mergers, and is based upon the argument that a single firm can produce more cheaply or gain access to technology and markets more easily than two separate firms. The term 'synergy', summarised as '2 + 2 = 5' or 'the whole is greater than the sum of the parts', is often used to describe this effect.

3. *Control of supplies.* A firm may wish to ensure access to supplies of raw materials and take over suppliers to ensure this.

4. *Control of outlets.* Firms may purchase retail or other outlets, for example television manufacturers have bought TV rental companies.

5. *Widening product range.* A business may wish to acquire a firm which produces a similar but slightly differentiated product. For example Volkswagen bought the Audi car business for its quality brand name. Mergers may offer a quicker way of building a presence in a new market.

6. *Diversification* If a firm feels that expansion in its present market is impossible, or that the market is likely to decline, it may acquire businesses in other markets. For example many oil and tobacco companies have diversified because of fears that demand for their main products would decline.

7. *Financial reasons.* Mergers may occur mainly for financial reasons. The acquiring firm may have large reserves of cash which are available for takeovers. Alternatively, a firm may be 'undervalued' on the Stock Exchange. In some cases the value of a firm's assets are more than its share value. It may be profitable to buy the firm, close it down and sell off its assets. This is called *asset-stripping.*

Arguments against mergers

Although many advantages have been claimed for mergers, both for individual firms or the economy as a whole, integration has two significant disadvantages. It can be argued that reducing competition is the main motive for many mergers, which are a substitute for producing more efficiently and developing new products.

There is little evidence that acquiring firms made any rational appraisal of their proposed takeover, or that merging led to increased competitiveness or profitability. It can be argued that the acquirer will inevitably pay more than a company is worth because the share price will rise above the 'correct' value when a merger is announced.

During the 1980s many takeovers were undertaken with high levels of borrowing. These are called *leveraged* or *highly-geared* buyouts. Many of these rapidly became unprofitable in the late 1980s, when a combination of high interest rates and falling share prices caused problems for businesses such as the Bond Corporation, Magnet and MFI.

Joint ventures

Joint ventures occur when two or more independent firms agree to work together on specific projects. These may take different forms, for example:

- Rover used Honda designs and engines for its cars;
- Royal Bank of Scotland and Banco Santander (Spain) provide services for each other in their home countries;
- Allied Lyons (UK) and Suntory (Japan) market each other's drinks in Britain and Japan respectively.

Ventures may be arranged in different ways, for example a new company may be set up, one firm buys shares in another, the firms may buy each other's shares or jointly take over an existing customer.

The aim of joint ventures is to gain advantages such as access to new technology and markets, benefit from economies of scale and reduce competition. This can be done without the problems of mergers, such as expense, costs of restructuring, objections from Governments and permanent commitment. A joint venture is also more logical in cases such as Royal Bank of Scotland and Banco Santander where there is only limited overlap between the firms' businesses.

Despite their advantages over full-scale mergers, joint ventures are often unsuccessful because of factors such as communication difficulties, conflicts between staff of different firms, extra pressures on management time and failure to think through the reasons for a joint merger.

De-integration

De-integration refers to the process of a firm or group reducing the scope of its activities. It may take different forms such as:

- De-merging – splitting into two or more firms as in Figure 1.10;
- Divestment – selling off subsidiaries, such as Asda selling MFI;
- Contracting-out – for example large firms selling ancillary services or departments such as transport or printing;
- Management buyouts (see Worked example **2.4**).

There are four major reasons for de-integration:

1. *Raising finance.* For example Asda sold MFI to pay for expansion of its store chain.

2. *Saving management time and expertise.* One of Courtaulds' main aims was to allow directors and senior managers to concentrate upon a more limited range of products.

3. *Increased efficiency.* By contracting-out services, a firm might hope to have more choice and competition between suppliers.

4. *Defensive reasons.* A holding company may feel that its shares are undervalued and therefore vulnerable to takeover because of the poor performance of certain companies in the group.

Problems of growth

Rapid growth can lead to significant problems for a company, especially a new small firm. These can be related to the four basic functions of business outlined at the start of this chapter. Possible problems include:

1. *Shortages of working capital.* A rapidly-expanding firm may find itself taking on orders which it does not have the working capital to finance. This is called *overtrading.* One common cause is where a firm offers generous credit to attract business and has to pay for materials, wages and overheads before receiving its revenue from customers.

   The firm may be trading at a profit, but its working capital is insufficient to pay creditors, who may refuse to continue supplies. Customers may also be frustrated

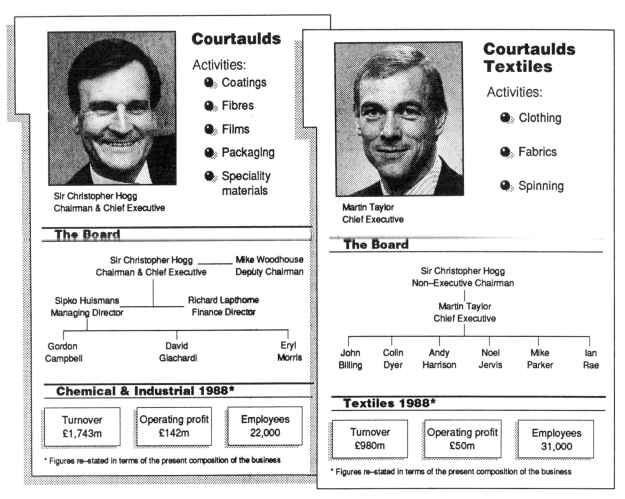

Figure 1.10 Courtaulds' demerger

because the firm has taken on too many orders to be able to meet delivery deadlines. The cost of borrowing will rise and at some point banks may be unwilling to increase credit.

The result is that a potentially profitable business can actually collapse because of poor cash control. Over-trading is one of the major causes of business failure, particularly for small firms.

2. *Production capacity becomes inadequate.* At some point the firm will only be able to increase production with heavy investment in new equipment, premises or other capital assets. This may involve large-scale borrowing with the risk that the investment may be unprofitable. Organisation of production processes may become more complicated.

3. *New markets are needed.* As the firm expands it will find itself trying to develop new products or sell to new markets. This may be expensive and risky. In extreme cases, such as Sock Shop's entry into the US market, such expansion may threaten the firm's existence.

4. *Management of people becomes more difficult.* As the business expands, new workers will have to be recruited and trained. Employees will expect the pay and conditions normally provided by large companies. It is also difficult to select appropriate managers, and for the original owners of the business to relax their control and delegate to others.

Increasing size will also lead to a more formal structure of the workforce. *Spans of control* may get wider and *hierarchies* become steeper. Communication becomes more complex, especially if the firm has more than one location and there will be more administrative work to co-ordinate a larger workforce (see Worked example **10.6**).

Worked Examples

Short-answer question

1.1 Give two reasons why an enterprise might wish to acquire a controlling interest in the share capital of a major supplier of its raw materials.

(AEB)

Answer For example security of supply, lower costs, more control over quality and terms of delivery.

10

1.2 The following passage is adapted from 'Business Brief' (*The Economist*, 29/10/83). Read the passage carefully and answer the questions which follow.

The recent decision of Nissan's chairman to drop his opposition to building cars in Britain means that a formal announcement of the controversial investment is only weeks away. Arriving at that decision took three years of indecision. This was caused by anxieties over:

1. The duration of the recession in the United Kingdom economy.
2. The amount of UK manufactured components to be used in Nissan's cars.
3. Whether or not Britain would continue to be a member of the Common Market.
4. The number of unions the Nissan Company would have to deal with. It would prefer to work with only one negotiating body.

N.B. Nissan is a multinational company which manufactures cars.

(a) Define the term 'multinational company'. *(2 marks)*

(b) State and explain
  (i) **two** reasons why a multinational might be welcomed by the host country;
  (ii) **two** reasons why a country might be suspicious of a multinational's wish to invest in it. *(8 marks)*

(c) Explain why the four anxieties of Nissan listed in the passage made the company reluctant to invest in the UK. *(15 marks)*

(AEB)

Answer **(a)** Company which produces and/or sells a large proportion of its output in several different countries.

(b) (i) For example increased investment, creates jobs, creates orders for domestic suppliers (such as UK car component manufacturers), transfer of new technology, improves skill of workforce, improves country's reputation so might attract other foreign firms.

(ii) For example difficult for Government to exert control over multinationals, may replace domestic producers, may import parts and materials from abroad, may pull out of country later, may take profits out of country without re-investing.

(c) 1. Recession – may reduce demand for Nissan cars.

2. % UK content – might wish to use Japanese components which are cheaper or better quality, but UK Government insisted on orders being placed with British firms.

3. EC membership – if Nissan build cars within EC they can be sold throughout Common Market. If UK withdrew from EC this advantage would be lost.

4. Unions – more complicated and time-consuming to negotiate with several unions, may lead to demarcation disputes or some unions rejecting settlements accepted by others, therefore Nissan might prefer one union.

1.3 Study the extract from the advertisement by Computerland and answer the questions which follow:

Between 1979 and 1981 sales of personal computers rose from £500 million to £2.5 billion. By 1985 they are expected to reach £18.6 billion. As a ComputerLand® franchise owner you would be a member of the world's largest chain of franchised computer retail stores.

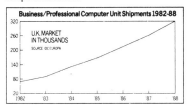

Business/Professional Computer Unit Shipments 1982-88

U.K. MARKET IN THOUSANDS
SOURCE: DC EUROPA

Yet you would still manage your own independent business. The huge advantage of franchising is that it allows you to combine your own entrepreneurial spirit with the unparalleled buying power of a major chain.

How do you begin?

A ComputerLand franchise needs a $35,000 franchise fee, plus a minimum investment of £150,000 – £200,000 (depending upon location), of which 50 per cent must be in liquid assets. For this, ComputerLand will set you up as the independent boss of your own ComputerLand store. This includes stock, working capital, professional help with the complete store design, and intensive training. As a ComputerLand owner you will have access to the very best names in computers, software and peripherals, at the very best prices.

Trademark of the ComputerLand Corporation USA

You will also benefit from our national advertising support and marketing expertise.

How safe is it?

That really depends on you. No ComputerLand owner needs to be a total computer boffin – but you should have a considerable degree of sales or marketing experience and natural business acumen.

One thing is for sure – the ComputerLand franchising formula does work: in 1976 there was only one ComputerLand store. Today there are over 600 successful franchise stores worldwide.

If you are interested in owning your share of the fastest-growing business in the world, just fill in the coupon below. We'll send you a complete portfolio of everything you need to know about becoming a ComputerLand franchise owner.

Source: *The Economist*, 28 July 1984

(a) Explain the term franchise in this context. *(2 marks)*
(b) Give **three** reasons for buying a franchise. *(3 marks)*
(c) What reasons might there be for the company selling franchises instead of opening the shops themselves. *(6 marks)*
(d) Examine the graph and identify **three** ways in which it may be misleading. *(9 marks)*

(AEB)

Answer **(a)** Ready-made business format containing all the elements necessary to run the business, such as products, advertising strategy, training packages, etc. Usually given a monopoly for a small area. The *franchisee* buys a licence to use the format from the *franchisor*, in this case Computerland.

(b) For example proven product, established brand name, geographical monopoly, assistance with setting up, training for staff, back-up services such as advertising and specialised equipment, lower costs for research and development and marketing, claimed to be less risky than setting up alone, easier to obtain finance as banks have franchise divisions and special packages for some franchises.

(c) For example can expand rapidly without having to raise large amounts of capital, can achieve growth quickly before idea is copied, economies of scale from large-volume purchases, tied customers for their products, franchisees own their business so many be more motivated and efficient than employed managers, with expansion new franchises can command higher licence feees.

(d) For example produced in 1984 so figures shown for then onwards are only forecasts (possibly very optimistic), not clear what 'shipments' means (may mean production rather than sales), figures are for computer market as a whole and not necessarily representative of Computerland's sales, definition of business/professional computers is vague, scale does not start at zero therefore exaggerates growth.

Essay questions

1.4 'Company directors are ultimately responsible to one group alone – the shareholders'. Critically evaluate this statement.

(AEB)

Answer (i) Explain the basis of the statement ie that shareholders are the owners of the firm and having risked their capital are entitled to the reward of maximum profits. They appoint directors for this purpose and have the right to remove them. Also, directors have a legal obligation to act in the best interests of the shareholders.
(ii) Outline the other groups to whom shareholders have responsibility, such as employees, customers, Government, community. Some of these are legal duties such as providing safe working conditions and products, paying taxes, obeying laws, etc. These may conflict with profitability.
(iii) Outline other reasons for recognising obligations to other groups, and explain why these may be necessary to achieve maximum profits in the long-run, such as poor relations with employees may reduce productivity and provoke industrial action, poor public relations may harm sales, such as Barclays lost many student customers through former links with South Africa, whereas a 'good' image may be a company's major selling point, such as Body Shop's or Oriflamme's refusal to use products tested on animals. (*ethics*)

1.5 (a) Explain the benefits to a self-employed sole trader of forming a private limited company to conduct his business. *(10 marks)*
(b) Discuss factors which would limit the size of a firm within an industry. *(15 marks)*

(UCLES)

Answer **(a)** Main benefits are *limited liability* for firm's debts, that is an individual would be responsible only up to the value of his or her shares in the company, and *incorporation*, that is the business is a separate legal body (see also Chapter 2). Limited companies have access to sources of finance not available to unincorporated businesses, such as shares, certain types of loans and Government schemes (like the Business Expansion Scheme). There are some tax advantages, such as reliefs for investment, which are not available to sole traders. There may be some prestige in being a limited company as compared with being a sole trader.

(b) Factors might include:

- size of the market as a whole, for example very specialised products;
- size of established competitors who have benefit of economies of scale;
- barriers to entry, for example small brewers have difficulties because many pubs are owned or 'tied' to large breweries;
- difficulties in persuading retailers to stock products such as 'health foods' or 'green' products until comparatively recently;
- difficulties in raising finance;
- inability to offer a full range of products;
- limited abilities of owners or managers.

Self-test Questions

Short-answer questions

1.6 A businessman decides not to increase the size of his enterprise. List three possible business reasons for such a decision. *Lack of finance*

(AEB)

1.7 Indicate three problems a businessman might encounter in the initial establishment of his organisation.

(AEB)

1.8 Distinguish between vertical and horizontal integration.

(AEB)

Data-response questions

1.9 Study the table and extract and answer the questions which follow.

Table 1 Share of Retail Trade 1961–1996 (%)

	1961	*1966*	*1971*	*1978*	*1983*	*1996*
Co-operatives	10.9	9.1	7.1	6.8	6.6	6.8
Multiples	29.2	34.5	38.5	46.5	50.4	55.0
Independents	59.9	56.4	54.4	46.7	43.0	38.2

Source: Census of Distribution 1961/6/71
Retail Inquiry 1978
CEG 1983
CEG Forecast 1986

Economies of shop size
The fall in shop numbers is mainly, though not entirely, accounted for by the decline of small shops. Small shops tend to be less efficient and are more vulnerable to increases in operating costs, unless this is offset by some other factor such as good location. The economies of scale in shop size are particularly strong in grocery where there has been a large increase in average size of shop. Productivity (defined as sales per full-time equivalent employee) is also much more favourable in larger than in smaller stores. Consequently co-operatives and multiples have tended to close many of their smaller stores, while the problems of independents are frequently a reflection of the adverse costs of smaller trading units.

Adapted from 'The Changing face of British Retailing'
National Westminster Bank Review

(a) What is meant by the term 'full-time equivalent employee'? *(2 marks)*
(b) Using the information contained in Table 1 produce a graph, in conventional form, showing the changes occurring in the shares of retail trade over the period from 1961 to 1996. *(7 marks)*
(c) Give **four** examples of the economies of scale which may be available to grocery shop owners and explain why these may arise. *(8 marks)*
(d) What effect might the changes in market share illustrated by Table 1 have on a major importer and distributor of perishable foodstuffs such as fruit? *(6 marks)*

(AEB)

1.10 Read the following extract and answer the questions below.

"The Bolton Committee (1971) suggested that the three main characteristics of a small firm were that it had a relatively small share of the market; that it was managed in a personalised way by its owners who took all the principal decisions and exercised the principal management functions; and that it was independent in the sense that it did not form part of a larger enterprise.
   These characteristics provide an economic definition of a small firm, but in censuses and surveys, firm size is determined by means of statistical measures such as employment or sales, and in terms of employment, for example, the largest size of firm which will typically conform to the Bolton characteristics varies with industry. In some manufacturing industries firms with 500 employees will often conform, while in retailing a firm with 200 employees will be relatively large, and in the world of finance firms with fewer than 50 employees will typically not conform. Since similar remarks also apply to any other statistical measure of size, considerable care needs to be

taken when using such measures to define a small firm. However, provided account is taken of industry, they do give at least a rough guide. In the manufacturing industry, for example, nearly all firms with less than 200 employees will also be small according to the economic definition.''

'The importance and Position of Small Firms' by R. Allard.
The Economic Review, Vol. 1, No. 2, Nov. 1983

(a) State **three** methods of comparing the size of firms in the same industry, other than by 'number of employees'. *(3 marks)*

(b) Explain why 'number of employees' on its own might be a misleading indication of the size of firms. *(2 marks)*

(c) Explain **two** reasons why small firms tend to be less capital intensive than large ones. *(6 marks)*

(d) Explain **four** different methods governments have employed in an attempt to encourage the small firm sector. *(8 marks)*

(e) Outline **two** reasons why the small firm sector is considered to be important to the UK economy. *(4 marks)*

(AEB)

Essay questions

1.11 Makeshift Tools PLC has enjoyed a period of enormous expansion over the past thirty years under the guidance of its founder and managing director Brian Surridge. From a company employing a handful of workers, it has become the major local employer. It also has two manufacturing plants in different countries overseas. Growth has brought pressures on the company both from within and outside.

Identify some of these pressures and analyse the ways of dealing with them.

(AEB)

1.12 What contribution can small business enterprises make to the economy? Evaluate the strengths and weaknesses of small businesses in making this contribution.

(AEB)

TYPES OF BUSINESS ORGANISATION

Types of Business

Businesses can be classified into two types: *private sector* and *public sector*, owned by private individuals and the Government respectively.

Principles of Business Organisation

Limited liability

Limited liability means that if a business is unable to pay its debts, the owners of the company can only lose the money that they have paid for shares or the *fully paid-up* value of the shares (see below).

Sole traders and partnerships have *unlimited liability*. If the business cannot pay its debts, the owners have to pay them out of their own money. They may have to sell their house and other personal possessions to pay the business's creditors.

The importance of limited liability is that people can put money into a firm by buying shares, without risking the loss of all their money if the company fails. If limited liability did not exist, people would be less willing to risk investing in firms.

Companies limited by *guarantee* are usually 'non-commercial' bodies such as clubs, professional associations and examination boards. The members of the company agree to guarantee its debts up to a certain amount (often £1). This is only paid if the company is wound up. A company limited by guarantee may also be allowed to omit the term 'limited' from its title.

The vast majority of companies are limited by *share*. In this case the shareholders are only liable for the value of their shares. Sometimes shares are only *partly-paid* with the shareholders only paying over a proportion of their value. In this case they may be forced to pay the full value to creditors if the company becomes bankrupt.

A very small number of companies are *unlimited*, with their shareholders being liable for all of the company's debts.

Joint-stock companies

Limited companies are sometimes called *joint-stock* companies because their shares or 'stock' is held jointly by a number of people.

The general rules for the running of joint-stock companies are set out by various Companies Acts dating from 1844 onwards. Most of these were consolidated (brought together) and amended in the Companies Act 1985. Rules are also made by Government Ministers and bodies such as the Stock Exchange. The purpose of these laws and regulations is to protect people who buy shares in or lend money to businesses.

Incorporation

An *incorporated body* has a legal existence separate from its owners. Contracts can be signed in its name, and it has

15

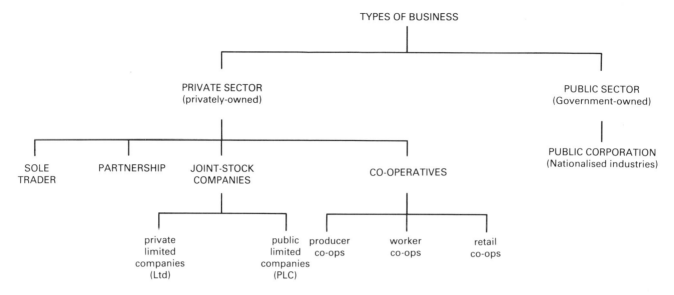

Figure 2.1 Types of business

legal rights and duties of its own. Its owners also usually have limited liability.

Business names

Joint-stock companies have to register their name with Companies House, a Government organisation. The name cannot be the same as an existing company, or close enough to suggest a link with another firm. Titles which include terms such as 'British', 'Royal' or 'Bank' are not allowed without permission from the relevant body.

Other types of business do not have to register their name, but must display the name and address of the owners on their premises and stationery (for example Fartown Stores, proprietor G. Smith).

Sole Trader

Features of the sole trader

A *sole trader* (also known as *sole proprietor* is a business owned and controlled by one person, usually trading under his or her own name. The sole trader is *unincorporated*, that is the owner is legally the same as the business.

Sole traders are usually small businesses and are common in industries such as farming, hairdressing, window cleaning and retailing. They are most often found in industries where production is *labour-intensive*, that is labour is a high percentage of costs and little capital is needed to set up in business.

Advantages of the sole trader

1. The business is to set up. Apart from any necessary licences or planning permission, there are very few legal formalities.
2. Although accounts are seen by the Inland Revenue, they do not have to be made public.

3. The business is usually small, and the owner is in charge of the day-to-day management. Decisions can be made quickly.
4. The owner gets all of the profit from the business, so he or she has an incentive to work hard.
5. Being small, the business can provide personal attention for its customers.

Disadvantages of the sole trader

1. Prices may be higher. Sole traders are unlikely to be big enough to get the benefits of large-scale production. However, if *expenses* are kept down, for example by using the owner's home as premises, a sole trader may be able to keep prices low.
2. It may be difficult to raise finance to expand the business. Capital is usually obtained from personal savings, borrowing and putting profit back into the business. The sole trader does not have access to the larger capital markets.
3. The sole trader has unlimited liability, and is personally responsible for the business's debts. He or she may have to risk home and savings to start the business.
4. The business depends very heavily upon the owner's abilities. He or she may be good at some tasks of running the business, but poor at others. For example, a person may have a technical skill as a car mechanic, but find it difficult to cope with accounts or staff when running a garage.
5. If the owner is ill, the business may have difficulty in continuing.
6. Sole traders often have to work very long hours, particularly when setting up a business.

Partnership

Features of the partnership

A partnership is legally defined as 'two or more persons

If there is no legal agreement the provisions of the Partnership Act 1890 apply. These are basically that:
- Profits and losses are shared equally.
- All partners have an equal say in the running of the business.
- All partners must agree before new partners can be admitted.

If a Partnership deed or agreement is drawn up it is likely to cover matters such as:
- The amount of capital to be contributed by each partner.
- The proportion in which profits and losses are to be shared.
- The management responsibilities of each partner.
- The maximum drawings of cash for personal use by each partner.
- Provisions for introducing new partners and the ending of the partnership.

Figure 2.2 Partnership deed

carrying on business in common with a view to profit' (Partnership Act 1890). This definition excludes non-profit-making organisations such as charities and sports clubs.

Partnerships have a legal maximum of 20 partners, with some exceptions such as solicitors and accountants. They can be set up without legal documents, although this is inadvisable. The partnership is an *unincorporated* business and partners have *unlimited liability*. There are *limited partners* in a very small number of partnerships, but all must have at least one partner with limited liability.

Advantages of partnerships

1. Compared with a sole trader, there are more people to put money into the business.
2. Can include people with different skills.
3. Fairly easy to set up.
4. As with sole traders, accounts do not have to be made public.
5. Partners are usually involved in the day-to-day running of the business, and have an incentive to see that it works efficiently.
6. Small partnerships can provide personal service.

Disadvantages of partnerships

1. Usually too small for large-scale production, although there are exceptions to this.
2. The partners have unlimited liability (except for *limited partners*) and are responsible for any debts.
3. With more people in charge, decisions may take longer than for the sole trader.
4. Small partnerships may find it difficult to raise capital.
5. Each partner is legally and financially liable for the others. If one partner makes a mistake, the others may lose money. It is usually possible to insure against this, for example doctors have insurance against being proved negligent.
6. There may be problems if one of the partners leaves or dies. The Partnership Deed (see Figure 2.2) should allow for such changes.

Private Limited Company

Features of private limited companies

A private limited company is a *joint-stock* firm owned by two or more shareholders. Under the Companies Act 1980 a private limited company is defined as any company which is not a public limited company.

Until 1980 private limited companies were legally obliged to have restrictions on the sale of their shares. They no longer have to do this, although many do have rules to make take-overs difficult. A private company cannot however advertise its shares for sale to the general public or through the Stock Exchange.

Shareholders have limited liability and the company must use the word 'limited' or abbreviation 'Ltd' in its title (in Wales 'Cyfngedig' or 'cyf' may be used). Some shareholders may not take part in daily management of the firm.

Advantages of private limited companies

1. Limited liability makes it easier to pursuade people to put money into the business.
2. Many private limited companies are large enough to obtain the benefits of large-scale production.
3. Limited companies gain certain tax advantages compared with unincorporated businesses.
4. There is no minimum authorised capital.
5. Accounts are less complicated than those of public limited companies.
6. It is possible to restrict transfer of shares, for example to preserve ownership by family members.

Disadvantages of private limited companies

1. There are legal formalities to set up the business.
2. Accounts have to be filed with Companies House, and it is therefore difficult to retain privacy. However, depending on the size of the company, it may be possible to keep parts of the accounts secret.
3. Shares cannot be sold to the public or on the Stock Exchange.
4. It may be difficult for shareholders to sell their shares and get their investment back, especially when companies have restrictions on transferring shares.

Public Limited Company

Features of public limited companies (PLCs)

A public limited company is a *joint-stock* firm owned by two or more shareholders, although most have hundreds or even thousands (see Figure 2.3). They are all very large firms, with a legal minimum of £50 000 authorised capital.

Many were originally private limited companies.

A public limited company must use the term 'public limited company' or abbreviation 'PLC' in its title ('Cwmni cyfngedig cyhoeddus' or 'ccc' is allowed in Wales). It is permitted to advertise shares for sale to the public, and about a third of all PLCs are *listed* on the Stock Exchange.

Most PLC shareholders do not take part in the management of the firm, which is run by a Board of Directors elected by shareholders, who have limited liability.

SHAREHOLDER INFORMATION

ANALYSIS OF ORDINARY SHAREHOLDINGS AT 30 JUNE 1990

	Number of holdings	Shares held – thousands	% of total shares
By Category of Shareholder			
Individuals	36,162	38,857	17
Banks, nominees and other corporate bodies	4,185	151,936	68
Insurance companies	239	28,222	13
Investment companies and pension funds	138	5,157	2
	40,724	**224,172**	**100**
By size of holding			
-500	14,905	3,609	2
501-1,000	10,740	8,251	4
1,001-50,000	14,684	40,399	18
50,001-100,000	133	10,249	4
100,001 and over	262	161,664	72
	40,724	**224,172**	**100**

TAXATION OF CAPITAL GAINS

For the purposes of capital gains tax the middle market quotations of the shares and debentures of the company on 31 March 1982 were as follows:

Ordinary Shares	157.5p
4.85% Cumulative preference shares	47.5p
6½% Redeemable debenture stock 85/95	£53.25
8¼% Redeemable debenture stock 88/93	£64.25

FINANCIAL CALENDAR
Dividends

Ordinary shares:
– Interim	Announced February, paid July
– Final	Proposed in September, paid January
Preference shares	Paid 1 February and 1 August

Annual General Meeting

11.30 a.m. on 16 November 1990 in the Methven Room, Centre Point, 103 New Oxford Street, London WC1.

Figure 2.3 Dalgety PLC shareholdings 1989

Advantages of public limited companies

1. Shareholders have limited liability.
2. They are large and can get the benefits of large-scale production.
3. PLCs can raise large amounts of capital through share issues and borrowing. They can usually borrow more cheaply than smaller firms.
4. If the company has a Stock Exchange listing shares can be bought and sold easily, so shareholders can get their money back (unless the value of the shares has fallen).
5. Because of their size, PLCs should get the benefits of *economies of scale*.

Disadvantages of public limited companies

1. PLCs are expensive to set up, because the regulations involved are very complicated. There are detailed laws about the presentation of accounts, disclosure of information and the duties of directors.
2. Because of the size of the firm there may be *diseconomies of scale* such as decisions taking a long time to make.
3. As a large firm, the company may seem impersonal to customers and employees.
4. Shares in PLCs are often owned by people who buy them in order to make a quick profit (most large shareholdings are kept for less than two years). This means that they are always vulnerable to takeovers by other firms.

Registration of Joint-stock Companies

When a joint-stock company is established, certain documents must be submitted to the Registrar of Companies, a Government Department. The two most important documents are the *Memorandum of Association* and the *Articles of Association*.

Memorandum of Association

This governs the firm's external relationships with other people and organisations, and provides the world at large with certain basic information about the company. It contains several items:

1. Name of the company.
2. Address of the Registered Office.
3. *Objects Clause*. This states the type of business in which the company will be involved, such as 'retailing' or 'building services'.
4. *Limitation Clause*. This is a statement that shareholders have limited liability, by share or guarantee.
5. *Capital Clause*. This gives details of the amount of authorised share capital and the amounts and categories of shares to be issued.
6. *Association Clause*. This includes the names of the founder members and the number of shares for which each has subscribed.
7. The memorandum of a public limited company must also state that it is a public company.

Articles of Association

These are the rules governing the internal affairs of a company, covering matters such as:

1. Voting rights of shareholders.
2. Election of directors.
3. Conduct of meetings of shareholders and directors.
4. The buying and selling of shares.
5. Payment of dividends.

The Companies Act 1985 contains a set of model rules which can be used, and which automatically apply if the company does not register its own Articles.

Statutory Declaration

This is a statement that the company has been set up within the regulations of the Companies Acts. It is sent to the Registrar of Companies along with the Memorandum and Articles of Association.

Certificate of Incorporation

This is issued by the Registrar of Companies, and is necessary before the company can start trading. In effect it is the company's 'birth certificate'. A private limited company can start trading immediately upon receipt of its Certificate of Incorporation, but a public limited company must also obtain a Certificate of Trading.

Certificate of Trading

This is also issued by the Registrar, and must be obtained by a public limited company before it can commence business. To obtain the Certificate of Trading the PLC must have raised a minimum amount of money. This is to ensure that the company will have sufficient capital to start trading.

Co-operatives

Co-operatives are special types of private sector businesses. They are a fairly minor proportion of the total number of businesses. The Co-operative Development Agency (CDA) estimates that in 1986 there were 1500 co-ops employing 14 000 workers, and that the number was growing every year.

There is no legal definition of a co-operative, but there are certain features which make most of them different from other types of firm:

1. Each member has one vote, no matter how much work or money he or she puts into the co-op.
2. Shares keep the same value.
3. All profits made belong to the members. Some may be kept for future investment, but the remainder is distributed to members in a previously-agreed way. Like shareholders of joint-stock companies, members of co-operatives have limited liability.
4. The level of interest that can be paid for borrowing is limited.

19

5. Many are involved in political and social work, for example the Co-operative movement sponsors several Members of Parliament.

It should be noted, however, that these principles are not applicable to all co-operatives.

There are several types of co-operative. *Producer co-operatives* involve a central organisation such as the Milk Marketing Board buying and selling products on behalf of its members. In Britain these are very common in agriculture.

Worker co-operatives are businesses owned by their workers. The most famous examples are the Mondragon co-operatives in Spain. In Britain there are only about 2000 worker co-operatives, a fairly small proportion of the total number of businesses. The main advantage of worker co-operatives is that the workers have an interest in the success of the business because they own it.

Retail co-operatives are the largest group of co-operatives in Britain. The 'Co-op' is made up of 90 separate locally-based societies. These societies own the Co-operative Wholesale Society (CWS), which produces 60% of the goods sold in Co-op stores.

The CWS is involved in many industries (see Figure 2.4), such as farming, insurance and undertaking. Its Board is elected from the member societies.

The Co-op's customers receive a dividend on their purchases (some societies do not pay a dividend as such,

---

UK CO-OPERATIVE MOVEMENT FACTS AND FIGURES

Co-Operative Retail Societies

Turnover	£5,350 million
Trading surplus	£99 million
Staff	82,000
Number of Societies	90
Members' Benefits/Dividend	£19 million
Number of shops	5,000 (65 Superstores)
Number of members	8,345,000

The Co-Operative Wholesale Society

Turnover	£2.4 billion
Staff	22,386
Factories	33
Farms	37,000 acres
Distribution centres	18
Co-op Brand Lines	2,000
Number of shops	320

The Co-Operative Bank Group

Assets	£1.64 billion
Staff	4,409
Branches	100
Handybanks	586
ChequePost (with cash-a-cheque support)	370
Cash-a-cheque points	2,370
Customer accounts	1.5 million
Financial Centres	49

The Co-Operative Insurance Society

Premium income	£768 million
Assets	Over £5 billion (market value)
Number of policies in force	12 million
Number of families insured	3.9 million
Staff	11,200
District Offices	220
Surplus on Life business for 1987	£234 million

Co-Operative Travel (all societies)	160 branches	
Shoefayre	180 branches	
Co-Operative Opticians	93 practices	
National Co-Operative Chemists	150 branches	
Worker Co-Operatives (UK)	2,000	May 1988

Figure 2.4 The Co-operative Movement – facts and figures

but keep prices low). Dividends are often paid by giving customers stamps which can be exchanged for cash, goods or shares in the society.

Public Corporations

Nationalisation

Nationalised industries (also called *public corporations*) are firms owned wholly or mainly by the Government.

The list of nationalised industries which remained in the public sector at the end of 1990 is as follows:
British Coal
North of Scotland Hydro-Electric Board
South of Scotland Electricity Board
Post Office
British Railways Board
British Waterways
Scottish Transport Group
Civil Aviation Authority

The following industries have been privatised since 1979:
British Steel Corporation
British Telecom
British Gas Corporation
British National Oil Corporation
British Airways
British Airports Authority
British Aerospace
British Shipbuilders (Warships)
British Transport Docks Board
Electricity (England and Wales)
London Regional Transport
National Freight Company
Enterprise Oil
National Bus Company
Water (England and Wales)
Girobank

Figure 2.5 The nationalised industries 1990

Most of the nationalised industries were created by the Labour Governments of 1945–51, 1964–70 and 1974–79. Usually this was done by the Government buying several firms from their private owners and merging them into one large public corporation.

A list of the nationalised industries at the end of 1990, and those already *denationalised* (sold to the private sector) is given in Figure 2.5. Further sell-offs to the private sector are planned for the early 1990s.

Features of the public corporation

A public corporation is a firm which is owned wholly or partly by the Government. The definition is not absolutely clear, but a public corporation has two features which distinguish it from a Government Department such as the National Health Service or Education.

A public corporation earns most of its revenue by selling its goods and services, whereas a Government Department 'gives away' its product. The corporation is controlled by a Board of Directors appointed by a Government Minister, whereas a Department is supervised directly by a Minister.

Being owned by the Government, public corporations are answerable to the public for their activities (see Figure 2.6). They work to financial and performance targets set by the Minister responsible for supervising them.

Most present and past nationalised industries are very large firms in terms of sales, employment and capital employed. Their products might be regarded as 'strategic', in that they are vital to people and firms throughout the economy.

Arguments for nationalisation

1. Nationalised industries may provide socially important services such as rural railway lines and postal services, which might not be supplied by a private firm because they are unprofitable.
2. Some industries are *'natural monopolies'*. It may not be financially worthwhile for more than one firm to provide a service such as gas and water. In these industries it is argued that it makes sense to have one producer, which should be owned by the Government to protect consumers.

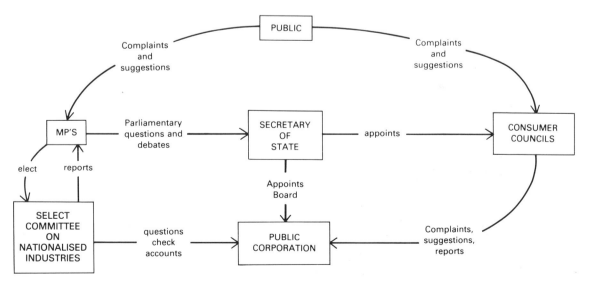

Figure 2.6 Control of nationalised industries

3. Many industries require investment in expensive equipment and technology. For example an electricity power station costs several billion pounds. A private firm might be unwilling to risk such a large investment.
4. Industries such as fuel and steel are vital to the economy, and may be important in times of war. It can be argued that the Government should have control of these industries to ensure ample supply of important goods and services.
5. The Government should control the economy on behalf of its citizens. This is the major political argument for nationalisation.
6. Occasionally a private firm is nationalised to stop it going bankrupt and causing unemployment or other economic problems. British Leyland (now called Rover) was rescued in 1975 to prevent large job losses in the West Midlands. Rolls-Royce Engines (not the car firm) was taken over in 1971 to ensure that Britain did not lose its capacity to make aircraft engines.

Arguments against nationalisation

1. Nationalised industries are inefficient because the Government will pay any losses that they make. The taxpayer is forced to support inefficient firms.
2. Lack of competition does not encourage efficiency or good service to customers. Most of the nationalised industries have had a *statutory monopoly*, which means that no other firm is allowed to compete with them.
3. Even vital industries can be trusted to private firms, as the Government can encourage or control production if necessary. For example, most defence equipment is provided by private-sector companies.
4. State control of industry is politically undesirable, giving the Government too much power over the way in which people make their living.
5. Nationalised industries are always subject to interference by the Government.

Privatisation

The three methods of privatisation

The Conservative Government which was elected in 1979 had *privatisation* as one of its major aims. Privatisation means switching production of goods and services from the public to the private sector. There are three basic methods of privatisation:

1. *Denationalisation* – selling Government-owned enterprises to the private sector, such as British Steel or Girobank.
2. *Deregulation* – removing statutory monopolies, for example abolishing restrictions upon bus services.
3. *Contracting-out* – allowing private firms to bid for the supply of public services, for example hospital cleaning, refuse collection.

Arguments for privatisation

1. It will lead to greater competition and efficiency. With more competition, producers will have to provide better and cheaper goods and services.
2. Consumers will benefit from greater choice and better services.
3. Taxpayers will benefit from cheaper Government services and lower payments to support nationalised industries. Denationalisation has provided several billion pounds of revenue to the Government.
4. Privatisation has increased the number of people owning shares in companies. By increasing share ownership by consumers and workers, the Government hopes that people will have a stake in the success and efficiency of British industry.

Arguments against privatisation

1. Privatisation does not necessarily increase competition or efficiency, for example the privatisation of British Telecom and British Gas has converted public sector monopolies into private sector monopolies. Contracting-out of public services has also led to complaints about the standard of work of private contractors in hospitals and Government offices.
2. Consumers have not always benefited, especially where competition has not been increased.
3. Privatisation costs the Government money. In some cases public corporations have been sold at less than their real value, and the profits from industries such as gas and telecommunications will be lost to future Governments. The Government has had to 'write off' debts to sell the corporations.
4. Increased share ownership has made little difference. Many people have sold their shares for a quick profit. They are still unwilling to buy shares with any real risk, such as those of Eurotunnel.

Worked Examples

Short-answer question

2.1 A sole trader called William Hicks names his business the 'Metal Drum'. State two administrative actions he must take because of this.

Answer Display own name on premises. Print own name on stationery. Give own name to creditors, suppliers, etc. on request.

2.2 The following extract is part of a document sent to Trafalgar House shareholders informing them, among other things, of a proposed acquisition. Read the article and answer the questions which follow.

Trafalgar House and its activities

Trafalgar House was incorporated in England on 22nd December, 1965 as a private limited company under the Companies Act 1948 with registered number 867281 and was re-registered on 20th January, 1982 as a public limited company pursuant to the Companies Act 1980. The Company now operates under the Companies Act 1985. The registered office of the Company which is also its principal place of business is at 1 Berkeley Street, London W1A 1BY. The principal objects of Trafalgar House, as set out in clause 4 of its Memorandum of Association, are to act as a holding company and to invest in and develop property and to enter into financial and commercial transactions of all kinds.

Trafalgar House is the holding company of a group whose principal activities include property and investment, construction and engineering, shipping, aviation and hotels, and oil and gas.

(a) What distinguishes a public limited company from a private limited company? *(6 marks)*
(b) Explain the main purpose of the Memorandum of Association. *(4 marks)*
(c) List **two** pieces of information, other than the Memorandum of Association, required by the Registrar of Companies when forming a public limited company. *(2 marks)*
(d) Explain the term 'holding company'. *(2 marks)*
(e) Suggest and explain **three** factors that might be considered by Trafalgar House when assessing whether to go ahead with any acquisition. *(6 marks)*

(AEB)

Answer **(a)** Legal definition – any limited company which is not a public limited company (PLC) is a private limited company (Ltd). Differences, are, for example:

- PLC can advertise shares to general public, Ltd not legally allowed do so;
- public limited company has 'PLC' after name, private limited company has 'Ltd';
- PLC £50 000 minimum authorised capital, Ltd no minimum;
- PLC minimum 2 directors, Ltd minimum 1;
- Ltd less detailed accounting and disclosure requirements;
- PLCs have more restrictions upon officials and directors;
- PLC needs Certificate of Trading to start business, Ltd does not;
- PLC may be quoted on Stock Exchange, Ltd cannot.

(b)
- Shows the aims and objects of the company, that is what its main business will be. Activities not allowed by Memorandum are *ultra vires* (beyond the powers) and therefore may be declared void.

- Regulates the external affairs of the company with other people and organisations.

(c) For example Articles of Association, Statement of Authorised Capital, details of directors, Statutory Declaration.

(d) Company which has ownership/controlling interest (not necessarily more than 51% of shares) in other companies. Most holding companies do not trade in their own right but control other companies, for example Tesco PLC owns Tesco Stores Ltd which owns the supermarkets.

(e) For example, potential profitability of acquired firm, shareholders' reaction in both firms, risk of Government intervention such as Monopolies and Mergers Commission reference, cost and availability of finance, employees' reaction, management skills in both companies, effect on share price, compatibility with existing activities (such as purchase of competitor, supplier, customer or complete diversification).

2.3 Study the extract and answer the questions that follow.

Nationalised Industries' Performance
At the end of the 1970s nationalised industries (NIs) as a whole were performing badly, after years of financial problems and subsidisation. The Government's main response has been to privatise. So far 16 major businesses have been returned to the private sector. For those still in the public sector the Government have tightened up financial disciplines, exposed their activities wherever possible to market competition, and generally demanded higher standards of management and efficiency.

Table 1

	Employment (annual % change)			Productivity (annual % change)		
	NIs	Manu-facturing	Whole economy	NIs	Manu-facturing	Whole economy
1975–76	−1.0	−5.3	−1.9	−5.1	−2.8	−1.8
1976–77	−2.3	−1.7	−1.0	2.1	6.1	3.7
1977–78	−1.9	0.2	0.4	1.2	−0.3	1.1
1978–79	−1.0	−0.6	1.3	3.2	1.7	1.7
1979–80	−1.0	−1.0	1.2	0.1	0.9	0.7
1980–81	−3.1	−6.9	−2.0	−0.5	−5.3	−3.8
1981–82	−5.5	−8.3	−3.9	6.5	6.9	3.5
1982–83	−5.5	−6.0	−2.2	2.4	6.4	4.0
1983–84	−6.1	−4.4	−0.2	7.2	8.3	4.0
1984–85	−4.5	−0.8	2.2	6.0	4.8	2.9
1985–86	0.0	0.6	1.4	0.8	2.4	1.1
1986–87	−6.0	−2.3	0.5	6.2	4.8	3.6

Table 2 Nationalised industries

	Gross trading surplus		External finance	
	£ bn	% GDP	£ bn	% GDP
1975–76	0.7	0.7	n.a.*	—
1976–77	0.8	0.6	2.1	1.6
1977–78	1.2	0.8	1.6	1.1
1978–79	1.3	0.8	2.0	1.2
1979–80	1.1	0.5	2.8	1.3
1980–81	1.5	0.6	3.2	1.4
1981–82	2.1	0.8	2.6	1.0
1982–83	2.7	1.0	2.4	0.9
1983–84	2.7	0.9	2.3	0.8
1984–85	3.1	0.9	2.0	0.6
1985–86	3.9	1.1	1.5	0.4
1986–87	4.5	1.2	1.2	0.3

(*not available)

Source: Adapted from *Economic Progress Report*,
December 1987, HM Treasury

(a) List **two** existing nationalised industries. *(2 marks)*

(b) On the same axes, graph the annual percentage changes in both employment and productivity for nationalised industries between 1980 and 1987. *(10 marks)*

(c) Using the information in Tables 1 and 2 and your graph from part (b) comment on the performance of the nationalised industries. *(12 marks)*

(d) Outline **two** economic arguments for and **two** economic arguments against privatisation. *(8 marks)*

(AEB)

Answer **(a)** See list in Figure 2.5, but note that some nationalised industries were planned for privatisation at a later date.

(b)

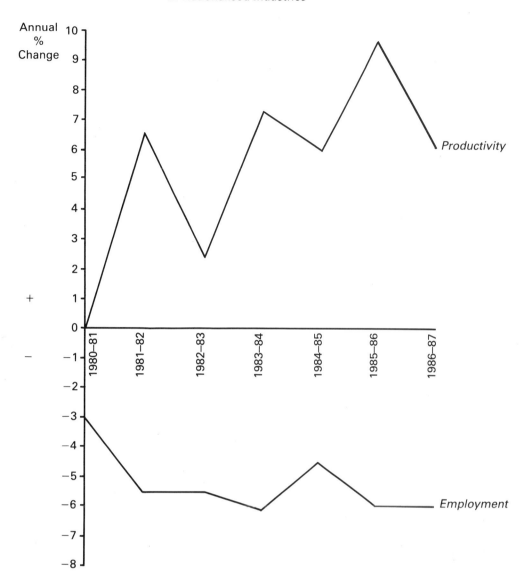

Changes in employment and productivity
in Nationalised Industries

Source: Economic Progress Report
(Dec. 1987)

(c) An answer to this question should focus on *analysis* rather than *description* of the data, and should relate the data specifically to Nationalised Industry performance.

Four basic variables can be identified from the data – employment, productivity, gross trading surplus, that is profit, and external finance, that is the amount that nationalised industries are allowed to borrow.

Employment has fallen every year since 1980 (note that the figures show the *change* and not the *level* of employment). It has fallen faster than that in manufacturing or the economy as a whole. This might be regarded as an indicator of increased efficiency because of elimination of over-manning. However it may also be due to falling sales or denationalisation. These effects cannot be seen from the data shown.

Productivity has improved in every year, although the rate of increase has varied significantly. It has also increased more rapidly than that of manufacturing and the whole economy. The productivity rise may be due to factors such as more capital-intensive production, improved technology, more flexible labour practices and cutting out of less efficient production units such as exhausted coal-mines.

Gross trading surplus has risen steadily, and faster than GDP, which implies that NIs have increased profitability more rapidly than the rest of the economy. This may have been due to factors such as better management, cost-cutting, greater productivity and higher prices. Figures for inflation during the period would be useful to verify the increase in *real* profits.

External finance has fallen, both in absolute money terms and as a percentage of GDP. This may be due to factors such as greater profitability, denationalisation and reductions in investment.

25

(d) *For*: for example more competition, increased efficiency, better consumer choice, improved quality of goods and services, lower prices, lower financial burden on Government, privatisation receipts can be used for other Government services, lower taxes, reduced Government control of economy, increased share ownership.

Against: for example public monopolies become private monopolies so little increase in competition, Government loses control of strategic industries, essential but unprofitable services not produced, often sold too cheaply, higher prices.

Essay questions

2.4 Before 1981 management buyouts were unknown in the UK. In 1986 there were 281 with a total value of £1.2 billion. Analyse the reasons for this growth.

(AEB)

Answer (i) Start by defining 'management buyout' (MBO) as the purchase of all or part of a business by its existing management.

(ii) Factors creating the growth of management buyouts (MBOs) can be divided into general economic changes and the advantages claimed for MBOs, which encouraged lenders to finance them.

Economic factors include:

- The merger boom of the mid-1980s, when many new parent companies sold off parts of the businesses they had taken over.
- The growth of privatisation. Some small public corporations and Government organisations were sold to their employees or managers. Contracting-out of local authority services such as school meals and bus services also led to the formation of many MBOs.
- Large firms started to decentralise and contract-out some of their ancillary services such as transport and printing.
- In many cases employees preferred a MBO to the prospect of redundancy or a hostile take-over.
- Interest rates were low and many lenders were prepared to lend high proportions of the cost of a buyout (leading to 'highly-geared' or 'leveraged' MBOs). Managements could therefore buy their firms with relatively little of their own capital invested in them.
- The rapid rise in share prices encouraged managers to take the risk of buying their companies with the expectation of a high profit when they sold their shares.

The main advantage claimed for MBOs is that managers are 'set free' to manage the company efficiently without interference from outside shareholders or directors who do not know the business well. The managers' close contact with workers and customers allows them to spot weaknesses and new opportunities. They also have the incentive to make the business as profitable as possible because they benefit directly from its success.

2.5 It is a widely-held belief that industrial co-operatives have failed, and yet there are over one thousand, mainly of a small-scale nature, operating in the UK. What advantages do they possess over ordinary companies and to what extent is their small scale inevitable?

(AEB)

Answer (i) Explain the term 'industrial co-operative', that is firm owned and controlled jointly by its workers, who elect directors and share any profits made. Shares are not transferable to outsiders and are redeemed (bought back) if the worker leaves the company.

(ii) Explain the advantages claimed for worker co-operatives, that is workers have a direct financial stake in the firm's success and also participate in management decisions. Because of these two factors they are more motivated and involved in their work, which leads to greater productivity and better quality goods and services.

(iii) Outline the reasons for many co-operatives being small-scale:

- Many are deliberately set up to be small-scale, for example with a few people setting up a craft co-operative.
- It is difficult to raise finance for co-operatives. Banks are often suspicious because they feel that co-operatives are not likely to make a profit since this is not their main aim. The value of shares is fixed (in most cases) which discourages large-scale investment in equity.
- Many co-operatives are set up as a result of a private firm going bankrupt, for example the Meriden co-op was established when Norton closed its factory – it eventually collapsed.

2.6 'Privatisation, through the profit motive, ultimately maximises consumer satisfaction'. 'Certain industries are too important to be left in private ownership'. From your study of business, how far can you reconcile these two views?

Answer (i) Define privatisation as transfer of production from public sector to private sector. Describe briefly the 3 types (denationalisation, deregulation and contracting-out).

(ii) Explain the rationale behind the first statement, that is managers of private sector organisation should be more efficient than public sector managers because they have to make a profit for their shareholders.

They also need to persuade customers to buy their products, often in competition with other producers. Therefore the consumer gets good quality goods and services at reasonable prices.

(iii) Explain the reasoning behind the second statement, that is some industries, such as electricity, telecommunications and rail transport, might be regarded as vital to the rest of the economy. Private producers may not provide adequate quantity or quality of service, for example rural railway lines or postal services may be unprofitable and therefore abandoned. *External benefits* may be lost because of the profit motive.

Private firms may also ignore *external costs* such as pollution or unemployment caused by closures of plants. A firm in the public sector may be more willing to act in the public interest, for example by locating in areas of high unemployment.

(iv) Finally, criticise these two statements. For example there is little evidence that privatisation has increased competition or made production more efficient. Similarly, nationalised industries have also created external costs such as pollution and regional unemployment, for example British Steel halved its workforce during the 1980s while still under Government control.

Self-test Questions

Short-answer questions

2.7 Suggest two possible reasons for the Government's privatisation policy.

(AEB)

2.8 Under the Partnership Act how would the profits of a partnership be divided between three partners if a formal agreement did not exist?

(AEB)

2.9 Explain the term 'limited liability'.

(AEB)

2.10 Distinguish between a public company and a public corporation.

(AEB)

Data-response question

2.11 The following passage is adapted from Buy-outs and British Industry (*Lloyds Bank Review*, October 1982). Read the passage carefully and answer the questions which follow.

> The buy-out of companies by their management has been one of the more important changes in the UK commercial and industrial scene in recent years: a development which was taken one step further in 1982 with the staff buy-out of the National Freight Corporation. This experience can be seen in the wider context of change within industry which has shown an increasing tendency to emphasize smaller scale, more autonomous, units of control. In many aspects we are seeing a reaction to the increased concentration which took place through the merger activities of the 1960s and 1970s.
>
> In general, the view is that big has been disappointing, and that much of the problem can be accounted for through either the diseconomies of managerial control, or more pertinently, the effects of an increased divorce between ownership and control. The management buy-out has primarily been seen in terms of a remarriage of ownership and control. The resultant companies have had a substantial portion of the equity owned by a small management group.

(a) What do you understand by the expression 'buy-out' in line 1 of the passage? *(3 marks)*
(b) The extract argues that 'big has been disappointing' as a result of either 'diseconomies of managerial control' or 'increased divorce between ownership and control'. Elaborate on each of these arguments. *(10 marks)*
(c) Describe **three** examples of the problems which the new owners may face following a buy-out. *(6 marks)*

(AEB)

Essay questions

2.12 **(a)** The Government has decided to privatise public libraries. How might this decision be implemented?
(b) As the Chief Librarian of a Public Library, write a report to the local Member of Parliament *either* supporting *or* condemning the proposal.

(UCLES)

2.13 In 1988 a number of firms decided to revert to private limited company status after being quoted on the Stock Exchange for some time. Discuss factors which might influence them to make such a move.

(AEB)

INFORMATION AND DECISION-MAKING

Business Information

The nature of business information

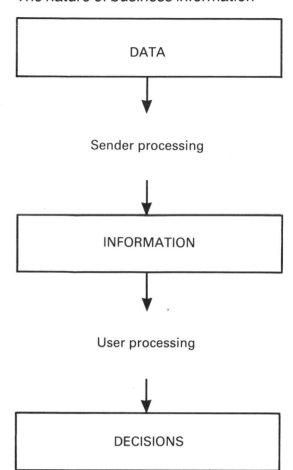

Figure 3.1 Information and decision-making

1. Data and information

The terms *data* and *information* are often used inter-changeably, but this is rather loose usage. In simple terms, data may be defined as basic facts which need *processing* in order to be of any practical use.

For example the personnel director of a large firm may be able to obtain a list of facts such as age, grade, salary and experience for every single worker in the business. However, lengthy unprocessed lists would be of little practical use for the personnel director's work.

Appropriate re-working or *processing* of data makes it useful *information*. If the personnel director wished to calculate the number of staff likely to retire, for example, he or she could ask for the raw data to be re-arranged to show the number of workers in each age-group. This would provide information which might be of use in planning replacement of workers.

It is important to remember that the processing of data must provide information in a form which is readily understandable by the user. The information has to be understood and processed by the user before it can be used as the basis for decisions.

2. Quantitative and qualitative data

Quantitative data, as its name implies, is data which records measurable facts such as sales or profit figures. It

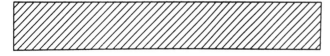

is often seen as superior to *qualitative data* which may represent opinions or vague ideas.

For example a manager may be aware that staff are becoming increasingly unhappy, but may be unable to produce any statistical information to prove the point. This does not mean that the manager's hunch should be ignored.

Despite this objection to the superiority of quantitative data, it can be argued that there is nearly always some form of numerical data which can be used to point to potential strengths or weaknesses of an organisation. For example, low morale among workers will often lead to measurable occurrences such as higher absenteeism, labour turnover or lower productivity.

In summary, it should be said that quantitative and qualitative data are complements to each other rather than alternative sources of guidance. Numerical data is useful for highlighting potential successes or problems or for helping to confirm their existence. *Ratio analysis* (see Chapter 5) is a good illustration of this.

3. Internal and external data

Internal data consists of facts which are available from the organisation's own records. Some of this information, such as employee or sales records, will be automatically recorded during day-to-day activity.

External data is data which is available from sources outside the business. It may come in various forms such as Official Statistics and market reports. Some of these are listed in Chapter 7.

Effectiveness of information

In order to be used effectively, information needs to be provided:

- at the right time;
- to users who need and can act on it;
- in a format understandable to the user;
- in enough detail for the user (but not in more detail than is necessary);
- at an appropriate cost.

It can be seen that providing too much information can be as bad as providing too little. A balance has to be struck between the cost of providing information (in time, wages and other costs) and the usefulness of the information to users. This is illustrated in Figure 3.2, where any

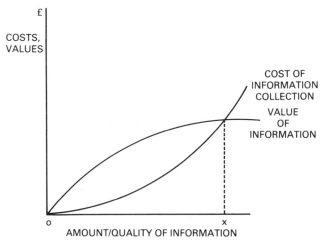

Figure 3.2 Cost-effectiveness of information

quantity or detail of information beyond OX costs more than its value to the organisation.

Accuracy and bias

Even numerical and statistical information can suffer from problems which mean that it has to be treated carefully. For example a major cause of increased burglary figures in the last twenty years has been the fact that more people have insurance and now report crimes which they might not have done before.

Common sources of potential inaccuracy in statistics include:

1. *Inadequate sample size*, for example not enough people interviewed in a market survey or opinion poll.
2. *Under-reporting*, for example incomes not declared for tax.
3. *Changes of definitions*, for example the method of calculating unemployment was changed about 20 times during the 1980s.
4. *Non-comparable definitions*, for example when comparing inflation or unemployment in different countries.
5. *Different interpretations and measures*, for example there is considerable argument about whether the Retail Price Index, which measures UK inflation, should include the cost of mortgage repayments (see Figure 3.3 for a comparison).

Figure 3.3 Alternative measures of inflation

6. *Deliberate distortion*, for example presenting figures in different ways. A common method is to cut the bottom off a scale to exaggerate the growth of sales, shares prices, profits, etc. An example can be seen in Figure 3.4 which shows how the same information can be presented to give widely different impressions.

Presentation of Information

Principles of presentation

In presenting information for use by others, the way in which it is presented may be as important as the factual

(a)	(b)

LETTERS POSTED   1979–89

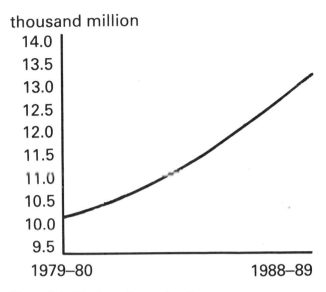

thousand million

LETTERS POSTED

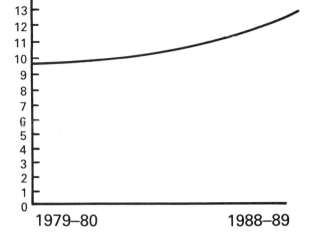

Figure 3.4 The importance of scale

details it is intended to show. This is explained in Worked example **3.8**.

Whatever the information presented, certain principles are seen as 'good practice':

- *appropriate quantity and detail of information*;
- *clarity and attractiveness of presentation*;
- *appropriate techniques for the user*, for example the correct level of difficulty and statistical technique;
- *lack of bias*, that is users should as far as possible be allowed to interpret the data themselves and reach their own conlusions about its content and relevance;
- *listing of sources*, including those from which further information can be obtained.

Whatever the presentational method used, any tabular or visual presentation should include all or most of the following:

- title(s);
- axes or columns labelled with units and/or scales;
- headings and labels for lines, parts of diagrams, etc.;
- sources and dates of data.

Tables

Tables are one of the commonest and most simple methods of summarising and presenting data. Labelled columns and rows can quickly show accurate information which can be quickly and easily comprehended.

Tables can also be used to interpret data partially. For example the table in Figure 3.5 shows what has happened to both dividends and earnings per share for Glaxo PLC during the 1980s. Although it is possible loosely to follow the trends in each variable, it is easier to compare their growth by presenting a third column such as that in Figure 3.6, which gives a direct comparison of the two variables by showing the proportion of earnings paid to shareholders.

The main disadvantages of tables are that they are often

Figure 3.5 Tabulation of Glaxo share statistics 1979–89

YEAR	DIVIDEND PER SHARE (pence)	EARNINGS PER SHARE (pence)
1979	2.0	7.0
1980	2.4	6.2
1981	2.8	8.9
1982	3.5	11.7
1983	4.5	14.9
1984	6.5	22.9
1985	10.0	37.4
1986	14.0	54.1
1987	19.0	67.0
1988	25.0	77.1
1989	35.0	92.4

Source: *Glaxo Holding PLC Annual Report 1989*

Figure 3.6 Refinement of Glaxo share statistics

YEAR	DIVIDEND PER SHARE AS % OF EARNINGS PER SHARE
1979	28.6
1980	38.7
1981	31.5
1982	29.9
1983	30.2
1984	28.4
1985	26.7
1986	25.9
1987	28.4
1988	32.4
1989	37.9

visually boring and do not usually show trends or comparisons as well as other methods of presentation.

Graphs

Graphs are used to show information in a more attractive and easily comprehensible form. The most common form

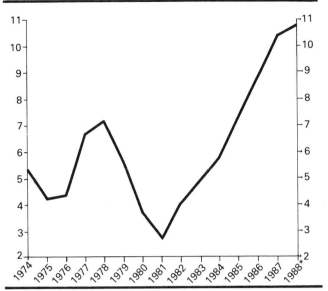

Profitability of UK companies

%

*Estimate

Note: Rate of return on capital employed by UK industrial and commercial
companies excluding North Sea Companies

Source: DTI, *British Business*

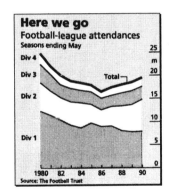

Figure 3.7 Time-series graphs

is the *time-series graph*, which shows changes in a variable such as profitability or oil reserves over a period of time.

Bar-charts

Bar-charts are used to compare different quantities by drawing bars or lines with their height or length proportionate to the quantity measured. They can be used in several ways, as shown in Figures 3.8 and 3.9.

It is traditionally regarded as proper to leave spaces between different bars, but this requirement is often ignored in practice. Bar-charts can be constructed in many different ways. Figure 3.9 gives a few commonly-used examples.

Pie-charts

Pie-charts are used to show proportions of a whole, for

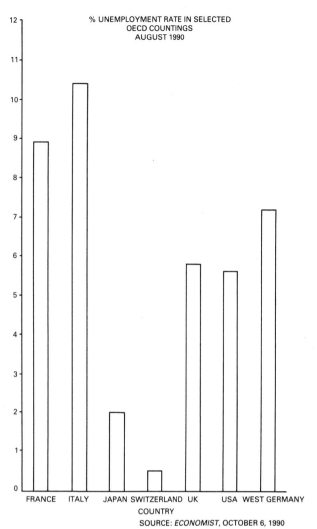

Figure 3.8 A simple bar-chart

example to divide a firm's sales by region or product. The area of each segment is proportional to each proportion. For example the 'bank borrowing' segment of the pie-chart in Figure 3.10 is 64% of the circle, which represents its 64% of external funding.

Histograms

A *histogram* (see Figure 3.11) shows the frequency of different variables. It looks similar to a bar-chart except that the bars are drawn touching each other. The height or length of the bars is proportional to the frequency of the variable (in this case, the amount spent per customer).

Pictograms

Pictograms are used for visual impact, with the purpose of attracting attention rather than reading data precisely. They are likely to distort data and are sometimes deliberately used for this purpose.

For example the 'Bananatronics' pictogram in Figure 3.13 actually shows sales as rising by 50%. However, by increasing the width as well as the height of the computer graphic, the impression of a much greater increase is given.

31

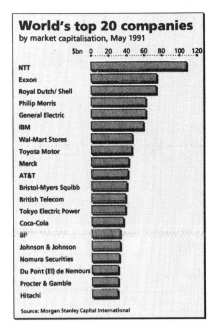

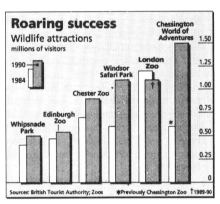

Figure 3.9 Varieties of bar-chart

1988,%

U.K. companies' external funding

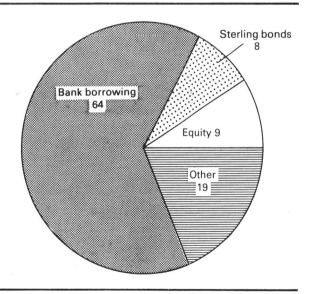

Source: CSO, *Financial Statistics*, and Bank of England

Figure 3.10 A pie-chart

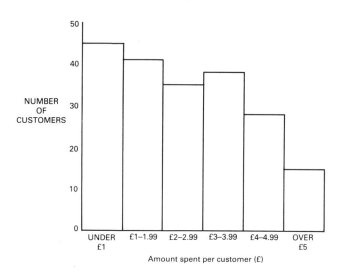

Value of individual customer purchases in O'Malley's chemists, June 1, 1991

Figure 3.11 A histogram

Index numbers

Index numbers are used when it is necessary to reduce different figures to a common base for easy comparison. A *base year* is chosen and all figures for that year are given a value of 100. Other figures are then expressed as a percentage of the original.

For example, the price of a good rises from £10 to £15. The original price is given a value of 100. The new price is 150% of £10, so it is given an index number of 150.

Index numbers make it easy to compare figures. For example the data in Figure 3.5 can be converted to indices and presented in a graph (see Figure 3.14). This makes the relative changes in earnings and dividends per share more obvious.

Decision Trees

Decision trees are a method of quantifying the best strategy for a business to use when the outcomes of alternative decisions are uncertain. They use the concept of *probability* for this purpose.

Probability is the likelihood of an event occurring, expressed as a fraction of 1. An event which is certain to take place, such as that a person will eventually die, has a probability of 1. An event which will definitely not occur, such as that a person will live forever, has a probability of 0.

Figure 3.12 Pictograms

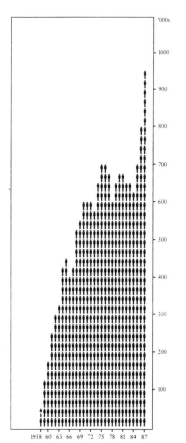

Membership of Consumer Association 1957–1987

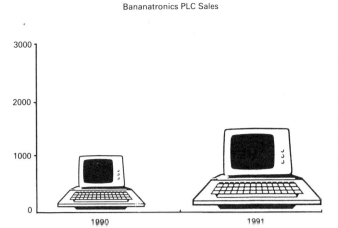

Figure 3.13 Pictogram distortion

Most probabilities fall between these two extremes, for example the chance of a coin landing on heads is 0.5. Decision trees assume that it is possible to assess in advance the probability of an event such as a new product being successful.

In constructing a decision tree it is necessary to make an accurate forecast of both the probability of an outcome and its likely effect on variables such as sales, costs or profits. Therefore it is insufficient for example to know the probability of a product being successful; the forecaster must also be able to place a numerical value on its effect on the business.

For example, suppose a retail chain has acquired a small shop as part of a takeover. It has three basic choices about what to do with the shop:

1. *Sell it.* This will earn revenue of £10 000.
2. *Open immediately.* Success has a probability of 0.6 and would earn £20 000 profit. Failure has a probability of 0.4 and would earn only £8000 in profit.
3. *Open after market research and extra promotion.* This would cost £5000 and reduce the return from success or failure by that amount. However it would increase the likelihood of success to 0.9 and reduce the probability of failure to 0.1

The company is therefore faced by a range of possible outcomes, as shown in Figure 3.15, with returns varying from £3000 to £20 000. Only the immediate sale has a certain outcome, but this is lower than will be earned if the shop is opened successfully.

One way of evaluating whether the risk of opening is worthwhile is to calculate the *expected values* of each decision. This is done by 'weighting' the returns from success or failure by their probabilities.

Open immediately

$$\text{Expected Value (EV)} = (£20\,000 \times 0.6) + (£8000 \times 0.4)$$
$$= £12\,000 + £3200$$
$$= £15\,200$$

Open after market research and extra promotion

$$\text{Expected Value (EV)} = (£15\,000 \times 0.9) + (£3000 \times 0.1)$$
$$= £13\,500 + £300$$
$$= £13\,800$$

Both of the expected values for opening are higher than

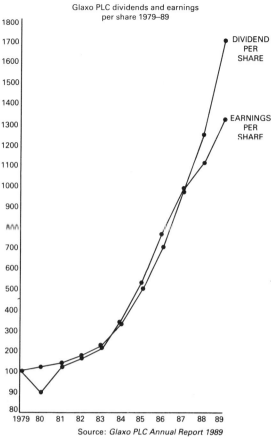

Glaxo PLC dividends and earnings per share 1979–89

Source: *Glaxo PLC Annual Report 1989*

	DPS	EPS
1979	100	100
1980	120	88
1981	140	127
1982	175	167
1983	225	213
1984	325	327
1985	500	534
1986	700	773
1987	950	957
1988	1250	1101
1989	1700	1320

Figure 3.14 Indexation of Glaxo share statistics

the £10 000 which would be received by selling the shop, so the decision tree analysis suggests that the firm should open the shop. Since the expected value for opening immediately is the highest, the expense of market research and extra promotion cannot be justified.

Decision trees have the advantage of clarifying the risks and possible outcomes from different business strategies. The act of constructing them helps to highlight the information which is necessary to assess risks.

Use of decision trees does however assume that all of the events which affect final outcomes can be foreseen, and that their probability can be accurately forecast. It is also assumed that the alternative outcomes in sales, costs, profits, etc. can be predicted accurately.

Even where a decision tree analysis indicates a logical decision, the attitude of management may be as crucial as

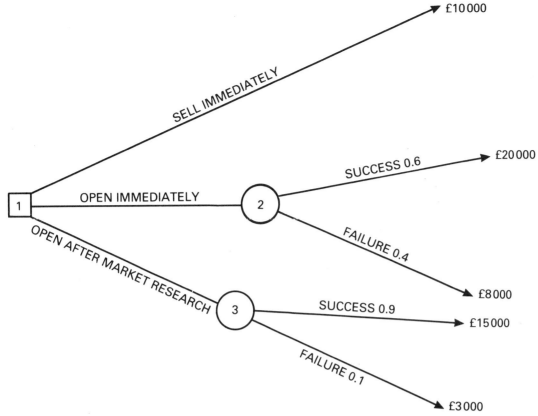

Figure 3.15 A simple decision tree

any quantitative analysis. In the example given above a cautious manager might prefer to pay for market research and extra promotion on the grounds that this made success very likely. An extremely cautious manager might even sell the shop immediately because there is a certain return.

Because of the impossibility of identifying risks accurately, and other factors such as managerial pessimism or optimism, decision trees are often used as an aid to planning rather than a fail-safe method of decision-making.

Networks

Uses of networks

Network analysis, also known as *critical path analysis* (CPA) or *project evaluation and review technique* (PERT), is used to plan complex tasks such as large-scale building or engineering projects.

Network analysis is most commonly used where different tasks have to be performed in a particular order. For example the foundations of a house have to be laid before the walls can be built, and the roof cannot be erected until the walls are finished. This sequence is illustrated in the network in Figure 3.16.

The circles in a network are *nodes*. They symbolise the start and finish of a particular activity and separate it from other activities.

The processes in Figure 3.16 are *consecutive activities* because they must follow each other in sequence. *Simultaneous activities*, as their name suggests, can take place at the same time.

For example once the walls are built, roof erection and window-fitting can be undertaken independently of each other. When the roof and windows are both finished, internal work such as plastering can start.

A simple network for these processes is illustrated in Figure 3.17. Note that there are alternative ways of illustrating simultaneous activities.

Planning with networks

1. Network notation

Networks can be used to determine the likely duration of a project, the sequence in which different activities must take place and the effect of delays in individual activities upon the completion date of the whole project. For example a network should be able to assess the likely impact of a delay in constructing the walls of a building because of bad weather or slow work.

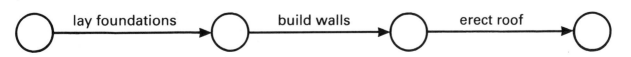

Figure 3.16 Network analysis – consecutive activities

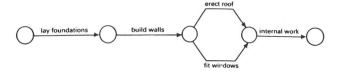

NB: This network could be drawn using a 'dummy' node with a dotted arrow (as below)

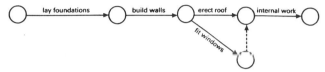

Figure 3.17 Network analysis – simultaneous activities

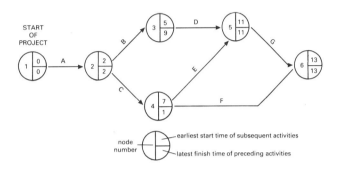

Activity	Duration (days)	Immediate predecessors
A	2	—
B	3	A
C	5	A
D	2	B
E	4	C
F	2	C
G	2	D, E

Figure 3.18 A simple network

It is customary to number nodes in the left-hand side of the circle. In Figure 3.18, node 1 is the start of the project and node 6 represents its completion. The right-hand side of the node circle is used to show the *earliest start time* (EST) and *latest finish time* (LFT).

2. *Earliest start time* (EST)

The EST of a node is the earliest date at which immediately following activities can be started. For example, at node 2, activities B and C cannot start until A is finished, that is 2 days after the beginning of the project.

Activity D cannot start until A and B are completed, that is after 5 days (2 + 3). The EST for node 3 is therefore 5.

E cannot start until C is completed, that is after 7 days. The EST for node 4 is therefore 7. Activities E and F cannot start until this date.

G cannot start until both D and E are finished. D could be finished by day 7 (2 + 3 + 2). However activity E cannot be completed until the 11th day (2 + 5 + 4). G therefore cannot start until day 11, which is the EST for node 5.

Finally, completion of the project will occur when both

F and G are completed. F can be finished in 9 days (2 + 5 + 2) but G will take until day 13 (2 + 5 + 4 + 2). The minimum completion time for the whole project is therefore 13 days.

3. *Latest finish time* (LFT)

The *latest finish time* (LFT) for an activity is the latest date at which it must be completed without delaying the whole project and extending the time taken to complete it. It is calculated by working back from the minimum completion date.

For example activities D and E must be finished in time for G to be completed by day 13. Since G takes 2 days, both D and E must be finished by day 11.

Working back, D must be started by day 9 at the latest. This means that B must be completed by day 9 and the LFT for node 3 is thus 9.

E takes 4 days and must therefore be started by day 7 if it is to finish by the 11th day. C must be completed by day 7 which is the LFT for node 4.

The LFT for node 2 is calculated by working back from the LFTs of nodes 3 and 4. B must be finished by day 9 (LFT of node 3) and could be started as late as day 6. However C takes 5 days and must be finished by day 7. Activity A must be completed by day 2 to allow this and to avoid delaying the whole project. The LFT for node 2 is therefore 2.

4. *The critical path*

The *critical path* through a network is the sequence of *critical activities*. Critical activities are those which will increase the project's duration if they are late in starting or take longer than expected to complete.

The critical path goes through all the nodes for which EST = LFT. In Figure 3.18, these are 1, 2, 4, 5 and 6. This means that the activities on the critical path must start and finish exactly as planned, or the whole project will take longer than the planned 13 days.

The critical activities in Figure 3.18 are therefore A, C, E and G. The other activities B, D and F are *non-critical activities* because even if they are delayed or over-run their planned time, it may still be possible to complete the project within 13 days.

For example activity F has to be finished by day 13. Assuming that previous activities are completed on time, it could start as early as day 7 (see node 4). However it could be delayed until day 11, its *latest start time* (LST). Alternatively it could start on day 7 and take 6 days instead of its planned 2. Neither of these problems would stop the project from being completed on day 13.

Activity E is a different case. It cannot be started until day 7 (its EST). However, unlike activity F it must also start on its EST, and must be completed within its planned time. For example if its start was delayed to day 8, it would not be completed until day 12. G could not then be completed until day 14, resulting in the project going over its planned finish time. If E took longer than 4 days a similar effect would occur.

These examples illustrate the basic advantage of critical path analysis, which is that it shows which activities must be planned and monitored most thoroughly if the project is to be completed in time. Whereas the timing of non-critical activities cannot be ignored completely, some delay or over-run can be tolerated. The extent to which this is possible is measured by its *float*.

5. Float

Float measures the extent to which activities can be allowed to run late without increasing the project duration. Since critical activities must not over-run, it is only non-critical activities which have a float.

The *total float* of an activity is measured by the equation:

Total float = Latest start time − Earliest start time
(LST)　　　　　　(EST)

For example activity D in Figure 3.18 can start as early as day 5, but could start as late as day 9 and still be completed by its target date of day 11. Therefore

Total float = LST − EST
　　　　= 9 − 5
　　　　= 4 days

Assuming that other activities go as planned, activity D can be delayed or over-run by up to 4 days without delaying the entire project.

A critical activity has no float, since it cannot be delayed at all. For example activity C's EST is day 7. This is also its LST, since if it starts any later activity E cannot be completed by day 11 and the project will go beyond 13 days. For project C:

Total float = LST − EST
　　　　= 7 − 7
　　　　= 0

As stated above, an activity can over-run by its total float if all other activities are completed on time. However this assumption may not be valid and it is not necessarily possible for an activity to be delayed up to its total float.

For example activity B could start on day 6 and finish on day 9. This would still leave time for D to start on day 9 and finish on day 11. B's LST is therefore 9 and

Total float = LST − EST
　　　　= 9 − 5
　　　　= 4 days

B and D thus both have total floats of 4 days. One or the other may be delayed up to 4 days. However, as both are delayed by 4 days the project will over-run. B will finish on day 9. If the start of D is then delayed by a further 4 days, it will begin on day 13 and be completed on day 15. The project will not be completed until day 17.

In real life this situation might occur if the managers of B and D did not communicate with each other and assumed that they could delay or take 4 days longer than planned. For example B and D might be different parts of a plane or suspension bridge made by unconnected firms.

To avoid this 'knock-on effect' it is necessary to allocate the total float between the activities. There are 9 days between the completion of A and the start of G. B takes 3 days and D takes 2, leaving a float of 4 days which can be shared between the two activities. This allocation is made by calculating the *free float*.

The *free float* of an activity is the length of time it can be delayed without increasing the EST of subsequent activities. It is measured by the equation:

Free float = EST of subsequent − Activity − EST of
　　　　　　activity　　　　duration　　activity

For activity B:

Free float = EST of − Duration − EST of
　　　　　activity D　of B　　activity B
　　　　= 5 − 3 − 2
　　　　= 0

Activity B cannot be delayed because it has no free float.

For activity D:

Free float = EST of − Duration − EST of
　　　　　activity G　of D　　activity D
　　　　= 11 − 2 − 5
　　　　= 4

If activity managers are allowed to over-run up to the free float, the manager of B would be given no leeway, whereas the manager of activity D would be allowed an over-run of up to 4 days. It may seem rather unfair that the total float for the two activities should be given to D, but this is the best method of ensuring that the project is completed on time.

Another way of using the float on an activity is to conserve resources such as labour and equipment by re-allocating them to other activities or projects. Instead of allowing B or D to over-run, the project manager might switch resources temporarily to other projects or to critical activities. This should reduce costs and/or reduce the completion time for the project.

Worked Examples

3.1 **(a)** Outline briefly the operational research approach to problems. *(5 marks)*

(b) Johnston Ltd is a small firm of jobbing builders. They have received an order for the construction of a small prefabricated building and are using network analysis to plan the project. Draw the network for the project, given the following information.

Activity	Must be preceded by:
A	—
B	A
C	A
D	C
E	B
F	B
G	D
H	D, E
I	H, G

(4 marks)

(c) The company is involved in a second project. The network is shown below:

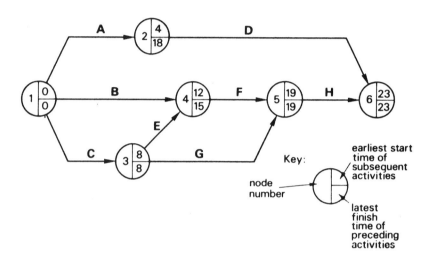

Activity:	A	B	C	D	E	F	G	H
Estimated Duration (days)	4	7	8	5	4	4	11	4

(i) Show that the total floats on activities A and D are both 14 days. What would the total float on activity D be if activity A over-ran by 3 days? Explain your answer. *(5 marks)*

(ii) Calculate the total float for all other activities and, using your answer, confirm that the critical path is via nodes 1, 3, 5 and 6. *(4 marks)*

(iii) The number of men needed for each activity is shown below:

Activity:	A	B	C	D	E	F	G	H
No. of men:	2	2	4	6	2	4	4	2

Each activity uses employees of the same skill level and no activity can be started with fewer than the number of employees required to carry out the activity. There are only six employees available for the project.

Explain how you would use float to ensure the optimum allocation of employees and show that the project cannot be completed in 23 days. *(7 marks)*

(UCLES)

Answer **(a)** Define OR simply, for example as a scientific approach to business problems and decisions, typically involving models, hypotheses, collection of data, analysis of risk, etc. A typical process might follow stages:

- vague recognition of problem;
- definition of problem;
- construction of model, such as network;
- use of model, such as by alteration of variables;
- choice of strategy;
- review of results of decisions;
- refinement of model/change of strategy.

(b) (i)

Activity A: Total float   = LST − EST
                                    = 18 − 4
                                    = 14 days

Activity D: Total float   = LST − EST
                                    = 18 − 4
                                    = 14 days

If A over-runs by 3 days, D cannot start until day 7 so:

Total float   = LST − EST
                      = 18 − 7
                      = 11 days

(ii)

Activity B: Total float   = LST − EST
                                    = 8 − 0
                                    = 8

Activity C: Total float   = LST − EST
                                    = 0 − 0
                                    = 0

Activity E: Total float   = LST − EST
                                    = 11 − 8
                                    = 3

Activity F: Total float   = LST − EST
                                    = 15 − 12
                                    = 3

Activity G: Total float   = LST − EST
                                    = 8 − 8
                                    = 0

Activity H: Total float   = LST − EST
                                    = 19 − 19
                                    = 0

The activities leading to nodes 1, 3, 5 and 6 have no float because LST = EST. If they are delayed, the project will take longer than the planned 23 days.

(iii) The float can be used to show where non-critical activities can be delayed and resources diverted to other activities.

There are various methods by which it can be shown that the project will over-run with only 6 employees. For example if the duration of each activity is multiplied by the number of men required to complete it, the number of man-days required is 160, compared with the 138 (6 × 23) which have been allocated to the project.

Another method is to consider the resources which must be devoted to critical activities which cannot be delayed. C takes 8 days and must be immediately followed by G, which has a duration of 11 days. This means that 4 men will be needed for the critical activities during the first 19 days.

However, activity D, which requires all 6 men, must start by day 18 at the latest. Therefore the project cannot be completed by 6 men in 23 days.

3.2 The data given below refer to a manufacturing company, XYZ Ltd. In 1970 the company employed a workforce of 2000, but by 1983 this number had dropped to 1000.

Fig. 1. Analysis of XYZ Ltd. workforce, by occupation

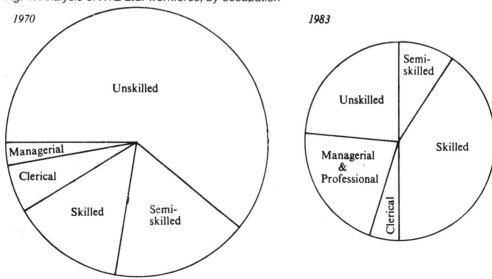

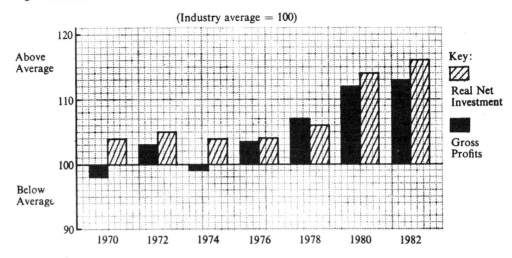

Fig. 2. Indices of Real Net Investment and Gross Profits for XYZ Ltd.

(a) State **one** advantage and **one** disadvantage of presenting data in the form of a pie chart. *(4 marks)*

(b) Give **one** reason why the pie-charts in Fig. 1 are of different sizes. *(3 marks)*

(c) Describe briefly the changes that have taken place in Company XYZ between 1970 and 1983. *(5 marks)*

(d) Using the data given above, state and explain **one** possible reason for the decline in the number of people employed by XYZ Ltd. *(4 marks)*

(e) Outline **three** problems the company might have faced as a result of the changing occupational structure of the workforce. *(9 marks)*

(AEB)

Answer (a) *Advantages*: for example shows proportions clearly, easy to compare categories quickly, attractive.

Disadvantages: for example poor display of absolute numbers or trends, such as workforce has halved but this is not exactly clear from pie-chart.

(b) Size of XYZ workforce halved between 1970 and 1983.

(c) For example:

- number of workers has fallen;
- composition of workforces has changed, for example higher % of skilled and managerial/lower % of unskilled workers;
- gross profits rose faster (or fell more slowly than) the industry average between 1970 and 1982 (no profit figures are given for 1983);
- real investment (that is after allowing for inflation) rose faster (or fell more slowly than) the industry average between 1970 and 1982 (no investment figures are given for 1983).

(d) For example labour replaced by machinery. Unskilled workforce has fallen by larger % than rest of workforce, investment appears to have risen more than average.

(e) For example:

- redundancy procedures and costs;
- job losses leading to lower morale;
- higher wages for more skilled/educated workforce;
- may be difficult to attract skilled workers;
- higher training costs;
- greater expectations by workers, such as for more satisfying work.

3.3 Newlin's Ltd. has to decide whether to continue producing its traditional range of goods next year or whether to produce an entirely new line. To help in making this decision, it is considering spending £5000 on a market research survey to assess the level of interest in this new line, which may be high, medium, or low. Whichever range Newlin's finally produces, it believes that the sales will be either 'successful' or 'unsuccessful'. The decision tree below illustrates the situation.

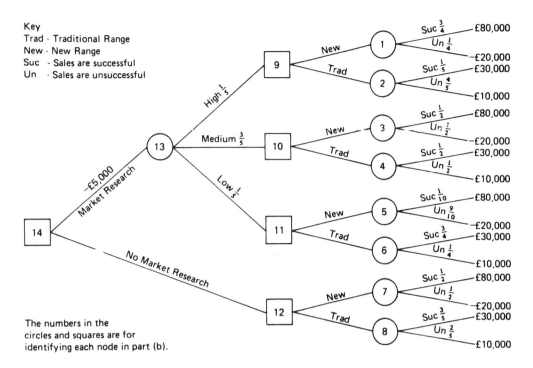

Key
Trad - Traditional Range
New - New Range
Suc - Sales are successful
Un - Sales are unsuccessful

The numbers in the circles and squares are for identifying each node in part (b).

(a) In the diagram, explain the significance of:
   (i) the squares;
   (ii) the circles;
   (iii) the fractions on the lines;
   (iv) the numbers at the end of the lines. *(4 marks)*
(b) (i) What do you understand by the term 'expected value' in the decision tree analysis? *(2 marks)*
   (ii) Calculate the expected values at each node in the decision tree. *(7 marks)*
(c) What action would you recommend Newlin's to take? Give reasons for your recommendation. What reservations might you have about your recommendation? *(3 marks)*

(UCLES)

Answer **(a)** (i) Squares are *decisions* to be made.
   (ii) Circles are *nodes* showing possible *outcomes* of decisions.
   (iii) Fractions are the *probabilities* of alternative outcomes.
   (iv) Numbers are the *value of sales* from different outcomes.

(b) (i) 'Expected value' (EV) is the sales expected as a result of alternative decisions, weighted according to the probability of different outcomes.
   (ii)
$$EV(1) = (\pounds 80\,000 \times \tfrac{3}{4}) + (-\pounds 20\,000 \times \tfrac{1}{4})$$
$$= \pounds 60\,000 - \pounds 5000$$
$$= \pounds 55\,000$$

$$EV(2) = (\pounds 30\,000 \times \tfrac{1}{5}) + (\pounds 10\,000 \times \tfrac{4}{5})$$
$$= \pounds 6000 + \pounds 8000$$
$$= \pounds 14\,000$$

$$EV(3) = (\pounds 80\,000 \times \tfrac{1}{2}) + (-\pounds 20\,000 \times \tfrac{1}{2})$$
$$= \pounds 40\,000 - \pounds 10\,000$$
$$= \pounds 30\,000$$

$$EV(4) = (\pounds 30\,000 \times \tfrac{1}{2}) + (\pounds 10\,000 \times \tfrac{1}{2})$$
$$= \pounds 15\,000 + \pounds 5000$$
$$= \pounds 20\,000$$

$$EV(5) = (\pounds 80\,000 \times \tfrac{1}{10}) + (-\pounds 20\,000 \times \tfrac{9}{10})$$
$$= \pounds 8000 - \pounds 18\,000$$
$$= -\pounds 10\,000$$

$$EV(6) = (£30\,000 \times \tfrac{3}{4}) + (£10\,000 \times \tfrac{1}{4})$$
$$= £22\,500 + £2500$$
$$= £25\,000$$

$$EV(7) = (£80\,000 \times \tfrac{1}{2}) + (-£20\,000 \times \tfrac{1}{2})$$
$$= £40\,000 - £10\,000$$
$$= £30\,000$$

$$EV(8) = (£30\,000 \times \tfrac{3}{5}) + (£10\,000 \times \tfrac{2}{5})$$
$$= £18\,000 - £4000$$
$$= £22\,000$$

To calculate the EV for node 13 take the highest EV possible from decisions 9, 10 and 11, that is £55 000, £30 000 and £30 000 respectively:

$$EV(13) = (£55\,000 \times \tfrac{1}{5}) + (£30\,000 \times \tfrac{3}{5}) + (£25\,000 \times \tfrac{1}{5})$$
$$= £11\,000 + £18\,000 + £5000$$
$$= £34\,000$$

(c) If market research is undertaken the EV is:

£34 000 − £5000 = £29 000

Without market research, the highest EV is £30 000 (see node 7). The best decision from the decision tree is therefore to introduce a new range without market research.

Reservations about the decision might include doubts about the accuracy of the assumptions about probability and expected sales.

3.4 The following information is taken from the article 'The development and future applications of pneumatic handling systems' by Tweedy and Collins (*The Mining Engineer*, June 1983). The pneumatic hoisting system costs £720 000 and the figures for the cumulative revenue given below are calculated on 3500 tonnes handled by the hoisting system and sold each month. The revenue figures are net of out-goings, that is running costs, interest and depreciation.

Pneumatic hoisting system: Payback on capital expenditure

Month	Cumulative net revenue at £5 per tonne (£000s)	Cumulative net revenue at £10 per tonne (£000s)	Cumulative net revenue at £15 per tonne (£000s)
1	70	140	210
2	140	280	420
3	210	420	630
4	280	560	840
5	350	700	1050
6	420	840	1260
7	490	980	1470
8	560	1120	1680
9	630	1260	1890
10	700	1400	2100
11	770	1540	2310
12	840	1680	2520

(a) Define the term 'payback'. *(4 marks)*
(b) From the data given and using the same axes in each case, draw a graph to illustrate the payback on the pneumatic hoisting system for each of the three rates per tonne. *(10 marks)*
(c) Assuming that the net revenue was £5 per tonne, approximately how long would it take a business using the pneumatic hoisting system to recover its initial capital outlay? *(2 marks)*
(d) Outline **three** advantages to a business of using the payback method of assessing the viability of an investment project. *(9 marks)*

(AEB)

Answer **(a)** Time taken for cash inflows from an investment to equal outflows, that is expenditure on an asset, is recovered from profits made as a result of the firm acquiring the asset.

(b)

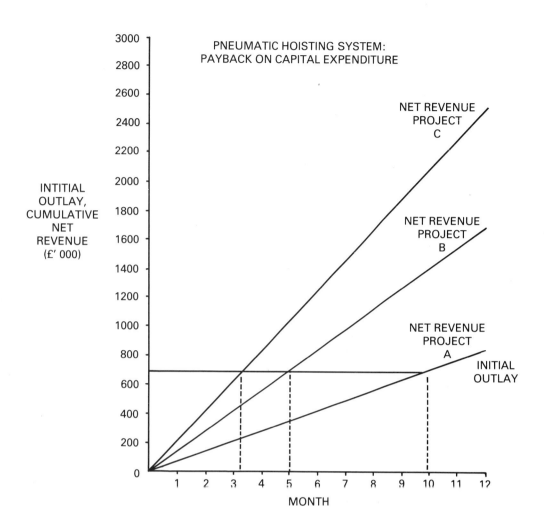

(c) Just over 10 months.

(d) For example:

- simple to calculate;
- easy to understand;
- good indicator of risk (faster payback = lower risk);
- takes timing of cash inflows into account (to a limited extent);
- can be used to 'screen' projects, for example if payback period longer than life of asset/life of product, asset should not be acquired;
- can be used to 'sift' alternative projects to see which pay back most quickly.

3.5 Machines Ltd. is about to choose between three projects:

Project A is for the purchase of a new machine;
Project B is for a promotional campaign;
Project C is for the rationalisation of a part of the production department.

The cost and expected returns for each project are as follows (£):

	Project A	Project B	Project C
Initial Cash Outlay			
Year 0	10 000	10 000	10 000
Cash Inflow			
Year 1	1 000	4 000	3 000
2	2 000	3 000	3 000
3	3 000	3 000	3 000
4	3 000	2 000	3 000
5	3 000		2 000
6	3 000		1 000

Present Value of £1 receivable at the end of a number of years, at 10%

After	1 year	2 years	3 years	4 years	5 years	6 years
PV of £1 (£)	0.91	0.83	0.75	0.68	0.62	0.56

(a) What is the Net Cash Flow for Project C? *(2 marks)*
(b) (i) Calculate the Net Present Value of each project using Discounted Cash Flow methods. *(11 marks)*
   (ii) On the basis of your calculations in (b) (i), which project should be selected? *(1 mark)*
(c) Suggest and explain **four** factors that might be taken into account when making an investment decision. *(8 marks)*
(d) State **three** different methods of financing the purchase of capital equipment. *(3 marks)*

(AEB)

Answer **(a)**

Net Cash Flow = Total of cash inflows – Initial cash outlay
= £15 000 – £10 000
= £5000

(b) (i)

Project A

Year (£)	Cash Inflow	× Present Value	= Net Present Value (£)
1	1 000	0.91	910
2	2 000	0.83	1 660
3	3 000	0.75	2 250
4	3 000	0.68	2 040
5	3 000	0.62	1 860
6	3 000	0.56	1 680
		Total	10 400

Project B

Year (£)	Cash Inflow	× Present Value	= Net Present Value (£)
1	4 000	0.91	3 640
2	2 000	0.83	2 490
3	3 000	0.75	2 250
4	3 000	0.68	2 040
		Total	10 420

Project C

Year	Cash Inflow (£)	× Present Value	= Net Present Value (£)
1	3 000	0.91	2 730
2	3 000	0.83	2 490
3	3 000	0.75	2 250
4	3 000	0.68	2 040
5	2 000	0.62	1 240
6	1 000	0.56	560
		Total	11 310

(ii) Project C – has largest Net Present Value (NPV).

(c) For example:

- purchase cost of asset;
- cost of capital, for example interest rate on borrowing;
- opportunity cost, for example interest on cash reserves;
- profitability of investment;
- future market trends, for example consumer demand;
- timing of cash inflows;
- changes in technology;
- quality of existing equipment;
- cost and profitability of alternative investments.

(d) For example:

- owners capital/shareholders funds;
- borrowing/leasing;
- equity capital;
- Government grants (in some cases).

3.6 **(a)** Why is 'weighting' necessary in constructing index numbers? Give a brief example. *(5 marks)*

(b) Identify the limitations of a typical retail price index. *(4 marks)*

(c) The following figures were provided by the Utopian Statistical Service for compiling a retail price index:

Item	Price Relative (June 1988, Jan 1980 = 100)	Weights (1987 average)
Food	110.3	25
Fuel	122.1	20
Housing	141.3	25
Services	126.9	15
Clothing	130.8	5
Miscellaneous	118.2	10
		100

(i) Explain why the weights refer to a period other than the base period (January 1980). *(3 marks)*

(ii) What is meant by the term 'price relative'? *(1 mark)*

(iii) Calculate a weighted aggregate price index for June 1988. *(6 marks)*

(d) A company calculates details of wage rates, material costs and factory overheads in index form, and in June 1988 these stood at 150, 60 and 130 respectively (January 1980 = 100). A particular product had the following cost structure in January 1980:

	£/unit
Labour	0.80
Materials	0.80
Factory Overheads	0.40
	2.00

(i) Estimate the mean percentage increase in the costs of producing the product between January 1980 and June 1988. *(4 marks)*

(ii) State any assumptions you have made. *(2 marks)*

(UCLES)

Answer **(a)** Weights reflect the importance of an item of expenditure/costs, etc. compared with the total, for example food is approximately a fifth of average UK consumer expenditure and thus has a weighting of about 200 out of 1000 in the Index of Retail Prices.

(b) For example:

* statistics based upon small sample;
* weighting is based upon 'average household', for example lower income households spend more than average proportion on food, higher income households spend higher than average proportion on consumer durables and holidays;
* new products make weights outdated;
* quality of goods may change;
* advertised prices may be more or less than those actually charged, for example because of discounts.

(c) (i) Weights have been updated to allow for changes in consumer spending. 1987 is most recent year.
(ii) Index of a single item in the index.
(iii)

Item	Price Relative	×	Weight	=	Weighted Index
Food	110.3		25		2 757.5
Fuel	122.1		20		2 442.0
Housing	141.3		25		3 532.5
Services	126.9		15		1 903.5
Clothing	130.8		5		654.0
Misc	118.2		10		1 182.0
					12 471.5

$$\text{Weighted price index} = \frac{\text{Total of weighted indices}}{\text{Total weights}}$$

$$= \frac{12\,471.5}{100}$$

$$= 124.715$$

(d) (i)

* Proportion of costs is the same in both 1980 and 1988.
* Quality of materials, labour, etc. are the same in both years.

Essay questions

3.7 State and discuss the criteria on which a statistical report should be based. Comment on the extent to which the presentation of data is as important as its accuracy.

(AEB)

Answer (i) Outline with examples the basic criteria which should be used in a good statistical report, such as:

* purpose clearly defined and explained;
* clarity and attractiveness of presentation;
* explanation of sources of data and further information;
* correct volume of detail and supporting explanation;
* complexity appropriate to the audience;
* variety of presentational methods;
* constraints of time and cost of collecting information;
* lack of bias;
* avoidance of over-reliance upon statistical information.

(ii) Evaluate the statement explaining the importance of presentation. Points might include:

* unattractive presentation will bore readers and may put them off reading it at all;
* large volumes of statistics may be used to confuse audience or hide facts;
* presentation may be designed to deceive or give a favourable impression, for example broken scales or pictograms.

3.8 **(a)** What is the role of the average rate of return when evaluating investment
projects? *(5 marks)*
(b) When might the payback period be a better technique? *(5 marks)*
(c) What advantages and disadvantages would the discounted cash-flow technique have over other methods when evaluating investment decisions? *(15 marks)*

(UCLES)

Answer　**(a)** Explain that the average rate of return is used where the life of the project and the expected profits can be forecast in advance. It is measured by the equation:

$$\text{Average rate of return (ARR)} = \frac{\text{Annual average profit}}{\text{Cost of initial investment}}$$

ARR is a quick easy way of comparing the profitability of alternative investments or of comparing the cost of financing an investment project with its profitability. However it takes no account of the timing of profits, for example profits received in the fifth year are regarded as equally worthwhile to those received 5 or 10 years later.

(b) Define the payback period as the time taken for the profits from an investment to equal its initial cost. Its advantage over ARR is that it recognises that the earlier that profits are received the better they are for the firm.

Payback also shows the length of time needed to recover the cost and may be important where investment capital is limited or there is a risk of capital assets or products becoming obsolete in the near future.

The main criticism of the payback methods is that it does not weight cash inflows according to when they are received. For example any profits received after the payback period are ignored. It is therefore better used as a quick 'screening' device to reject projects which cannot repay their initial cost within their useful life.

(c) Explain the basic rationale of discounted cash-flow (DCF) methods, that is allowance is made for the fact that earlier profits are more valuable. Give a simple numerical example of how Net Present Value (NPV) is calculated.

Explain factors which might affect the rate of discount, such as interest rates, 'normal' rate of return in the industry and 'riskiness' of investment.

Describe possible advantages of DCF methods over ARR and payback, for example:

- take full account of timing of payments and receipts;
- measure the 'opportunity cost' of capital more accurately;
- discount rate can be adjusted according to variables such as interest rates and the risk associated with different projects;
- can be used to rank projects in order of merit.

Explain possible disadvantages, such as:

- more complex than other methods;
- discount factors are only an intelligent guess, for example based upon forecasts of interest rates or 'normal' rates of return;
- forecasts of profits are less valid in later years.

Self-test Questions

Data-response questions

3.9　**(a)** Define the concept of marginal cost.　　　　　　　　　　　　　*(2 marks)*

(b) A hospital X-ray department has a machine which cost £250 000 five years ago, when it still had an expected life of 10 years. It costs £2500 a year to maintain and, in addition, a new special part costing £6600 is needed, on average, every 18 months. The life of this part is directly related to the number of investigations carried out by the machine, which averages 400 per year. In order to reduce film costs the X-ray department is considering the purchase of a camera at a cost of £35 000 to replace the existing X-ray film unit. This camera will cost £200 per year to maintain and is estimated to have a residual value of £2000 in five years' time. The direct costs per investigation under both systems are given in the table below:

	Machine with X-ray film unit	Machine with camera
Film costs:		
Average number of pictures	35	50
Fixed cost	—	£1
Cost per picture	£1	10p
Drugs	£5	£5
Minor Equipment	£30	£30
Contrast injections		
(@ £14 per bottle)	2 bottles	2 bottles – 75% of the time
		3 bottles – 25% of the time
Labour (@ £5 per hour)		
Day	Not applicable as it can be regarded as a fixed cost	
Night	2 hours	2 hours

(i) On the assumption that the X-ray film unit is in use, calculate the marginal cost of an investigation, both during the day and as a night-time emergency.　　*(4 marks)*

(ii) What additional costs should be included if you were calculating the total cost of an investigation in order to charge the patient.　　*(3 marks)*

(c) (i) Show that the annual cash flow can be reduced by £10 000 per year if the camera is bought. *(3 marks)*

(ii) Calculate the pay-back period for the purchase of the camera. *(1 mark)*

(iii) If the camera is bought, the present value of the *change* in cash flow over the next five years is £4100, using a discount rate of 10%. You are required to undertake the same calculation using a discount rate of 16%. *(5 marks)*

(d) (i) Discuss the relative merits of the methods of investment appraisal used in (c) (ii) and (c) (iii). On numerical grounds, would you recommend that the camera ought to be bought? *(4 marks)*

(ii) What other factors should be taken into consideration before a final decision is made? *(3 marks)*

Present values of £1 in future are given below at various rates:

	10%	12%	14%	16%
One year hence	0.91	0.89	0.88	0.86
Two years hence	0.83	0.80	0.77	0.74
Three years hence	0.75	0.71	0.68	0.64
Four years hence	0.68	0.64	0.59	0.55
Five years hence	0.62	0.57	0.52	0.48

(UCLES)

3.10 CKL is a manufacturer of capital equipment who set up in business 15 years ago (Year 1 in the table below). Its yearly sales, and the five and eight period moving averages, are shown below in index form.

Year	1	2	3	4	5	6	7	8
Sales Index	100	132	160	173	181	174	158	140
5 period moving			149.2	164	169.2	165.2	160.2	156.8
8 period averages					155.25	159.75	163.75	167.25

Year	9	10	11	12	13	14	15	16
Sales Index	148	164	184	205	209	198	178	164
5 period moving	156.8	168.2	182.0	192.0	196.8	190.8		
8 period averages	171	174.25	177	179.75				

(a) Time-series data, such as that in the table above, can be analysed into three major components. Identify these three components. *(3 marks)*

(b) (i) What factors should you bear in mind when choosing the number of observations you will use in a moving average? *(2 marks)*

(ii) Show how the five and eight period moving averages for year 10 have been calculated. *(6 marks)*

(iii) Plot a graph of the sales index and trend lines and comment on your result. *(9 marks)*

(c) (i) Stating clearly any assumptions you make, predict a trend value for year 18. *(2 marks)*

(ii) How would you attempt to make a useful forecast of the actual sales for year 18? *(3 marks)*

(UCLES)

3.11 The owner of a UK company selling coats, dresses and hats is considering expanding by setting up another shop in Europe.

(a) What commercial information should the owner seek before making any decision? *(4 marks)*

(b) The pie-charts below are taken from the company's reports and accounts for 1986.

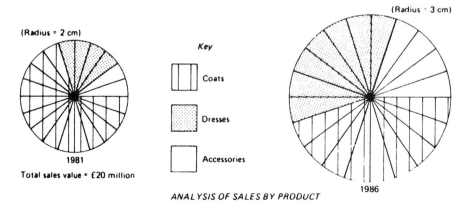

(Radius = 2 cm)

1981
Total sales value = £20 million

Key
Coats
Dresses
Accessories

(Radius = 3 cm)

1986

ANALYSIS OF SALES BY PRODUCT

(i) Discuss whether these pie-charts satisfy the main principles one should always bear in mind when presenting data. *(4 marks)*

(ii) Show that the total sales in 1986 were £45 million. *(3 marks)*

(iii) Calculate the percentage increase in the sales value of accessories between 1981 and 1986. *(3 marks)*

(iv) If total sales continue to increase by the same average amount over the next three years as they did in the five years 1981–1986, and sales of dresses increase by 40% in total over the next three years, what angle of a pie-chart for 1989 would represent the contribution to total sales by the dress department? *(4 marks)*

(c) The managers of the three departments each claim that their product is 'doing best'.

(i) How could each manager use the above pie-charts to support his claim? (You are not required to undertake any calculations to answer this question.) *(3 marks)*

(ii) Suggest an appropriate graphical method for displaying sales information. Give reasons for your answer. *(4 marks)*

(UCLES)

3.12 Castons Ltd. produces a casting for a car which has a design specification of 600 mm ± 2 mm. The machine has been set to produce no more than 0.3% defectives, but due to variation in the settings the actual number produced is usually much higher. Castons is considering changing its system of quality control in order to reduce the number of defectives which reach the customers.

(a) At the moment, Castons operates a quality control system whereby a single sample of 100 pieces is taken, and if more than one defective is found in the sample, the whole batch must be sorted.

Write down a simplified expression for the probability of the batch being sorted if:

(i) the batch contains no defectives, *(1 mark)*

(ii) the batch contains 1% defectives. *(2 marks)*

(b) (i) Define consumer's and producer's risks and show these on a sketch graph. *(5 marks)*

(ii) Explain how you would judge whether Castons is operating a good system of quality control at present and suggest any modification that could be made to improve the sampling system. *(5 marks)*

(c) Castons is considering the introduction of a quality control chart such as that shown below.

Upper action limit
Upper warning limit
Mean
Lower warning limit
Lower action limit

An operator would be required to sample two castings every five minutes. If the lengths of both castings were outside the warning limits or if the lengths of either was outside the action limit then the machine should be stopped immediately.

(i) What values should the action and warning limits take if, when the machine is correctly set, no more than 0.3% of all castings should lie outside the action lines and 95% should lie within the warning lines? (You may find the table at the end of the question helpful.) *(5 marks)*

(ii) What is the probability that a machine will be stopped unnecessarily (that is be stopped when it is still producing within the required tolerances)? *(3 marks)*

(d) What are the main differences between the two schemes and what additional factors should Castons bear in mind when deciding between them? *(4 marks)*

Distance from mean in terms of standard deviation	±1	±1.96	±2.58	±3
Proportion of area in given range	68%	95%	99%	99.7%

(UCLES)

3.13 The following information was taken from *The Economist*, 21 August 1982. Study it carefully and answer the questions.

Key indicators: **Commodity prices**

Big dipper

The long slide in commodity prices has brought the all-items dollar index to its lowest point for four years, 37% down from its peak in November, 1980. Prices of industrial commodities continue to weaken in the grip of world recession and a high dollar, while oversupply of many foods – notably grains, soya beans and sugar – has resulted in a slump in the food index. The relative buoyancy of the sterling indices over the past 18 months merely reflects the weakening pound.

The Economist commodity indices

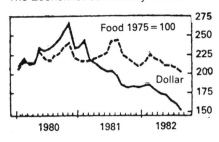

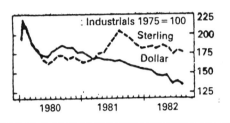

1975 = 100
Dollar index

	Aug 10	Aug 17	% change on the month	year
All items	149.2	147.8*	−3.8	−20.9
Food	156.1	154.2*	−4.2	−22.2
Industrial				
All	136.9	136.6*	−3.0	−18.4
Fibres	149.6	147.9*	−3.0	−6.3
Metals	123.4	124.5	−3.5	−22.1

Sterling index

	Aug 10	Aug 17	% change	year
All items	194.9	192.3*	−2.0	−15.2
Food	204.1	200.5*	−2.4	−16.7
Industrial				
All	178.9	177.6*	−1.2	−12.6
Fibres	195.5	192.3*	−1.2	+0.3
Metals	161.3	161.8	−1.7	−16.7

*Provisional.

(a) Define the term 'index' as used above. *(3 marks)*
(b) Explain briefly why 'Prices of industrial commodities continue to weaken in the grip of world recession and a high dollar'. *(8 marks)*
(c) Construct a bar-chart to compare the percentage changes in the year of the dollar commodity price indices for food, fibres and metals with those of sterling. *(8 marks)*
(d) Give **three** ways in which the trends illustrated above might affect a manufacturing company. *(6 marks)*

(AEB)

3.14 Figure 1. Total sales of sports equipment by UK manufacturers for the period 1961–77:

Sales (£m)

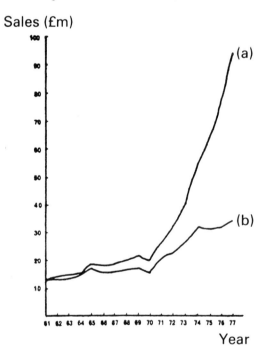

Year

(a) Sales at current prices.
(b) Sales deflated by sports equipment price index.

50

Figure 2. Exports and Imports of sports equipment:

	Exports (£ thousand)	As proportion of total UK manufacturers sales	Imports (£ thousand)	As proportion of total UK manufacturers sales
1970	9 888	50.99	3 105	15.99
1971	13 562	48.47	4 285	15.31
1972	15 209	46.01	5 775	17.47
1973	20 393	48.76	8 981	21.47
1974	25 935	47.05	13 850	25.12
1975	32 184	50.42	18 168	28.46
1976	36 187	47.30	20 500	26.80

Source: *Business Monitor PQ 494.3.*

(a) Briefly explain why the two lines on the graph diverged between 1971 and 1977. *(2 marks)*

(b) On graph paper, construct a bar-chart to compare Exports and Imports for the years 1971, 1973 and 1975. *(10 marks)*

(c) (i) Calculate the relative increase in both Exports and Imports between the two years 1970 and 1976. *(4 marks)*

  (ii) Identify **four** economic and social factors which might have led to these changes. *(4 marks)*

(AEB)

Essay questions

3.15 What are the quantitative techniques of investment appraisal? Assess the extent to which they should be used to plan future investment.

(AEB)

3.16 **(a)** What do you understand by the term 'critical path analysis'? *(5 marks)*

(b) As a management consultant, write a report to a client in the house-building industry recommending the adoption of this system as an aid to project control. *(20 marks)*

(UCLES)

3.17 **(a)** Outline three different situations where models might be used as an aid to decision-making. *(10 marks)*

(b) Discuss in detail how you would set up **one** of these models and explain how you would interpret and utilise the results. *(15 marks)*

(UCLES)

FINANCE

The Need for Finance

All firms need finance to stay in business. The finance required may be divided into two categories:

- *fixed capital* for purchasing assets such as buildings, vehicles and equipment;
- *working capital* for running costs such as wages, materials and rent.

The amount of finance required by the business is affected by factors such as:

- the size of the business;
- the level of stocks retained;
- the credit terms obtained from suppliers and given to customers;
- the amount of research and new product development undertaken;
- the type of technology used in the industry.

Finance may be obtained from either *internal* or *external* sources.

Internal Finance

Internal finance is obtained from within the business itself. It is by far the most important source of capital for firms, accounting for over two-thirds of the total. For smaller businesses it may be the only means of raising finance. It can be obtained from:

1. *Retained profit*

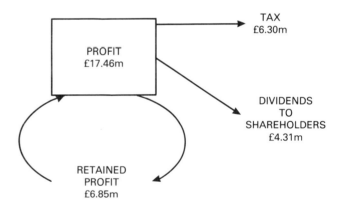

Figure 4.1 Allocation of profit by Boots Company PLC 1989

This is also referred to as **ploughed-back profit**, or undistributed profit. At the end of the financial period (usually every 6 or 12 months), the firm will divide its profits in three ways, as shown in Figure 4.1.

2. Shareholders' reserves, that is profit earned and retained in the past. These are sometimes listed as *General Reserve* in company accounts.
3. Reducing the credit period allowed to customers, or persuading suppliers to give longer credit. A *factor* may be used.
4. Reducing the level of stocks of materials and goods kept.
5. Selling off assets such as buildings or subsidiary companies.

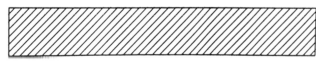

THE ECONOMIST MARCH 19 1988

Figure 4.2 TI divestment

External Finance

External finance is money obtained from outside the business, through means such as the following.

Borrowing

This accounts for 20–30% of firms' capital. There are several different types of lender to business.

1. Commercial banks

These are the major High Street banks such as Barclays and Midland. They offer two major types of loans to business:

Overdraft. This allows the firm to spend more than it has in its account, up to an agreed limit. The period of the overdraft is fixed, but is often continued indefinitely. This is the cheapest form of borrowing, as the borrower pays interest only upon the actual sum owed at any particular time.

Overdrafts are suitable in cases such as a shop stocking up for Christmas or a manufacturer supplying goods on credit.

Fixed-term loan. These are suitable for a business wishing to invest in fixed assets such as premises or machinery. A fixed amount is borrowed and paid back in instalments over a definite period.

Apart from these basic loans, banks often have schemes specially designed for particular types of business such as farms or franchises.

2. Specialist banks and finance houses

These specialise in lending to commercial borrowers. A well-known example is Investors in Industry (3i), which lends to firms in return for a proportion of the shares. Institutions such as this are sometimes referred to as *venture capital* firms.

3. International banks and consortia

Large public limited companies may need to borrow millions of pounds. A single bank might be unwilling to risk lending all of this money, so an international bank such as Chase Manhattan or Barclays International will arrange for a number of lenders to share the loan and risks. This is called a *consortium loan.*

4. Leasing

If a firm needs expensive equipment or vehicles it may lease them through a bank or finance house. The leasing house buys the equipment and hires it out to the user over an agreed period. The firm does not have to commit large amounts of capital.

5. Factoring

A *factor* will pay a proportion of all the debts owed to a firm, which gets immediate payment instead of having to provide credit. The factor then collects the full amount owing from the firm's debtors.

Figure 4.3 An international consortium loan

Factors may also offer a full credit control service, assessing potential customers and setting credit limits on the value supplied and length of credit term.

6. Debentures

Public limited companies can issue debentures on the Stock Exchange. A debenture is an IOU from the firm, which promises to repay it in a few years' time. The holder of the debenture receives interest every year. Debentures are *negotiable*, that is they can be bought and sold freely. They are not shares, and their holders have no say in the running of the firm. They are forms of *loan stock.*

Issuing shares

Limited companies can obtain capital by issuing shares (known as *equity finance*). *Private limited companies* cannot advertise shares for sale, but are allowed to admit new shareholders – often banks and finance companies. A private company can also 'go public' by becoming a public limited company.

Public limited companies can issue two main types of shares:

(i) *Preference shares* are paid a dividend before other

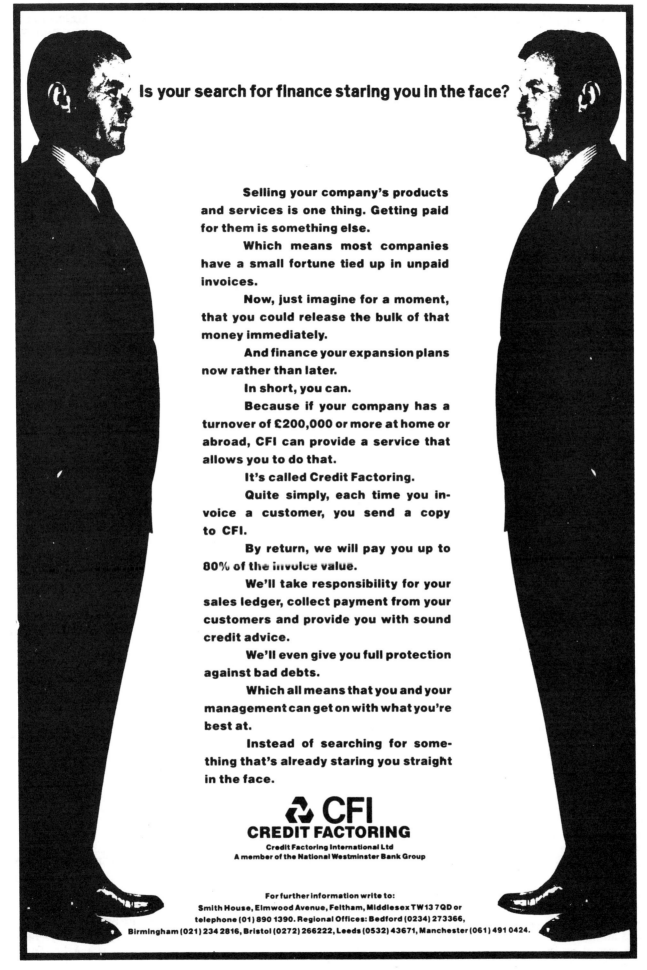

Figure 4.4   Credit factoring

types of shares. They carry a fixed dividend rate; for example the holder of £100 worth of 9% preference stock would receive £9 per year.

Preference shares may be *cumulative* – if profits are too low to pay a dividend in one year, they get double dividends the next year.

Participating preference shares have a fixed return, plus an extra dividend (usually a fraction of the ordinary share dividend) which varies according to the annual profits.

Redeemable preference shares are repayable by the company at some future date (usually at their nominal value).

Convertible preference shares give their holders the right to swap them for ordinary shares by a certain date.

Preference shares provide a steady and safe income, and because their prices are more stable than ordinary shares, less risk of capital loss. They are usually non-voting shares, with exceptions for important decisions such as whether to postpone payment of preference dividends or to issue new shares.

Overall, however, preference shares are a very small proportion of total shares and many companies have no preference shares at all.

(ii) *Ordinary shares* are the majority of company shares. The rate of dividend varies from year to year, depending upon the level of profits. Ordinary shareholders only receive their dividend after preference shareholders have been paid. Most ordinary shares carry a vote for each share held, although some companies have non-voting or 'A' shares. In a good year they will usually receive a higher return than preference shares.

Government assistance

The Government has various schemes which assist firms for certain purposes such as investing in particular regions or types of production. Some of these are listed in Chapter 12.

The Stock Exchange

Functions of the Stock Exchange

The Stock Exchange (full name, the International Stock Exchange of the United Kingdom and the Republic of Ireland) has several functions, as illustrated in Figure 4.5. It is a market for both new and second-hand shares, debentures and Government securities. It is also responsible for supervising *new issues* of shares when firms become public limited companies.

By providing a market for new and second-hand shares the Stock Exchange makes it possible for firms to raise capital, and for investors to convert their shares into cash. Without a market of this type it would be more difficult for companies to persuade people to invest their money in new shares.

In December 1987 there were 3062 companies listed on the Stock Exchange. 400 of these were quoted only on the *Unlisted Securities Market* (USM) and the *Third Market*. These are intended to allow shares in smaller companies to be traded on the Exchange. The Third Market was disbanded in 1990.

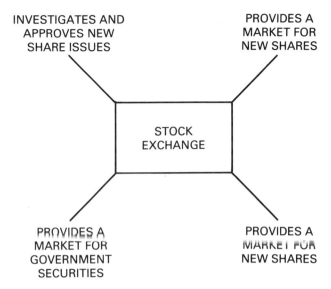

Figure 4.5 Functions of the Stock Exchange

The 'Big Bang'

Until October 1986 there were two types of members of the Stock Exchange.

1. *Brokers* worked as agents for buyers and sellers, who could only trade in shares through a broker. The broker received a commission (which had a fixed minimum rate) for buying and selling shares.
2. *Jobbers* bought and sold and sold shares for themselves. They made their living from profit (called *jobber's turn*) on their dealings.

The main feature of the system was 'single capacity'. A person could only be a broker or a jobber. Brokers were not allowed to buy or sell shares for themselves. Jobbers were not allowed to deal directly with the public. This was to prevent members of the Stock Exchange from advising their clients to buy shares in which they had a personal interest.

In October 1986 this system was completely changed by the 'Big Bang'. The aim of Big Bang was to make dealing in shares more competitive and efficient. The key changes were:

1. All members could now operate in 'dual capacity', trading shares for themselves and clients.
2. Scales of minimum commission were abolished.
3. 'Corporate membership' by banks and financial institutions was allowed. Members can now have limited liability.
4. Protection for investors was increased, particularly through electronic recording of all transactions.
5. A computerised dealing system called the *Stock Exchange Automated Quotation* (SEAQ) system (Figure 4.6) was established.

There is now only one type of Stock Exchange member – the broker/dealer. Some members will act as *market-makers* in particular types of shares, such as oil or chemicals, buying and selling these shares on a regular basis.

All members can deal with the public, but they must always tell the client whether they are buying or selling the shares themselves, or for a client. The SEAQ system is designed to ensure that the client gets the best price available at the time.

The Stock Exchange

New Technology

SEAQ – Stock Exchange Automated Quotations – shows information on share prices which until 'Big Bang' was only available on the Stock Exchange floor. The information is shown on television screens in *brokers'* offices anywhere in the UK or overseas giving them all access to the same information simultaneously.

The information is updated continuously as market makers inform the SEAQ central system of trading which has taken place. The introduction of this sophisticated system has resulted in trading taking place over a television screen rather than on the market floor.

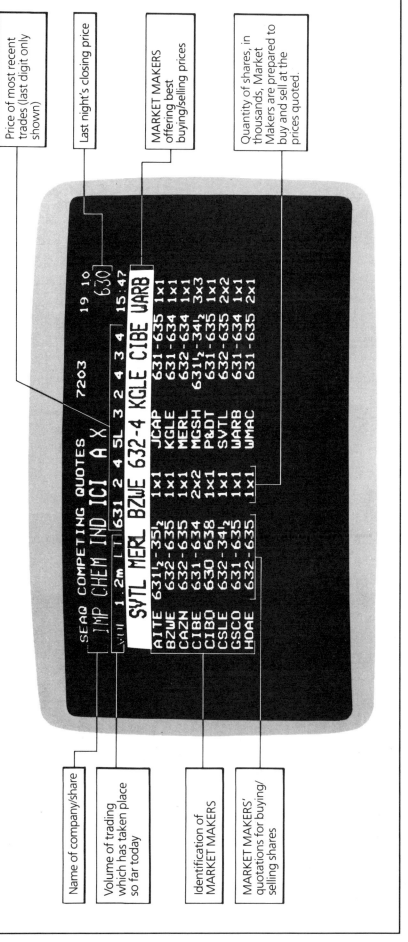

Price of most recent trades (last digit only shown)

Last night's closing price

MARKET MAKERS offering best buying/selling prices

Quantity of shares, in thousands, Market Makers are prepared to buy and sell at the prices quoted.

Name of company/share

Volume of trading which has taken place so far today

Identification of MARKET MAKERS

MARKET MAKERS' quotations for buying/ selling shares

Figure 4.6 The SEAQ system

57

The Directors of the Company, whose names appear in Part IV of this document, accept responsibility for the information contained in it. To the best of the knowledge and belief of the Directors (who have taken all reasonable care to ensure that such is the case), the information contained in this document is in accordance with the facts and does not omit anything likely to affect the import of such information.

This document comprises listing particulars relating to the Company prepared in accordance with the listing rules made under section 142 of the Financial Services Act 1986. Copies have been delivered to the Registrar of Companies for registration in accordance with section 149 of that Act.

Application has been made to the Council of The Stock Exchange for the whole of the issued ordinary share capital of the Company to be admitted to the Official List. It is expected that admission to the Official List will become effective and that dealings in the ordinary shares will begin on Wednesday, 12th July 1989.

ABBEY NATIONAL

ABBEY NATIONAL plc

(Incorporated under the Companies Act 1985. Registered in England number 2294747)

Offer

by

Kleinwort Benson Limited

of

750,000,000 ordinary shares of 10p each at 130p per share

Part I	Key Information	5
Part II	Background to the Offer	9
Part III	The Business of Abbey National	14
Part IV	Management and Staff	22
Part V	Financial Summary	27
Part VI	Profit Forecast and Dividends	30
Part VII	The Strategy of Abbey National	33
Part VIII	Use of Proceeds and Prospects	35
Part IX	Accountants' Report	38
Part X	Statutory Statement of the Society	49
Part XI	Additional Information	57
Part XII	Share Entitlements	73
Part XIII	Offer Arrangements	79
Part XIV	Terms and Conditions of Application	81

The business

Abbey National is one of the largest personal financial services groups in the United Kingdom, providing a wide range of financial products and services. At 31st December 1988, over eight million customers had a savings or mortgage account with Abbey National. The Group operates in four major personal finance sectors:

Personal lending. The Group provides an extensive and flexible mortgage service, as well as a range of other secured and unsecured loans. At 31st December 1988, the Group had total personal lending of over £25 billion and over 1.1 million borrowers.

Savings and investments. Abbey National provides a range of savings accounts to meet the varied requirements of its customers. At 31st December 1988, the Group had 8.2 million savers with total savings of over £25 billion. The Group also offers personal pension plans, and independent financial advice is provided through a professional consultancy service.

Insurance. The Group is a large distributor of insurance services in the United Kingdom, earning significant income from the sale of life policies linked to endowment mortgages and from property insurance. The Group has expanded its insurance operation by increasing the types of policy offered and by marketing insurance products generally to its customers.

Money transmission. The Group entered the money transmission market in 1988, when it launched its current account nationally and opened a banking centre in London.

Profit forecast

The Directors consider that, in the absence of unforeseen circumstances, the Group's profit before tax for the six months ending 30th June 1989 will be not less than £195 million, compared with an unaudited profit before tax for the six months ended 30th June 1988 of £203 million. Further details of the profit forecast are set out in Part VI.

Offer statistics

Offer price	130p
Number of shares being offered	750 million
Net amount of capital being raised (1)	£890 million
Shares in issue following the Offer (2)	1,310 million
Market capitalisation at the Offer price	£1,703 million
Pro forma 1988 earnings per share (3)	24.5p
Price earnings multiple on pro forma 1988 earnings per share	5.3 times
Notional gross dividend yield at the Offer price (3)	7.9 per cent.
Notional dividend cover on the basis of the pro forma 1988 earnings per share (4)	3.2 times
Pro forma net tangible assets per share at 31st December 1988 (5)	168p

Timetable

Completed application forms to be received in branches by	5.00 p.m. on Wednesday, 28th June 1989
Completed application forms to be received by post by	10.00 a.m. on Thursday, 29th June 1989
Basis of allocation expected to be announced by	Tuesday, 4th July 1989
Despatch of share certificates and notices of allocation expected on	Monday, 10th July 1989 and Tuesday, 11th July 1989
Dealings expected to commence on	Wednesday, 12th July 1989

Figure 4.7 Extracts from Abbey National prospectus

New share issues

A firm wishing to issue shares through the Stock Exchange must follow the rules made by the Stock Exchange Council. These are intended to ensure that a firm advertising shares to the public is reputable and safe for investors to trust with their money.

The firm will employ an *issuing house*, which is usually a department of a merchant or commercial bank. A *prospectus* must be issued, containing information such as:

- the company's financial record, such as past profits, turnover and assets;
- the number and type of shares to be sold;
- future plans;
- date of share issue;
- an application form to buy shares, with details of how shares will be allocated if the issue is *oversubscribed*.

Applications for shares are unlikely to equal exactly the number offered for sale. The issue will usually be *undersubscribed* (too few applications) or *oversubscribed* (too many).

If the issue is undersubscribed the shares will be paid for by the *underwriters*, usually one or more financial institutions which have agreed in advance to buy any unsold shares at a particular price.

If the issue is oversubscribed, shares will be allocated according to the formula described in the prospectus.

Worked Examples

Short-answer questions

4.1 Give two reasons why business may sell a debt to a factor.

(AEB)

Answer For example to improve cash flow, cut credit control costs.

4.2 Give three items of information a businessman might be expected to supply when seeking to negotiate a loan.

(AEB)

Answer For example current profits, expected profits, what loan is for, security provided, term of loan, timing of proposed repayments, cash-flow forecasts, balance sheet.

4.3 Give three methods of issuing new shares in a public limited company.

(AEB)

Answer For example:
- *Offer for sale* – issue to public at large for fixed price.
- *Placing* – issue placed by merchant bank with selected clients at fixed price.
- *Tender* – potential buyers invited to bid for shares.
- *Rights issue* – shares offered to existing shareholders

 4.4 The directors of a company recommend a dividend on their £1 ordinary shares of 8%. How much would a company pay to an investor holding 100 shares, if the current market price was £1.20 each?

AEB)

Answer The dividend is calculated on the *nominal value* of the shares, that is £1. The market price is therefore ignored.

Dividend per share   = £1 × 8%
                       = £0.08
Shareholder's dividend = 100 × £0.08
                       = £8.00

4.5 Give two reasons for a public company preferring to raise additional capital by means of debentures rather than by issuing more shares.

AEB)

Answer For example to retain control, may be cheaper, do not have to share profits.

Data-response questions

4.6 Purton Plastics Ltd is considering making a bid for control of Marsham Mouldings. The company's directors have taken a five year view. Marsham's predicted cash flow for the first year is a surplus of £800 000, and it is expected that this will rise by £100 000 p.a. for each of the next four years. If Purton's bid is successful, it is believed that the annual surplus can be increased by a further £400 000 p.a., but only if £1 million is invested at once and a further £300 000 is invested at the end of each year thereafter, to maintain the plant.

(a) Construct a table of cash flows for each of the coming five years. *(5 marks)*

(b) What is the maximum price that Purton should pay for Marsham? Assume a discount rate of 10% and a five year time horizon for the acquisition.

No. of years hence Present day value of £1 at 10% discount rate (cash flows assumed to arrive at the end of year)	0	1	2	3	4	5
	1.000	0.909	0.826	0.751	0.683	0.621

(5 marks)

(c) The European Economic Community (EEC) is considering introducing the following measures:

(i) investment grants. *(3 marks)*

(ii) tax allowances. *(3 marks)*

Briefly discuss how each of these might affect Purton's decision.

(d) What factors might the company consider when deciding on a discount rate of 10%? *(4 marks)*

(UCLES)

Answer **(a)**

	Year 0	1	2	3	4	5
Cash in £'000 000		0.8	0.9	1.0	1.1	1.2
+ additional surplus		0.4	0.4	0.4	0.4	0.4
Total:		1.2	1.3	1.4	1.5	1.6
Cash out £'000 000	1.0	0.3	0.3	0.3	0.3	0.3
Net cash flow	(1.0)	0.9	1.0	1.1	1.2	1.3

(b)						
Disc factor	1	0.909	0.826	0.751	0.683	0.621
NPV £m	(1.0)	0.8181	0.8260	0.8261	0.8196	0.8073

PDV = £3.0971 m

Thus, Purton Plastics should pay a maximum of £3.0971 m for Marsham Mouldings – less dependent on market risk.

(c)

(i) Could delay purchase decision until details of EEC scheme are ready. If applicable, would reduce investment cost (£1 m) and thus increase return (PDV) so, perhaps, increasing the amount Purton would pay.

(ii) Tax allowances would raise return to company – reduces taxable profit. Improvement to cash flow in *year* when tax *payable*.

No use when no profit is made, that is Year 0 and also in purchase decision: matches PDV of flows with or without tax allowances.

(d) Cost of capital (WALL), cost of borrowing, opportunity cost of capital.

Next best alternative project.
Risk of project.

Essay questions

4.7 Indicate the major advantages and disadvantages of leasing as opposed to the purchase of an item of capital equipment, and comment on the factors to be considered in deciding whether or not an asset should be acquired by lease or purchase.

(AEB)

Answer (i) Explain what is meant by leasing, that is a form of long-term hire of fixed assets such as buildings, vehicles or equipment.

(ii) Describe the potential advantages, such as

- helps cash flow/liquidity because there is no need to tie up capital in assets;
- firm can easily change to new technology/products;
- maintenance and other services are usually provided;
- temporary replacement may be provided for faulty vehicles or equipment;
- the repayments are constant and known in advance, as opposed to loans for purchase which may be at variable interest rates;
- there may be tax advantages such as special reliefs for interest paid under leasing agreements;
- assets can often be bought cheaply after expiry of lease, for example employees may be offered cars for personal ownership at a discount price;
- the business does not have the problem of having to dispose of capital equipment such as vehicles or machinery which have reached the end of their useful life.

(iii) Describe possible disadvantages, such as:

- the business is committed to payments over a long period;
- payments may be higher than for outright purchase, for example the chance of obtaining discounts for cash payments may be lost;
- equipment cannot be used as security for loans.

(iv) Factors which might be considered include:

- cost of the asset;
- current and expected interest rates;
- cost as compared with outright purchase or other forms of borrowing;
- availability of other forms of finance such as retained profits;
- long-term potential sales;
- rate of technological change;
- tax provisions, such as rate of tax relief on borrowing.

4.8 The following is an extract from the balance sheet of a public limited company.

Ordinary shares	£	£
Authorised 800 000 at £1 each	800 000	
Issued and fully paid 700 000 at £1 each		700 000
General Reserve		50 000
Long-term borrowing		
Debentures 10% (2010)		250 000
Capital employed		£1 000 000

The company now wishes to raise an additional £500 000 to finance the development of a new product. Assess the implications of the relevant alternative sources of finance.

(AEB)

Answer (i) Explain the two basic sources of finance, internal and external. In the case described internal finance is not a realistic option at present, for example the firm has reserves of only £50 000 compared with the required £500 000. Without further information it is difficult to say whether any assets could be liquidated and the firm is unlikely to be able to obtain the sum required from trade credit.

(ii) Explain that given the need for external funding there are two basic types of finance, equity and loans. Explain briefly how the firm may raise finance through shares and borrowing.

(iii) Compare the merits of equity and loans, for example:

- equity finance may lead to loss of control, loans leave current owners in legal control;
- new share issues may require change of the Memorandum of Association, loans will not (unless the purpose of the loan is *ultra vires* at present);
- issuing equity may ultimately be a cheaper option for existing shareholders if interest rates are high;
- the proposed investment is a high risk for shareholders, for example it is 50% of the firm's current capital employed, so loan capital may spread the risk.

Self-test Questions

Short-answer questions

4.9 A company wishes to install a new machine. Give four methods of financing the purchase.

(AEB)

4.10 Give three examples of how a firm might raise finance by liquidating its assets.

(AEB)

Data-response question

4.11 **(a)** Describe the main options open to British companies if they wish to raise long-term capital. *(5 marks)*

(b) A small engineering firm (Blacklock Ltd) consists of four departments, three of which are production departments (P_1, P_2 and P_3), while the fourth (D) deals with the administration of the whole business. Data for the four departments are given below:

	P_1	P_2	P_3	D
Number of employees	10	8	8	5
Average wages per employee per week	£225	£200	£150	£100
Fixed costs per week	£2500	£1000	£1500	£1000
Other variable costs – average per employee per hour	£40	£20	£40	None
Capital used, at cost ('000)	£150	£100	£50	£10
Working hours per week	30	30	30	30

(i) Which of the methods described in answer to part (a) above would you recommend if Blacklock wished to raise a modest amount of capital and obtain a quotation on the Stock Exchange for the first time. Explain the reasons for your recommendation. *(5 marks)*

(ii) From the data above, prepare a weekly budget of costs for the total business and for each of the four departments. You should assume that each department is to be charged with interest at 10 per cent per annum (assume a 50 week year) and that since D does not earn revenue, its costs are to be aggregated and then allocated to P_1, P_2 and P_3 in the proportions of 40:40:20 respectively. *(10 marks)*

(c) What other sources of finance are available to Blacklock Ltd, if they finally decide not to get a quotation from the Stock Exchange, and what might be their advantages and disadvantages from Blacklock's point of view? *(5 marks)*

Essay questions

4.12 For what reasons do business enterprises purchase new fixed assets? Discuss the major problems associated with such investment.

(AEB)

4.13 A family-owned private limited company is contemplating the issue of further shares, as a public company. Consider the factors which might influence this decision.

(AEB)

ACCOUNTING

The Need for Financial Records

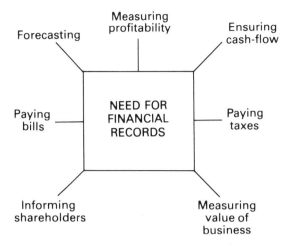

Figure 5.1 The need for financial records

All firms have to keep financial records, which serve various purposes, as illustrated in Figure 5.1. Accounts are used for management and control of the organisation, providing information such as:

- which customers/products are most profitable;
- which products/departments consume the most working capital;
- when the organisation may need to borrow;
- which products are most frequently returned because of faults;
- whether the firm can afford new investment.

Costs, Revenues and Profits

Costs

Costs are the money paid by a firm to workers and suppliers. They are usually divided into *fixed* and *variable* costs, although the distinction is rather artificial in most businesses.

For example labour is often described as a variable cost, but most firms cannot increase or reduce the quantity of labour employed at will. Similarly, depreciation of equipment might be regarded as a fixed cost, but will generally rise with output.

(i) *Fixed* costs (also called *overheads* or *indirect* costs) stay the same whatever the business's sales or production. Fixed costs include items such as rent and rates, hire of machinery and vehicles and management salaries.

Because fixed costs are not affected by output, average fixed cost falls with output, as shown in Figure 5.2.

(ii) *Variable* costs (also called *direct* costs) increase as output increases. They include items such as materials, fuel and wages. It is often assumed that variable costs increase constantly with output. However, it is possible for variable costs to increase more rapidly than output, for

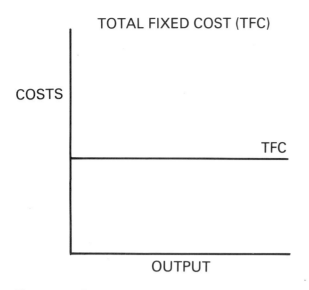

Figure 5.2 Fixed costs

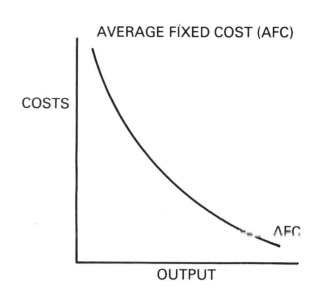

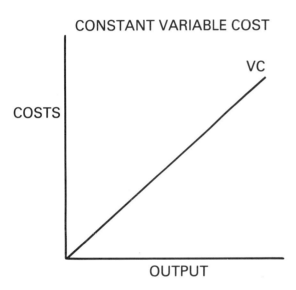

Figure 5.3 Variable costs

example if it is necessary to pay overtime for extra production.

Reference is sometimes made to *semi-variable* costs. These are costs which are fairly constant, but which may increase or decrease with sharp changes in output. For example an increase in overtime to fulfil a large order may result in fuel bills rising as machines are used more intensively.

(iii) *Total* costs = Fixed costs + Variable costs. Total costs rise with output.

(iv) *Average* or *unit* costs = Total costs/Output.

This is the cost of producing one unit of a product, such as a single car or a ton of sand. The average cost curve may be 'U'- or 'L'-shaped, as shown in Figure 5.5.

A U-shaped cost curve is likely when economies of scale occur at low levels of output. For example in industries such as hairdressing or window-cleaning there are few significant cost-savings to be made by large-scale production.

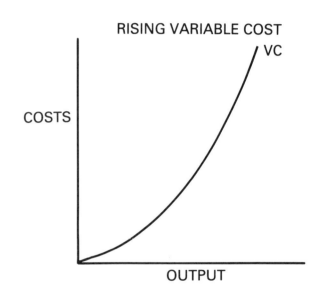

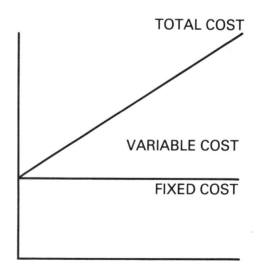

Figure 5.4 Total costs

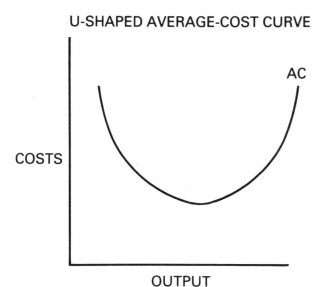

Figure 5.5 Average cost curves

The average-cost curve is likely to be L-shaped in industries where fixed costs are a high proportion of total costs. As output rises, this large fixed cost is spread across a larger output, so that average fixed cost falls rapidly. For example in the chemical or car industries, unit cost falls rapidly throughout any feasible output.

Revenues

Revenues are the money received by a business for selling its goods or services.

Profits

Profits are the difference between revenues and costs, that is:

Profit = Revenues − Costs

In accounting terminology, it is customary to distinguish between *gross* and *net* profit (discussed later in this chapter).

The Balance Sheet

Purpose of the balance sheet

A *balance sheet* is a picture of the business at any particular time. It records *assets* (items owned by the firm) and *liabilities* (items owed by the firm).

An example is illustrated in Figure 5.7. There are different ways of presenting a balance sheet. This is the particular style specified in current Companies Acts.

The balance sheet can be used to find facts such as:

- 'net worth' or value of the business;
- capital employed;
- amount of working capital;

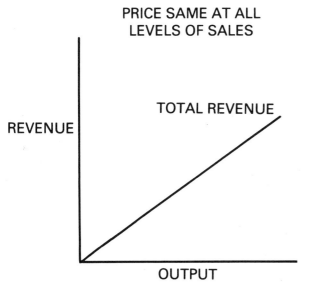

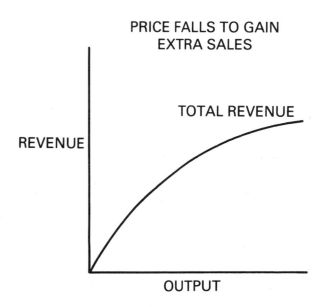

Figure 5.6 Revenues

Company Balance Sheet at 30th June 1989

	1989 £m
Fixed assets	
Tangible assets	1.1
Investment in subsidiaries	18.1
	19.2
Current assets	
Due from subsidiary companies	242.2
Debtors	8.9
Bank and cash	0.3
	251.4
Current liabilities	
Due to subsidiary companies	20.3
Creditors due within one year	122.6
	108.5
Total assets less current liabilities	127.7
Creditors due after more than one year	2.9
	124.8
Capital and reserves	
Called up share capital	17.9
Share premium	82.4
Profit retained	24.5
	124.8

Approved by the board on 20th October 1989

J S R Swanson

R W R James — Directors

Figure 5.7 Barrall's PLC balance sheet

- liquidity;
- gearing.

Items in the balance sheet

1. Fixed assets

These are assets which will stay in the business for more than a year. They may increase in value (*appreciate*) or fall in value (*depreciate*). Some balance sheets give more detail, for example about acquisitions and disposals of assets. Others include an allowance for *intangible assets* such as goodwill, patents and brand names.

2. Current assets

Current assets are the short-term assets of the company such as materials, work-in-progress and stocks. These change constantly during the year as the business buys and sells goods and services.

3. Current liabilities

These are debts which have to be paid within a year.

The *creditors* include suppliers, banks and tax authorities to whom the firm owes money.

4. Capital and reserves

This is the money that the owners have put into the business plus the net profit which has been retained in previous years. It is often referred to as 'Reserves' or 'General Reserve'.

The Funds Flow Statement

STATEMENT OF SOURCE AND APPLICATION OF FUNDS
FOR THE YEAR ENDED 31ST MARCH, 1989

		1989 £ million
Profit on ordinary activities before taxation		796.7
Adjustments not involving the movement of funds		
Depreciation	222.8	
Currency translation adjustments	19.7	
Decrease/increase in provisions	*33.9Dr*	
Undistributed profit of associated companies and changes in minority interests	*85.6Dr*	
		123.0
		919.7
Funds from other sources		
Sales of interests in subsidiaries and associated companies	41.0	
Sales of fixed assets	16.7	
Sales, less purchases of fixed asset investments	12.7	
Increase in payments received in advance	38.4	
Issues of ordinary shares	4.5	
		113.3
		1,033.0
Application		
Purchases of subsidiary companies *	173.0	
Investments in associated companies †	131.2	
Increase in loans to associated companies	31.3	
Decrease/increase in loan capital	1.0	
Purchases of fixed assets	286.3	
Taxes paid in the year	398.1	
Dividends paid in the year	182.8	
Increase in debtors	85.1	
Increase/decrease in inventory	27.2	
Decrease/increase in creditors	14.7	
		1,330.7
Decrease in net balances with bankers and current asset investments		*297.7*

Figure 5.8 GEC funds flow statement

Now a compulsory document in the Annual Report of all public limited companies, the funds flow statement shows changes in the firm's assets and liabilities during the year. It is usually listed as the 'Statement of Source and Application of Funds'. Its purpose is discussed in more detail in Worked example **5.7**.

The Profit and Loss Account

Purpose of the profit and loss account

The profit and loss account illustrates the performance of the business during a certain time period (often a calendar year). An example is given in Figure 5.8.

Important items in the profit and loss account

1. Turnover

Sometimes listed as *sales*, this is the income received from selling goods and services.

2. Cost of sales

Also called *purchases*, this is the amount spent on buying goods for resale plus the net value of any stocks used up during the year.

Etam Public Limited Company and subsidiaries

Group Profit and Loss Account
for the 52 weeks ended 28th January 1989

	Note	1988/9 £000's	1987/8 £000's
Turnover	2	**140,715**	113,868
Cost of sales	3	**(121,573)**	(94,122)
Gross profit		**19,142**	19,746
Administration expenses		**(3,953)**	(2,997)
Interest receivable		**2,010**	1,451
Trading profit including interest receivable	4	**17,199**	18,200
Interest payable	8	**(77)**	(308)
		17,122	17,892
Other income, net	9	**338**	(21)
Profit before taxation		**17,460**	17,871
Tax on profit on ordinary activities	10	**(6,304)**	(6,390)
Profit for the financial period	11	**11,156**	11,481
Dividends	12	**(4,312)**	(3,920)
Retained profit for the period	23	**6,844**	7,561
Earnings per share	13	**17.08p**	19.56p

Figure 5.9 Etam PLC profit and loss account

3. Gross profit

Gross profit is the profit made from buying and selling goods or services before expenses involved in the sale are subtracted:

Gross profit = Sales − Cost of sales

Expenses are the costs involved in selling goods and services, such as wages, transport, advertising and rent.

4. Trading profit or net profit

This is the profit made after expenses have been deducted:

Net profit = Gross profit − Expenses

Working Capital

Cash flow

All businesses have to make or receive payments at different times. It is often necessary to pay for purchases or expenses before payment is received from customers. This is particularly likely in businesses where customers normally buy on credit. Small firms may also have to pay cash for supplies because they are regarded as a bad risk.

This means that a business may be operating profitably, but will need to have cash or borrowed money available at certain times. A *cash-flow* forecast such as that in Figure 5.10 sets out the likely cash position of a company over the near future.

The forecast is prepared by Healden Crafts, a small business making toys and novelty gifts. Some are sold direct to the public through Healden's own shop and at craft fairs. The firm also sells to large retailers, who insist upon being allowed 3 months' trade credit.

As can be seen from Figure 5.10, the peak sales periods are in the summer and just before Christmas. However the goods have to be made throughout the year, with materials and other expenses being paid for. Although the business makes a profit during the six months, it is not until December that the firm actually has cash in its account.

This situation will not be serious if it is anticipated, and loans can be arranged to keep the business going. However, many small firms fail because of cash-flow problems, even though they are actually making a profit.

Working capital flows

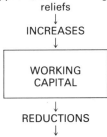

Payments from debtors, retained profits asset sales, borrowing, equity issues, lower stock levels, increased credit from suppliers, Government grants/loans/tax reliefs

↓

INCREASES

↓

WORKING CAPITAL

↓

REDUCTIONS

↓

Payments to creditors, dividends, asset purchases, loan repayments, increased stock levels, increased credit to customers, tax payments

Figure 5.11 Working capital flows

As can be seen from Figure 5.11, working capital is a much wider concept than cash flow, but the basic principle of needing the means to pay creditors is the same. Inadequate working capital is one of the major problems for small firms in particular, causing problems such as:

Month	Jul	Aug	Sept	Oct	Nov	Dec	Total (July–Dec)
Balance at start of month	(4000)	(4000)	(5000)	(6000)	(4000)	(1000)	–
Sales	4000	5000	3000	6000	7000	8000	33 000
Purchases	2000	2000	2000	2000	1000	1000	10 000
Expenses	2000	4000	2000	2000	3000	3000	16 000
Net profit for month	0	(1000)	(1000)	2000	3000	4000	7 000
Balance at end of month	(4000)	(5000)	(6000)	(4000)	(1000)	3000	–

Notes
1. Figures in brackets are negative
2. Balance at start of month is the amount of cash the firm has in the bank e.g. at the start of July the firm has an overdraft of £4000
3. Net profit = sales − (purchases + expenses)
4. Balance at end of month = net profit + balance at start
   This figure becomes the balance at start for the next month.

Figure 5.10 Cash-flow forecast

- inability to pay suppliers;
- loss of trade discounts;
- difficulties in repaying loans;
- lack of finance for investment;
- underpriced sales of assets or goods to raise cash;
- vulnerability to unforeseen events such as lost orders, strikes and cost increases.

Controlling working capital

Policies to ensure an adequate supply of working capital might include:

- reducing credit amounts and periods for customers;
- offering discounts for prompt payment;
- obtaining more extensive credit facilities from suppliers;
- using *credit factors* to obtain payments more quickly;
- increased borrowing, especially if loans can be switched from short- to long-term;
- reducing stock levels;
- leasing rather than purchasing assets.

Stock Turnover

Stock turnover or *rate of stock-turn* measures the speed with which stock moves in or out of the business, that is the time taken from buying goods until they are sold.

To calculate the rate of stock-turn it is necessary to work out the *average stock* held during the year:

$$\text{Average stock} = \frac{\text{Stock at start of year} + \text{Stock at end of year}}{2}$$

For example, if a business has £10 000 in stock at the beginning of the year, £20 000 at the end, and its cost of sales is £60 000:

$$\text{Average stock} = \frac{£10\,000 + £20\,000}{2} = £15\,000$$

The rate of stock-turn is measured by the equation:

$$\text{Rate of stock-turn} = \frac{\text{Cost of sales}}{\text{Average stock}} = \frac{£60\,000}{£15\,000} = 4$$

In this case, goods are replaced on average 4 times a year, that is, goods are held in the business an average of 3 months. If stock was being turned over every day, such as fresh milk or newspapers, the rate of stock-turn would be 365.

The firm will try to achieve the highest possible rate of stock-turn, since keeping stock ties up capital and storage space. If goods are kept too long they may deteriorate or go out of fashion.

The ideal rate of stock-turn will depend upon the type of goods stocked. A rate of 4 might be acceptable for jewellery or furniture, which could be stored for several months. It would be far too low for fresh fruit or fashionable clothes.

Ratio Analysis

Types of ratio

There are several measures and ratios which are important in showing a business's value, efficiency and profitability. These are commonly used in assessing the performance and viability of a business. However, as explained in Worked example **5.8**, ratios on their own are only a partial guide. Past ratios and those of other firms in the same industry must be taken into consideration, together with current market and economic conditions.

There are three basic types of ratio:

- *Profitability* or *performance* ratios are a guide to how well the business is being run. They compare a business's profits with its sales and capital invested by its owners and creditors. Profitability ratios are of interest to the firm's owners and potential borrowers and lenders.
- *Liquidity* ratios measure the 'security' of a business,

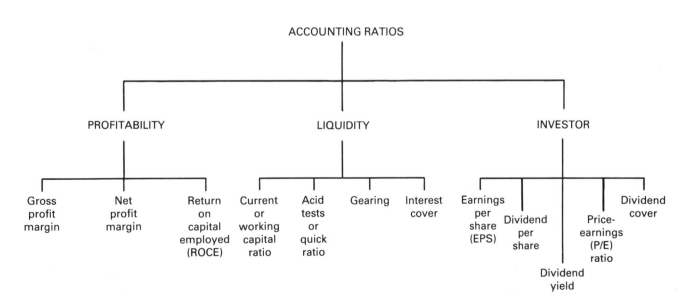

Figure 5.12 Types of accounting ratio

that is its ability to meet its debts. They are particularly important to creditors, who wish to ensure that any loans or trade credit given to the business is safe from the danger of non-payment.

- *Investor* or *shareholder* ratios measure the potential return on the purchase of shares in a company. They are very important to Stock Market investors, and are related to the levels of dividends and the market price of shares.

Profitability ratios

1. Gross profit margin

Gross profit margin is measured by the formula:

$$\text{Gross profit margin} = \frac{\text{Gross profit}}{\text{Sales}} \times 100$$

The average gross profit margin will vary between different types of business. For example, if goods have to be kept for a long time, or expenses are high, the profit margin will tend to be high. Storing goods ties up capital, and expenses have to be paid from the gross profit. if goods are sold quickly and expenses are low, the gross profit margin is likely to be lower.

2. Net profit margin

Net profit margin is calculated using the equation:

$$\text{Net profit margin} = \frac{\text{Net profit}}{\text{Sales}} \times 100$$

The net profit margin will also tend to vary between businesses. For example it will tend to be lower when there is strong competition or falling sales in an industry.

3. Return on capital employed (ROCE)

This is measured by the formula:

$$\text{Return on capital} = \frac{\text{Net profit}}{\text{Capital}} \times 100$$

This relates the profit made by the firm to the capital invested in it by shareholders. The ROCE should be higher than could be earned by investing capital elsewhere.

Liquidity ratios

1. Current or working capital ratio

$$\text{Current ratio} = \frac{\text{Current assets}}{\text{Current liabilities}}$$

This reflects the firm's ability to repay its short-term debts. A normal current ratio would be between 1.5 and 2.

2. Acid test or quick ratio

$$\text{Current ratio} = \frac{\text{Current assets} - \text{Stocks}}{\text{Current liabilities}}$$

The acid test ratio compares the current liabilities with those assets of the business which can be quickly converted into cash. Stocks of goods are not included because

they take time to sell, and could only be sold quickly at less than their true value. A 'safe' ratio is about 1.

3. Gearing

$$\text{Gearing ratio} = \frac{\text{Debt}}{\text{Equity capital}}$$

Gearing (sometimes called *leverage*) is a measure of the financial risk of the company for potential lenders. There are several different ways of measuring gearing, but all show the proportion of finance obtained from shareholders relative to that provided by borrowers. Using the above formula, a ratio of more than 1 would be regarded as 'high' gearing, whereas less than 1 would be regarded as 'low'. Gearing may also be expressed as a percentage, with over 100% being regarded as 'high'.

Both high and low gearing have advantages. A simple analogy would be similar to that of a bicycle, which uses high gears to go downhill and low gears to go uphill. High gearing is advantageous in favourable conditions, when sales are expanding and interest rates are low. It allows more assets to be employed and can finance rapid expansion. This leads to greater profits which can offset high interest payments.

In periods of recession and high interest rates, however, high gearing can cause huge financial problems. Profits may decline while interest payments are rising. In severe cases this may lead to the company being unable to repay its loans, as happened with many highly-leveraged management buy-outs in the late 1980s.

4. Interest cover

$$\text{Interest cover} = \frac{\text{Net profit}}{\text{Interest payable}}$$

Interest cover shows the business's ability to pay debt interest from its profits. If this is less than 1, the firms cannot pay interest from current profits, and may have to reschedule loans or draw on reserves. A ratio of 3 or more is usually considered safe.

Investor ratios

1. Earnings per share (EPS)

$$\text{Earnings per share} = \frac{\text{Profit after tax}}{\text{No. of ordinary shares}}$$

Earnings per share is a measure of the amount of profits which is available for distribution as dividends to shareholders. Some of these earnings will however be retained for future investment.

2. Dividend per share

$$\text{Dividend per share} = \frac{\text{Dividends}}{\text{No. of ordinary shares}}$$

This measures the amount actually paid out as dividends per ordinary share. If all profits were distributed as dividends, the dividend per share would be the same as the earnings per share.

Financial review — five-year charts

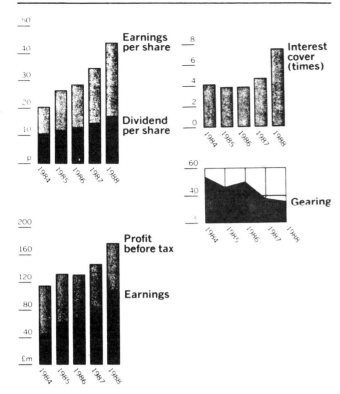

Figure 5.13 GKN PLC investor ratios

3. Dividend yield

$$\text{Dividend yield} = \frac{\text{Dividend per share}}{\text{Market price per share}} \times 100$$

The dividend yield is the percentage return on the shareholders' investment, and will be compared with alternative investments such as bank accounts, Government securities and shares in other companies.

4. Price-earnings ratio (P/E ratio)

$$\text{Price-earnings ratio} = \frac{\text{Market price of share}}{\text{Earnings per share}}$$

This is used as a measure of market confidence in a particular company. It will tend to be high if the market expects future profits to rise, and low when the prospects look poor. It is also affected by the type of industry and the general state of the market.

5. Dividend cover

$$\text{Dividend cover} = \frac{\text{Profit after tax}}{\text{Dividends}}$$

Dividend cover shows how many times the dividend could have been paid out of current profits. For example a dividend cover of 4 shows that shareholders are being paid a quarter of the after-tax profits, with three-quarters being retained as reserves.

Dividend cover is also equal to earnings per share divided by dividend per share. If dividends are increased by less than the rise in profits, dividend cover will fall. For example in Figure 5.13 it can be seen that GKN's dividend cover rose from 2 to 3 (approximately) between 1984 and 1988.

Worked Examples

Short-answer questions

5.1 A businessman is considering buying a small firm. The following information is available from the firm's balance sheet

	£
Fixed assets	48 000
Goodwill	18 000
Stock	12 000
Debtors	9 000
Cash	2 600
	89 600

(a) What is goodwill?
(b) Why should the businessman be prepared to pay for it?

(AEB)

Answer   **(a)** Benefits arising from business's reputation or connections, such as existing customer base and personal skills of employees.

(b) Goodwill allows business to earn higher return on capital than would be expected from the assets employed.

5.2 An aircraft manufacturer has total fixed research and development costs of £100 million; variable costs of £1 million per aircraft; sales price of £3 million per aircraft.
How many aircraft does it need to sell to break even?

(AEB)

Answer

$$\text{Break-even output} = \frac{\text{Fixed costs}}{\text{Contribution per unit}}$$

$$= \frac{\pounds100m}{\pounds3 - \pounds1m}$$

$$= 50 \text{ aircraft}$$

Data-response questions

5.3 A machine costs £20 000 to purchase. It has a useful life of 5 years and a residual value at the end of this period of £3000.

Depreciation figures, using the Reducing Balance Method are as follows:

Year	Depreciation Provision (£)	Net Book Value (£)
1	6315	13 685
2	4321	9 364
3	2957	6 407
4	2023	4 384
5	1384	3 000

(a) Explain the term 'depreciation'. *(3 marks)*
(b) Suggest **three** factors that influence the useful life of an asset. *(3 marks)*
(c) Calculate the annual depreciation provision using the Straight Line Method. *(3 marks)*
(d) Compare the Reducing Balance Method with the Straight Line Method of depreciation. *(6 marks)*
(e) On a graph, show the annual Net Book Value for each of the following methods of calculating depreciation:
(i) the Straight Line Method
and
(ii) the Reducing Balance Method. *(7 marks)*
(f) Why is depreciation a provision rather than an expense? *(3 marks)*

Answer (a) For example method of allocating accurate values of assets in Balance Sheet, divides cost of asset over its life, allowance for obsolescence/wear and tear, makes profit more realistic.

(b) For example physical conditions of use, fashion, technological change, changes in market demand, quality of asset, regularity and quality of maintenance.

(c)

$$\text{Annual depreciation allowance} = \frac{\text{Original value} - \text{Residual value}}{\text{Forecast life of asset}}$$

$$= \frac{\pounds20\,000 - \pounds3000}{5}$$

$$= \pounds3400$$

(d) For example:

- RB allocates larger % of cost in early years (possibly more realistic) whereas SL has constant depreciation allowance;
- RB is more complicated to calculate than SL;
- RB has effect of making company look less profitable in early years, more profitable later – SL has opposite effect.

Net Book Value

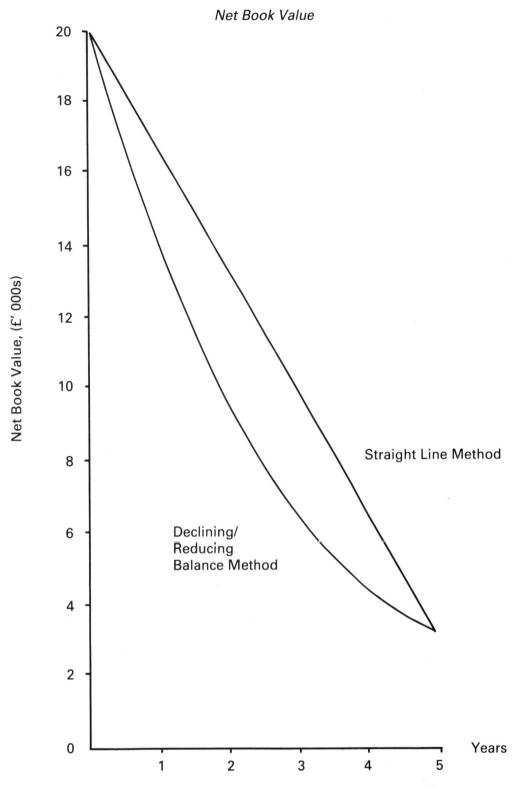

(f) 'Expense' implies that money is flowing out of the business, whereas depreciation does not involve any cash outflow. The money has already been spent. Firm's liquidity is not affected by depreciation.

5.4 ABC Ltd. had the following cost information for the year ending 31st December, 1988:

Sales for the year	20 000 units
Direct costs per unit:	
Materials	£100
Labour	£150
Fixed costs	£1 000 000
Selling price per unit	£500

The following changes were expected from 1st January, 1989:

   Sales to increase by 10%
   Material costs to increase by 25%
   Labour costs to increase by 33.3%
   Selling price to fall by 10%

(a) Produce a break-even chart to show the break-even quantity in 1988. *(9 marks)*
(b) Calculate the break-even quantity for 1989. *(7 marks)*
(c) Calculate the estimated change in profit between 1988 and 1989. *(9 marks)*
(d) Outline the advantages to a firm of the use of break-even analysis. *(5 marks)*

Answer   **(a)**

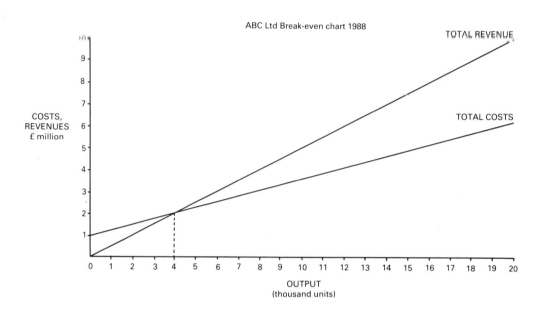

ABC Ltd Break-even chart 1988

(b) 1989 direct costs per unit

Materials	£100 + 25% = £125
Labour costs	£150 + 33% = £200
Total direct cost per unit	£325

Selling price per unit = £500 − 10% = £450

$$\text{Contribution per unit} = \text{Price} - \text{Direct cost}$$
$$= £450 - £325$$
$$= £125$$

$$\text{Break-even output} = \frac{\text{Fixed costs}}{\text{Contribution}}$$

$$= \frac{£1\,000\,000}{£125}$$

$$= 8000 \text{ units}$$

(c)   *1988*

$$\text{Total revenue} = \text{Sales} \times \text{Selling price}$$
$$= 20\,000 \times £500$$
$$= £10\,000\,000$$

$$\text{Total costs} = \text{Fixed costs} + (\text{Sales} \times \text{Direct costs per unit})$$
$$= £1\,000\,000 + (£20\,000 \times £250)$$
$$= £6\,000\,000$$

$$\text{1988 Profit} = \text{Total revenue} - \text{Total costs}$$
$$= £10\,000\,000 - (£6\,000\,000)$$
$$= £4\,000\,000$$

                                          1989

$$\text{Total revenue} = \text{Sales} \times \text{Selling price}$$
$$= 22\,000 \times £450$$
$$= £9\,900\,000$$

Total costs = Fixed costs + (Sales × Direct costs per unit)
$$= £1\,000\,000 + (22\,000 × £325)$$
$$= £8\,150\,000$$

1989 Profit = Total revenue − Total costs
$$= £9\,900\,000 − (£8\,150\,000)$$
$$= £1\,750\,000$$

Therefore profit has fallen by £4 000 000 − £1 750 000, that is £2 250 000.

(d) For example shows minimum quantity which must be sold before profit occurs, simple and cheap to compile, easy to understand, can be used to 'screen' new product ideas, useful model for predicting effects of changes in costs or revenues.

5.5 Barton Ltd make sets of cooking utensils. They are currently making and selling 16 000 sets a year, 4000 units below the maximum capacity of the plant. Mr Barton is preparing for a meeting of the marketing and production managers to discuss proposals for the next year. He has decided to use a straight line break-even approach to analyse the company's position. The company earned a 5% return on its net assets which are currently £320 000. Unit total costs at this level of output are £39.00 of which variable costs are £24.00.

(a) (i) What is the present profit? *(2 marks)*
  (ii) Calculate the present selling price per unit. *(2 marks)*
  (iii) Calculate the present contribution per unit. *(1 mark)*
  (iv) What is the company's revenue at break-even? *(4 marks)*

(b) As a means of raising the company's return on assets to 10%, Mr Barton is keen to increase sales by reducing prices by 10%. The plant's capacity can be increased from 20 000 units to 30 000 units per year but this will involve additional fixed overheads of £52 000 per year. Net assets will not rise because Mr Barton is considering leasing the new equipment. The lease agreement would last for ten years.
  (i) How many additional sets would the company have to sell? *(4 marks)*
  (ii) Consider the marketing and production implications of the new, higher output. Would you advise Mr Barton to go ahead with this plan? *(7 marks)*

(UCLES)

Answer   (a) (i) Present profit
      Return = 5% of Assets.
      Therefore profit = 5/100 × £320 000
      $$= £16\,000$$
    (ii) Selling price/unit
      ATC + profit.
      16 000 sets at £39 + £16 000 = Total Revenue
      $$= £640\,000$$
      Therefore price/unit $= \dfrac{£640\,000}{16\,000}$
      $$= £40$$

      Or Profit = £16 000
      Therefore profit/unit = £1
      Therefore price = ATC + profit/unit = £40
    (iii) Contribution per unit = Price − AVC
      $$= £16 \text{ p.u.}$$
    (iv) Revenue at break-even
      Fixed cost = 16 000 × £15 = £240 000
      At Break-even

      $$\frac{FC}{Counter/unit} = \frac{£240K}{£16K} = 15\,000 \text{ units}$$

      Therefore Revenue = 15 000 × £40 = £600 000

  (b) (i) New return on Assets = 10%
      Therefore profit = £32 000
      New price = 90% × £40 = £36
      Total fixed costs increase by £52 000
      Let new output be x

      Price × output = VC × x + FC + Profit
      Therefore £36 x = £24 x + £292 000 + £32 000
      Therefore £12 x = £324 000
      Therefore x = 27 000 units
      Therefore company must sell an additional 11 000 units
    (ii) Sales have risen by 68.8%
      Would VC remain constant?
      Economies/diseconomies of scale.
      Promotional expenditure? Higher fixed costs.

75

Will demand remain high for 10 years? Perhaps look at subcontracting of overtime/shift work on existing plant.
Availability of skilled labour?
Funding for new machinery?
State of market, competition.
Promotion to create awareness of drop in price.
Selling and distribution.

Essay questions

5.6 Outline the objectives of funds flow statements and discuss the usefulness of such statements to a business.

(AEB)

Answer (i) Explain the basic purpose of a funds flow statement, that is to show the 'sources and applications of funds' during the firm's accounting year, namely where did money come from and where did it go?

Sources include any transactions which increase working capital, such as retained profit, sales of assets, increased loans, share issues and longer trade credit.

Applications include transactions which reduce working capital, such as payments to creditors, purchase of assets, loan repayments and longer credit to suppliers.

(ii) Explain the relationship to the balance sheet, that is the funds flow statement shows net effect on balance sheet during the year. The balance sheet is a 'snapshot' at one moment, showing the historic accumulation of assets and liabilities. The funds flow statement shows changes in assets and liabilities during the accounting period.

(iii) Compare funds flow statement with the profit and loss account, which does not include capital movements. For example the profit and loss account may show an increase in profits, but the firm may have significant cash outflows for investment or stock purchases. The funds flow statement can thus show changes in liquidity or the firm's capital structure.

5.7 To what extent would ratio analysis enable you to draw meaningful conclusions about the performances of different public companies?

(AEB)

Answer (i) Explain briefly that ratio analysis is designed to compare figures from the company's accounts or stock market performance. Classify ratios into the three basic types – profitability, liquidity and investor. Explain briefly the parties who are likely to be interested in using the ratios.

(ii) Give examples of some of the major ratios, such as ROCE, acid test, gearing and dividend yield, explaining what they are meant to measure. Where possible give numerical examples of 'safe' or 'normal' ratios.

(iii) Comment on the limitations of ratio analysis, for example:

- different methods of accounting for certain variables such as stock valuation, depreciation, valuations for property, equipment and other assets;
- accountants sometimes 'dress up' accounts to make them look more attractive;
- ratios need to be compared with past performance and other firms in industry/economy;
- economic and stock market conditions affect profitability and share prices, and must be allowed for – factors such as high interest rates or 'fashions' for particular types of shares may lead to large changes in ratios.

(iv) Explain that it is foolish to assess a company simply on the basis of accounting information. Other factors such as management skill, brand names and trade prospects have to be allowed for. Ratios might be regarded as a pointer to further research rather than the answer to all important questions.

5.8 **(a)** Distinguish between *contribution* and *profit*. *(5 marks)*
(b) Under what circumstances would 'contribution' be used as an indicator of the value of a cost centre to a firm? *(8 marks)*
(c) Is profit important to a business? Explain your answer. *(12 marks)*

(UCLES)

Answer **(a)** Explain that contribution is the revenue earned by a product, department, etc. less its variable costs. Fixed costs are ignored in the calculation of contribution.

Profit takes into account fixed costs and is therefore equal to revenue less total costs.

(b) (i) Define the term 'cost centre' as an area of production to which direct costs can be allocated. This may be a factory, department product, piece of equipment or even a person. A cost centre will usually have its own budget.

(ii) Explain that it is only possible to determine the contribution made by a cost centre if a significant part of its costs can be allocated and if it is possible to determine the revenue it earns for the firm.

(iii) Outline factors which may make it easier to calculate contribution, such as:

- accuracy of records, for example a retailer using laser scanners and computerised stock control may be able to calculate the contribution earned by individual products;

- number of cost centres monitored;
- labour, equipment and premises are used principally by one cost centre rather than being shared
- overheads are a low proportion of total costs.

(c) (i) Explain the basic purposes of profit that is:

- survival – if the firm loses money it will eventually fail unless the owners are prepared to finance losses indefinitely;
- a reward for owners for risking their capital if the business fails – they expect a higher return than can be obtained from safer investment such as bank deposits or fixed-interest securities;
- source of finance for fixed and working capital;
- a measure of management effectiveness;
- a stimulus to efficiency, for example discourages waste, may encourage effort on part of employees or be used as a target for managers.

(ii) Explain that although some business such as co-ops or nationalised industries may not be run principally for profit, maximisation of profit is generally considered to be the main objective of privately-owned firms. Even where profit is a secondary objective, it may still serve purposes such as measuring efficiency or ensuring a supply of capital for re-investment.

5.9 (a) What does an accountant understand by the term *liquidity*? (5 marks)
(b) Outline a method by which a firm might predict future liquidity problems and explain how these may be averted. (10 marks)
(c) Does the method of depreciation of fixed assets have any bearing on a firm's cash position, and if so, why? (10 marks)

(UCLES)

Answer (a) Define liquidity as ability to meet current liabilities by converting assets to cash quickly. Explain how it may be measured by the current or acid test ratios.

(b) (i) Explain how a cash-flow forecast may be used to highlight future shortages of working capital. A simple example could be constructed.
(ii) Outline possible policies, such as:

- arranging credit facilities such as an overdraft;
- factoring;
- reducing stock levels;
- obtain longer credit from suppliers;
- obtain quicker payments from customers, for example through discounts for prompt payment.

(c) (i) Describe the main possible policies for depreciating assets, such as straight-line, reducing balance, replacement cost.
(ii) Explain that depreciation does not directly affect the firm's cash position because the money has already been spent and depreciation allowances are not actual cash outflows.
(iii) Outline possible indirect effects, such as:

- tax relief may be different for different methods because of amounts written off affecting profit level;
- firm may use depreciation allowances as a guideline for assessing future replacement investment finance;
- depreciation affects the balance sheet and may therefore affect investors' or lenders' willingness to provide finance.

Self-test Questions

Short-answer questions

5.10 Why might a company decide to revalue its fixed assets?

(AEB)

5.11 *Sales at cost divided by Average stock*

(a) What is the name of this ratio? – Rate of Stock turnover.
(b) What information does it provide? measures speed at wh stock moves in an out of a business

(AEB)

5.12 State three items which might be shown as current assets in the balance sheet of a company.

Debtors
Cash in bank
Stocks

(AEB)

77

5.13 The following information relates to a company which produces a single product:

	£
Direct Labour per unit	11
Direct Materials per unit	6
Variable Overheads per unit	3
Fixed Costs	200 000
Selling Price per unit	30

(a) Explain the term 'Break-Even'. *(2 marks)*
(b) Using these figures, produce a chart to show the minimum number of units which must be sold for the company to break-even. *(9 marks)*
(c) Market research has indicated potential sales for the coming period of 30 000 units at the current price, or 37 500 units if the selling price were lowered to £28 per unit. Which strategy would you advise the company to adopt and why? *(10 marks)*
(d) Outline the factors which **any** business should take into consideration before using Break-even analysis as a basis for decision making. *(9 marks)*

(AEB)

5.14 Fisher's Furniture Ltd. is a small furniture retailer whose accounts for the year ending 30th April 1986 are given below.

	£		£	£
Shareholders' Funds		*Fixed Assets*		
Share capital	100 000	Land & Buildings		120 000
Reserves	30 000	Van	12 500	
		Depreciation	(2 500)	10 000
Long-term liabilities				
Loans	60 000	*Current Assets*		
		Stock		85 000
Current Assets		Debtors		8 000
Creditors	24 000	Cash		3 500
Provision for tax	12 500			
	226 500			226 500

(a) Explain what you understand by the following terms which appear in the balance sheet above:
  (i) Shareholders' Funds;
  (ii) Long-term liabilities.
(b) During the year ending 30th April 1987, the following transactions took place.

  £240 000 of goods were bought.
  £300 000 of goods were sold. These were originally bought by Fisher's for £195 000.
  £220 000 was paid to suppliers.
  £7500 was paid on average each month to cover wages, the running expenses of the shop and van, and interest on the loan.
  £12 500 was paid for last year's tax.
  £2500 allowance was made for depreciation on the van.

  All profits are retained within the firm and tax is chargeable on them at the rate of 50%. Debtors have risen by £2000.
  (i) Calculate the profit made for the year ending 30th April 1987 and the cash in hand at this date. *(6 marks)*
  (ii) Draw up a balance sheet for the year ending 30th April 1987. *(5 marks)*
(c) Explain how the following assets which appear in the balance sheet have been valued and identify alternative methods that could have been used.
  (i) The van (which was purchased on 1st May 1985 and was expected to have a five year life). *(3 marks)*
  (ii) Stock. *(4 marks)*
(d) What else is legally required (other than the balance sheet and profit and loss account) to appear in all published accounts? *(3 marks)*

(UCLES)

5.15 Study the extract and answer the questions that follow.

New pattern for Sirdar

(25p ordinary Share Price 137p)

Year to 30 June	Turnover £m	Pre-tax profit £m	Stated earnings per share (p)	Gross dividend per share (p)
1982	27.3	6.18	8.2	2.93
1983	30.0	7.15	10.1	3.61
1984	33.1	9.01	12.5	4.64
1985	36.5	9.53	12.6	5.89
1986	38.7	10.26	13.7	7.25

Sirdar is a highly efficient manufacturer of hand knitting yarns – and with a good profit record too. That efficiency is due to a sustained capital programme (£27m spent over ten years). The last acquisition was made in 1972.

But now comes a change of policy. Sirdar's capital investment has become self financing, and it has decided to invest its large cash balance in new activities . . .

. . . In August Sirdar announced the £6m cash purchase of Eversure Textiles, a manufacturer of ready made curtains. The price payable does not look dear in terms of Eversure's promised annual pre-tax profits of £850 000 (£808 000 in the year to March) and to widen the product range, introduce more own label items and cut back stock levels.

Then earlier this month Sirdar announced an agreed £17m takeover of Burmatex, which makes carpet tiles. . . . Sirdar believes it can best help Burmatex through marketing and developing its export business.

Together the acquisitions will account for about a quarter of Sirdar's enlarged profits.

The new businesses will also help counter swings in demand for knitting wools. Three years ago there were two clear knitting seasons – pre/post Christmas for chunky and lighter garments. Since then lighter wools have dominated sales for most of the year – which caused Sirdar problems in 1985–86.

When put together, the new group should make pre-tax profits of £13m in 1986–87, including first contributions from Eversure and Burmatex.

Source: *Investors Chronicle*, 17–23 October 1986 (Vol. 1 78/986)

(a) Calculate:
- (i) Sirdar's profit as a percentage of turnover for 1986
- (ii) Dividend Yield for 1986
- (iii) Price/Earnings Ratio for 1986. *(9 marks)*

(b) Explain why 'a sustained capital investment programme' assists efficiency. *(4 marks)*

(c) Why do you think Sirdar made each of the **two** acquisitions mentioned in the text? *(4 marks)*

(d) Give **two** examples of vertical integration that Sirdar could make to benefit the organisation. Identify **two** motives for such acquisitions. *(4 marks)*

(e) If Sirdar's profits increase as expected in 1986–87, what general effect will this have on its Price/Earnings Ratio? *(4 marks)*

5.16 Micro Ltd is a small private electronics company run by Anne Little, who owns 60% of the equity. It is a fast-growing profitable business with sales of £800 000 over the last year ending 30 April 1986, giving a post-tax profit of £60 000. The company is anxious to expand, as the market demand for its product is growing fast. It needs finance, however, to do this.

(a) (i) What are the main external sources of finance available to Micro Ltd?
(ii) What factors should Anne Little consider in choosing which to use? *(8 marks)*

(b) Over the next two years, Micro is planning rapid expansion and it expects sales and profits to increase each year by 25% of the present level. It also aims for:

    stocks   = 3 months' sales
    debtors   = 2 months' sales
    creditors = 1 month's sales.

As no new capital equipment has been bought during the last year, Micro plans to spend £100 000 on replacing existing machines during the next two years, and the same again on new machinery.

The present situation of the company is shown on the balance sheet below.

Balance sheet for Micro Ltd year ending 30 April 1986

1985 (£000s)		1986 (£000s)	1985 (£000s)		1986 (£000s)
410	Shareholder funds	430	150	Land and buildings	150
120	Long-term loan	120	220	Machinery	200
110	Creditors	120	245	Stock	250
170	Bank overdraft	130	195	Debtors	200
810		800	810		800

Stating clearly any assumptions made, calculate the following:
  (i) the cash required to support this expansion;   *(4 marks)*
  (ii) the extent to which internal funds will contribute.   *(5 marks)*

(c) Using the information given in the balance sheet above calculate the following ratios: (i) Current, (ii) Acid test and (iii) Gearing. On the basis of these ratios, make recommendations as to how the company should raise any external finance necessary for its expansion?   *(5 marks)*

(d) If it cannot raise the necessary cash, what alternatives are open to the company?   *(3 marks)*

(CLES, 1986)

5.17 Examine this extract from the published accounts of Redland and answer the questions which follow.

Redland

	YEAR ENDED	
	March 1985	March 1984
Sales	**£1,247m** + 5%	£1,184m
Profit before tax	**£108.2m** + 15%	£93.8m
Earnings per share	**28.0p** + 14%	24.6p
Dividends per share (gross)	**15.00p** + 10½%	13.57p

I want to emphasize our commitment to realizing a consistently high return on capital employed. In every one of the last ten years, despite considerable variances in the levels of construction activity, Redland has earned returns of over 20 per cent and averaging 25 per cent.

(Extract from the statement by the Chairman, Mr Colin Corness, at the
Annual General Meeting held on 26th September, 1985)

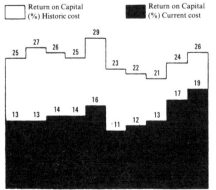

75/76 76/77 77/78 78/79 79/80 80/81 81/82 82/83 83/84 84/85
ECONOMIST OCTOBER 5, 1985

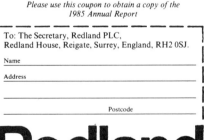

Please use this coupon to obtain a copy of the 1985 Annual Report

To: The Secretary, Redland PLC,
Redland House, Reigate, Surrey, England, RH2 0SJ.

Name

Address

Postcode

Redland
**CONSTRUCTION MATERIALS
AND SERVICES IN OVER 30 COUNTRIES**

(a) (i) Using Ratio Analysis comment on the profitability of the company. *(5 marks)*

(ii) Give **three** factors which must be taken into consideration before using financial ratios to analyse company performance. *(6 marks)*

(iii) Explain why Earnings per Share is greater than Dividend per Share. *(1 mark)*

(b) The Chairman's statement gives figures for the return on capital of 'over 20%' and '25%'.

(i) How would the return on capital figures be calculated? *(2 marks)*

(ii) Outline **three** specific valuation problems which would be faced when calculating capital employed. *(6 marks)*

(c) Examine the diagram and explain the bases on which it has been prepared. *(4 marks)*

(AEB)

Essay questions

5.18 'Ratios extracted from one company's accounts are virtually useless without additional information'.

What other information would you need in order to make them valuable?

(AEB)

5.19 **(a)** Differentiate between *fixed* and *variable* costs. *(5 marks)*

(b) How would you anticipate Sunday Trading affecting a large retailer's cost structure and its overall profitability? *(20 marks)*

(UCLES)

5.20 How is it possible for a profitable firm to run out of cash, or for a cash-rich firm to be unprofitable?

(AEB)

5.21 'The simple break-even model provides an easily understood and effective aid to decision-making'. Discuss limitations to its usefulness and evaluate possible modifications that might be made to overcome them.

(UCLES)

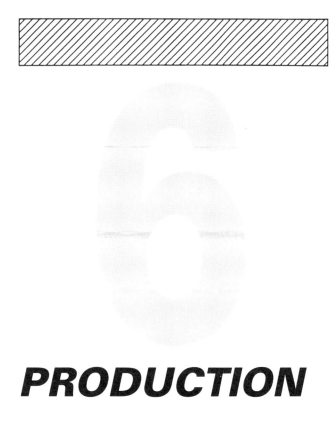

PRODUCTION

The Production Function

Production means creating goods and services which satisfy people's needs. It is sometimes used in the narrow sense of *manufacturing production* (making goods in factories). However, a bus-driver or a disc jockey is also involved in production because they provide services which fulfil consumer needs. Some of the activities described below are used mainly or solely in the manufacture of goods, but others such as quality control and purchasing are as vital in service industries.

Production involves converting *inputs* of materials, labour, capital and management into a good or service which can be marketed to the customer. In simple terms, if marketing is concerned with creating the demand for a product, production is concerned with creating the supply to meet the demand.

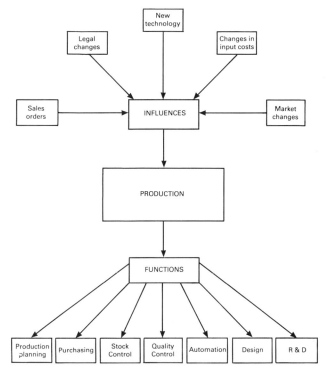

Figure 6.1   Production functions

Methods of Production

Methods of production are often divided into three basic types, according to the output of individual products. Firms often employ a mixture of these methods for different products.

Job production

Job production occurs when a single product is designed and made, such as a cruise-liner or made-to-measure kitchen units. The product is made to order and therefore designed and made to exact requirements for a special purpose. Typically, job production is used for specialised products with a high profit margin.

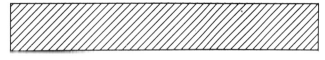

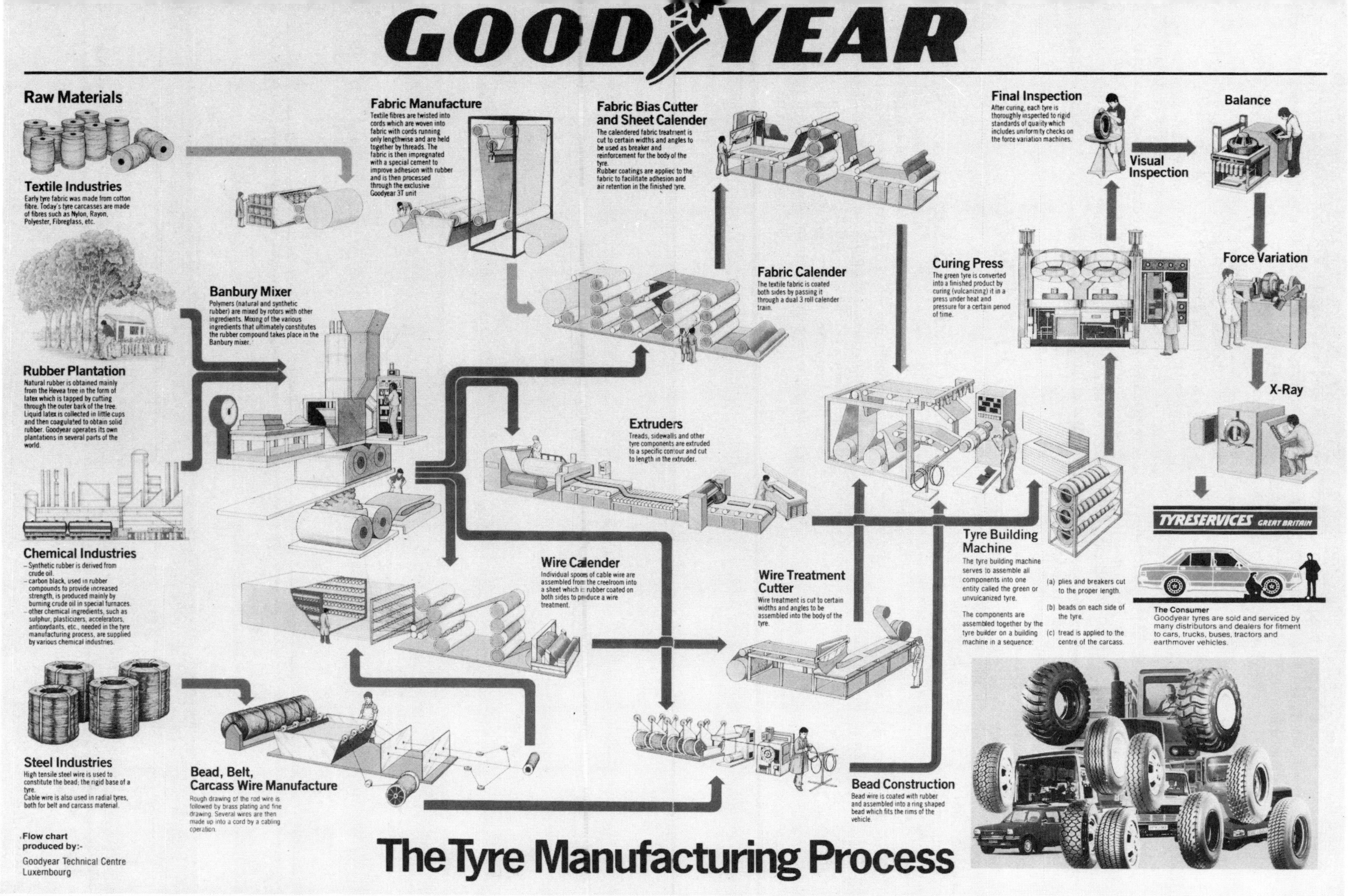

GOODYEAR

The Tyre Manufacturing Process

Raw Materials

Textile Industries
Early tyre fabric was made from cotton fibre. Today's tyre carcasses are made of fibres such as Nylon, Rayon, Polyester, Fibreglass, etc.

Rubber Plantation
Natural rubber is obtained mainly from the Hevea tree in the form of latex which is tapped by cutting through the outer bark of the tree. Liquid latex is collected in little cups and then coagulated to obtain solid rubber. Goodyear operates its own plantations in several parts of the world.

Chemical Industries
– Synthetic rubber is derived from crude oil.
– carbon black, used in rubber compounds to provide increased strength, is produced mainly by burning crude oil in special furnaces.
– other chemical ingredients, such as sulphur, plasticizers, accelerators, antioxidants, etc. needed in the tyre manufacturing process, are supplied by various chemical industries.

Steel Industries
High tensile steel wire is used to constitute the bead, the rigid base of a tyre.
Cable wire is also used in radial tyres, both for belt and carcass material.

Flow chart
produced by:-
Goodyear Technical Centre
Luxembourg

Fabric Manufacture
Textile fibres are twisted into cords which are woven into fabric with cords running only lengthwise and are held together by threads. The fabric is then impregnated with a special cement to improve adhesion with rubber and is then processed through the exclusive Goodyear 3T unit

Banbury Mixer
Polymers (natural and synthetic rubber) are mixed with other ingredients. Mixing of the various ingredients that ultimately constitutes the rubber compound takes place in the Banbury mixer.

Bead, Belt, Carcass Wire Manufacture
Rough drawing of the rod wire is followed by brass plating and fine drawing. Several wires are then made up into a cord by a cabling operation.

Fabric Bias Cutter and Sheet Calender
The calendered fabric treatment is cut to certain widths and angles to be used as breaker and reinforcement for the body of the tyre.
Rubber coatings are applied to the fabric to facilitate adhesion and air retention in the finished tyre.

Fabric Calender
The textile fabric is coated both sides by passing it through a dual 3 roll calender train.

Extruders
Treads, sidewalls and other tyre components are extruded to a specific contour and cut to length in the extruder.

Wire Calender
Individual spools of cable wire are assembled from the creelroom into a sheet which is rubber coated on treatment.

Wire Treatment Cutter
Wire treatment is cut to certain widths and angles to be assembled into the body of the tyre.

Bead Construction
Bead wire is coated with rubber and assembled into a ring shaped bead which fits the rims of the vehicle.

Tyre Building Machine
The tyre building machine serves to assemble all components into one entity called the green or unvulcanized tyre.

The components are assembled together by the tyre builder on a building machine in a sequence.

(a) plies and breakers cut to the proper length.

(b) beads on each side of the tyre.

(c) tread is applied to the centre of the carcass.

Curing Press
The green tyre is converted into a finished product by a curing (vulcanizing) it in a press under heat and pressure for a certain period of time.

Final Inspection
After curing, each tyre is thoroughly inspected to rigid standards of quality which includes uniformity checks on the force variation machines.

Visual Inspection

Balance

Force Variation

X-Ray

TYRESERVICES GREAT BRITAIN

The Consumer
Goodyear tyres are sold and serviced by many distributors and dealers for fitment to cars, trucks, buses, tractors and earthmover vehicles.

Figure 6.2 Goodyear flow production

The main disadvantage of job production is that it is usually expensive because of the need for specialised labour and management. Large projects may be difficult to cost in advance and some, such as the Humber Bridge and the Channel Tunnel, have cost far more than the original estimates.

Batch production

Batch production involves a number of identical products being produced. Equipment and labour are then switched to another product. Examples include bakeries which will make different loaves and cakes using the same equipment, and engineering firms which make components to order. This allows benefits such as bulk purchasing and the use of less skilled labour on occasions.

Batch production requires careful planning to ensure that the batch is economic, justifying the cost of setting up machinery and other equipment. Administration costs may be increased by the variety of products. If the product is not made to order, the firm must avoid the problem of the batch size being too large which might result in unsold goods having to be put into stock.

Flow production

Flow production is used to make thousands or millions of standardised products. It is used to manufacture goods such as cars and baked beans. An *assembly line* may be used, with a product being transported along a conveyor belt or track.

Flow production is often cheap because of lower setting-up costs and the advantages of bulk purchasing. It often allows for the use of semi-skilled or unskilled labour, saving wages and training costs.

However flow production usually involves large investments of capital, requiring correspondingly large and regular sales. Co-ordinating production can be complicated. Flow production also relies on extensive *division of labour* which may lead to boring work and therefore significant labour problems.

Division of Labour

Division of labour by process

Division of labour means that workers concentrate upon doing one particular job. The simplest form of this is for a worker to concentrate upon producing one good or service such as making clothes or repairing cars.

Modern manufacturing frequently relies upon *division of labour by process*, which splits jobs up even further. Each worker carries out one or two very simple tasks,

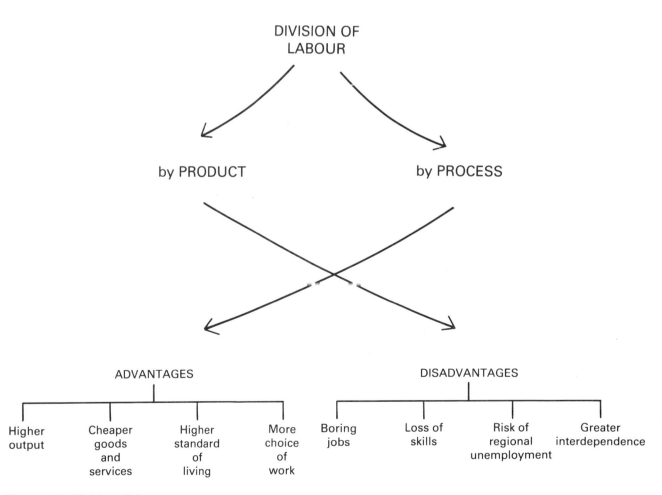

Figure 6.3 Division of labour

repeating the same operation hundreds of times a day.

A famous example of this was in the Ford car factory in Detroit during the early 20th century, which was one of the first to use an assembly line. By breaking production down into such small stages, Ford was able to produce the Model T in far greater numbers and much more cheaply than its competitors. Although changes in technology and attitudes to work have changed rapidly, almost all large car manufacturers still use a similar system.

Advantages of division of labour

1. *Higher output.* People can do what they are best at, and by doing the same job continuously, can get better at it. Jobs can be made very simple, requiring shorter training. Time is saved moving from one job to another.
2. *Cheaper goods and services.* By increasing workers' *productivity*, division of labour reduces the unit costs of production.
3. *Higher standard of living.* If the economy produces more goods and services at lower cost, its citizens should be better off.
4. *More choice of work.* Division of labour should allow people to choose work that they enjoy and have a talent for.

Disadvantages of division of labour

1. Boring jobs

Division of labour can involve jobs which are very simple and repetitive. A typical assembly line operation, for example, lasts less than two minutes. This means that the worker is doing the same thing more than thirty times an hour. Boring jobs can cause problems such as poor quality work, absenteeism, stress and illness, strikes and high labour turnover.

2. Loss of skills

If workers are only trained in one job or part of a process, they may have difficulty in adapting to new techniques of production. If their industry is declining, they may find it difficult to find work elsewhere.

3. Risk of regional unemployment

Many industries are concentrated in particular areas. If a town depends heavily upon an industry which is declining, the result may be high unemployment. The fastest rise in unemployment during the 1980s was in the West Midlands, which depended heavily upon engineering and car manufacture.

4. Greater interdependence

Division of labour leads workers and organisations to be very dependent upon each other. Disruptions to production or poor quality in one part of a business or its suppliers may lead to loss of production or quality in another. Some producers such as McDonalds and Marks & Spencer exert strict control over their suppliers in order to avoid such problems.

Production Planning and Control

Planning production of a good or service involves several different activities such as:

- forecasting future demand patterns to determine when and where products will be needed;
- setting production targets based on market forecasts;
- purchasing materials, components and other supplies;
- planning the use of equipment and physical facilities such as factory, warehouse, office or retail space;
- forecasting labour requirements such as new employees, training and changes to working hours;
- maintaining adequate stock levels of materials, components and finished goods;
- arranging for physical distribution of goods to the customer.

It will also be necessary to set up control procedures (see Chapter 9) to monitor production and adjust where necessary. Many firms employ *progress chasers* whose job is to check that production schedules are being kept to and sort out problems which might cause production delays.

Production Activities

Purchasing

Purchasing involves ensuring that the organisation can obtain adequate supplies of inputs such as materials, components, stationery, finished goods and services economically and in good time for use during production. The basic purchasing functions are:

- co-ordinating purchases of inputs;
- negotiating appropriate discounts for large purchases or quick payment;
- ensuring that orders are made in time and that delivery dates are kept;
- checking invoices and other documents from suppliers against the goods or services actually supplied;
- ensuring that suppliers are paid within an appropriate time to obtain discounts and preserve the organisation's credit rating.

One of the main issues in purchasing policy is whether supplies should be ordered by a centralised Purchasing Department or by individual departments or plants. In centralised organisations, purchasing decisions may be made at a Head Office for a large number of geographically dispersed offices, shops or factories. This may lead to longer *lead times* between ordering and delivery.

Centralised purchasing has advantages such as the ability to obtain bulk discounts and bargaining power with suppliers over technical specifications or delivery terms.

Quality control

The term *quality control* is often interpreted as the process of inspecting goods to ensure that they are the right size, shape or weight. However inspection is only one part of

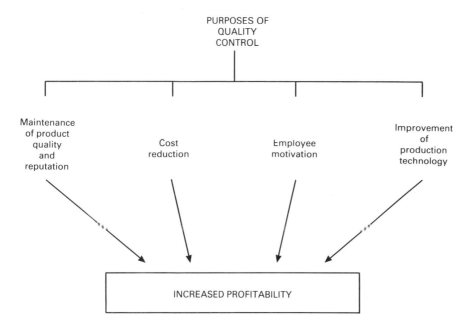

Figure 6.4 Purposes of quality control

quality control, which is as relevant to service organisations as to manufacturing firms.

As can be seen from Figure 6.4, quality control can contribute to profitability in several ways:

1. *Maintenance of product quality and reputation.* High quality goods and services enhance the organisation's reputation and lead to repeat orders. Many industries have legal restrictions such as health or medical regulations for food and pharmaceutical products. They also allow the firm to charge higher prices because customers will pay for quality and reliability.
2. *Cost reduction.* As well as upsetting customers and driving them away, defects cost the firm money through the costs of returns, repairs and replacements. Labour, materials and goods are wasted by inefficient production.
3. *Employee motivation.* Studies have shown that employees are often motivated by being associated with high quality products. Many firms have bonus payments or other incentives for meeting quality targets and *self-inspection* by workers of their own production is becoming more common in manufacturing industry.
4. *Improvement of production technology.* The process of improving quality will help to point out possible problems in production processes such as defective machines or poor storage of materials.

Some organisations, especially Japanese manufacturers, have *quality circles*, where small groups of workers from different levels meet to discuss production problems such as wastage or high defect rates. Despite their name, quality circles have a much wider scope than just quality control, being designed to foster employee participation in control of production.

Research and development

Research and development (R&D) is the process of enquiring into new processes, materials and products. Re-

search is the process of enquiry and generation of ideas, whereas development is the process of turning ideas into marketable products.

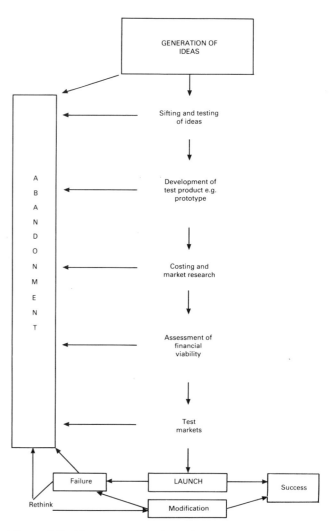

Figure 6.5 The research and development process

The process of research and development of a product may be generated in several ways, for example:

- accidental, such as the discovery of penicillin;
- adding to a product range, such as unleaded petrol or diet drinks;
- a by-product of other developments, for example Teflon was developed as a part of the US space programme;
- responding to customer feedback, for example the idea for Blu-tack was suggested by industrial adhesive salesmen who saw customers using blobs of Bostik to stick up notices;
- individual inspirations, for example Post-it notes were suggested by a man who wanted removable stickers in his hymn-book;
- in response to legal or market requirements, such as lighter car components and more economical engines in response to rises in the prices of oil;
- through pure research, for example 3M orders its scientists to spend 15% of their time on their own individual projects.

As can be seen from Figure 6.5, R&D is a lengthy and expensive process. Many ideas will be rejected at each stage, often with only a small percentage actually being launched on the market. Of those which are launched, many will be unsuccessful and fail to last more than a short time.

Location of Industry

The choice of location for a firm or industry is affected by several factors.

1. Cost of inputs

Input costs such as materials, labour and equipment may have a significant effect upon firms' locational decisions.

Industries which rely upon particular materials may locate near to natural resources, for example Sheffield became a major iron and steel-making area because it was near to sources of iron ore, coal and limestone. Modern steelworks are near the coast because most raw materials are imported.

With improved transport many industries are now *footloose*, with their location having little effect upon transport costs. For example the cost of office space in London has caused many firms and Government organisations to move their Head Offices or important departments to other areas.

2. Power

The first major industries in Britain were located near to fast-flowing rivers because they used water-power. When steam-driven machines came into use, factories were set up near coalfields. In twentieth-century Britain, access to power is rarely a problem.

3. Nearness to markets

Until the twentieth century, many industries had to be near their main markets. This was particularly important for heavy low-value goods such as beer and bricks. This factor is no longer as important for firms producing goods, but service industries such as retailing and banking have to be convenient for their customers.

Generally the degree of geographical concentration of an industry depends upon whether the customer has to come to the product, as in retailing or banking. In this case the industry will tend to be dispersed. If the product can be taken to the customer, as with manufactured goods, the industry is more likely to be concentrated in one or a few areas.

4. Transport

Firms may choose an area because it has good transport links for their customers, suppliers and workers. Many

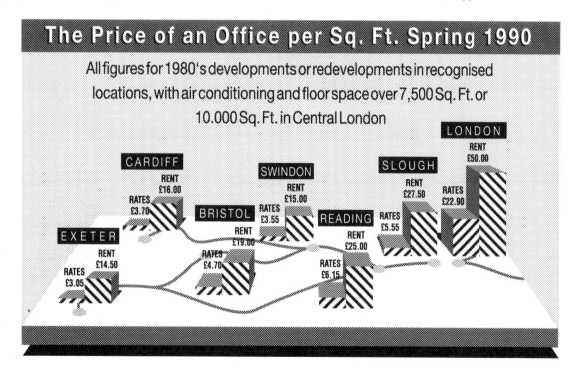

Figure 6.6 Regional differences in office rents

towns have grown up around railways, airports and motorway junctions for this reason. Motorways such as the M4 have led to increased industrial development along the 'Western Corridor' from London to South Wales.

5. Climate and landscape

This is important for industries such as agriculture and tourism. Some industries have special requirements such as flat land for chemical and oil refineries or remote locations for nuclear power plants.

6. Supply of labour

Many areas have a ready supply of labour with particular skills, such as metal-workers in Sheffield or financial analysts in the City of London. The cost and availability of labour may also vary between areas. For example many organisations in London and South-east England have found it difficult to recruit labour.

7. Government influence

The Government gives grants, loans and other assistance to firms locating in Assisted Areas (see Chapter 13). British Steel and British Coal also give assistance to businesses which provide employment in areas where they have closed plants and pits. Firms can also obtain grants for locating in other countries such as Singapore.

8. Industrial inertia

An industry may remain in a particular area after its original advantages have disappeared. For example the pottery industry remains in North Staffordshire although the deposits of china-clay in that area ran out many years ago. Pottery manufacturers have stayed because of tradition and the area's reputation.

Firms may also prefer not to move to another location because of the costs associated with relocation. In some cases they may remain in an existing location because the owners and managers do not wish to move house.

9. Economies of concentration

When an industry is well-established in an area, firms obtain benefits such as skilled workers, local school and college courses and a reputation for a particular product. These benefits are called *economies of concentration*.

Information Technology

Information technology (IT) is defined by the Department of Trade and Industry as

> "the acquisition, processing and dissemination of vocal, pictorial, textual and numeric information by a micro-electronics based combination of computing and telecommunications"

Figure 6.7 British Steel (Industry) Ltd

88

Figure 6.8 International locational incentives

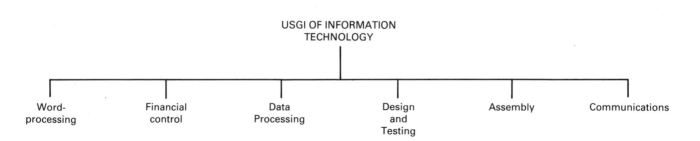

Figure 6.9 Uses of information technology

Over the past 20 years computers have become smaller, cheaper, faster and more powerful. The quality and speed of telecommunications have improved rapidly, whereas the cost has fallen. Because of these changes the number of businesses using information technology has increased rapidly. Some of the main uses of IT will now be considered.

Text-handling

The main method of handling text is by using word-processors, which may be specialist machines or general-purpose computers using a word-processing program. The advantage compared with a typewriter is that mistakes can be quickly and easily corrected by changing one word rather than an entire document. Longer documents such as reports or book manuscripts can be altered quickly and easily.

Word-processors are particularly useful when the same list or letter is used many times for different people. A document can be altered each time by typing in the name and address, without the bother of retyping the same message every time. This allows companies to send out mailshots such as advertising brochures for new products.

Financial control

Many firms keep financial records on computers, which can quickly recalculate figures such as costs or sales. The cash-flow forecast shown in Figure 5.10 could be adjusted to check the effects of a fall in sales or an increase in costs.

Computers connected to telephone lines can also be used to transfer funds between different locations, as is done by banks and stock-broking firms. Eftpos (electronic funds transfer at point-of-sale) systems such as Switch and Connect allow transfer of funds without using cheques.

Data processing

Businesses collect large volumes of data such as information on their customers. These can be kept in a *database*, which is a list of certain information about a customer. The computer can also be instructed to act automatically upon the information. For example reminders can be sent to customers who have not paid their accounts.

Design and testing

Many manufacturers use computers when developing new products or testing the quality of their products. For example cars can be tested for weak points by robots. The quality of a service can be tested by examining records to find out how many customers use it more than once.

Production

Many factories use computerised robots to assemble goods, particularly where repetitive and heavy work is involved. Information technology also allows efficient stock control, with automatic re-ordering when lines reach a minimum level. Laser-based supermarket checkouts using barcodes on products are one example of the use of IT to make production more efficient.

Communications

An increasing proportion of communication in business uses computers. Some of these services are described in Chapter 9.

CUSTOMERS TAP IDENTIFICATION NUMBERS INTO KEY-PAD, LINKED TO THEIR CURRENT ACCOUNTS

DEBIT CARDS ' WIPED ' THROUGH AN ELECTRONIC SENSOR ON CASH REGISTER

PHONE LINES LINK SHOP WITH BANK OR BUILDING SOCIETY SO ACCOUNT AUTOMATICALLY DEBITED

Figure 6.10 EFTPOS

Worked Examples

Short-answer
questions

6.1 Suggest three features of product design which might be considered important by a firm producing hi-fi equipment.

(AEB)

Answer For example, complaints, modification of products, changes in product range, changes in production schedules, delivery dates, after-sales service.

6.2 Name three ways in which the Production Department is influenced by the activities of the Marketing Department.

(AEB)

Answer For example changing design of existing/new products, consumer feedback about price/quality/choice/delivery/after-sales service.

*Data-response
questions*

6.3 The following passage has been adapted from 'Working with robots is a bore' by Harry Scarborough (*New Scientist*, 28 May 1981). Read the passage carefully and answer the questions which follow.

"Observers believe that the number of robots (defined as programmable manipulators that can do a range of manufacturing jobs) employed in factories will multiply by something like 25% per year during the 1980s. Robots are introduced mainly to save labour and so increase productivity. Studies in West Germany suggest that for every job created by robots, between five and seven jobs are eliminated.

Supporters of automation often claim that workers should welcome the machines into their plants not only because they increase productivity, but also because they eliminate menial jobs that people find boring or dangerous. Employers define the dirty jobs that robots take over and where they are eliminated it may be the consequence of an employer's desire to reduce absenteeism or shop floor militancy through new technology.

A small robot may be programmed with a simple computer language. With this an operator instructs his robot simply by typing instructions on a keyboard. Employers are afraid that if their workers use this equipment, they will demand regrading and higher wages. Programming will often be done by staff in computer departments away from the shop floor.

Robots are most suitable to industries that turn out lots of standard parts on assembly lines; the motor industry is, therefore, the biggest user. Firms generally adopt one of two approaches to their introduction. In one option, which Fiat and Olivetti have followed in Italy, the company restructures its production processes, and redefines manual tasks to make them more interesting. In the second approach, firms simply replace people with machines.

Since the early days of robots, there have been few industrial disputes directly concerning the technology. However, as robots have been used more and more, unions have drawn up strategies to influence the way in which technology affects their members' work. In 1979 Ford workers in the United States of America, members of the United Auto Workers, demanded that all tasks created by new technologies such as the programming and maintenance of robots, should be done by shop-floor workers who would receive special training where necessary. Because of the recession in the US car industry, the union could not get Ford to agree to its requests. But the episode showed that increased demands by unions over new technology, with the more intense international competition that is forcing firms to automate, are putting a strain on the accords between managements and unions, that, so far, have secured the peaceful assimilation of robots in industry."

(a) Explain briefly the statement 'to save labour and so increase productivity'. *(2 marks)*
(b) Give **one** reason why an increase in productivity might be of benefit to the workers. *(2 marks)*
(c) State and explain **three** possible advantages to employers of the potential flexibility of robots described in paragraph 3. *(6 marks)*
(d) Outline **three** possible advantages to a company introducing robots into the production process of following the example of Fiat and Olivetti (paragraph 4). *(9 marks)*
(e) Assume that the United Auto Workers had been successful in their negotiations with the Ford Motor Company (paragraph 5). Explain **three** possible consequences on the company. *(6 marks)*

Answer (a) Reduced wage bill and increased output/revenue per employee.

(b) For example makes firm more profitable, higher profit/value added per employee, therefore possibly better job security and prospects, higher wages.

(c) For example greater precision/reliability of operation, higher quality, faster work, more flexible production, lower labour costs, reduced unit costs.

(d) For example more interesting work, higher labour morale, increased productivity, more skilled and adaptable workforce, lower labour turnover, less absenteeism, fewer industrial relations difficulties.

(e) For example cost of retraining workers, some workers not very flexible/cannot cope, cost of retraining, slower and dearer to retrain rather than introduce new workers, difficult to break down demarcations, workers may want higher wages.

6.4 Read the extract and answer the questions which follow.

Just-in-time for Britain

The Toyota car company is credited with introducing the philosophy of just-in-time manufacturing. Company executives reputedly got the idea from a US supermarket which re-stocked its shelves as customers plucked groceries from them. In any event, Japan has enthusiastically embraced the idea of keeping stocks of raw materials in line with production requirements.

Now British managers are waking up to the idea, according to a survey carried out by management consultants Peat, Marwick, Mitchell. A poll of 100 industrialists reveals that over half are actively investigating just-in-time manufacturing. While a further 22% are considering installing computerized materials requirement plan-ning systems.

Although just-in-time manufacturing does not depend on computers, the ability of flexible manufacturing systems to work on small batches plays an important part in reducing raw materials stocks. Automatic ordering of parts from components suppliers also helps reduce stock overheads. British companies which have implemented just-in-time techniques report hefty reductions in inventory and waste. GKN Light Alloys claims a 50% drop in scrap and rework. The Cummins Engine Company, for instance, claims cost savings of £1.75 million and a drop in working capital required of £6.2 million.

(Source: An article by John Lamb in *Management Today*, November 1986)

(a) What is meant by the term 'working capital'? *(4 marks)*
(b) Explain
   (i) the possible benefits, and *(5 marks)*
   (ii) the possible problems to a company of introducing 'just-in-time manufacturing'. *(5 marks)*
(c) Assess the importance of integrating stock control with sales, marketing and production strategies. *(6 marks)*

Answer (a) Technically the difference between current assets and current liabilities. Working capital represents the resources available to pay for materials, wages and other short-term expenses. Working capital is especially important for costs which occur before the revenue needed to cover them is generated, for example where a firm has to give credit to customers but pay for its supplies before payment is received.

(b) (i) For example lower costs of holding stocks of materials, work-in-progress and finished goods, reduced wastage/deterioration/theft of stocks, more flexible production, lower working capital requirements.
   (ii) For example requires accurate forecasting and control of stock requirements, firm vulnerable to strikes/late deliveries/sudden orders, expensive computerisation/flexible manufacturing systems usually needed.

(c) The question may be divided into the 3 categories:

Sales   For example finished goods must be available to meet consumer demand, overstocking may lead to physical deterioration/obsolescence.

Marketing   For example poor stock control may lead to stockholding costs pushing up prices, good stock control helps a firm to respond quickly to customer requirements such as new orders.

Production   For example cost of storing/financing stock control, need to have materials/goods for production runs, importance of ordering stocks in time, stocks allow 'smoothing' of production, for instance stocks increased when demand high/decreased when demand low.

6.5 Read the following information and answer the questions which follow.

'And you'll find it all here!

As a thriving centre for business and industry, Angus has a few surprises up its sleeve.

Of course there's everything you'd expect, including readily available factory units, some of which are listed below.

It's also an area with excellent communications and there's a trained and trainable workforce ready and willing to work for you.

All this you'd expect (though you might well be surprised by the amount of extra help we can offer).

What you won't find elsewhere is the Angus lifestyle.

The area's beautiful surroundings include a stunning coastline and some of Scotland's most majestic glens.

And in addition to the scenery and places of historical interest, there's plenty to occupy your leisure time.

If you enjoy golf, tennis, swimming, sailing, football, rugby – in fact just about any sport you care to mention – you'll find it in Angus.

If there's a factory or site that suits you requirements from those listed below, you'll soon discover many other reasons to move to Angus.

CARNOUSTIE

A town with development area status, offering 0.5 acres of land and 5000 sq. ft of workshop units being developed 1987/88.

ARBROATH

The Kirkton Industrial Estate has a 16 000 sq. ft modern factory available and 25 acres of fully serviced land. Further workshop building in progress 1987/88. All of course benefit from this being an Enterprise Zone.

MONTROSE

In the town, 7 acres of serviceable ground, 5000 sq. ft workshop units being developed and storage areas of 13 600 sq. ft and 6800 sq. ft.

Also, the Montrose Harbour Trust can offer a whole variety of sites, including office blocks, warehousing, open and closed storage areas and workshops. The Harbour can accommodate ships up to 10 000 tons and supply full stevedoring services. The Harbour is also used by Oil Supply vessels and has all the facilities needed for such operations.

At every stage Angus can give you a helping hand through an impressive range of financial packages.

All this plus Angus ITEC, which was established to assist local business in training for specific needs in Computing and Electronics, Technical Colleges, good labour relations and training incentives.

And though no area can actually promise to hand you success on a plate, Angus can certainly put it within your grasp.

To find out more, send us the coupon or phone Robin King on 0307 65101.

Angus
Put it there!

Adapted from a leaflet provided by the Industrial Development Section of Angus District Council

Brocton Engineering Ltd is considering opening a new factory. As yet no decisions have been finalised on a specific location. As a junior member of the management team, you have been asked to report on Angus as a possible area for location.

Write a formal report (format *5 marks*) to the Managing Director outlining the following:

(a) The importance and significance of Enterprise Zones and Development Areas. *(6 marks)*

(b) Six business advantages, other than those mentioned in (a), of Angus as a possible location for the new factory. *(6 marks)*

(c) Four further factors that might need to be considered before deciding to locate in Angus. *(8 marks)*

(AEB)

Answer **(a)** (i) *Enterprise Zone* – small geographical areas, usually a few hundred acres, with various financial incentives, such as exemption from uniform business rate/planning controls.

(ii) *Development Area* – larger area, usually with high unemployment rate or other economic difficulties, which offers Government incentives for location such as grants, loans and tax reliefs.

(b) For example:

- ready-made workshops and factories;
- trained workforce;
- pleasant surrounding;
- social and sporting facilities;
- good labour relations;
- local colleges and training facilities;
- sea transport.

(c) For example:

- availability/cost of sites;
- cost of relocation;
- transport links, for example Angus remote from rest of UK;
- need for new suppliers;
- reaction of existing customers.

93

6.6 The following passage has been adapted from the article 'Hard cash for bright design' by Hugh Pearman (*Your Business*, October 21 1983). Read the passage before answering the questions which follow.

Truvox Flooring, a specialist Southampton firm making industrial cleaning equipment, is one of the 1100 small businesses which have found that there is more to the 'Design for Profit' scheme than Whitehall rhetoric. There's £10m hard cash available to help British firms create first class products. Under the scheme the Government will pay an approved industrial design firm for 15 'man days' design work on a new machine with a further 15 'man days' at half price.

The first stage involved the designer in producing a number of concept designs which evolved into a clear idea of what the machine would look like – strong, unfussy, attractive – then came the task of getting the components arranged logically and economically for ease of assembly.

When the product was launched in the UK an order was placed which took care of the entire first month's production run. Confident that production targets can be reached the technical director of Truvox Flooring is turning his eyes away from the home market.

He (the technical director) is sure that strong design is increasing in importance in the UK. 'The influence from the Continent is hitting hard. We know that if somebody likes to use a piece of equipment then the productivity of that person goes up.'

(a) Explain why Truvox Flooring might not find it economic to employ its own design team. *(4 marks)*

(b) Give **two** reasons which might explain why the government decided to launch the 'Design for Profit' scheme. *(4 marks)*

(c) The passage draws attention to the work of the industrial designer with reference to the appearance and technical aspects of product design. State and explain **two** reasons for the importance of
(i) the appearance of the product,
(ii) the technical design of the product. *(8 marks)*

(d) Outline **three** reasons why the technical director would want to be convinced that production targets could be reached before considering the expansion of the markets (third paragraph). *(9 marks)*

Answer **(a)** For example not enough work for them to do because firm is small, could not afford cost of full-time design team because skilled designers get high salaries, cheaper to subcontract.

(b) For example increase exports/reduce imports by making UK firms more competitive, lower costs, increase employment, higher profitability, encourage investment, keep UK products up-to-date.

(c) (i) *Appearance* – will attract/repel buyer, user works better if they like the product therefore more likely to sell well.
(ii) *Technical design* – increased efficiency/productivity for user, more reliable, easier and cheaper to manufacture.

(d) For example possibility of not fulfilling orders, unfilled orders may harm company's reputation and sales, technical director's reputation at stake, may need overtime/more equipment leading to higher costs, may lead to resources being diverted away from other products, more pressure on workers/management.

Essay questions **6.7** How might a manufacturing company determine the level of stocks it should hold?

(UCLES AS)

Answer (i) Start by explaining that 'stocks' may be of different types, for example raw materials, work-in-progress and finished goods held for production and future sales.
(ii) Explain the basic reasons for holding stocks, for example for immediate production, unexpected orders, replacement components for equipment, goods in the process of manufacture, as a precaution against disruption, such as strikes/transport problems affecting suppliers or firm's own production.
(iii) Describe the major principles on which the decision about stock levels should be made, that is the higher the stock level the greater the security against disruption or failure to fulfil orders, but the higher the cost of stockholding and the greater risk of products deteriorating or becoming obsolete.
(iv) Outline factors considered by firm when deciding stock levels, such as reliability of suppliers, closeness of ties to suppliers, rate of price increases, durability of product (for example, against physical deterioration or fashion changes), warehousing capacity, range of components and finished goods, lead time for delivery of supplies, cost of holding stocks, discounts for bulk purchases, speed at which customer expects to obtain product (for example parts for machines may be needed immediately so higher stocks will be needed).

6.8 Why might an organisation experience a reduction in profitability following the introduction of information technology?

(AEB)

Answer   (i) Define information technology (IT), for example as the use of computers and telecommunications to transmit information.

(ii) Explain the basic reason why the introduction of IT may be initially unprofitable, that is the benefits are often long-term whereas in the short-term there may be high financial and other costs.

(iii) Outline potential difficulties of introducing IT. These may be placed under three basic headings:

- Initial financial costs, for example 'hardware' (computers, fax machines, etc.), 'software' such as customised computer programs, changing of office layout to accommodate machinery, need for more light and cleaner environment, training of staff, use of management time, altering stationery.
- Employee problems, such as insecurity, loss of morale, lack of flexibility, redundancy, higher labour turnover, boring jobs, changed jobs, reduced promotion chances. These may decrease productivity, increase unit costs and lead to lower quality goods and services.
- Customer/supplier problems, such as payments and deliveries may be slower at first, level of service may be lowered because of disruption, data such as customer records may be lost in transfer to computer.

6.9 When emphasising the importance of consumer orientation Peter Drucker wrote:

"The business enterprise has two – and only two – basic functions: marketing and innovation. Marketing and innovation produce results; all the rest are 'costs'."

How would you reconcile this statement with the importance of production?

(AEB)

Answer   (i) Describe the basis of the statement, that is the purpose of business is to produce/supply what the customer wants, rather than 'production-orientation' where the business simply produces its good or service and then tries to sell them. Production may thus be regarded as subservient to marketing.

(ii) Explain that even if Drucker's statement is accepted, the production function is still vital to the firm. In simple terms the business can only market products successfully if they can be produced profitably. Marketing and production are completely interdependent.

(iii) Outline the marketing advantages that a firm may obtain from efficient production functions, such as skill of employees, quality of customer service, lower costs than competitors, technological innovation. In many cases the firm's reputation and profitability may be largely based upon factors such as these. Examples might include Black and Decker's low-cost production and leadership in developing new products, Honda's reputation for reliable engines and Toshiba's use of similar technologies and components in different products.

Self-test Questions

Short-answer question

6.10 Give four problems which a firm might face when automating its production.

(AEB)

Data-response questions

6.11 Study the extract and answer the questions which follow:

Any company adviser who's done his homework can confidently recommend Hampshire, England, and its neighbouring Isle of Wight as, potentially, Western Europe's most profitable business location.

The reason is simple: in Hampshire doing business is truly cost-effective.

• Cost-effective premises. Modern buildings, ready to move into for a fraction of the cost of similar accommodation in, say, London. Town-centre locations, out-of-town business parks, sites for development.

• Cost-effective manpower. The skills you need backed by good training facilities for information technology, integrated circuits, optical fibres, frontiers-of-knowledge projects, university research . . . . Already, Hampshire's hi-tech industries employ more than twice the national proportion of the local work-force.

Where people like to work
HAMPSHIRE DEVELOPMENT ASSOCIATION

• Cost-effective environment. The quality of life every family wants – villages, cities, downlands, forest, coast and sea, providing excellent recreation and top value living – including housing.

• Cost-effective communication. Excellent land, sea and air routes connect you economically with London, Europe and the world. Southampton is Britain's largest deep-sea container port and the site of one of its first freeports. **Among profit-conscious companies already located in this area are Cyanamid, IBM United Kingdom, Plessey, Pirelli General, Sun Life of Canada and Zurich Insurance.** To discover how to join them, call Hampshire Development Association on Winchester (0962) 56060. From overseas, dial +44 962 56060. Or telex 477729. Ask for Peter Scruton. Or use the coupon.

> To Hampshire Development Association, Winchester, Hampshire SO22 5BS, England.
>
> Please contact me about relocation opportunities.
>
> Name_____
> Position_____
> Company_____
> Address_____
>
> _____
>
> Type of Business_____
>   TE 13/4

Source: *The Economist*, 14 April 1984

(a) A major Japanese company is proposing to establish a UK manufacturing and distribution base for zip fasteners. Write a *brief* report, using a suitable format *(5 marks)* to show the advantages *(10 marks)* which the advertisement claims for Hampshire.   *(15 marks)*

(b) Identify **five** other items, not mentioned in the advertisement, which would need to be clarified before a decision on location could be made and show in each case why it would be important to the company.   *(10 marks)*

6.12

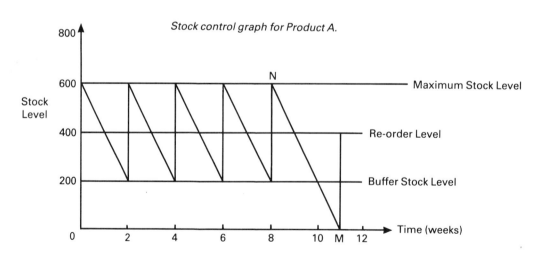

Stock control graph for Product A.

(a) What are the weekly issues of the product to the nearest whole number?   *(1 mark)*

(b) State the length of time which normally elapses between the ordering of new stock and the delivery.   *(2 marks)*

(c) What quantity of the product is re-ordered each time?   *(2 marks)*

(d) What minimum amount of the product is normally required to be kept in stock at all times?   *(2 marks)*

(e) Give **two** reasons to explain the change in the level of stock held between N and M. *(4 marks)*

(f) State and briefly explain the main factors which might influence the quantity at which
  (i) the minimum stock level
  (ii) the maximum stock level
  could be set. *(12 marks)*

(g) Give **one** reason why it is important for an enterprise to set a realistic stock level. *(2 marks)*

Essay questions

6.13 Why is it becoming possible for manufacturing business to be less geographically concentrated than in the past?

(AEB)

6.14 (a) Differentiate between job and batch production systems. *(5 marks)*

(b) How might a biscuit manufacturer benefit from changing production processes from batch to flow? *(10 marks)*

(c) Discuss the potential problems that might arise from such a change. *(10 marks)*

(UCLES)

6.15 (a) Do entrepreneurs always aim to minimise average costs when deciding on a location for a new factory? *(10 marks)*

(b) Identify other factors which might influence the decision and explain difficulties which are likely to arise in reaching such a decision. *(15 marks)*

(UCLES)

7

MARKETING

What is Marketing?

There are many different definitions of marketing, each with a slightly different emphasis. The most commonly quoted in the UK comes from the Institute of Marketing;

> "the management process responsible for identifying, anticipating and satisfying consumer requirements profitably"

This definition implies that successful marketing involves

1. recognising the goods and services that customers want at present and in the future;
2. ensuring that these products are available to the customer in acceptable quantities and prices;
3. selling at a profit.

A classic definition of marketing was written by Peter Drucker in 1954:

> "Marketing . . . encompasses the entire business. It is the whole business seen from the point of view of its final result, that is, from the customer's point of view" (*The Practice of Management*, Harper & Row, 1954)

This definition stresses that all activities in the business may be regarded as marketing, which is much more than simply promoting and selling the product. All activities of the company should be subordinated to marketing.

Even wider definitions of marketing would include non-customers as part of the marketing audience. The business has an effect and an image with many people and organisations who are not actually customers. Thus, for example, an oil company must avoid being seen by people and pressure groups as environmentally 'unsound', because as voters and political lobbyists they may have a damaging effect upon the firm's business by persuading the Government to restrict its activities. This would involve activities not directly related to their main business such as sponsorship of environmental or other causes.

The Marketing Process

Marketing involves integrating the various activities of the business in order to produce the 'best' result. For a privately owned business this will usually be concerned with maximisation of profits, although as indicated in Chapter 1, even private businesses may have other aims.

Marketing is also relevant to 'non-profit-making' organisations such as charities or Government organisations. For example Oxfam has to convince potential givers of the benefits of its work, and schools and colleges have to attract students.

Figure 7.1 summarises the marketing process, which has to be integrated with the rest of the business's activities. The organisation must consider external constraints such as changes in the economy or consumer tastes. It will also be necessary to examine the organisation's production costs and ability to sell its products.

There is also a need for the organisation to continually review and change its *marketing mix* whenever necessary. Businesses which fail to change their products or the ways in which they are priced, promoted and sold will quickly decline.

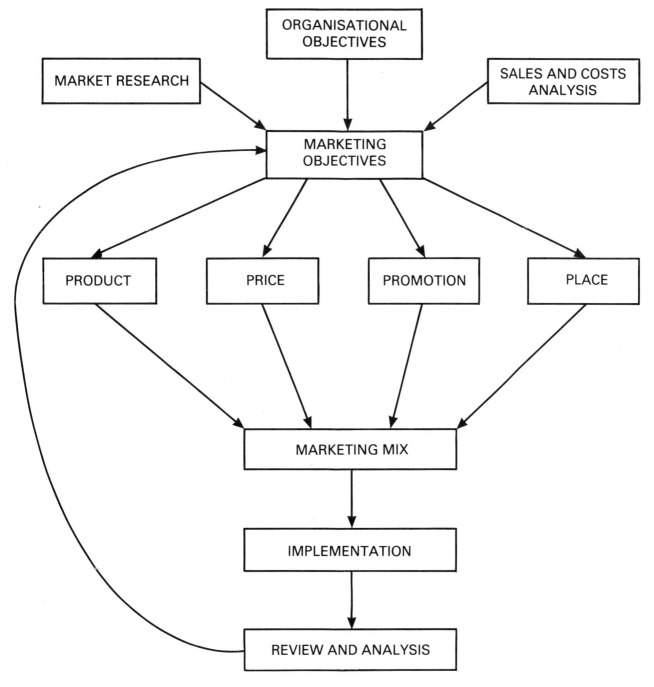

Figure 7.1 The marketing process

The importance of good marketing is stressed by A. R. Morden in *Elements of Marketing* (D. P. Publications, 1987);

"If the business does not provide the would-be customer with:

- the right information about the product, and
- the right product, accessible and available to the customer
- at the right time
- at the right price
- and with the right guarantees, after-sales service etc.

then, in a competitive market the customer will NOT buy the product. He or she, not surprisingly, will take their custom elsewhere."

Consumer and Industrial Markets

Classifying markets

Markets for goods and services can be split into two broad categories with different characteristics. *Consumer markets* are those where customers buy goods and services for their own personal use. *Industrial markets* are for goods or services which are used in production or may be resold to other customers. A firm may well be involved in both types of market, for example car manufacturers sell to the general public and to firms and Government organisations.

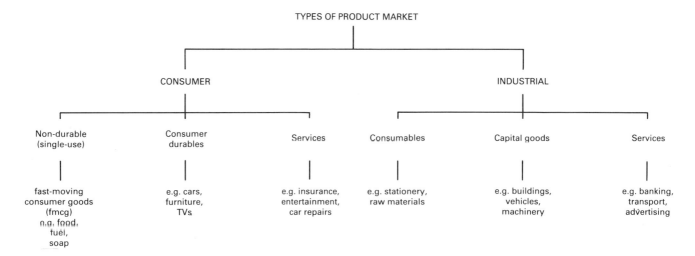

Figure 7.2 Consumer and industrial markets

Consumer markets

Consumer products can be divided into three distinct categories:

1. *Non-durable goods* such as food, fuel and small household goods have a short economic life and are bought frequently. They are sometimes called *fast-moving consumer goods* (fmcgs) or *single-use goods*. Demand for these tends to be relatively *income inelastic*, with sales being only mildly affected by economic booms or recessions.
2. *Durable goods* such as televisions, cars, furniture and clothing are used over a longer period of time. Typically they are more expensive than non-durables and are bought on a less frequent basis. Sales of durables are very responsive to changes in income or other economic variables such as interest rates.
3. *Services* such as car and house repairs, insurance, entertainment and legal services have become an increasing proportion of consumer expenditure as incomes have risen in recent years.

Consumer markets tend to have common characteristics which distinguish them from industrial markets:

- large numbers of final consumers;
- sales often made through intermediaries such as wholesalers and retailers;
- standardised products with limited specification by customers;
- high spending on advertising, especially through mass media;
- prices and terms of supply normally fixed by supplier with no consumer negotiation.

Industrial markets

Industrial markets can be divided into three different types:

1. *Consumables* such as stationery, fuel and raw materials are used quickly and purchased frequently.
2. *Capital goods* such as buildings, vehicles and machin-

ery are purchased infrequently and have a long economic life.
3. *Services* such as banking, advertising, transport and telecommunications are purchased on a regular basis in order to fulfil basic business functions.

Industrial markets tend to have common characteristics:

- demand is *derived* from the demand for the final product, for example the demand for building materials depends upon the demand for construction;
- demand for industrial goods and services fluctuates much more rapidly than that for consumer products;
- often based around a relatively small number of final customers;
- relationships with customers are often close and conducted through personal selling;
- customers often specify the content of the product;
- advertising spending may be low and concentrated in trade media such as specialist press;
- prices and terms of supply such as discounts and credit are often negotiable by individual customers.

Market Demand, Supply and Price

Although businesses are responsible for setting their own prices (see Chapter 8) they are always influenced to some extent by the prevailing market price.

The market price of a product depends largely upon the market demand and supply. In this case the term 'market' refers to the sale of a product in general rather than specific 'segments', such as 'furniture' rather than 'self-assembly kitchen units'.

Market Demand

Effective demand

The demand for a good or service is the amount that customers wish to buy:

- in a particular market, such as a fruit market, a country, the world market;
- over a period of time, such as week, day, year;
- at a particular price.

Effective demand means that customers have the money to buy a good and are willing to pay for it.

Demand and price

Generally the higher the price of a product, the lower the demand. This occurs for two basic reasons:

- customers will be able to afford less;
- customers will switch to a substitute.

When the price rises the opposite occurs, with consumers being able to afford more and also switching from a substitute. Demand will therefore normally fall.

This relationship can be illustrated by a *demand curve* such as that shown in Figure 7.3. The extent to which demand will change depends upon the product's *price elasticity of demand*. Note that the three factors listed above (market, period and price) are shown.

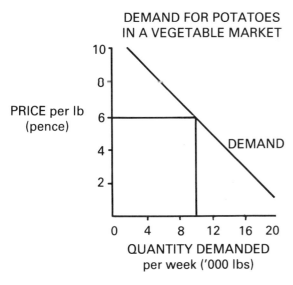

Figure 7.3 Demand curve

By reading off the demand curve it is possible to work out how much of a good or service will be demanded at any given price. Using the schedule the opposite way, it can also be seen what price would result in any given quantity being sold.

Because price and demand usually vary in the opposite direction, the demand curve normally slopes downward from left to right. There are some exceptions, where consumers use price as an indicator of the product's quality. Perfume and some types of jewellery are often quoted as examples.

Shifts in demand

Demand may also be affected by factors other than a change in price. These factors will cause a *shift in demand*. The demand curve will move to the right if demand increases and to the left if it decreases, as shown in Figure 7.4.

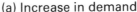

(a) Increase in demand

(b) Decrease in demand

Figure 7.4 Shifts in demand

Influences on demand (other than price) include the following.

1. Income

A rise in income will increase the demand for most products. There are some exceptions, referred to by economists as *inferior goods*, for which demand falls as income rises, because customers switch to 'superior' substitutes. Examples include bus-rides and basic foods such as bread and sausages.

Incomes have risen steadily in the UK over the last 40 years, but this has had more effect upon demand for some products than others. This is reflected in the *income elasticity of demand*.

Two terms which are commonly used when discussing income levels are *real* and *disposable*. *Real* means after allowing for price changes. *Disposable* means after allow-

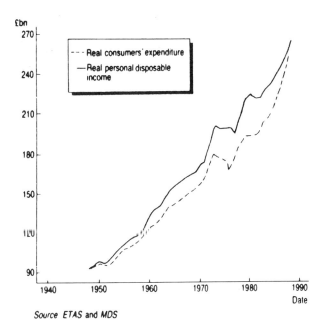

Source ETAS and MDS

Real consumers' expenditure and real personal
disposable income in the UK, 1948–88

Figure 7.5 Income and consumer spending 1948–88

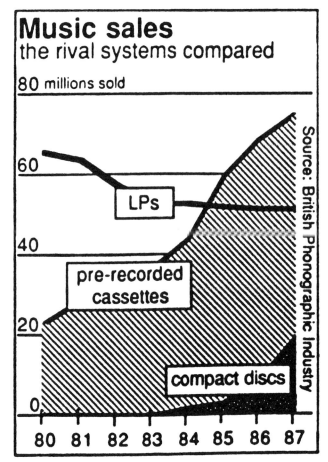

Figure 7.6 Demand for pre-recorded music

ing for taxes on income (sometimes referred to as *direct taxes*).

As well as personal income, market demand may depend heavily upon the purchasing power of firms and Government organisations. For industrial suppliers the profitability of firms and their investment plans can be very important.

2. Prices of other goods

Demand can be affected by changes in the price of *substitutes* or *complements*.

Substitutes are products which are in *competitive demand*, that is when the price of one rises, demand for the other also rises. Examples include butter and margarine, tea and coffee or compact discs and LP records.

Technically all products are substitutes for all other products, because if customers spend their money on one good or service they will not spend it on another. The relationship will not always be obvious. For example cars and foreign holidays might be regarded as substitutes. Although many people may buy both, others may do without one to buy the other.

Complements are in *joint demand*, that is when the price of one rises, demand for the other falls. Examples include petrol and new cars or cups and saucers. The term *derived demand* is sometimes used when the relationship is more 'one-way' as with houses and bricks or cars and steel.

3. Population changes

Demand is greatly affected by the population structure of a potential market. This can be based upon factors such as:

Size – The greater the population, the greater the potential market. For example Eastern Europe, China and 'newly-industrialised countries' such as Taiwan and

Singapore offer large potential markets. However allowance has to be made for income and other factors.

Age – The proportion of the population in different age groups can change dramatically, as shown in Figure 7.7. This has obvious effects upon certain products such as children's clothes, education, medical services and sheltered accommodation.

Geographical distribution – Producers such as firms and Governments also need to consider where people live within their target regions. For example cars tend to sell more in rural areas, mainly because of the lack of alternatives such as public transport.

4. Social changes

Social changes such as an increased divorce rate and a higher proportion of women workers can affect the demand for products. For example, the rising divorce rate has led to an increase in the number of households and therefore demand for smaller flats and houses. The higher numbers of women workers have increased the demand for convenience foods.

5. New products

A new product may create a market for itself, and reduce or increase the demand for other products. For example in-car and personal stereos boosted the market for cassettes and compact discs, but helped steadily to destroy the demand for vinyl LPs.

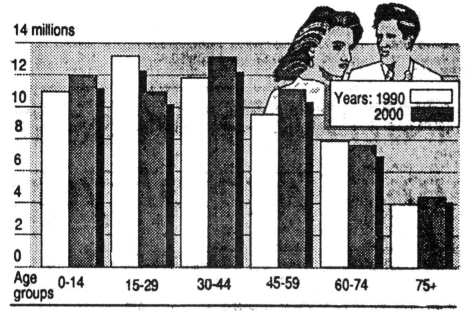

Figure 7.7 Age distribution of UK population 1990–2000

6. Seasonal demand

Sales of many goods and services vary with the time of year or the type of weather. Obvious examples are ice-cream and anti-freeze, but there are many other products which depend heavily upon seasonal sales. Books, records and perfume all rely heavily upon the pre-Christmas peak period.

7. Tastes, fashions and crazes

Demand may rise or fall steadily because of long-term change in tastes. Sales of dairy foods, football tickets and motorcycles have fallen consistently for many years. During the same period there has been a steady increase in demand for products such as lager, wine and denims.

Sometimes the change in demand may be more short-lived, as in the case of 'crazes' such as Rubik cubes, CB radio and skateboards. Demand for a product may also change rapidly for unusual reasons such as football attendances and equipment sales rising when England won the World Cup in 1966. Perhaps the most famous example occurred in the 1930s in the USA when Clark Gable took off his shirt in a film. He was seen not to be wearing a vest, and sales of vests halved during the following year.

8. Cost and availability of credit

Many goods and services are bought with borrowed money. Their demand may therefore be sensitive to the level of interest rates and the ease with which consumer and firms can borrow money. This is particularly important for more expensive items such as housing, cars and consumer durables.

9. Government influence

Government policies affect demand for many goods and services. The Government is a major buyer of products such as books, medical equipment and construction services. Its economic policies, such as changes in taxes, interest and foreign exchange rates, have a large effect upon demand.

Market Supply

The supply of a good or service is the amount that suppliers wish to sell:

- in a particular market, such as a fruit market, a country or the world market;
- over a period of time, such as week, day or year;
- at a particular price.

Supply and price

Generally the higher the price of a product, the greater the supply. This occurs for two basic reasons:

- existing suppliers supply more because it is profitable to increase production;
- new suppliers will enter the industry.

When the price falls the opposite occurs, with some suppliers reducing production and others leaving the industry altogether. Supply will therefore normally fall.

This relationship can be illustrated by a *supply curve* such as that shown in Figure 7.8. Note that the three factors listed above (market, period and price) are shown.

By reading off the supply curve it is possible to work out how much of a good or service will be available for purchase at any given price. Using the schedule the opposite way, it can also be seen what price would result in any given quantity being supplied. Because supply increases as price increases, the supply curve normally slopes upward from left to right.

Shifts in supply

Supply may also be affected by factors other than a change in price. These factors will cause a *shift in supply*. The supply curve will move to the right if supply increases and to the left if it decreases, as shown in Figure 7.9.

103

SUPPLY OF POTATOES IN A VEGETABLE MARKET

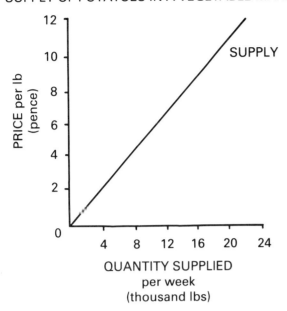

Figure 7.8 Supply curve

(a) Increase in supply

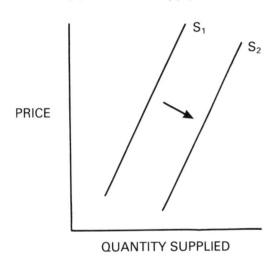

(b) Decrease in supply

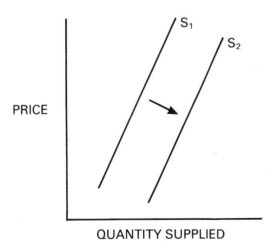

Figure 7.9 Shifts in supply

Influences in supply (other than price) include the following.

1. Costs of inputs

If input costs such as wages, materials, rents and fuel increase, it will be more expensive to supply goods and services. At any given price, suppliers will supply less. On the other hand, a fall in input costs will increase supply.

2. Productivity

An increase in productivity will tend to reduce unit costs and therefore increase supply. For example new technology has caused a fall in the real cost of producing many goods and services, as a result of faster production and increased productivity.

3. Competition

Competition can force suppliers to produce more efficiently and cut prices, therefore increasing supply. This has happened in many legal and financial services, as a result of the rapid increase in competition during the 1980s.

4. Seasonal supply

The supply of many goods and services is significantly affected by the time of year or the weather. For example some crops can only be grown at certain times of year, and their supply is largely determined by the weather.

It is important not to confuse seasonal supply with seasonal demand. For example toys and records are in seasonal demand but not in seasonal supply, because they could be supplied evenly throughout the year.

Because of better transport, refrigeration, imports and changing agricultural techniques, seasonal supply is not as marked as it used to be for many products.

5. Natural resources

Supply of some primary products can be affected by the discovery of new reserves. For example exploration of the North Sea has increased the supply of oil and natural gas.

6. Government policy and political events

The Government can influence the supply of a product, usually through *subsidies* or by producing services such as education, health care and defence itself. In other cases, it increases production costs by imposing taxes such as VAT and tobacco tax, which help to reduce supply.

Political events, particularly wars and international issues, have sometimes influenced the supply of goods and services. Middle East wars have often resulted in lower supply of oil, and decisions by the Soviet and South African Governments can affect the world supply of gold and diamonds.

Market Price

Equilibrium price

The market price is determined by the interaction of the demand and supply of a product. For example, if the

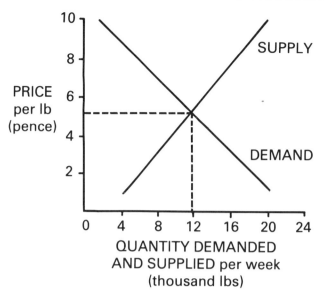

DEMAND AND SUPPLY OF
POTATOES IN A VEGETABLE MARKET

Figure 7.10 Determination of market price

demand and supply curves shown above are put together, as in Figure 7.10, the market price can be determined.

In this case the market price will be 5 pence per pound. At this price consumers will wish to buy 12 000 pounds of potatoes per week, and suppliers will be willing to supply the same amount.

The market price is often referred to as the *equilibrium price*, because it will stay the same unless either demand or supply changes. At any other price, market forces will cause the price to change until the equilibrium price is reached.

This can be seen from Figure 7.10. If the price was set at 8 pence per pound, that is ABOVE the equilibrium price, suppliers would want to supply 18 000 pounds per week, but consumers would only be prepared to buy 6000 pounds at this price. This would create a *surplus* and suppliers would be forced to cut their price. The market price would fall. Consumers would buy more, suppliers would reduce supply, and the equilibrium will be restored at a price of 5 pence.

If prices are allowed to change freely, any surplus will automatically be cured by a fall in price. If, however, the price is not allowed to fall, the surplus will become permanent. One famous example of this is the market for some agricultural products, whose suppliers are guaranteed minimum prices by the European Community. This leads to 'butter mountains' and 'wine lakes' because farmers produce more than consumers are prepared to buy at the guaranteed prices.

If the price was set BELOW equilibrium price, the opposite situation, that is a *shortage* would occur. For example at a price of 3 pence consumers would want to buy 16 000 pounds, but sellers would only wish to supply 8000 pounds. Suppliers would increase their prices. Demand would fall until the equilibrium price was restored at 5 pence per pound.

As with surpluses, any shortage will be automatically cured by a change in price. If, however, prices are not allowed to rise freely, other methods of resolving the shortage must be found, such as rationing, queuing, waiting lists or 'black markets'. Examples of these situations occurring include rationing of food during the Second World War and the allocation of FA Cup Final tickets to clubs. In both cases 'black' or 'unofficial' markets occurred as people bought from spivs or ticket touts.

Demand and supply curves are often drawn using algebraic notation, that is without using numbers. This is shown in Figure 7.11.

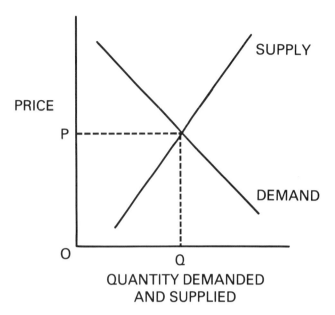

Equilibrium price = OP
Equilibrium quantity = OQ

Figure 7.11 Demand and supply in algebraic notation

Changes in equilibrium price

The equilibrium price of a good or service will only change if there is a shift in either demand or supply. There are four possible situations in which this may occur, as shown in Figure 7.12, using the example of the market for new houses.

Elasticities of Demand

Price elasticity of demand

Price elasticity of demand (PED) measures the responsiveness of demand for a product to changes in its own price. It is measured by the formula:

$$PED = \frac{\% \text{ change in demand}}{\% \text{ change in price}}$$

For example if the price of a product rises from £2 to £3 and demand falls from 1000 to 800 per week:

$$PED = \frac{-20\%}{50\%} = -0.4$$

For most products, price elasticity is negative, because if price rises demand falls and vice versa. However, FOR

105

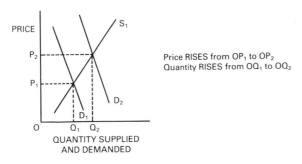

(a) Increase in demand e.g. caused by rise in incomes

Price RISES from OP_1 to OP_2
Quantity RISES from OQ_1 to OQ_2

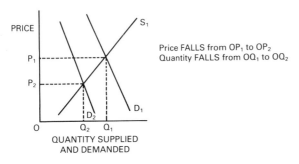

(b) Decrease in demand e.g. caused by higher mortgage rates

Price FALLS from OP_1 to OP_2
Quantity FALLS from OQ_1 to OQ_2

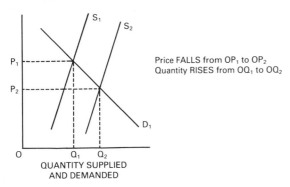

(c) Increase in supply e.g. caused by land prices falling

Price FALLS from OP_1 to OP_2
Quantity RISES from OQ_1 to OQ_2

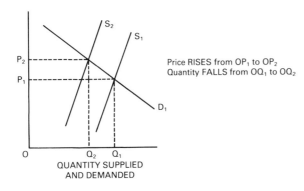

(d) Decrease in supply e.g. caused by dearer building materials

Price RISES from OP_1 to OP_2
Quantity FALLS from OQ_1 to OQ_2

KEY: D_1, S_1, OP_1, OQ_1 ORIGINAL DEMAND, SUPPLY, PRICE, QUANTITY
D_2, S_2, OP_2, OQ_2 NEW DEMAND SUPPLY PRICE QUANTITY

Figure 7.12 Changes in equilibrium price

PRICE ELASTICITY ONLY, the negative sign is usually ignored.

Depending upon the effect of a price change upon revenue, demand may be classified as *price elastic* or *price inelastic*.

If demand is price elastic, the percentage change in demand is GREATER than the percentage change in price, that is PED is greater than 1. In this case a price rise will lead to a FALL in spending on the product. A reduction in price will lead to an INCREASE in spending.

Demand is likely to be relatively price elastic for one of two basic reasons – a product has close substitutes, such as butter and jam, or is a high percentage of spending, such as cars and consumer durables.

The opposite situation occurs when demand is price inelastic. The percentage change in demand is LESS than the percentage change in price, that is PED is less than 1. A price rise will lead to an INCREASE in spending on the product. A reduction in price will REDUCE spending.

Demand is likely to be relatively price inelastic if a product has few close substitutes, such as petrol and cigarettes, or is a very small percentage of spending, such as matches and salt.

Income elasticity of demand

Income elasticity of demand (YED) measures the responsiveness of demand for a product to changes in consumers' incomes. It is measured by the formula:

$$\text{YED} = \frac{\% \text{ change in demand}}{\% \text{ change in income}}$$

For example if income rises by 10% and demand for a product rises by 20%:

$$\text{YED} = \frac{20\%}{10\%} = 2$$

For most products, income elasticity is positive, because demand rises and falls with income. The only exceptions are *inferior goods* such as bus-rides and bread.

Depending upon the effect of an income change upon revenue, demand may be classified as *income elastic* or *income inelastic*.

If demand is income elastic, the percentage change in demand is GREATER than the percentage change in income, that is YED is greater than 1. This is likely for more expensive products which represent a high percentage of consumer spending, such as cars, consumer durables and services like entertainment and holidays. It is also likely to occur where purchases can be postponed or brought forward as income changes.

The opposite situation occurs when demand is income inelastic. The percentage change in demand is LESS than the percentage change in income, that is YED is less than 1.

Demand is likely to be relatively income inelastic if spending on a product is a small percentage of spending. This is particularly likely in the case of regular low-price items such as basic foodstuffs and electricity.

Cross-elasticity of demand

Cross-elasticity of demand (XED) measures the responsiveness of demand for a product to changes in the price of a *substitute* or a *complement*. It is measured by the formula:

$$XED = \frac{\% \text{ change in demand for product A}}{\% \text{ change in price of product B}}$$

For example if the price of product B rises from £10 to £15, and demand for product A (a complement) falls from 5000 to 4000 per week:

$$XED = \frac{-20\%}{50\%} = -0.4$$

Cross-elasticity of demand is positive for substitutes, because if demand for one good or service rises, demand for its substitutes also rises. Similarly demand for a product will fall if the price of a substitute falls.

For complements, cross-elasticity is negative, because if the price of a product rises, demand for its complements falls and vice versa.

The level of cross-elasticity between two products depends upon the closeness of the relationship between them. The closer the substitutes or complements, the greater the cross-elasticity. For example, the cross-elasticity of demand between butter and margarine will be higher than that between cars and holidays.

Market Research

Scope of market research

Market research is the process of obtaining information about the market for new and existing products. A business may look for information about matters such as:

- potential sales of a new or existing product;
- consumers' attitudes to a product, such as do they like the colour/taste/packaging/name?
- strengths and weaknesses of competitors;
- future trends in a market such as fashions and trends;

Market research checklist
While there are many hundreds of areas that could be investigated, the following list should alert you to the significant points.

Size of the market
1. What is the total market – industrial, consumer, home and overseas?
2. Is it growing or shrinking?
3. Are there any regional biases or preferences?
4. What are the seasonal influences?
5. Where are the big users?
6. Proportion met by imports?
7. It is a well-developed, sophisticated market or are new competitive products entering?
8. Is it prone to fashions, short runs, cyclical changes?
9. Is new technology likely to alter the market?
10. What changes may affect demand?
    a) Government legislation, taxation, trading standards, credit restrictions?
    b) Obsolescence?
    c) Innovation by competition?
    d) Your firm's variation in policy?

The competition
1. Who are the main competitors and what share do they enjoy?
2. What is their product range and where lies their appeal?
3. What are their strengths and weaknesses?
4. Where do you have a competitive edge?
5. What are the trends?

Your own performance
1. How do you measure up in the market?

2. Where do you make most profit and where is the growth?
3. What extra lines or services are needed?
4. Are you positioning yourself correctly?
5. How do you promote yourself and compare with your competition?
6. What is the cost of marketing, broken down into product lines, channels of distribution, enquiry or order value, market segment etc?
7. What changes have been made or are intended?

The product
1. Who uses the product?
2. Frequency of purchase?
3. Who else could use the product?
4. Are there related lines or extra service that could be sold?
5. How can it be improved?
6. What do customers think of it?
7. Is it branded?
8. Is the price right?
9. Where does it lie on the product life cycle?
10. Are specials produced? Can it be personalised?
11. What are the returns?
12. What is the life?
13. What new products are envisaged and how will they tie in with existing lines?

The customer
1. What else can you sell them?
2. Where are the decision makers?
3. How can you reach them?
4. Is the buyer the user?
5. What is the customer profile?
6. What are their needs?
7. How can you best reach them?

Figure 7.13 Questions posed by market research (from D. Patten, *Successful Marketing for the Small Business*)

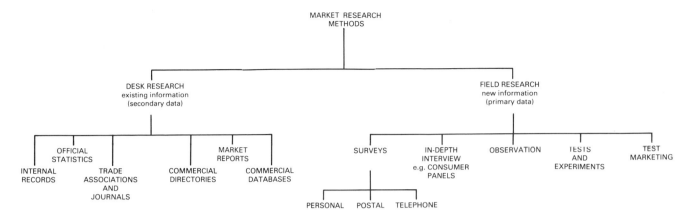

Figure 7.14 Methods of market research

- potential new markets, such as in different areas or countries;
- image of the business with customers/public;
- possible effects of changes in products or prices;
- effectiveness of advertising, promotion and distribution channels.

Marketing information is sometimes classified into *quantitative* and *qualitative* data. A crude distinction is that quantitative data is concerned with facts, for example about sales in different areas or size of the total market, whereas qualitative data is concerned with assessing attitudes, such as opinions of different products or the company image.

Market research methods

Market research includes many different activities. At its simplest it might involve checking the suitability of a site for a shop by counting the number of people going past it at different times of the day. A sophisticated campaign may involve spending thousands of pounds upon questionnaires, consumer interviews and test marketing.

Research may be carried out internally by the organisation's own staff, or by one of the many specialist market research agencies, who may also plan a complete promotional campaign for a product.

Market research methods are traditionally classified into *desk* and *field* research. Desk research is concerned with using existing information such as internal records and published information, often referred to as *secondary* data. Field research involves obtaining new information.

Desk research

Desk research involves using existing information or *secondary data*. There are many potential sources of secondary data:

1. *Internal data*, such as records of how much certain types of customer spend and which areas have the best sales for particular products.
2. *Official statistics.* The Government publishes statistics and reports on many topics such as population changes, foreign trade and consumer spending. Examples of relevant publications include *Business Monitors* and

Economic Trends and Monthly Digest of Statistics.
3. *Trade associations* and *trade journals* supply information for almost all types of business.
4. *Commercial directories* of different types of company and buyers of particular products.
5. *Market reports* on different products are published by firms such as Mintel and the Economist Intelligence Unit (see Figure 7.16).
6. *Commercial databases* such as ACORN contain valuable information for finding customers.

Field research

If the information the business wants is not already available, it will be necessary to use field research to find it. Methods of field research include the following:

1. Surveys

These involve interviewing, often based upon a *questionnaire*. Interviews consist of three principal types: face-to-face, postal and telephone. A *sample* of people will be chosen, as it is impossible to interview every potential customer or relevant party.

The sample may be *random*, with no attempt to choose the type of person interviewed. This is likely to be used for a product such as biscuits which is bought or used by many different types of people. Random sampling is not suitable for products aimed at particular groups, for example a 40-year-old man's opinion about a teenage girls' magazine or brand of perfume is unlikely to be useful for market research.

Because of this disadvantage, *stratified random* sampling is often used. This involves choosing people of a particular type, such as professional women between 25 and 40 or car-owners.

Quota sampling involves interviewing a weighted cross-section of different people according to pre-defined criteria. To take a very simple example, if sales of a product are divided between four geographical areas in the proportions 40:30:20:10, a quota sample would also involve interviews in these proportions. Other variables which might be allowed for include income level, occupation, sex and household type.

Do you sometimes find yourself barking up the wrong tree?

Survey Research Associates' experience in researching promotions can help you make the right decisions.

Our experience includes researching into specific market expenditures, reducing the risks on special promotions and testing promotions awareness. This is just one of the services offered by SRA.

SRA is one of the leading market research companies in the UK offering the complete range of research facilites; data processing, field and hall tests, telephone research...

SURVEY
RESEARCH
ASSOCIATES

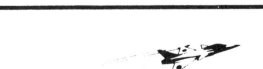

SAAB asked us for research. We told them where to go!

Figure 7.15 Specialist marketing agencies

WALL FOR SALE

The wall, long a symbol of the communist threat, is now a symbol of opportunity and is being bought and sold on the streets of Berlin. But when the wall came down last year so did all the old rules about doing business in the rest of Eastern Europe. What was once a quiet but predictable backwater for Western companies is now wide open. Business International's weekly newsletter — **BUSINESS EASTERN EUROPE (BEE)** — can help business executives, like yourself, to take advantage of these opportunities.

★ **BEE** has been published for 18 years
★ **BEE** is a *weekly* newsletter — it delivers the facts 51 times a year
★ **BEE** covers the whole of Eastern Europe — that includes Albania!
★ **BEE** is a concise 8 page newsletter
★ **BEE's** focus is strictly business and finance
★ **BEE** tells you what your competitors are doing in Eastern Europe
★ **BEE** is *the* best source of intelligence on this key region

What's more every week **BEE** includes:

What's New in Your Industry — 3 pages of Western sales, JVs, M&As, privatizations, licensing deals — classified into 35 sectors and listed by country. Last year **What's New** reported over 3,000 EE deals.

Focus on Financing — one page on new investment credits, bank offices, leasing and insurance trends.

Plus four pages of up-to-the-minute stories — all with the angle for business right up front. Recent issues have included articles on: How

higher oil prices will affect the economies of Eastern Europe; and Boris Yeltsin's 500 day market transition plan for the Russian Republic.

Since **BEE's** inception in 1972 it has covered over 60,000 deals. To acquire this information yourself, you would need to monitor dozens of newspapers and trade journals — East and West — every day, and maintain a full network of correspondents in Eastern Europe. We know because we do!

Let us show you what our regular readers have known for 18 years —that **BUSINESS EASTERN EUROPE** can become an integral part of your business decision-making in the Soviet and East European markets.

And two final points. Subscribe to **BEE** *NOW* and you will take advantage of both these offers:

MONEY OFF
★ 10% discount off your first year's subscription.

THE BI GUARANTEE
★ If you are not entirely satisfied with **BEE** you may cancel your order at any time for a full refund of the unused portion of your subscription — an offer you cannot refuse.

GET INSIDE EASTERN EUROPE — GET BEE.

Figure 7.16 EIU market report

HOW WELL DID WE HANDLE YOUR CONTACT WITH US?

1. Which ONE of the following statements best describes the way you feel about the action taken in response to your recent contact with our Customer Support Centre?

   ☐ I was completely satisfied
   ☐ I was not completely satisfied but the action taken was acceptable
   ☐ I was not completely satisfied but some action was taken

   ☐ I was dissatisfied with the action taken
   ☐ I was very dissatisfied — I don't consider any action was taken at all

2. How satisfied were you with the Customer Support Centre on EACH of the following:

A. **PERSONNEL**

	Very satisfied	Somewhat satisfied	Neither satisfied Nor dissatisfied	Somewhat dissatisfied	Very dissatisfied
Professionalism	☐	☐	☐	☐	☐
Responsiveness	☐	☐	☐	☐	☐
Knowledge	☐	☐	☐	☐	☐

B. **RESPONSE**

	Very satisfied	Somewhat satisfied	Neither satisfied Nor dissatisfied	Somewhat dissatisfied	Very dissatisfied
Timeliness	☐	☐	☐	☐	☐
Clarity	☐	☐	☐	☐	☐
Helpfulness	☐	☐	☐	☐	☐

3. As a result of our action, how likely is it that you will recommend Polaroid to a friend or business associate who needed equipment or supplies?

I definitely will	I probably will	I might or might not	I probably will not	I definitely will not
☐	☐	☐	☐	☐

PLEASE TEAR OFF THIS PART OF THE CARD AND POST — POLAROID HAS PAID THE RETURN POSTAGE

Figure 7.17 Polaroid market research questionnaire

2. In-depth interviews and group discussions

These allow more detailed questions to be asked. They are often used to discover people's attitudes to new products or advertisements before they are tried out on the public. *Consumer panels* may be used to measure changes in behaviour and attitudes over time.

3. Observation

This involves watching people in different situations. It is sometimes used in shops to see how people react to displays of products. One ice-cream manufacturer discovered that its products were selling badly because children could not see over the top of the freezer. The problem was solved by altering the design.

4. Test marketing

A product may be tried out on a small scale before launching it to all customers. For example the Wispa chocolate bar was sold in North-east England as an experiment.

Testing marketing has the advantages of trying a product out with real customers. Faults can be ironed out and unsuitable goods or services dropped quickly. Sales and distribution efforts can be concentrated and advertising may be obtainable at discount rates, especially on television.

Some marketers, however, argue that test marketing creates more problems than it solves. Ideas are given away to competitors, who may try to sabotage the test by extra advertising or promotional effort. The test market may be unrepresentative or sales staff may make abnormal effort which cannot be sustained for the full market.

Worked Examples

Short-answer questions

7.1   Explain what a rise in 'real' wages means, and give one effect it might have on a supplier of consumer durables.

(AEB)

Answer   Wages rise faster than prices/inflation. Would lead to higher demand or higher costs.

7.2   Demand for a particular product is price inelastic. What is the significance of this for a firm when considering a change in the price of its product?

(AEB)

Answer   If demand is inelastic the change in demand for any given price rise or cut will be less than the percentage price change. Therefore a price cut will reduce revenue and a price rise will increase it. Also, if price rises, demand will fall which should lead to lower costs and higher profitability.

7.3   A business decided to increase the price of its product from £1.00 to £1.20. As a result, sales fell from 1200 to 900 per week. Calculate the price elasticity of demand for the product.

(AEB)

Answer

$$\text{PED} = \frac{\text{Percentage change in demand}}{\text{Percentage change in price}}$$

$$= \frac{25\%}{20\%}$$

$$= 1.25$$

Alternatively:

$$\text{PED} = \frac{\text{Change in sales}}{\text{Original sales}} \div \frac{\text{Change in price}}{\text{Original price}}$$

$$= \frac{300}{1200} \div \frac{£0.20}{£1.00}$$

$$= 1.25$$

7.4   Identify two ways in which the Government may deliberately influence the demand for a given product.

(AEB)

Answer   Could include:

- heavy taxes on goods, for example tobacco and alcohol;
- tax relief, for example on mortgages and pension plans;

- tax exemptions, for example on food, books and domestic fuel;
- subsidies, for example on bus travel;
- Government purchases, for example defence equipment.

Data-response question

7.5 A company has developed a consumer product of advanced technological design. A decision was made to subcontract manufacture and for the company itself to concentrate on marketing. It was thought that an initial output of 10 000 units per month would be adequate to meet demand in the first year of the product's life. The diagram below illustrates the relationship between projected demand, actual demand and output levels for the first six months of trading. Study the diagram and answer the questions which follow.

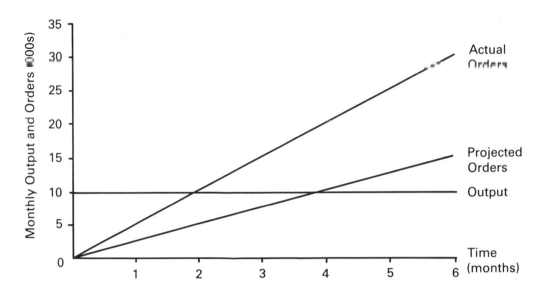

(a) State at approximately which point in time a back-log of orders will begin to build up, and why. *(5 marks)*

(b) Give **three** marketing problems the company may encounter if the trend of actual orders is maintained. *(4 marks)*

(c) If the company is unable to deliver on time, customers may decide to cancel their orders. State and explain **two** ways in which the company may seek to prevent this happening. *(4 marks)*

(d) Give **three** reasons why the subcontractor might find it difficult to expand his production to meet the unanticipated demand. *(6 marks)*

(e) Outline briefly **two** reasons why the company might have decided on a low initial level of output. *(6 marks)*

Answer

(a) After 3 months:

Cumulative output = $3 \times 10\,000 = 30\,000$
Cumulative orders = $5000 + 10\,000 + 15\,000 = 30\,000$

After this point, demand exceeds output and there are no stocks to meet the excess demand.

(b) For example longer delivery times, inability to meet existing orders, cannot take on new orders, may hurt reputation.

(c) For example take on new subcontractors, increase orders to existing subcontractors, manufacture product itself, reduce price to compensate for slow delivery.

(d) Answer should be linked to product being technologically advanced, such as finding skilled workers, obtaining materials, availability of technical equipment, insufficient working capital.

(e) For example limited capital to finance development and production, try out product first to discover and iron out faults, restrict output to 'skim' the market, insufficient resources or knowledge for large-scale marketing.

Essay questions

7.6 Examine the factors which might influence the demand for cars in the short-term.

(AEB)

Answer

(i) Explain that cars are not a single *homogeneous* product and may be divided in various ways, most obviously by size and price. As well as the demand for cars as a whole, some factors may cause a shift between different types.

(ii) Discuss the influence of factors such as:

- *Price*, especially in *real* terms. It is likely that demand will tend to be relatively price inelastic, since there are few close substitutes.
- *Incomes*, especially *real* incomes. Demand for cars is *income elastic* that is highly responsive to changes in income. Car-buying is a major expensive purchase, which may well be postponed when income is falling or brought forward when income is rising. It is also worth mentioning that actual changes in income are often less important than people's *expectations* about future income or general feelings about being worse or better off. For new cars, *company profits* are also important, since just over half are bought by firms. Company cars are also concentrated in the middle-price sector.
- *Prices of substitutes*. There are few direct or close substitutes, but there is some competition with other forms of transport.
- *Price of complements* such as petrol or insurance can have an effect. The large price rises of the 1970s reduced demand, and also caused a shift from large to small cars in the short-term.
- *Seasonal demand* is very important for new car sales, with August (new registration) and January (new calendar year) the main peak months. The previous months of July and December have the lowest demand.
- *Cost and availability of credit* is vital, as a high proportion of new cars are bought with borrowed money. Interest rates, credit restrictions and special finance deals all affect demand.
- *Government policy* on taxes, road spending and general economic control have significant effects. For example about a sixth of the price of a new car and half of the price of petrol consist of tax.
- *Population and social changes* are important influences upon demand for cars, although these will tend to be more long-term, for example the proportion of women qualified to drive rises steadily every year.

(iii) Explain that demand is affected by a combination of these factors, and that sales cannot be predicted by using only one variable such as petrol prices or interest rates. For example even if both of these rose sharply car sales might still increase because of higher incomes and company profits.

7.7 **(a)** 'Marketing managers need to know about elasticity'. Why? *(10 marks)*

(b) If the Bank of England introduced a tighter monetary policy, what, in your opinion, would be the consequences of this for a firm producing video machines? *(15 marks)*

(UCLES)

Answer **(a)** Explain that demand elasticities measure the responsiveness of demand for a product to changes in its own price, income and prices of other products. They therefore have a significant effect upon businesses, which need to carefully consider the potential effects of changes in these variables.

For example a product with a close substitute is likely to have high price and cross-elasticities. It will be difficult for a firm to increase its price without losing a large proportion of its sales. However, if the firm is able to reduce prices without the danger of retaliation, it can benefit from a price-cutting strategy.

Income elasticity of demand affects the steadiness of a product's sales. Non-durables such as food and domestic fuel tend to fluctuate very little as income rises and falls. Spending on these does not rise significantly in a boom. Consumers also tend to maintain their spending during a recession.

(b) (i) Outline the likely features of a 'tighter monetary policy' such as higher interest rates, possibly combined with some restrictions on credit, such as minimum deposits or maximum repayment terms. Either as deliberate policy or as a result of tighter monetary policy, it is also possible that the exchange rate of sterling would rise.

It is likely that one of the major Government aims would be to reduce the level or growth of spending on consumer products such as video machines, to control inflation and/or reduce imports.

(ii) Explain possible effects of these policies, such as the demand for consumer goods is likely to fall, resulting in a loss of orders for a video machine producer. Video machines might be described as a 'discretionary' or 'deferrable' purchase which can be postponed until people feel better off.

If the exchange rate does rise, imported machines will be relatively cheaper to British customers, and the firm's products will be more expensive in export markets. If the firm cuts prices to stay competitive, its profit margins will fall.

7.8 Describe briefly the methods of market research available to a company manufacturing consumer products. How may the work of the marketing and production departments be affected by the findings of market research?

(AEB)

Answer (i) The questions ask for a *brief* description, so it is only necessary to outline the basic methods. For example while questionnaires may be mentioned, there is little need to go into enormous detail about open and closed questions. It is important to attempt some classification of research methods, such as desk and field, quantitative and qualitative, with some indication as to how and why each method might be used.

(ii) Explain ways in which the Marketing Department may use the results of market research.

The answer could focus upon the four elements of the *marketing mix* (see Chapter 8), for example:

- altering quality/design of product;
- setting prices for different products or markets;
- altering advertising and other promotional activity to change the product's image, emphasise its strengths or reach new markets;
- expanding distribution networks for its products.

(iii) Explain possible effects upon the Production Department. This is more than knowing how much to produce. It may involve factors such as:

- a maximum price which the consumer will pay, therefore making it necessary to produce at below this price;
- feedback about the design and quality of the product, such as do consumers like the shape/find it easy to use?
- estimates of possible peaks and troughs in demand so that the Production Department can plan for busy and slack periods;
- estimates of demand may be used to plan orders so as to ensure best possible terms, such as for bulk orders;
- advice on packaging and presentation;
- information on likely requirements for spare parts, after-sales service, repairs.

Self-test Questions

Short-answer questions

7.9 List three types of information a manufacturer might acquire from market research.

(AEB)

7.10 What effect would a rise in interest rates be likely to have upon house prices?

(AEB)

Data-response question

7.11

'Don't panic' is the message for shoppers from Britain's retail pepper suppliers following the latest sharp increase in world prices. The increase shows a slowly dawning awareness that an acute world shortage is looming, because of crop setbacks in many parts of the world. Unusual weather patterns this year have hit production, with losses probably most severe in Brazil, where crops could drop by as much as 50%. Brazil, Malaysia, India and Indonesia produce more than 95% of the world's pepper. Provided shoppers do not go out and buy a year's supply of pepper tomorrow, McCormick – the world's largest spice company – believes that it should be able to hold prices at least for a couple of months. Its stock holdings are fairly comfortable.

Supply scares in the past have seen pepper disappear quickly from Britain's supermarket shelves. A small pot is comparatively cheap at about 20p, so shoppers can easily stock up without breaking their budget.

The boom has been fuelled by heavy speculative buying.

(Adapted from 'The pepper market hots up', R. Stainer, *The Guardian*, 10/11/83)

(a) The article suggests that the retail price of pepper may rise. Using the information in the passage explain **two** possible causes of such a price rise. *(8 marks)*
(b) Draw a labelled diagram to show the variation in retail stock levels that might occur as the result of panic buying on the part of the consumer. *(6 marks)*
(c) 'Brazil, Malaysia, India and Indonesia produce more than 95% of the world's pepper'. What is the significance of this statement in explaining the shortfall in supply? Use information given in the passage to support your argument. *(5 marks)*
(d) The article implies that the demand for pepper is not very responsive to changes in price.
  (i) Give **three** possible reasons for this situation. *(6 marks)*
  (ii) Explain the effect of this situation on the pricing policies of the spice companies. *(3 marks)*
  (iii) Comment briefly on the possible effect of the situation on the revenue of the spice importers. *(2 marks)*

(AEB)

Essay questions

7.12 A firm is about to extend its product range. Under what circumstances might the firm engage in market research and how might it be undertaken?

(AEB)

7.13 Review the constraints on a marketing director when formulating his marketing plan.

(AEB)

7.14 A Ford Escort manufactured and sold in the USA contains many features not found in the equivalent Ford Escort assembled in the UK and yet it is several hundred pounds cheaper. Explain why this is so.

(AEB)

THE MARKETING MIX

The Marketing Mix

Having formulated its marketing objectives, a business has to decide on the appropriate *marketing mix*. The marketing mix is often referred to as the '4 Ps':

1. *Product* – the type of good or service produced, such as size, quality, design and packaging.
2. *Price* – this includes discounts, credit terms and special offers.
3. *Promotion* – products have to be advertised and brought to customers' attention.
4. *Place* – how and where products are sold, such as through shops or direct to customers; this is often referred to as *distribution*.

These four components of the mix cannot be totally separated, as they are interdependent. For example, if a higher-than-average price is to be charged for a product, it will be necessary to ensure that other elements such as the quality, type of packaging and channel of distribution are sufficiently 'upmarket'. As a simple example, it is difficult to sell high-priced fashion clothes through a market stall.

Product

What is a product?

Products come in many different forms. A business producing goods or services must consider factors such as:

- size, shape and colour;
- packaging;
- quality of materials;
- services offered, such as delivery and after-sales service;
- image;
- brand name;
- credit terms;
- price;
- fashion;
- type of customer.

The importance of these factors will vary between different products and customers. Colour, image and fashion are fairly unimportant for matches, but crucial for the sale of clothing.

Products are sometimes defined in terms of 'customer benefits' rather than what they actually are (hence the classic marketing slogan 'sell the sizzle not the steak').

A simple example of this was given by Akio Morita, Chairman of Sony, who described the video recorder as giving the buyer the power to 'grab a TV programme in the hand'. The real benefit was the freedom to rearrange the TV schedules, in just the same way as the buyer of a book could pick it up and put it down at will.

Another example is the computerised hotel key service supplied by Yale. This uses plastic cards instead of metal keys. The cards can be programmed and read by computer to give details of the hotel services used by an individual customer. The card is changed for every customer. The hotel gets the benefits of not losing keys and easy billing. By creating extra benefits compared with the conventional metal key, Yale is able to charge a much higher price.

THE MARKETING MIX

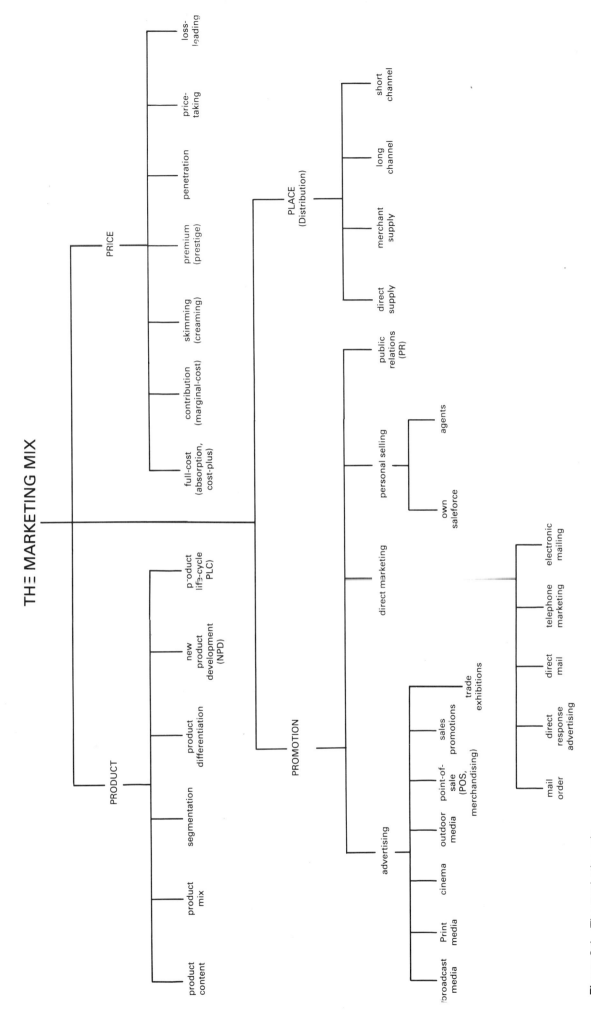

Figure 8.1 The marketing mix

117

The product mix

RETAILING	Market	Profile	Target Market Age	Size of Market People	Value of Market £	Total no of Outlets
BURTON	Men Youths	Mainstream formal and casual clothing and accessories	20-40	10.4 m	£3.6 bn	467
ALIAS	Men	Fashionable colour co-ordinated leisure and casual clothing	25-40	6.1 m	£900 m	33
TOP MAN	Men Youths	Fashion aware formal and casual clothing and accessories	11-30	8.5 m	£2.9 bn	252
RADIUS	Men	Individualistic formal and casual clothing and accessories	20-35	6.5 m	£2.9 bn	32
PRINCIPLES for MEN	Men	Modern classic clothing and accessories for business and pleasure	25-45	8 m	£2.5 bn	105
CHAMPION SPORT	Men Women Children	Fashionable sportswear and equipment	15-35	16 m	£1.6 bn	100
DOROTHY	Women	Mainstream formal and casual clothing and accessories	18-40	9 m	£4.1 bn	467
SECRETS	Women	Fashionable lingerie and nightwear	15-45	13.7 m	£1.7 bn	27
TOPSHOP	Women Girls	Fashion aware casual and occasion clothing and accessories	11-30	8 m	£3 bn	302
PRINCIPLES	Women	Sophisticated fashionable classic clothing and accessories	25-45	7.5 m	£3.5 bn	192
evans	Women	Mainstream fashion size 14+	25-60	10 m	£1.8 bn	196
DEBENHAMS	Men Women Children Home	Mainstream mass market fashion for the individual and home	All ages	45 m	£31 bn	71
HARVEY NICHOLS	Men Women Children Home	Exclusive and designer fashion for the individual and the home	All ages	–	–	1

RETAIL SUPPORT SERVICES

Retail Systems	Data processing, systems development and communications
Retail Distribution	Dedicated warehousing and distribution
Retail Planning	Monitor and evaluate retail space performance and opportunities
Retail Marketing	Strategic market analysis and research
Design Studio	Provide fashion trends, styles and colour information Design and develop merchandise ranges

Figure 8.2 The Burton Group 'product mix'

Almost all businesses sell different types of products. The range of products sold is called the *product mix.*

In choosing its mix a business may follow different policies such as:

1. concentrating upon a single market segment, such as sports cars, Far East holidays, or health foods;
2. covering all or most segments of a particular market, for example Honda sell cars ranging from small hatchbacks to large luxury models, the Burton Group has clothes shops for different types of customers (see Figure 8.2);
3. selling many different products, that is *conglomeration.*

Segmentation

Market segmentation is the process of dividing the total potential market for a product into distinct groups (*segments*). Each segment should be separate and large enough to justify devising a marketing mix for.

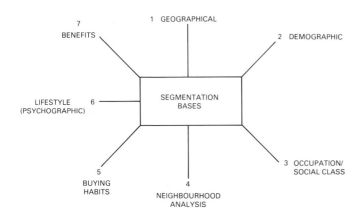

Figure 8.3 Bases for segmenting markets

There are many different segmentation 'bases', that is ways in which potential customers can be divided. Examples include:

1. *Geographical,* for example by region, country or continent. Tastes may vary tremendously, for instance more sweets per head are bought in Southern than Northern England, car ownership is higher in rural areas.
2. *Demographic,* for example banks and building societies have different types of accounts and advertising approaches for teenagers and over-forties, beer consumption declines with age.
3. *Occupation and social class* are usually linked, since the social class of a household is generally classified according to the occupation of its 'head'. Occupation is also a crude guide to income.
4. *Neighbourhood* analysis is best-known through the ACORN (A Classification of Residential Neighbourhoods) system which divides areas into 38 types. The data is referred to by using postcodes. The basis for this system is that different types of neighbourhoods have different habits and spending characteristics.
5. *Buying habits,* such as always plan carefully, buy on impulse, degree of customer loyalty, size of individual orders, etc. This is a complicated way of dividing customers, requiring careful use of customer records and market research.

6. *Lifestyle* (also known as *psychographic*) segmentation is based on the idea that people have a particular image which they try to live up to, for example 'homely', 'caring', 'sophisticated', etc. Products may be designed to suit such images. 'Boy-racer' cars such as the Escort XR3i or Golf GTi are examples of these. The markets shown for the Burton Group in Figure 8.2 are a simply defined segmentation for clothing retailers.
7. *Benefits* obtained by a customer may be a way of classifying particular markets. For example benefits provided by a café may include a quick snack, a rest during shopping, a way of keeping children from moaning too much, a social meeting point or a take-away sandwich. Each of these needs may require a slightly different approach, such as very quick service for takeaways, a pleasant atmosphere for 'sitdown customers', play equipment for children and so on.

Having identified its segments the business has to decide which it will aim to reach, and how it will do so. It may try to satisfy as many of the 'segments' as possible, or concentrate upon the most profitable.

Each segment requires a different 'marketing mix'. For example a food manufacturer trying to reach as many retail outlets as possible would probably have to negotiate personally with the buyers of the major supermarket chains. They would expect large discounts, long credit terms and influence over the content and quality of the product.

For the thousands of small independent retailers this approach would not be cost-effective. Marketing in this case will be conducted through wholesalers and the trade press, with mass media advertising to persuade customers to ask for the product.

Even comparatively small segments may be profitable if they can be targeted in a cost-effective manner. For example Heuga make oil-proof carpet tiles for car showrooms and wired carpet to prevent static in computer rooms. Although these are each small markets, the benefits offered are sufficient to make production profitable.

Concentrating upon a small segment of the market is often referred to as *niche-marketing.* During the 1980s many companies grew very rapidly as a result of 'nicheing'. Famous examples include Body Shop, Tie Rack and Sock Shop. However, the failure of many such companies shows that it is vital that the segment chosen should be more than just a passing fad, and that the company should always be looking to broaden its markets.

Managing the product mix

The composition of a firm's product mix may depend upon several factors:

1. *Profitability* or *return on capital* is the most obvious criterion, with unprofitable products being dropped or changed.
2. *Opportunity cost* of a product can be measured by the capital, management or staff time, plant use and other resources needed to produce it. The firm would need to consider if there is a more profitable alternative use for these resources.
3. *Working capital* has to be devoted to any product, and the profits have to justify the expense.
4. *Compatibility* between products is important to avoid wasteful competition between the firm's products. Careful segmentation can help to avoid this problem.

119

Characteristics of ACORN Types

	13	36	UK average	KEY
🏠	43.0%	89.7%	55.7%	% households owner-occupied (1981 census).
☂	24.6%	84.1%	48.8%	% economically active population employed in white collar jobs (1981 census).
🧒	21.8%	16.4%	19.3%	% population under 15 (CACI updates, 1985).
65+	14.6%	13.9%	15.0%	% population over 64 (CACI updates, 1985).
UB40	20.1%	4.4%	11.3%	% workforce unemployed (Dept of Employment/CACI July 1987).
📺	38.1%	6.6%	20.7%	% adult population watching 20+ hours IBA Channels weekly (National Readership Survey, 1986).
🚗	6.2%	44.2%	18.5%	% households with 2+ cars (BMRB Target Group Index, Apr 86-Mar 87).
	4.0%	38.0%	14.0%	% adults owning any stocks & shares (NOP Financial Research Survey, Oct 86-Mar 87).
	13.0%	61.0%	34.0%	% adults owning any bank credit card (NOP Financial Research Survey, OctMar 87).

The ACORN system divides addresses into 38 different types. 2 of these are illustrated here.

TYPE 13
Older Terraces, Lower Income Families

Type 13 includes those areas where local authorities have been active in purchasing and improving poor quality pre-1914 terraced housing.

This type is often seriously disadvantaged by low levels of industrial skill and high unemployment amongst its population. It is particularly common in cities such as Liverpool, Hull, Teesside and Sunderland where docks, steelworks and chemical plants have often provided well paid but physically strenuous work for an unskilled labour force.

In contrast to type 12, married women are less likely to work and families are much larger so that the proportion of children in the community is therefore much greater.

TYPE 36
Detached Houses, Exclusive Suburbs

Of all 38 types, this is the one with the highest status, whether measured by car ownership or by the proportion of professional or managerial workers.

These therefore are areas of large detached houses, in mature grounds, in locations of choice landscape value, such as Esher and Solihull.

Most of these areas were developed in the 1930's so that this type attracts mostly the older professional with school age or grown-up children. Younger families are seldom able to afford the house prices, and those who can do are more likely to prefer more modern executive estates.

Low unemployment and very affluent lifestyles predominate.

Figure 8.4 The ACORN system

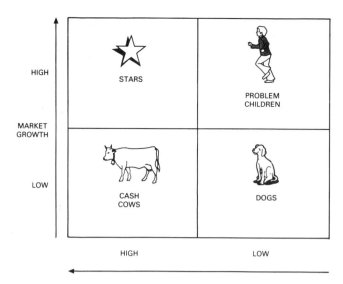

Figure 8.5 BCG growth/market share matrix

Figure 8.6 Ansoff product/market matrix

PRODUCT / MARKET	PRESENT	NEW
PRESENT	Market penetration	Product development
NEW	Market development	Diversification

There are many different formal methods of assessing a firm's product range. Two of the most famous are the Boston Consulting Group's (BCG) growth/market share matrix and the Ansoff product/market matrix.

The BCG matrix divides a firm's products into four categories, according to their market share and the overall growth of the market. This analysis is loosely related to the *product life-cycle* in that low growth rates are more likely in mature markets. The matrix is 'dynamic' in that products may change from one state to another, for example stars may become cash cows.

Stars need large injections of cash for promotion, investment in production, research and development, design, etc., in order to maintain high market share in what is likely to be a very competitive market. They may however generate cash if the firm is first in the market and can use *skimming* as a pricing policy. Properly managed stars should become cash cows when the market matures.

Cash cows require small amounts of cash compared with the profits that they bring in. Kelloggs Cornflakes, which could be regarded as a cash cow, are heavily advertised but also make huge sales. Cash cows help to cover overhead costs and support new products. Badly managed, however, they may turn into dogs.

Problem children, sometimes called *question marks* or *wildcats*, are difficult to decide what to do with, as their name implies. They may possibly become stars with heavy investment and good management, but are just as likely to become dogs when the market growth slows down. For example, many personal computer firms went bankrupt in the mid-1980s.

Dogs are heavy users of capital and are often unprofitable or have a low return on capital. They are at a double disadvantage, competing against larger competitors in a market with little room for expansion. For example the growing number of *joint ventures* formed by smaller European car manufacturers such as Volvo and Rover is the result of fears of being squeezed out of a saturated market. Normally, dogs will be disposed of unless there is some chance of improving their profitability.

Although the BCG matrix is a simplification, it does provide a useful basis for classifying products within a product range. A business needs to have a balanced portfolio of each type of product. In particular, unless it has one or more cash cows it will find survival difficult.

Stars are also needed to provide future growth.

The Ansoff product/market matrix (Igor Ansoff, *Corporate Strategy*, McGraw-Hill, 1965) is a method of analysing the ways in which a firm can increase its sales. A firm can sell more of its existing products or develop new ones. It can try to sell to existing customers or to new markets. Putting these decisions together gives four possibilities.

Market penetration means selling more of the existing products to present customers. On face value this is the least risky policy since both products and markets are familiar. However it can be expensive and unprofitable in mature markets because sales will have to be taken away from competitors. Market share may have to be increased by heavy advertising or price-cutting.

Market development means selling the present product range to new customers. This may involve geographical expansion, selling to different age groups (for example milk to young people), income groups (for example Ford buying Jaguar) or gender groups (Burton buying Dorothy Perkins).

Market development has the advantage of familiarity with the product, but new markets may be difficult to enter successfully. For example British retailers have often done badly in Europe and the USA, and Midland Bank lost heavily when expanding into American markets. It may be difficult to establish new sales networks and distribution channels.

Product development involves selling new products to existing markets. This often involves more intensive use of brand names or distribution networks, for example Lucozade Orange Barley, Marks & Spencer credit cards, newsagents renting videos and Post Office selling stationery.

The major problem with product development is that of 'overstretching' brand names or losing customer goodwill. The rapid decline of the Next retailing chain in the late 1980s was attributed by many people to the use of the name in too many different types of store.

Diversification is by far the most risky policy, because both products and markets are unfamiliar. It is typically employed as a policy when the firm is in a mature or declining market or when market share is stagnant or falling.

Product differentiation

Firms often try to *differentiate* their product from those of other firms in order to retain customers and create growth. Modern writers such as Michael Porter (*Competitive Advantage*, 1980 and *Competitive Strategy*, 1985) and Tom Peters (*Thriving on Chaos*, 1987) argue that high-quality products differentiated from those of competitors are vital for long-term success and even survival.

Factors involved in product differentiation may be

based on low prices, particularly where some 'psychological barrier' is breached. Successful examples include Ford's Model T car for $360, Laker Airways' £99 London–New York flight and Amstrad's PCW 8256, a complete word-processor and printer system for £399. However, it must be remembered that Ford lost its world leadership and Laker went bankrupt because competitors gradually eroded their price advantage.

In the long-term it is very difficult to sustain price leadership, and other factors may be important in differentiating products. These include customer service, high quality, reliability, brand names, packaging and variety of products.

The importance of non-price factors compared with other forms of differentiation can be seen by the success of the Sony Walkman, introduced in 1980. This was rapidly copied by many other firms, and sales halved in the first year. However, by constantly improving sound quality and adding features such as radios, Sony was able to bring sales back up to three-quarters of the 1980 level by 1990. The lost volume was compensated for by increased prices and profit margins.

Brand names are an important feature of product differentiation. Sometimes, as in the case of petrol and washing powder, there is little significant difference between the physical qualities of different products, and the brand name is the main distinguishing factor.

An established brand name such as Heinz or Kelloggs provides instant recognition, even for new products. A survey in the USA showed that three-quarters of 1920 brand leaders across a wide range of products were still the best seller 60 years later. Many important British brand names such as Polo, Shell and Cadbury were established before the Second World War.

Brands can also be *extended* to new markets. This has been particularly important in the drinks market, where names such as Coke, Ovaltine, Lucozade and Horlicks have all been 'stretched' to include new flavours such as 'light' and 'diet' drinks.

During the late 1980s the attraction of established brand names became particularly apparent through takeovers of firms such as Rowntree, Trebor, Lotus and Jaguar in order to gain control of brand names or trade marks. Many companies started to include a value for names in their balance sheets.

Against these trends, however, it can be argued that even successful brands can die or decline rapidly. Vitalis, Omo, Spangles, Double Diamond and Triang were all well-known in the 1960s, but are virtually unheard of now.

New product development (NPD)

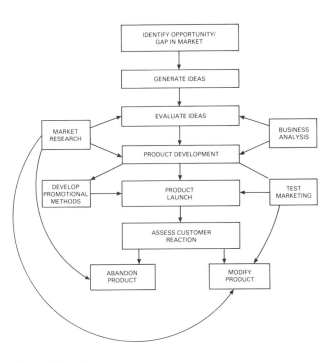

Figure 8.8 Stages in new product development

Figure 8.7 Brands used by Dalgety

New products are vital if a company is to survive in the long-run, but they are also very risky to launch. As can be seen from the *product life-cycle*, new products are rarely profitable in the early years. The investment can be very high. For example, a new drug costs over £100 million to develop and test before the company can recover any revenue from sales. New cars and passenger planes cost many times more than this.

The term 'new product' can include a variety of situations. Some products, such as the first televisions, microwaves and compact discs, might be regarded as *innovative.* The firm might also produce *replacements* such as new models of existing products. A third possibility is that the new product may be *imitative* of competitors. For example the Sony Walkman and the Ford Sierra were rapidly copied.

Developing new products may cause problems such as:

- risk of failure – about half of all new products last less than 4 years;
- competitors' reaction, for example copying;
- development and introduction costs placing high demands on working capital;
- devaluation of brand names/company image;
- distributor acceptance, such as mistrust about product's future;
- customer acceptance, such as will the product last?

The risk is likely to be particularly high for certain reasons where economies of scale are important, for example low-price branded consumer goods, or where support services such as computer software or motor spares are necessary. If customers do not feel that these will be available, or are mistrustful of long-term services or resale values, they will be less willing to buy the product.

The product life-cycle

All goods and services have a *product life-cycle* which describes the way in which sales rise and eventually fall. The life-cycle is divided into four stages.

1. Introduction

The product is developed and launched on the market. Sales will be low and there will be large spending upon advertising and promotion. Profits may be low, or the product may make no profit at all because of the costs of research and development or initial promotion. There may be limited distribution, frequent design modifications and high stockbuilding costs. Many products fail at this stage.

2. Growth

Sales and profits increase steadily. There may be more competition, but increased sales should create economies of scale. This is the best time to gain high market share and create the stars which will later become cash cows. It could also be the 'make-or-break' point for a product.

3. Maturity

This is usually the longest stage. Sales and profits may still be rising, but at a slower rate. Eventually the product will reach its *saturation point*, when sales are at their highest level. A high proportion of sales may be 'replacement' by existing customers, for example colour TVs or fridges in Britain. This is the period in which the business will need to defend its market share. A successful defence will create the cash cows of the future.

Sales may be maintained by price-cutting, heavy advertising or launching 'improved versions'. The key purpose will be to differentiate the product. Inefficient producers will be forced out of the market.

This is the stage in which new products or markets should be developed, before the 'decline' stage is reached. For example Sony bought CBS Records and the Columbia film studios because it saw the 'hardware' stereo and VCR markets as saturated. The 'software' market for recorded music and films was seen as more permanent.

4. Decline

Eventually sales for the total industry will start to fall. In order to preserve sales, firms may start to make deep price cuts. Profit margins may begin to decline.

The business may accept this or abandon the product altogether. Even if profits are still being made, the product may be taking up capital or management time which could be used profitably on other products.

This is traditionally regarded as the time to 'get out'. However, a firm may decide to maintain production while

(d) The Product Life-cycle

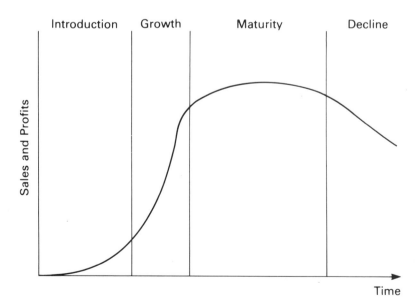

Figure 8.9 Product life-cycle

others leave or even enter a declining market. This can often be a successful strategy, as in the case of Amstrad entering the personal computer market in 1984.

The length of the product life-cycle and its different stages varies considerably between products. Citizen's Band radio and skateboards had very rapid growth for a couple of years, followed by almost instant decline. The maturity stage was very short. At the other extreme, basic goods such as salt and coal have had life-cycles lasting hundreds of years.

Price

The limits of pricing

The price that can be charged for a product has two basic limits:

1. *Cost of production.* Although a product may sometimes be sold below cost price, for example as a *loss-leader*, in the long-run prices must be sufficient to cover costs.
2. *Demand*, that is what the customer is prepared to pay.

In setting prices, a business must keep these upper and lower limits in mind. Although a distinction is sometimes made between *cost-based* and *market-based* pricing strategies, in practice the business has to consider both its own costs and customer demand.

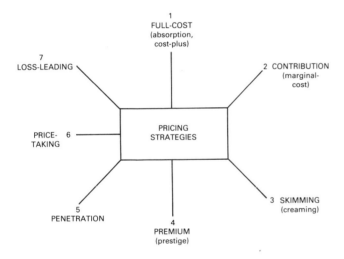

Figure 8.10   Pricing strategies

Full-cost pricing

Full-cost pricing, also known as *absorption* or *cost-plus* pricing, is the most traditional method of pricing. It involves detailed calculation of costs, which are divided into *fixed* (*overhead*) and *variable* (*direct*) costs.

Overhead costs are divided by the output expected to be sold during a particular period to obtain a fixed cost per unit. This is added to the variable cost per unit for a particular product or job in order to calculate the total cost per unit. An agreed mark-up is then added to give the final price.

124

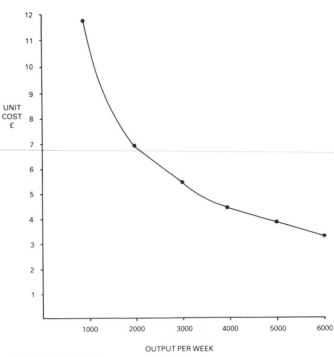

UNIT COST FIGURES

1000 – £12.00	4000 – £4.50
2000 – £ 7.00	5000 – £4.00
3000 – £ 5.33	6000 – £3.66

Figure 8.11   Jones Engineering unit costs

This can be seen in the example shown in Figure 8.11. Jones Engineering is producing a small component for textile machines. It has fixed costs of £10 000 per week, and the direct costs such as labour and materials are £2 per unit. Its capacity is 6000, and 25% is added for profit.

Jones' expects to sell 5000 units per week. Its price will be set by the calculation:

Fixed cost per unit $= \dfrac{£10\,000}{5000} =$	£2.00
Variable cost per unit =	£2.00
Total cost per unit =	£4.00
plus 25% mark-up	£1.00
SELLING PRICE	£5.00

At sales of 5000 per week the firm's total costs will be £20 000 (fixed costs £10 000 + variable cost of 5000 × £2 = £10 000). Total revenue will be 5000 × £5 = £25 000, so the firm is making a healthy 20% profit.

Full-cost pricing has the advantage of being simple to calculate, and attempts to ensure that all products pay their way by covering the firm's overheads. In theory it should result in all costs being covered and provide a profit margin. However, there are several problems associated with this pricing policy:

1. It is not always easy to forecast or allocate fixed costs (or even variable costs) in a multi-department, multi-plant or multi-product firm.
2. It assumes that all the output will be sold. If sales are lower than expected, the firm will either have to increase its prices or produce at a loss. For example if Jones Engineering sold only 3000 per week but kept its price at £5:

$$\text{Total revenue} = 3000 \times £5 \qquad = £15\,000$$
$$less \quad \text{Total costs} = £10\,000 + (3000 \times £2) = £16\,000$$

Loss	£1 000

To cover its costs and 25% mark-up, the firm would have to charge a fixed cost per unit of £3.33, leading to an eventual price of (£3.33 + £2.00 + 25%), that is £6.66. However if it attempted to do so, its sales would probably fall even further.

3. It largely ignores market conditions. This is the most fundamental criticism of full-cost pricing. Prices may be far higher or lower than the customer might be prepared to pay. Competition and market share objectives are ignored. The buyer is interested in the price to be paid and does not particularly care about the supplier's costs.

Contribution pricing

Also known as *marginal-cost pricing*, this is a more flexible system than full-cost pricing. All sales are expected to cover their marginal costs, which are equal to the increase in variable costs. As long as the price is higher than the marginal cost, a *contribution* will be made to paying overheads and earning an overall profit. For each unit of output:

Contribution = Price − Variable cost

For example, if Jones Engineering (Figure 8.11) charges £5 per unit, the contribution is equal to £5 − £2 = £3.

Contribution pricing may involve some sales at less than full-cost, as long as other sales make more than full-cost. For example to make £5000 profit on sales of 5000 per week, Jones Engineering needs to earn sales revenue of £25 000, an average of £5 per unit.

As long as an overall average revenue of £5 is achieved, the firm may charge different prices to different customers. Assuming that direct costs are to be covered, a price as low as £2.01 can be justified if some sales are at prices above £5.

For example if the firm obtains an order for 3000 units at £6 each, it will earn £18 000 in revenue. Total costs will be equal to £10 000 + (3000 × £2) = £16 000. All fixed costs have been covered and the firm has already made £2000 profit. Any contribution earned from remaining sales will be all profit.

To achieve its profit target of £5000 the firm needs to make a total contribution per unit of £3000 from the remaining 2000 units. The minimum contribution per unit should be:

$$\frac{£3000}{2000} = £1.50$$

This will be achieved if the average price per unit is at least £3.50, so the price can be lowered for subsequent customers.

Contribution pricing is most likely to be used when:

- Fixed costs are a high proportion of total costs.
- There is no alternative use for equipment or labour, which would otherwise be underemployed.
- The product is 'perishable'. This may be literally true in the case of food products. Other products may go out of fashion very quickly or simply not exist after a certain time, for example holiday bookings or seats on a train.

- A sale below full-cost will generate goodwill and bring in further sales. A firm may *loss-lead* or give introductory discounts to new customers.

Contribution pricing is often used in transport, where planes or trains may have spare seats. The marginal cost of extra passengers is very low, and empty seats are instantly perishable. It is therefore profitable to offer low-price deals such as stand-by or off-peak fares.

Contribution costing has the advantage of paying attention to market conditions, but can cause problems:

1. If one customer is offered a low-price deal, others may be resentful or look for the same discount. For example full-fare passengers may resent the student or pensioner who gets a seat for much less.
2. The firm may be tempted to offer big discounts to obtain business, but uncontrolled discounting will lead to losses if too many orders fail to cover the full-cost.
3. Discounted sales may start to squeeze out full-profit business. For example many people wait for last-minute bookings to get cheap holidays.

		PRICE		
		HIGH	MEDIUM	LOW
QUALITY	HIGH	PREMIUM	PENETRATION	SUPER VALUE FOR MONEY
	MEDIUM	OVER-PRICING	AVERAGE PRICE – QUALITY STRATEGY	VALUE FOR MONEY
	LOW	HIT AND RUN	SHODDY GOODS	CHEAP GOODS

Figure 8.12 Price/quality strategies

Skimming

Skimming or *creaming* is a pricing policy often used with new products, especially where patents or technology make it difficult for competitors to enter the market. It has been used successfully with consumer electrical goods such as video recorders and compact discs.

Skimming involves charging a very high-margin price to initial customers. These 'early adopters' are willing to pay a high price in order to get the product first. The price is then gradually reduced to attract new generations of customers, and as competitors enter the market.

Skimming has distinct advantages for a new product. Development costs can be recovered quickly and demand limited until production can be expanded. At the same time, the high price suggests value to the buyer and large profits can be made.

This policy can only work, however, if the product is distinctive and desirable enough. It failed with quadrophonic stereos and video-discs. The high price makes it risky for buyers to invest in the product. High profit margins will also attract competition quickly, especially if the barriers to entry are weak, as in the case of compact discs.

Premium pricing

Also called *prestige* pricing, this involves selling a high-quality product at a high-margin price. Unlike skimming, however, the intention is to maintain the high-margin price permanently. The aim is to keep prices higher than those of competitors by being seen as the best product.

The relationship between quality and price is two-way. The high quality enables a premium price. The price suggests high quality and may be used as an integral part of the advertising strategy (as is done by Heinz Baked Beans, Fairy Liquid and Stella Artois).

Premium pricing can be very profitable because of the high profit margins. Typically a brand-leader for a fast-moving consumer good might be able to charge 10% more than the industry average.

There are some problems of premium pricing, however:

1. High profit margins attract competitors.
2. Quality must be constantly improved as consumer demands increase and competitors improve their products.
3. Part of the image of the product may be exclusivity, which makes it difficult to increase sales without 'de-valuing' the product. For example in 1989 Gucci withdrew their products from many retail outlets to regain the exclusive image of their products.

Penetration pricing

Penetration pricing involves selling at a very low price in order to gain market share. It may be used as a permanent policy or to establish market leadership. It is particularly likely to be used where:

- the market is growing;
- the product is price-sensitive, and quality is secondary or taken for granted;
- significant cost-savings occur with high output;
- the firm has a significant cost advantage over its competitors.

Penetration pricing can enable a firm to achieve rapid growth and high market share. Competitors may be driven out or discouraged from entering the industry by the low profit margins. A low-price product can also create its own market by attracting new customers for a product, as in the case of the Amstrad PCW word-processor and cheap air travel.

For several reasons, however, penetration pricing is one of the most risky pricing strategies:

1. It requires very large price cuts, perhaps 30% or more below the industry average. Unless increased sales are very large, they will not compensate for low profit margins.

2. Low profit margins mean that even small errors in costing and pricing can create large losses.
3. It may lead to 'price wars' if competitors react. This is especially likely in mature markets.
4. The low price may suggest low quality to the customer.
5. It is very difficult to sustain in the long-run, especially with changing technology and international competition.

Price-taking

Price-taking involves charging at or around the average price for the industry. For example the second or third firm in the industry might typically charge about 5% more than average. A business wishing to build market share steadily might charge 10–15% below average.

Price-taking is particularly common in *oligopololistic* markets, where a few large firms dominate the industry. If one firm raises or lowers its prices, the others will tend to react in the same way in order to increase profits or defend their market share. In these industries, such as petrol-retailing and banking, there is a high degree of *non-price competition* such as heavy advertising and sales promotions.

Price-taking is a fairly 'safe' strategy, but not one which is likely to lead to rapid growth or profitability.

Loss-leading

Loss-leading involves selling a product at less than cost or with very low profit margins in order to attract new customers or increase sales of other products.

Promotion

What is promotion?

Promotion can be defined narrowly as the process of informing existing and potential customers about a firm's products. However wider definitions, often using the term *marketing communications*, include activities such as *public relations* (PR) which may be aimed at other targets such as pressure groups and Government Departments.

As can be seen from Figure 8.13, promotional activities can be divided into four broad categories: advertising, direct marketing, personal selling and public relations.

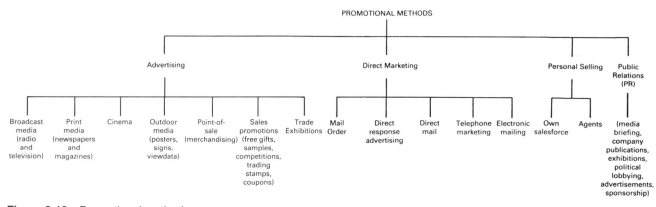

Figure 8.13 Promotional methods

Criteria for successful promotion

In considering its *promotional mix*, an organisation must take into account several factors.

1. Cost-effectiveness

Any promotional expenditure must be justified by its returns. This would normally be measured according to the increase in sales, although in highly competitive markets promotional expenditure may be needed simply to preserve market share.

One of the difficulties of assessing cost-effectiveness, however, is that it is hard to gauge what effect particular advertisement campaigns or other activities have. This is summarised by the famous comment by Lord Leverhulme about his company's advertising expenditure

"Half the money I spend on advertising is wasted, and the trouble is I don't know which half"

2. Integration

The different elements of the promotional mix must work together, and in conjunction with the rest of the firm's activities. For example if sales staff are expected to increase sales rapidly, they must be backed by appropriate advertising and pricing strategies, and goods must be available to service new customers quickly.

3. Targeting

The firm must evaluate different ways of reaching its target market, and how 'selective' targeting can be. For example buyers of specialised industrial machinery could be reached through television advertising, but this would waste money because of the wasted cost of advertising to people who had no interest in the product.

4. Image

Promotional activity must reflect the 'image' and quality of the product. For example an expensive perfume will need high-quality glossy adverts and packaging. The promotion may be used to project a particular image. For example recent advertising campaigns for milk have presented it as a 'healthy' alternative to soft drinks.

5. Timing

Since many products, especially in consumer markets, are subject to seasonal demand, promotional efforts need to

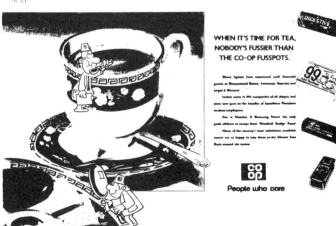

Figure 8.14 Co-op advertising campaign

be concentrated at particular times of year, for example holidays in December and January, cars in June and July.

6. Market conditions

For many products there will be accepted methods of promotion. For example buyers of bulk steel will expect personal selling and supermarket chains will usually want promises of mass media advertising before they will stock a new product. While it may sometimes be profitable to use new methods, firms will always need to consider what buyers of their products expect.

Advertising

For many products, advertising is very important, especially for branded goods and services such as Heinz baked beans and Avis car hire. Over £5 billion a year is spent upon advertising in Britain, from people selling second-hand goods to million-pound national advertising campaigns.

1. Broadcast media

Broadcast media consist of commercial television and commercial radio. Commercial television is the most effective medium for reaching large numbers of people, and has been proven by research to be most noticed and remembered. It is also the most expensive, with peak-time adverts costing £30 000 or more per minute.

Television advertising can be very effective, but has several drawbacks. Because of the cost, TV adverts have to be very brief, most being for less than 30 seconds. They cannot be very informative, and display images rather than information. Television advertising is not very selective – it is hard to reach a particular group of people.

Radio advertising is fairly cheap and can be effective in reaching certain types of people such as housewives. At present, however, there is no national commercial radio station in the UK, although national networks are planned for the early 1990s.

Broadcast media have the advantage of sound and movement (on TV), but are increasingly expensive and subject to much greater restrictions than other media. For example tobacco advertising on British television was stopped in 1991. Broadcast adverts are also very brief and cannot include significant detail or technical specifications.

2. Print media

Print media include a wide variety of publications such as:

- national daily and Sunday newspapers;
- local daily and weekly newspapers (including 'freesheets');
- national and local general magazines such as *Woman's Weekly* and *The Scots Magazine*;
- 'special interest' magazines such as *Amateur Photographer* and *Athletics Weekly*;
- trade and professional publications such as *Building* and *Materials Reclamation Weekly*.

Print media adverts make it easier to give detail which is not possible in broadcast adverts. Potential customers can be targeted very easily. For example an advert in *Amateur Photographer* will reach about 100 000 people who have a strong interest in photographic products. Advertising rates are cheaper and adverts can be studied at length. Tear-off slips or coupons can be included to generate replies. However, unlike broadcast adverts, print adverts cannot incorporate sound and movement.

3. Cinema

Cinema adverts are only a small part of advertising because they can only reach small audiences compared with other media. They have the advantage of a captive audience and can look impressive on a large screen. However the advertiser has little idea of what size or type of audience will be present to see the advert. Some large-scale advertisers have started to pay for 'plugs' or 'product placement' for their products in the actual films. For example Pepsi is heavily featured in the *Back to the Future* films.

4. Outdoor media

Outdoor media include posters and hoardings, signs on buses, trains and taxis, neon signs and electronic message boards or viewdata.

Outdoor media are cheap and effective if good locations or widely-used transport can be found. They have to be easy to read quickly, and are usually used together with other forms of advertising. In some cases, such as cigarette advertising, they are the major form of promotion.

5. Point-of-sale advertising

Point-of-sale (POS) advertising includes all activities which aim to promote the product in the location where it is sold. Examples include display containers such as book dump-bins and tool-holders, posters and special packaging. Sometimes referred to as *merchandising*, POS is often used in conjunction with *sales promotions* such as money-back coupons and competitions.

Merchandising is usually applied to fast-moving consumer goods such as food and small household goods. However, it may also be part of sales techniques for other products such as cars or industrial supplies in a trade warehouse. It has two main purposes – to obtain the optimum selling position in a retail outlet (for example the front of a shop, eye-level height, ends of aisles) and to provide rapid product recognition by the final customer.

POS has become regarded as increasingly important because many purchases, especially of consumer goods, are made on impulse. The typical supermarket shopper will be buying in a familiar shop and will know where most of the basic items are. Merchandising must attempt to grab the customers' attention to get them to buy new products or continue with current brands.

This is particularly difficult for manufacturers which sell their products through independent retailers. The manufacturer has little control over how and where the product is displayed.

6. Sales promotions

These include free gifts, competitions, giveaway samples, coupons, trading stamps and special offers. They are very common for products such as petrol, where there is little price competition. They are often used for consumer goods to persuade retailers to offer good positions in shops, garages and other outlets.

The main advantages of sales promotions are that it is

Figure 8.15 A trade press advertisement

129

Figure 8.16 Sales promotions

very easy to measure their effectiveness, for example by running them in one area and not in another. They can be a cheap way of generating sales and act as an additional weapon for sales staff. Some food manufacturers such as Weetabix regularly change their sales promotions to ensure that stock is not kept too long in shops.

Against these advantages are the facts that sales promotions are often short-lived and can possibly devalue the brand image of a product. Competitors may also introduce their own incentives, making a sales promotion uneconomic. This has happened with many national newspaper bingo promotions.

7. Trade exhibitions

Trade exhibitions are used in both consumer and industrial markets, although they are usually more cost-effective when selling to industrial buyers. British firms spend about £500 million a year on exhibitions.

The main advantage of exhibitions is that they make it possible to meet large numbers of potential customers very quickly and cheaply. In many industries a major part of sales are made or instigated at exhibitions. They are a useful way of displaying new products and obtaining publicity.

Against this, the disadvantages of exhibitions are the possible expense, ranging from a few thousand pounds for a small show to hundreds of thousands for exhibitions such as the Motor Show. It is often argued that exhibitions do not really sell the product effectively and are regarded more as a reward for staff than as a promotional tool.

Direct marketing

Direct marketing is a rather vague term which covers a number of selling methods by which a firm or other organisation approaches customers directly. Usually the product is sold without using intermediaries such as retailers and dealers. However, some forms of direct marketing do attempt to persuade potential customers to visit a dealer or agent, as in the example shown in Figure 8.17.

There are several types of direct marketing:

- *Mail order* is based mainly upon the use of catalogues, sometimes with part-time agents. This is used by firms such as Littlewoods and Kay's. Customers generally order by mail and receive goods through the post, although telephone-ordering has become more common.
- *Direct response advertising* sells products through customers responding to advertisements in the print and broadcast media, or to handbills and leaflets distributed by hand. Printed adverts usually include tear-off slips for the customer to order. Both print and broadcast adverts also often use telephone orders, usually using credit card numbers.
- *Direct mail* involves contacting people direct at their homes or place of work. It is usually 'personalised' by including the recipient's name and job title where relevant. *Reader's Digest* and the Automobile Association are heavy users of direct mail.
- *Telephone marketing* consists of people being solicited directly at home or at work. It is frequently used to generate sales leads for household services such as central heating and kitchen improvements. A sales representative will be sent to interested respondents.
- *Electronic mailing*, known as E-mail, works in a similar way to direct mail, using computers and telecommunications.

As well as selling products, direct marketing is used for purposes such as compiling lists of potential customers, charity fund-raising and market research.

Although methods used vary, direct marketing has distinct advantages:

- It can be very selective (a 'rifle' rather than a 'shotgun' approach). Using the firm's own customer records and databases such as ACORN (Figure 8.4) it is possible to reduce the wastage of advertising.
- It can be carefully organised to fit in with other promotional activity such as mass media advertising. For example TV campaigns for new washing powders are often combined with mailshots of small samples to households.
- It is easy to monitor the effects of a campaign through the response. For example coupons can be given different codes for different adverts, for example to test which newspapers bring the best response.
- Direct marketing can be cheaper than conventional advertising.
- By eliminating some or all of the involvement by intermediaries such as retailers, a firm can exercise greater control over its promotion and come into closer contact with its customers.

For Peugeot Talbot, Pearson Paul Haworth Nolan ran a 98,000 mailshot for the
Peugeot 205. The March campaign, on a "six-figure" budget, sold the most
cars from a single mailing and exceeded response projections by 70 per cent

Driving home the 205 message

THE PEUGEOT 205

See it

Feel it

The mailing reinforced TV and press advertising with the theme "See it, feel it, touch it, love it". The target was prospects generated by press advertising, questionnaire mailings, the 1988 Motor Show and ICD's Lifestyle Questionnaire, all of whom were previous Peugeot 205 buyers. Image-building was timed to counteract Ford's launch of the new Fiesta by positioning the 205 as the premier stylish small car

Factfile

Client: Peugeot Talbot

Agency: Pearson Paul Haworth Nolan

Account director: Giles Calver

Account manager: Tess Doughty

Creative directors: Don Paul and Ian Haworth

Touch it

Love it ♡

PEUGEOT 205

Take up Peugeot's special holiday Traveller's Cheque offer.

All bar 5,000 of those mailed also received an offer of £150-worth of traveller's cheques if they purchased a 205 between March 1 and April 28. Results of this test are still being evaluated

A key element of the mailing was the "Keep me posted" questionnaire on purchase intentions. This provided dealers with the equivalent of ten to 15 names each, while centralised telephone follow-up of the campaign by Merit Direct and individual dealers also generated significant test drive requests and marketing intelligence

Keep me posted.

IF YOU ARE NOT PURCHASING A NEW PEUGEOT 205 BEFORE THE 28TH APRIL 1989 PLEASE COMPLETE AND RETURN THIS CARD.

Monday June 5 1989

Figure 8.17   Direct marketing by Peugot

Despite these features, direct marketing suffers from several disadvantages:

- Promotion can be wasted if mailing lists are poorly constructed or out-of-date. Over 10% of households move every year and a similar proportion change jobs.

- Many people object to being bombarded with direct mail and throw it in the bin (hence the expression 'junk-mail'). Some insurance companies have to put a special notice on their envelopes to warn people not to destroy policies and other documents.

- Some forms of direct marketing, especially mail order

catalogues, have a very 'downmarket' image and are not popular with higher income groups.

- Direct marketing is often regarded as an invasion of privacy, especially when organisations sell lists of their members or customers.
- Many people have environmental objections because of the heavy use of paper.

Personal selling

Personal selling involves a firm employing its own sales force or agents to promote its product directly to customers. This may include a wide variety of situations such as:

- paper and printing materials to a large number of small local printers;
- industrial plant to a few large firms;
- cosmetics through part-time agents;
- a branded food range to a supermarket chain Chief Buyer;
- life assurance to individuals;
- passenger aeroplanes to airlines.

1. Own salesforce

In choosing its personal selling strategy, a firm needs to consider factors such as:

- The cost of servicing customers compared with potential order size. For example a food manufacturer would use senior sales representatives to sell to a supermarket chain. It would probably sell to corner shops through wholesalers, without direct contact.
- The technical knowledge needed by sales staff.
- After-sales services required by product.
- Frequency and size of orders.
- Consumer expectations, for example the buyer of a new Mercedes would expect a higher standard of service than the buyer of a ten-year-old car.
- How customers are to be divided among sales staff, such as regionally or by product.
- The amount of discretion given to sales staff to negotiate prices and other terms of delivery.

The advantages of personal selling are:

- Two-way personal communication with the customer makes it easier to obtain feedback and gauge the feelings of the customer. Possible doubts and problems can be resolved quickly.
- Sales staff should be enthusiastic about the firm's products and communicate this to potential customers.
- Personal selling allows negotiation and gives the customer an influence over prices and terms of supply such as credit and delivery times.
- Sales representatives can perform 'non-selling' tasks such as dealing with complaints, technical advice, training of staff and collecting ideas for new products or product change.

The disadvantages of personal selling are:

- The high cost – a 'typical' annual cost in 1990 was approximately £25 000 for a full-time sales representative.
- Staff work independently and may be difficult to motivate and control. Even 'results-based' systems such as commission may be demotivating, especially in a recession when income may fall.

- Sales staff may be overloaded with administrative tasks, taking away time from the selling process. Alternatively, essential 'non-selling' tasks may be ignored in the pursuit of commission.
- Sales staff traditionally have a high labour turnover.

2. Agents

Agents are independent people or firms used to sell a product, usually on a commission basis. They are often used for low-value accounts which are too expensive to serve with full-time sales staff. The firm's own staff will usually handle larger customers. Agents may also be used for *canvassing* potential customers who are then visited by the firm's own sales staff.

Agents are common in industries such as cosmetics, clothing and insurance. They can make it economic to service small accounts, but can be administratively expensive, difficult to control and of variable quality. However they can be used successfully, as Figure 8.18 indicates.

Public Relations

Public Relations (PR) is defined by the Institute of Public Relations as

"the deliberate planned and sustained effort to establish and maintain mutual understanding between an organisation and its publics"

The term 'publics' in this definition refers to people and organisations who are not an organisation's customers, but who may have influence over its activities. These may include existing and potential shareholders, employees, pressure groups such as consumer and environmental organisations, politicians, Government departments and the general public.

PR activities include:

- *press releases* and briefings for mass media such as newspaper journalists and TV producers in the hope of obtaining favourable stories in the mass media;
- company publications such as employee newspapers;
- exhibitions such as the Sellafield Visitors' Centre set up by British Nuclear Fuels Ltd (BNFL) to reduce worries about nuclear power stations;
- lobbying of politicians to vote or use their influence in the organisation's favour;
- mass media advertisements such as that illustrated in Figure 8.19;
- sponsorship of 'good causes' such as sporting and arts events.

Place

Place decisions

'Place' refers to the way in which a product is made available or *distributed* to the final customer. Place decisions have to be made on matters such as:

- choice of intermediaries such as retailers and wholesalers;

THE WORLD'S NO. 1 NAME IN DIRECT SELLING

Knowing what you're good at

Avon sells direct because that's what we know about and that's what we do best.

Avon is one of the acknowledged leaders in the field of direct selling – after all, we've been doing it for more than 100 years. We know the joys and sorrows, advantages and disadvantages of selling direct and we're a leader in the cosmetics world.

Advantages

The advantages of selling direct are numerous:

All of our products are factory fresh. Customers know our products have not been stored in a warehouse for months or displayed on a shop counter.

Customers can choose products in the comfort and convenience of their own home at times to suit them.

Every Representative provides her customers with a friendly and reliable service.

There is no competition for our products at the point of sale unlike a store where there can be several brands on the same counter.

Representatives seek out customers and their earnings opportunity – we don't have to wait for customers to come to us. We have a territory system that provides for every home within that territory to be serviced every campaign.

Since Avon sells in three-week cycles, it gives our customers time to plan their purchases and set money aside for those special occasions.

We have little need of advertising. Representatives talk to customers and place brochures in the homes in their territory. It's a tremendously personal way of advertising and it happens every three weeks.

Direct selling means we can quickly change or introduce new products to meet customers' demands and changes in fashion. We constantly strive to improve our customer service, because at the end of the day, direct selling represents service in a time of diminishing service and that's why a direct selling business such as Avon is good, and will remain good, for those who work at it.

Figure 8.18 The advantages of direct selling

Figure 8.19 British Nuclear Fuels Ltd PR advertisement

- mark-ups offered at different stages of the distribution process;
- transport and storage of goods;
- financing and credit arrangements;
- provision of after-sales service.

Although the term 'distribution' is often used in the narrow sense of transporting and retailing goods, distribution decisions are just as relevant to service industries such as insurance and travel, both of which use intermediaries to sell their products.

Factors influencing channel choice

In selecting the appropriate channels of distribution for its products, a firm needs to consider factors such as the following.

1. Cost-effectiveness

If a firm uses intermediaries it will have to pay for their services by offering trade discounts or commissions. These must be balanced against the cost of undertaking intermediary functions within the firm.

For example a consumer product with a final price of £15 might be purchased by a retailer for £10. The manufacturer 'loses' £5 of the money paid by the consumer. However selling the product directly might cost more than this, because the manufacturer would have to pay the costs of holding stocks, display and selling to large numbers of customers rather than a limited number of retailers.

2. Coverage of outlets

A firm may try to sell through as many outlets as possible, or try to maintain an 'exclusive' image by only selling through restricted outlets. The first policy is likely where the consumer is uninterested in the image of the outlet, as with cigarettes or sweets. Exclusive distribution is often used where a high standard of service is expected, as with cars or quality clothing, or technical knowledge is important, as for many industrial markets.

3. Control over outlets

Many firms like to exercise strict control over their outlets in order to preserve a high-quality product or image. For example Macdonalds own rather than franchise most of their UK stores to keep strict control of their product. Other producers such as petrol companies and breweries own garages and pubs to guarantee their sales.

4. Tradition

There may be certain outlets where customers habitually buy a product or which dominate the market. Food manufacturers usually have to sell through the large supermarket chains and fit in with retailers' distribution

THE YEAR IN BRIEF – a quick summary of the
highlights of British Rail's Annual Report and
Accounts for 1987/88

GROUP SURPLUS	:	The Group had a surplus of £113m, which became a surplus of £291m after interest and extraordinary items.
PASSENGER VOLUME	:	Passenger volume increased by over 8% to 20.6 billion passenger miles, the highest total for 27 years.
FREIGHT	:	Railfreight marked its tenth year as a fully commercial sector with an operating surplus of £43.6m before interest.
PRODUCTIVITY	:	Railway staff numbers were reduced during the year by 6,502 (5%). Staff productivity, measured in train miles per member of staff, rose by 8%, bringing the total increase since 1983 to 18%.
PUNCTUALITY	:	Overall punctuality of trains was maintained and 90% arrived within five minutes of scheduled time.
ELECTRIFICATION	:	Work was completed on 156 route miles of new electric railway.
PROPERTY	:	Property Board sales and letting contributed £263m gross to BR's cash flow.
STATION CATERING	:	Travellers Fare Ltd increased its operating surplus by 36% to £7.5m.
PAYMENTS TO BR		by government and local authorities for railways current operations totalled £894m.
PAYMENTS BY BR		and its subsidiaries on goods and services totalled some £1,308m, spent mainly in the private sector.
INVESTMENT		spending totalled £543m, of which £495m went on railway improvements, £48m on other businesses.

British Rail had a record breaking group surplus of £291m in 1987/88, and achieved the highest railway operating surplus in its history and the highest passenger volume for 27 years.

In his Chairman's Statement in the Board's Annual Report and Accounts for 1987/88 published today (6 July 1988), Sir Robert Reid says: "1987/88 was a record breaking year for British Rail.

– the group result, a surplus of £291m after interest and extraordinary items, was the highest we have ever achieved

– the surplus on ordinary activities was £47.3m after interest, compared with £2.4m in 1986/87;

– the railway operating profit of £109m before interest was the best result recorded in the 25 years history of the Board

– passenger volume at 20.6 billion passenger miles was the highest for 27 years and all three passenger sectors had record growth

– Railfreight had its best result for a decade with an operating surplus, before interest, of £43.6m."

"We paid for all our investment without recourse to long term borrowing. Our cash flow, helped by record input of £263m by our Property Board, was so healthy that we were able to lend money on a short term basis. Looking to the future we also decided to make early repayment of £86m of government loans, thus reducing the burden of interest payments in future years."

Income from property sales (£181.4m) and recovery of redundancy costs (£67.6m) accounted for the extraordinary items which produced a final group surplus of £290.9m compared with a net loss in 1986/87 of £82.6m.

"By any standards it was a very successful year," says Sir Robert, "but we do not yet produce a uniformly improved quality of service so that all our customers share the fruits of our improved financial position."

Figure 8.20 A British Rail press release (extracts)

systems, and holidays are traditionally bought through travel agents. There may also be legal restrictions upon where products can be sold, as in the case of alcohol, tobacco and prescription medicines.

Channels of distribution

There are four basic types of distribution channel, as

shown in Figure 8.21. Many producers use more than one. For example insurance companies sell directly to people and firms, but also sell policies through brokers.

1. Direct supply

This is common for industrial goods such as mainframe computers and aeroplanes. It is also used in many con-

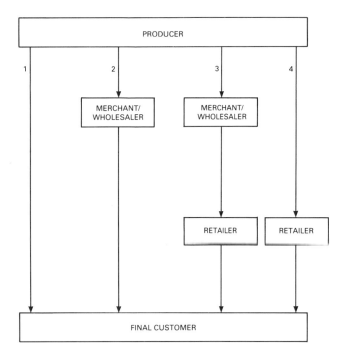

1 Direct supply
2 Merchant supply
3 Long channel
4 Short channel

Figure 8.21 Channels of distribution

sumer markets for services such as home improvements and insurance.

Direct supply is commonly used where the market has characteristics such as high profit margins, large order sizes, high-level customer service, discussion of technical details and customer-designed specifications for the product.

The advantages of direct supply are:

* direct contact with customers, with quick feedback and two-way communication – questions and problems can be addressed quickly;
* the producer obtains a higher proportion of the final selling price;
* greater control over servicing and pricing.

The disadvantages of direct supply are:

* it may be uneconomic for low-value sales because of higher administration costs;
* maintaining a permanent sales force is expensive;
* it may limit the number of potential outlets, especially for consumer and export markets.

2. Merchant supply

Merchant supply is common in industrial markets for low-value purchases such as building supplies or car parts. Sales are to other businesses rather than to consumers.

The advantages of merchant supply are:

* merchants provide services such as breaking bulk, storing goods, sorting and repackaging;
* merchants will make regular payments, removing some of the costs of stockholding.

The disadvantages of merchant supply are:

* the supplier is dependent on the efforts of the merchant, who may be selling competitors' products;
* merchants require a high proportion of the final selling price (typically 30%, although this varies between products);
* the manufacturer has little control over display or customer service.

3. Long channel

This involves two or more intermediaries, usually a wholesaler and a retailer. It is frequently used in consumer markets to sell *fast-moving consumer goods* (fmcgs) such as food and hardware to small retailers.

The advantages of long channel distribution are:

* a large number of retail outlets can be reached quickly and easily;
* physical distribution of goods is easier;
* distributing through wholesalers may be cheaper because of the saving in administrative and transport costs which might be incurred by supplying large numbers of retailers directly.

The disadvantages of long-channel distribution are:

* the producer is remote from the final customer, making it more difficult to obtain customer reaction to products;
* the producer has little control over the way in which products are presented to the final customer;
* the mark-ups required by intermediaries reduce the revenue received by the producer.

4. Short channel

Short channel distribution involves a producer dealing directly with retailers. It is used in many consumer goods markets, especially where there are a few retailers which dominate the market. Examples include branded foods, travel and books. The retailer may be 'tied' to the producer, as in the case of many garages and pubs.

Short channel's advantages are:

* co-operation with the retailer may be easier, for example the supplier can assist with product display or staff training;
* it may be possible to concentrate the marketing effort on a small number of large customers, possibly using other methods such as wholesale distribution for smaller customers.

The disadvantages of short channel are:

* There are more separate accounts than when dealing through wholesalers. This increases selling and administration costs if a large number of retailers are targeted.
* Large retailers have bulk-buying power and may try to obtain discounts and credit terms which are unfavourable to the supplier. This is a particular problem for smaller firms or firms without strong brand names.
* Retailers often stock competitors' products and it may be difficult to obtain favourable retail space or service.

Worked Examples

8.1 Give two examples of non-price competition.

(AEB)

Answer For example heavy advertising, sales promotions, extensive retail/sales networks, high level of service.

8.2 Give two examples of the costs that an enterprise may incur in ensuring that its products are of a high quality.

(AEB)

Answer For example dearer materials, packaging, better service, technology, research and development, skilled labour, inspection/quality control.

8.3 Explain the meaning of price discrimination, as practised by British Rail.

(AEB)

Answer Charging different prices (more technically, different mark-ups) for different customers/markets/times. British Rail has reduced fares for students, OAPs, off-peak travel, etc.

8.4 Suggest two points that must be considered for advertising to be effective.

(AEB)

Answer Choice of media, target customers, image/type of product, state of market demand, message/slogan used, cost of advertising, timing.

8.5 Give two reasons why a company may sell, for a limited period, part of its product range at a loss.

(AEB)

Answer For example to stimulate future sales of product, encourage sales of other products, raise cash, sell surplus stock, drive competitors out of market.

8.6 A business receives an order for £100 000 worth of components. The direct materials costs are estimated at £20 000, the direct labour costs at £40 000 and general overhead costs apportioned to this job at £25 000.
Calculate the contribution to fixed costs to be expected from accepting this order.

(AEB)

Answer
$$\text{Contribution} = \text{Revenue} - \text{Variable costs}$$
$$= £100\,000 - (£20\,000 + £40\,000)$$
$$= £40\,000$$

Note that the overhead costs are not deducted as these are fixed costs.

8.7 Coley Ltd. is an engineering firm. It is the largest supplier of a particular tool in a market where, at a standard price of £500, there is very little competition. The home market is reaching saturation point, but Coley Ltd. is not yet working at full capacity. Present output is 1500 units, while full capacity is 2500 units.
An order for 500 units has been received from an Italian firm on condition that the tools can be delivered to their factory all expenses paid at a price of £400 each.
Coley Ltd.'s present cost structures are:

		£
Materials		120
Direct labour	per unit	100
Variable overheads		60
Fixed overheads		300 000

However to these must be added the costs associated with exporting to Italy. A sum of £20 000 is thought to be ample to cover this order.

137

The company's first reaction was to reject the order on the basis that it meant a loss of £70 per unit, while at present, sales produced £20 profit per unit. However, further consideration of the financial and commercial aspects of the deal swung the decision in favour of accepting the order.

(a) Use appropriate financial calculations to demonstrate whether the decision to accept the order was justified. Show all your workings. *(9 marks)*
(b) Discuss **three** other reasons for accepting the order. *(6 marks)*
(c) Explain **two** problems that might be encountered if the order is accepted. *(6 marks)*

(AEB)

Answer (a) There are several different approaches to this question. The simplest is to calculate the contribution that the order makes to fixed costs, that is:

	£
Revenue	200 000
less variable cost	140 000
	60 000
less export costs	20 000
Contribution	40 000

Since the fixed costs have already been incurred in domestic production, the £40 000 will be an addition to profit, and the order is justified.

Note: variable cost = 500 × (£120 + £100 + £60) = £140 000.

Alternatively, the answer can be reached by calculating the total profit before and after the order, that is:

Before order

	£
Revenue	750 000
less variable cost	420 000
	300 000
less fixed costs	300 000
Total profit	30 000

Note: variable cost = 1500 × (£120 + £100 + £60) = £420 000.

After order

	£
Revenue	950 000
less variable cost	560 000
	390 000
less fixed costs	300 000
	90 000
less export costs	20 000
Total profit	70 000

Therefore total profits have increased by £40 000, making the order worth accepting.

Note: variable cost = £420 000 + [500 × (£120 + £100 + £60)]
= £420 000 + £120 000
= £560 000.

Other ways may be used to calculate the effect of the order, but it is important to show that profits will *increase* with the order.

(b) For example:

● home market saturated, so Coley need new markets;
● establish international reputation, may lead to further export orders, gaining export expertise;
● space capacity available, therefore fixed costs can be spread over larger output;
● competition may take order.

(c) For example:

● cultural/language differences;
● exchange rate fluctuations;

- transport difficulties;
- legal/Customs difficulties;
- other customers may demand same price;
- payment difficulties.

8.8 The following diagram illustrates sales revenue and profit for Product X over a number of years. During the period, Product X underwent two design changes.

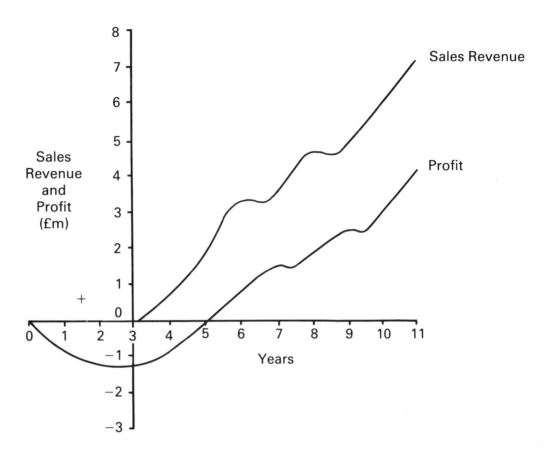

(a) Calculate the percentage profit on sales for Product X at the end of year 10. *(1 mark)*
(b) (i) In which years do the design changes occur? *(1 mark)*
    (ii) Comment on the relationship between design changes and profit. *(2 marks)*
(c) Why might design changes be necessary and at what point in the product life-cycle are they most likely to occur? *(3 marks)*
(d) Explain the shape of the profit line from year 0 to year 5. *(6 marks)*
(e) Discuss **three** factors which need to be considered when assessing a new product idea in a multi-product firm. *(6 marks)*
(f) Suggest and explain **three** factors that might influence the price charged for a product. *(6 marks)*

(AEB)

Answer **(a)**

$$\% \text{ profit} = \frac{\text{Profit}}{\text{Sales}} \times 100$$

$$= \frac{£3 \text{ million}}{£6 \text{ million}} \times 100$$

$$= 50\%$$

(b) (i) The graph is not clear, but the changes appear to have taken place in years 6/7 and 8/9, because sales and profits fall in these years.

(ii) Design change should increase sales but costs money to implement, for example change in materials/packaging, etc. Profits fall in the short-term but increase after a time-lag.

(c) A design change could take place at any stage of the product life-cycle, for example Introduction/Growth to iron-out initial faults/attract new customers, Maturity to extend the maturity stage, Decline to arrest the fall in sales.

(d) Note that the question asks for EXPLANATION, not just a description of what is happening.

139

Years 0–3: the product is not yet on market, therefore no sales revenue but costs are incurred in R&D, testing, etc., therefore the product is running at a loss.

Years 3–5: the product is launched at the end of Year 3. Sales increase slowly, and costs may be high because of promotional expense, modifications, small production runs, etc. Therefore it is not until the end of Year 5 that the product breaks even, and becomes profitable in later years.

(e) Note the emphasis on a *multi-product firm*. Possible factors include:

- effect on demand for firm's other products, for example replacing or complementing existing sales;
- effect on firm's image;
- production capacity available;
- will overheads be increased?
- available technical and managerial expertise;
- opportunity cost, that is what other uses are there for capital, management time, equipment, etc.?
- can existing brand names be used?
- can existing distribution channels be used?
- cost and availability of finance.

(f) For example:

- must cover costs in long-run;
- competitors' prices;
- stage of PLC, for example may 'skim' in early stages;
- costs of development;
- return on capital required;
- company objectives, for example market share, upmarket image;
- customer expectations;
- state of market demand, for example in recession;
- price elasticity of demand.

8.9 Read the attached extract on the marketing of the Cadbury Wispa and answer the questions which follow.

Marketing the Cadbury Wispa

The gigantic brands in the 'pure' chocolate market had, without exception, origins dating back to before the Second World War. Cadbury's Dairy Milk was launched in 1905 and has sold prodigiously ever since. Some twenty years later Cadbury launched Flake, which was discovered as a by-product of manufacturing milk chocolate.

These two products set the pace in the market for eighty years. There have been many attempts to launch a product to stand alongside CDM and Flake. None succeeded until the late 1970s when Cadbury started a secret R&D project.

It was found that the latest technology applied to chocolate manufacturing could confer a different texture and new eating characteristics on the classic milk chocolate product.

All the pre-launch research suggested that the product was a winner. However, as years of bitter experience have taught many manufacturers in this market, having a product that the public likes is not always enough. The complete marketing package is just as critical.

Nothing new under the sun

This was the attitude of most consumers to chocolate products. They simply didn't believe you could produce anything new. Reversing this belief was the problem facing the Young and Rubicam advertising agency when Cadbury brought them the product now named 'Wispa' in 1980.

In October 1983 the product was launched . . . . Cadbury spent heavily on Television Advertising . . . and on a massive poster campaign. Wispa is now the third largest brand in the total confectionery market and 11 weeks after launch spontaneous awareness among consumers reached 73%. Whichever way you look at it the product is a superb technical and marketing accomplishment, unique in a fiercely competitive market.

Source: adapted from a Cadbury advertisement, *The Economist*, March 1986.

(a) Give **three** examples of what would be included in the 'complete marketing package'. *(3 marks)*

(b) The initial launch may well have been accompanied by special pricing deals. What factors might the company have taken into consideration when setting the long term price? *(6 marks)*

(c) Outline the factors that the company might take into consideration before embarking upon a European launch of the product? Which do you think are most important and why? *(16 marks)*

(AEB)

Answer (a) For example mass advertising back-up, sales promotions, credit terms, packaging/point-of-sale material, appropriate pricing/mark-up for retailer and/or wholesaler.

(b) For example competitors' prices, pricing of other Cadbury products, mark-ups/discounts required by intermediaries, consumer demand, manufacturing costs.

(c) For example language and cultural differences, tastes in different countries, production capacity, costs of transport, establishing distribution networks, advertising strategies, legal/customs formalities.

Essay questions

8.10 Filocopy Ltd believes it has identified a market opportunity in a field dominated by one firm – the originator of a novel product. Filocopy have asked you as marketing consultant to advise them of actions they should take.

Answer

(i) Consider Filocopy's situation before suggesting possible actions. The firm needs to assess its strengths and weaknesses compared with the opposition. Some simple analysis of the market would indicate likely features such as:

- The original firm in the market may have an established reputation with potential customers. Its market share may allow for economies of scale through long production runs and established distribution networks.
- The original firm may have become complacent and failed to update the product because of the lack of competition.
- Filocopy will have to either take customers away from the existing firm and/or establish new markets for the product.

(ii) Approach the problem by considering the elements of the marketing mix – product, price, promotion and place. For example:

Product

- Can Filocopy produce a better quality product or a cheaper version?
- Can extra features be added to Filocopy's product. Alternatively, there may be some elements of the original product which some consumers do not require.
- Can the product be adapted to appeal to new consumer groups, such as given different colours or packaging?

Price

- Filocopy cannot 'skim' the market because it is not the first entrant. It may choose to undercut the original firm's price, or alternatively charge a premium price for a high-quality product. Filocopy will have to consider how the competitor will react, and the effect of the price on the image of its product, for example a low price may suggest a 'cheap and nasty' copy of a superior product.

Promotion

- If Filocopy is to attract new customers or take them away from the original product, the firm will need to promote its product heavily to consumers and retailers. However, promotion and advertising are expensive, and the costs may not be recouped if the new product fails.

Place

- Distribution channels will need to be arranged, but retailers may be unwilling to stock Filocopy's untried product as well as or instead of the established good. Filocopy may be forced into giving large discounts.

(iii) As well as the 4 Ps, Filocopy might consider its production capacity and ability to finance the launch of the product. Market research such as consumer surveys, discussions with retailers and test marketing may help to indicate the potential of the product.

8.11 **(a)** Why do suppliers of key products such as British Gas, an Electricity Board or Telecom operate a pricing policy which includes a fixed charge? *(10 marks)*
(b) Why do such organisations often charge different prices to various types of customer? *(15 marks)*

(UCLES)

Answer

(a) (i) Explain the common feature of these firms, that is heavy capital investment in equipment and distribution networks such as telephone and electricity cables, gas pipelines, etc. Because of this investment, fixed costs are a high proportion of total costs. They also have large numbers of customers, most of whom purchase only small quantities of their service.

(ii) Outline the consequence of this, that the supplier has to ensure that the costs of selling to individual customers is recovered. They levy a minimum 'standing charge' to ensure that each customer repays the fixed costs of supplying them.

(iii) The answer might be illustrated with a break-even chart showing that a minimum output must be sold to an individual customer to make supply profitable.

(b) Various reasons might be given for the different prices for different customers. These can be related to both supply and demand factors, for example:

- Suppliers faced with peaks in demand, such as electricity at meal-times, British Telecom during office hours. This means retaining production capacity which is unused for much of the time, so peak-time users are charged more to cover this.
- Off-peak charges may be lowered to attract custom, such as evening and night-time phone calls or electricity.
- Discounts may be given to large customers such as industrial users.
- Competition may be stronger in some sectors than others, for example BT has consistently increased prices for domestic users, where it has little competition, faster than business charges, for which competition is greater.

8.12 Why does a company manufacturing consumer durables spend money on advertising? Comment on the view that such expenditure must inevitably increase price.

(AEB)

Answer (i) The answer should be focused on advertising for consumer durables rather than in general. Reasons for advertising consumer durables might include:

- Purchases infrequent, so consumers may be cautious about buying, especially if the brand name is unfamiliar to consumers.
- Many purchases are 'deferrable', that is consumers do not have to buy immediately, for example they may keep a car longer rather than buy a new one. Advertising may be necessary to persuade them to replace current durables.
- Durables are usually sold through retailers and/or wholesalers, who expect advertising support for the product if they are to stock it.
- In many markets, such as washing powder, pet food and confectionery, rivals will be advertising extensively and it may be necessary to keep up.

(ii) It can be argued that advertising is very expensive, especially for national campaigns and TV advertising, which may be necessary for consumer durables. This has to be allowed for in costings, and the expenses have to be passed on in prices.

Against this, it can be argued that advertising increases sales, which may result in lower unit costs through mass production. The consumer may therefore benefit from lower prices than would be achievable for smaller-scale production.

Self-test Questions

Short-answer questions

8.13 Identify three factors likely to influence the choice of the channel of distribution for a product.

(AEB)

8.14 Define the term 'product differentiation'.

(AEB)

8.15 What are 'extension strategies' as related to a Product's Life-cycle? Give an example.

(AEB)

8.16 Give two examples of sales promotion.

(AEB)

Data-response questions

8.17 The Emperor Garment Company is a medium-sized clothing manufacturer specialising in the production of a small range of high quality shirts and blouses, trousers, skirts and jackets, which sell at the upper end of the price range. It grew rapidly in the 1970s as the public chose these less common products in the High Street clothing shops and department stores through which Emperor marketed its output. However between 1980 and 1983 sales began to level off and then decline. The Managing Director is considering the purchase of a small number of retail shops in prime sites. These shops would sell only 'Emperor' garments, supplemented by a range of ties, socks, knitwear and accessories bought in from other manufacturers.

As Marketing Manager you are required to prepare a report, using a suitable format *(6 marks)*, to help him in reaching a decision.

Your report should cover the following areas:

(a) Possible reasons for the decline in sales. *(8 marks)*
(b) Advantages and disadvantages to The Emperor Garment Company of having its own retail outlets. *(8 marks)*
(c) Alternative marketing strategies open to The Emperor Garment Company. *(8 marks)*

(AEB)

8.18 The following passage is based on an article concerned with the difficulties involved in marketing service industries.

"It is now estimated that over 60% of the United Kingdom workforce is employed in services. Far more small firms are involved in services than in manufacture . . . It is arguable that the special strengths of small firms, particularly the intimate involvement of top management in all aspects of the firm's operation, are a great advantage in the service sector.

People are far more important in service marketing than in manufacturing . . . The travel agent will help the customer choose his holiday on the basis of his understanding of the buyer's needs, comments and finance. The difficulties of the service firm are made even greater by the intangible nature of their offering and this leads to problems for the management. Simply communicating to staff the importance of carefully handling customers; probing to establish their real as opposed to their stated requirements and explaining differences of understanding are essential.

At the same time sectors of the service industry do fail to capitalise on their opportunities . . . . Salesmen tend to spend all their time selling the service and virtually no time selling their own firm.

This involvement of people creates massive problems of standardisation; on the other hand the close direct personal contact between the small service firm and its client provides a valuable opportunity for systematic information gathering . . . a characteristic of the market orientated service firm."

Tom Cannon, 'Make a Point of Making People Happy', *The Guardian*,
February 6th, 1980 (adapted).

(a) What is meant by the term 'intimate involvement of top management'? *(4 marks)*
(b) With reference to service industries give **three** advantages of such intimate management involvement. *(6 marks)*
(c) Give three reasons why 'people are more important in service marketing than in manufacturing'. *(6 marks)*
(d) State **one** reason why a salesman should spend time selling his firm as well as the goods or services which are offered. *(3 marks)*
(e) Give **three** ways in which this selling of the firm can be attempted. *(6 marks)*

(AEB)

The Post Office

Public Affairs
33 Grosvenor Place
LONDON
SW1X 1PX

Telephone 01-245 7132/3

BRIEFING: **Direct Mail**

December 1986

High growth and high standards of direct mail

Direct Mail – advertising by post – now represents 10 per cent of the Royal Mail's letter business.

It continues to be the fastest growing form of advertising in the country but, compared with the rest of Europe, the amount of direct mail per household is still very low.

The Post Office seeks to promote the use of mail advertising through discounts to major postal users. It is also encouraging high professional standards from direct mail companies and supporting a service which offers private consumers the means to select what, if any, personally addressed advertising they wish to receive.

Business increase

More than 1.3 billion direct mail items were handled by the Post Office last year – a growth of more than 30 per cent in the past five years.

Direct Mail now takes a 9 per cent share of all advertising expenditure – some £445 million a year – ahead of posters, radio and cinema combined. Postage charges represent about one-third of total direct mail costs.

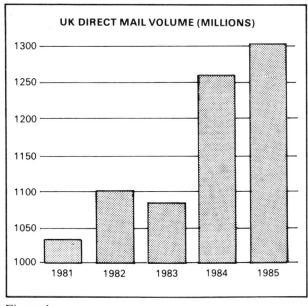

Figure 1

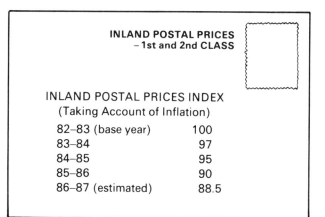

Figure 2

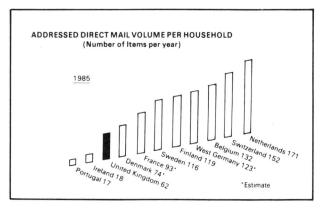

Figure 3

(a) How many items of direct mail were received by the average household in the UK and in Belgium in 1985? *(2 marks)*
(b) Explain (i) **two** advantages available from the use of direct mail advertising *(4 marks)*
and (ii) **one** disadvantage of using direct mail advertising. *(2 marks)*

(c) Why might an increase in direct mail, as shown in Figure 1, benefit not only its users, but all customers of the Post Office? *(6 marks)*

(d) Figure 2 gives the 'Inland Postal Prices Index' for the UK.
  (i) Explain the relevance of the 'base year' and how subsequent years are calculated. *(4 marks)*
  (ii) Explain **one** advantage of using an index rather than actual figures. *(2 marks)*

(AEB)

Essay questions

8.20 Outline the different pricing methods employed by firms and consider when each might be used. Do such pricing methods imply that consumers have little or no influence over prices?

(AEB)

8.21 Explain and illustrate what is meant by the 'product life-cycle'. Using appropriate examples, explore the implications for management of this concept.

(AEB)

8.22 A furniture manufacturer is concerned about a reduction in sales of its existing product range. What action should it take?

(AEB)

8.23 How might the manufacturer of a new chocolate bar decide to market the product?

(UCLES)

INTERNAL ORGANISATION

Functions of Management

Figure 9.1 Functions of management

One of the most commonly-quoted divisions of the functions of management was by Henri Fayol in *General and Industrial Administration* (1916). Fayol listed five basic functions;

Planning

Management must decide upon the *objectives* of the business and how these will be carried out. Plans must be made about matters such as which goods and services will be produced, where the firm will locate and how it will market its products.

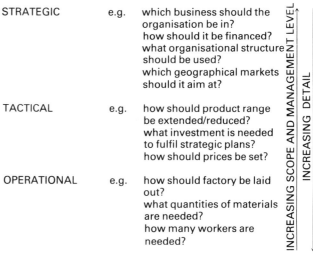

STRATEGIC	e.g.	which business should the organisation be in? how should it be financed? what organisational structure should be used? which geographical markets should it aim at?
TACTICAL	e.g.	how should product range be extended/reduced? what investment is needed to fulfil strategic plans? how should prices be set?
OPERATIONAL	e.g.	how should factory be laid out? what quantities of materials are needed? how many workers are needed?

Figure 9.2 Levels of planning

Planning may take place at various levels, according to the power and detailed knowledge of the manager involved. One method of dividing these levels is to distinguish between *strategic*, *tactical* and *operational* planning, as shown in Figure 9.2.

Organising

Organising involves ensuring that plans are carried out. People must be given responsibility for different functions of the business. Everybody must know who is responsible for making decisions and ensuring adequate supplies of materials, labour and equipment. It is often argued that the most successful managers are those who have the ability to *delegate* authority and tasks successfully.

Command

Managers must ensure that employees work towards the

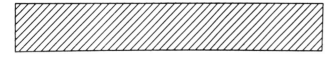

company's objectives. Fayol derived the term mainly from the practice of military leadership and the often authoritarian style of industrial management common in the early twentieth century. However the term 'motivation' is more commonly used nowadays, because it is generally believed that workers are more efficient if they are involved in their work rather than simply being told what to do.

Co-ordination

Within businesses, particularly larger firms, workers may have different objectives and priorities. If they are not co-ordinated to work together, problems may occur.

For example a machine may be the cause of complaints from customers. This may be because of production problems such as bad design or defective parts, or because sales staff are exaggerating what it can do. Whatever the cause, management must ensure that the problem is solved by getting production and sales staff to work with each other. This requires the establishment of effective communication within the organisation.

Control

Control means setting up systems to check that plans are being carried out. The business will usually have targets for items such as sales, costs and profits. There may also be performance targets for certain parts of the business (see Chapter 1).

A basic system of control procedures is shown in Figure 9.3. If a business's targets are not being achieved, the management must either set more realistic targets or take corrective action to improve performance in order to fulfil plans.

Organisation Charts

Functional charts

In small businesses, a single owner may be responsible for all the functions of management. In larger organisations, however, the business is likely to be split into departments. Figure 9.4 is an *organisation chart* showing the departments in a typical medium-sized manufacturer.

Product-based charts

The chart shown in Figure 9.4 is a fairly traditional one, and there are many possible variants. The Granada Group organisation chart in Figure 9.5 divides the group according to different markets, mainly based on its products, but with some geographical divisions.

Matrix charts

Some organisations use *matrix structures* such as the one shown in Figure 9.6. Each product manager is expected to co-ordinate all functions associated with his or her product. Specialist advice and assistance is provided by the production, marketing, finance and personnel staff.

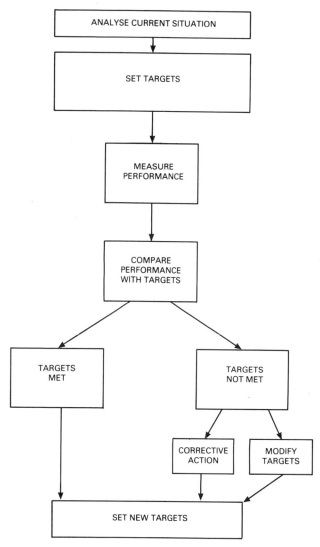

Figure 9.3 Control procedures

Customer-based charts

Many companies now use novel forms of organisation chart such as that used by Nordstrom, the US retailer (Figure 9.7). These types of chart typically show the customer at the top or side with the directors as a supporting force for staff who deal directly with customers.

Principles of Internal Organisation

Delegation

All organisations depend upon the *delegation* of authority. For example in a large public company the shareholders have ultimate control. However, they do not usually have the time or willingness to run the day-to-day business.

147

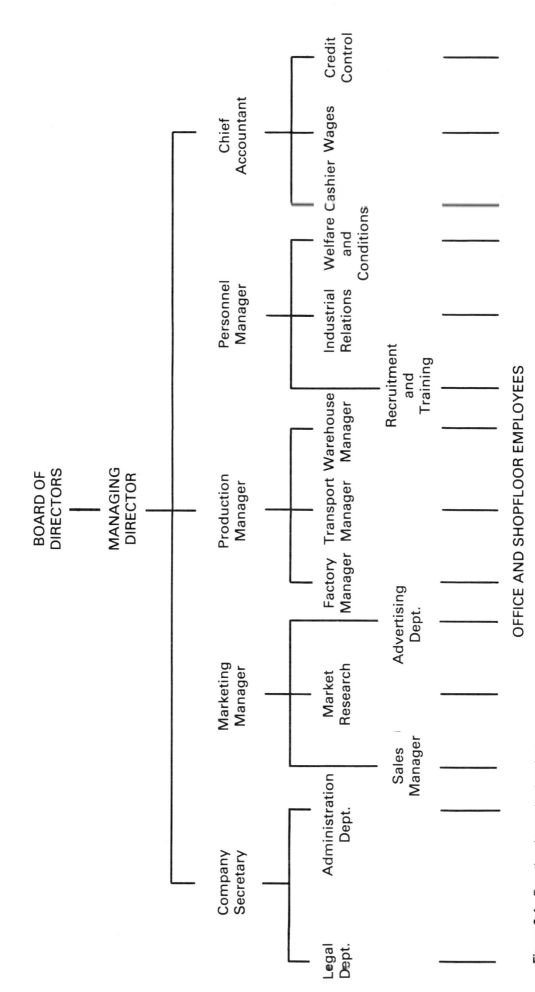

Figure 9.4 Functional organisation chart

GRANADA GROUP
ORGANISATION CHART

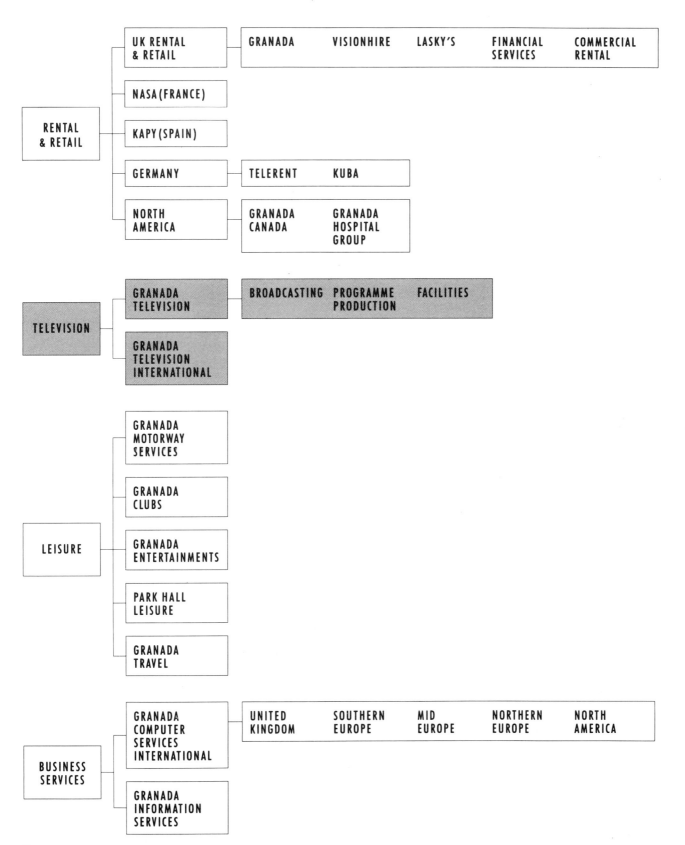

Figure 9.5   Granada Group organisation chart

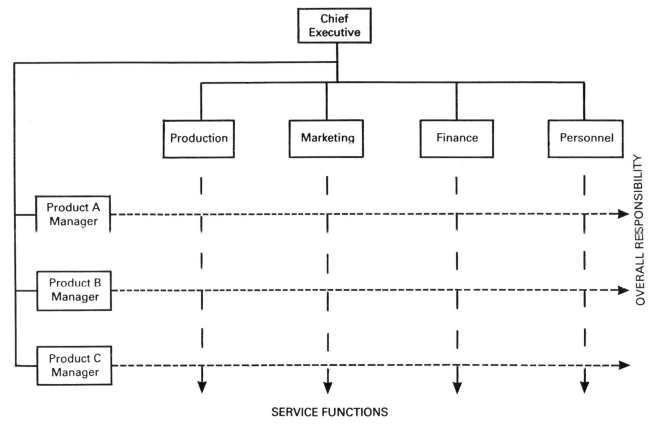

Figure 9.6 Matrix structure

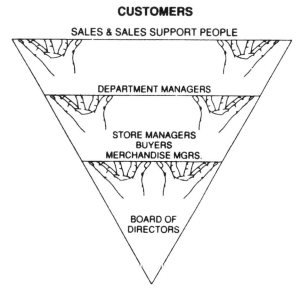

Figure 9.7 Nordstrom organisation chart

They elect a Board of Directors, which in turn delegates this responsibility to the Managing Director.

Although the Managing Director is responsible for management of all the business's activities, he or she cannot directly control hundreds or thousands of workers. Department Managers are appointed to control different activities, such as finance or production. Each manager then appoints other workers to take on smaller responsibilities, such as managing an individual factory or recruiting junior staff.

At each level, employees are given varying degrees of responsibility, together with the limited authority necessary to fulfil those responsibilities.

Delegation does not mean giving up responsibility. For example a product may sell badly because of poor work in the factory. The Managing Director does not directly control production, but may still be held responsible because he or she should have set up systems to ensure that such problems did not occur.

Chain of command

The *chain of command* refers to the way in which power is passed down through the organisation. In a small firm, workers may be directly supervised by the owner or manager. In larger firms, however, the chain of command will be more complicated. This is shown by Figure 9.8, which shows two possible alternative chains of command for an organisation.

The tall organisation has seven different levels of authority (often considered the largest number possible for an efficient organisation). This arrangement is fairly typical of large firms or Government Departments. Tall organisations usually have characteristics such as:

- long chains of command;
- lengthy decision-making times;
- senior management remoteness from 'shop-floor';
- narrow spans of control;
- narrow specialisation of employees;
- heavy reliance upon formal/written communications.

Tall structures are rather unfashionable in the 1990s,

150

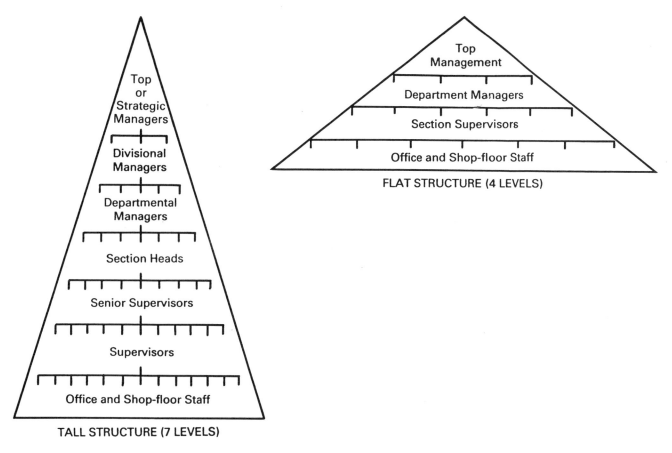

Figure 9.8 'Tall' and 'flat' organisations

and some organisations such as BP and the Civil Service have been attempting to 'flatten' the number of levels of authority. However such attempts are often resisted by employees because of potential losses of status, promotion opportunities and sometimes jobs.

Flat organisations tend to be smaller. A typical solicitor's office or medium-sized garage are possible examples. Likely characteristics of flat organisations are:

- short chains of command;
- quick decision-making;
- senior management closeness to shop-floor;
- broad spans of control;
- more versatile employees;
- reliance on informal/oral communication.

It should be remembered, however, that both of these sets of characteristics are only generalised assumptions and may not always apply.

Span of control

The *span of control* is the number of people directly controlled by one person. In Figure 9.4, for example, the Managing Director has a span of control of five managers.

The number of people which can be directly controlled varies according to the type of work involved. The five people in the Managing Director's span of control all have complicated responsibilities. It would be difficult to control a large number of people with similar jobs.

For simple work which can be checked easily, the span

of control can be larger. Skilled and experienced staff can be controlled effectively in larger spans than can new untrained employees. Other factors which may affect the width of the control span are the costliness of possible errors, the stability of the external environment and the ability of the manager.

An inappropriate span of control can be very costly to an organisation. Over-wide spans lead to problems in assisting, training and controlling subordinates. If the span is too narrow the manager may tend to exercise excessive control, which demotivates subordinates, stifles initiative and wastes labour by duplicating tasks.

Centralisation and decentralisation

Authority within an organisation may be *centralised* or *decentralised*. If it is centralised, decisions are taken by the top managers and passed down through the chain of command. Multiple chains of shops often work upon this basis. Individual shop managers have little or no control over which goods to stock and the prices to charge. In a *decentralised* company, local shop managers would have more power to make decisions.

Decentralised management has become increasingly fashionable during the last few years, particularly in public services such as education and health. It involves devolving authority to junior managers, who are given responsibility for the 'operational' or even 'tactical' decisions such as those illustrated in Figure 9.2. The main advantages claimed for decentralised management are:

- junior managers are closer to the customer and can respond more quickly to customer requirements;
- people feel more involved in their work because of increased responsibility;
- administration costs may be lower;
- attention can be focused on *cost centres*, for example by giving individual managers a budget to control;
- senior management have more time for strategic planning.

Despite these advantages, many organisations have resisted decentralisation. Sometimes this has been because senior managers are reluctant to relinquish their authority. This may be because of reluctance to lose power or because they are afraid to allow junior managers to take important decisions. A decentralised organisation is harder to control, and the process of decentralisation involves employees taking on more responsibility, which some may not wish for.

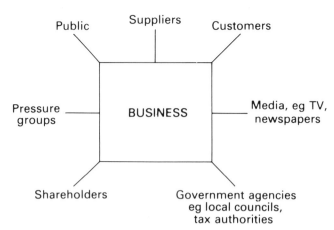

Figure 9.10 External communication

Communication

Reasons for communication

Good communication is vital to the effective running of a business. Figure 9.9 gives some examples of the ways in which people within a business will communicate with each other (*internal* communication) and Figure 9.10 with people and organisations from outside (*external* communication).

The elements of communication

Any form of communication has the following elements:

1. *Transmitter*. This is the person who sends a message.
2. *Message*. All of the statements in Figure 9.9 are messages. A message may be a simple sign saying 'No Entry' or a complex document such as a financial report or a book.
3. *Medium*. This is the method used to send the message, for example spoken, visual or electronic.
4. *Receiver*. This is the person or group of people to whom the message is sent.

Figure 9.9 Reasons for communication

5. *Feedback*. This is the response of the receiver to the message (which may consist of ignoring it altogether).
6. *Noise*. This refers to any factor which may prevent the message getting through. This may be noise in the literal sense or distractions such as alternative preoccupations.

An example of these elements combined is given in Figure 9.11.

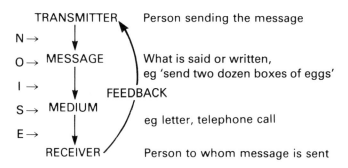

Figure 9.11 Elements of communication

Barriers to communication

Problems in communication can occur for several reasons:

- complex language or jargon is used;
- the message is too long;
- essential information is missed out because of poor planning;
- the 'lines of communication' are too long, for example a message is passed through too many people;
- the medium used is unsuitable, such as complex messages sent by phone;
- the receiver is distracted by 'noise';
- the tone of the message is wrong, such as a manager 'talking down' to workers;
- the message is sent too late for the receiver to act on it;
- the transmitter and receiver are in different places;
- the transmitter has low status in the view of the receiver, for example a person is more likely to take notice of a superior than of a subordinate;
- 'bias' and 'reflectivity', that is people hear what they want to hear, perhaps by selecting parts of the message which are agreeable to them.

Communication networks

Communication networks or *sociograms* are a method of indicating the flow of communication within an organisation. The type of network will depend upon factors such as the nature of the organisation, the style of leadership and the type of task being undertaken. Three basic types of network are illustrated in Figure 9.12. It should be remembered that both the number and shape of communication networks often vary between writers.

The *chain* network is typical of a hierarchical organisation with authoritarian leadership (an army is often suggested as an example). Orders and other communications are passed up or down the line only to immediate superiors or subordinates. A chain is more likely to occur in a 'tall' organisation.

A is the formal leader, but will have little or no contact with lower-grade personnel. In practice *C* (perhaps repre-

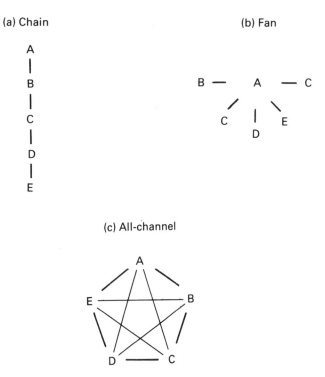

Figure 9.12 Communication networks

senting middle management) is likely to have considerable influence, particularly on day-to-day matters.

The *fan* network involves the leader *A* communicating individually with each member of the group, but no formal communication between the other members. This might be true of a sales manager with representatives in different regions, or a very traditional school lesson where pupils are not allowed to talk to each other. In both cases there is likely to be informal communication.

Fan networks may be quick and effective, but there is little co-ordination or sharing of information, at least formally, by people with similar functions.

An *all-channel* network allows every member of the group to have two-way communication with each other. It might be typical of a working group set up to develop a new product or undertake a task involving several departments, such as computerisation or relocation. There will often be no formal leader.

All-channel networks are particularly likely in organisations with a *matrix* structure. The main advantages are that knowledge and ideas can be exchanged quickly and there is likely to be more commitment to the group purpose. However, decisions may take longer to make because of the time spent in communication.

Methods of Communication

Oral communication

Oral communication is ideal when it is necessary to pass on a short message or find information quickly. It is unsuitable for communicating complex information.

1. *Face-to-face contact* is the most widely-used form of communication in business. It may be *informal*, such as simple requests or orders, or *formal*, such as meetings and interviews.

153

2. *Interviews* are formal and are commonly used to select employees or for purposes such as grievance or disciplinary procedures.
3. *Meetings* usually follow a particular procedure which is used by organisations of all types. An *agenda* listing the points to be discussed is sent to people who will be attending. The main arguments and decisions taken are summarised in the written *minutes* of the meeting.
4. *Telephones* provide a quick means of conversation with people in other rooms or outside the business.

Non-verbal communication

People's actions or *body language* are a form of communication which is as important as any other type. For example a supervisor may annoy workers by staring round the room while he or she is asking for help or making a complaint.

Written communication

Written forms of communication are used for situations where:

- speed is not particularly important;
- long or detailed messages are sent;
- the message is to be recorded for future use;
- it is necessary to contact several people at the same time;
- people cannot be contacted in person or by phone.

1. *Letters* are used mainly for *external* communication.
2. *Memoranda* or 'memos' are a short note sent to people within the same organisation.
3. *Brochures* and *advertisements* are designed to sell a firm's goods and services to outside people and firms.
4. *Reports* are collections of facts, often listing alternative solutions to a particular problem, for example a Health and Safety report may give details of accidents and illness, together with recommendations for reducing them.
5. *Manuals* give employees instructions about company products or procedures, for example on handling machinery or dealing with customers.
6. *Notices* are used to display information or instructions throughout the premises.
7. *Annual Reports* detailing the company's financial performance and plans must be sent to shareholders every year.
8. *Press releases* and *public relations material* are used by firms to inform the public and mass media about company affairs such as new products and orders or performance during the year.
9. *Micro-film* can store large amounts of data in a very small space. It is used by organisations such as credit-card companies, libraries and retailers of motor spares.

Electronic communication

During the last 20 years the cost of using computers has fallen dramatically, and electronic communication has become increasingly important. The speed and cheapness of electronic communication make up for the cost of buying special equipment. For example a small business can buy a sophisticated computer system for under £10 000, which is less than the cost of employing a worker for a year.

1. *Electronic mail* uses the telephone system to send messages from one computer to another. A *modem* is needed to connect a computer to the telephone network. The receiver's computer stores the message until he or she has time to read it.
2. *Telex* is one of the oldest forms of electronic communication. A message is typed into a special machine and transmitted to a Telex printer via a telephone line. Telex cannot transmit drawings or graphics.
3. *Facsimile transmission* (fax) sends a copy of a document or drawing through a telephone line without the need to type a message in. It is therefore faster and more flexible than Telex, which it is gradually replacing.
4. *Teletext* services such as Prestel link television screens, telephone lines and keyboards to send information of different types. The Stock Exchange's SEAQ system (Figure 4.6) is one example of this use.

Worked Examples

Short-answer questions

9.1 Distinguish between formal and informal communication in business.

(AEB)

Answer Formal – established and controlled by management, 'official', often dominated by 'vertical' communication up or down the chain of command.
Informal – not directly established by management, usually verbal rather than written, 'social' communication often not directly associated with work, more likely to be 'horizontal' or 'diagonal', ignoring chains of command, for example rumours and canteen conversations.

9.2 Distinguish between 'line' and 'staff' relationships as shown in an organisation chart.

Answer Line – contributes *directly* to production of good or service, such as production staff or delivery drivers; usually concentrated in one part of organisation.
Staff – provide services such as personnel and accounting to line functions, usually right across the organisation.

9.3 Discuss the difficulties and dilemmas faced by management in the long-term as opposed to the short-term.

(AEB)

Answer **(i)** Distinguish between the short-term and long-term. Main difference is the time, for example up to 2 years might be regarded as short-term, and any period beyond this as long-term. Studies show that few firms plan in any detail beyond 2 or 3 years ahead.

(ii) Explain that apart from actual time-periods it is possible to distinguish according to the character of decisions to be made in each case. Short-term decisions are 'operational' or 'tactical'. The phrase 'fire-fighting' is sometimes used to express the feeling that management tends to react to immediate pressures without thinking far ahead. There may also be little that can be done to change the firm's situation.
In the long-term, managers have much wider powers because there is more scope to change the firm's situation significantly.

(iii) Compare the management's situation in the short- and long-term. Short-term decisions are easier to make because the detail of the situation is much clearer and there is less risk of making the wrong decision. Managers may feel happier because they are working in familiar circumstances, and may put off long-term decisions.
However, it is long-term decisions which will ultimately determine the organisation's survival. This involves taking a much broader view and often making a blind guess at how the market will change over the next several years.

9.4 Why is delegation so necessary to the success of a business, and why is it so difficult to carry out?

(AEB)

Answer **(i)** Define delegation as the transfer of authority to a subordinate person or group. Give a simple illustrative example. Explain the basic reason for delegation, that is the owners/directors/senior managers cannot do or supervise everything themselves and therefore have to give subordinates some power and responsibility.

(ii) Outline possible advantages of delegation, for example:

- saves management time, which can be used for more complex functions or planning;
- decisions can be made more quickly if authority is shared;
- senior managers are often unaware of changes at shop-floor level;
- may motivate subordinates by giving more responsibility;
- helps to develop staff for future promotion;
- cheaper than constant supervision if well-managed;
- allows specialisms within the organisation, such as dealing with particular processes, customers, etc.

(iii) Describe possible difficulties in carrying out delegation, such as:

- managers may not be willing to 'let go' and refuse to trust their subordinates;
- care has to be taken to ensure that subordinates know the limits of their authority and responsibility – this may involve setting up complex control and administrative procedures;
- effective delegation requires a level of skill from both the manager and subordinates;
- some employees may not want or be able to exercise authority effectively;
- appropriate reward systems such as bonuses or fringe benefits may be necessary.

9.5 Examine the barriers to effective communication in a large company.

(AEB)

Answer This essay basically requires you to apply forms of communication barrier such as those described above to the situation of a large company. Examples of such application might include:

- long chains of command with remote management (use a diagram of a 'tall' organisation);
- limited knowledge of other employees apart from immediate colleagues;
- demarcations and rivalries between departments/offices/factories/shops, etc.
- less likelihood of communication being face-to-face;
- use of jargon, such as by computer or production staff;
- separate geographical locations, so more formal and slow communications between people who do not know each other.

Self-test Questions

9.6 Give two factors that determine the effectiveness of delegation.

(AEB)

9.7 Distinguish between autocratic and democratic styles of leadership.

(AEB)

9.8 State two functions of management.

(AEB)

Essay questions

9.9 It is claimed that leadership is important for the success of any group activity in business, although the styles of leadership may differ according to the situation.

What is meant by the term 'style of leadership'? Discuss the appropriateness of different leadership styles in a business context.

(AEB)

9.10 **(a)** Distinguish between *autocratic* and *democratic* styles of management.   *(5 marks)*
(b) Why is 'span of control' relevant in any discussion of management style?   *(8 marks)*
(c) Compare and contrast the advantages and disadvantages of the following methods of communication and say to which style they might be appropriate:
  (i) letters
  (ii) notice boards
  (iii) telephones
  (iv) meetings.   *(12 marks)*

(UCLES)

PERSONNEL MANAGEMENT

Functions of Personnel Management

Objectives of personnel management

Personnel management is defined by the Institute of Personnel Management as concerned with:

> "recruiting and selecting people; training and developing them for their work; ensuring that their payment and conditions of employment are appropriate, where necessary negotiating such terms of employment with trade unions, advising on healthy and appropriate working conditions; the organisation of people at work, and the encouragement of relations between management and work people."

This definition includes a wide range of functions and objectives for management of workers, whether undertaken by specialist personnel staff or by general managers. Even in very small organisations, most or all of these functions will have to be undertaken.

A more complex outline of personnel work is given in Figure 10.2. This relates the personnel function to the overall purpose of the organisation.

The quality of a business's workforce is vital to its success. If workers are happy and interested in their work they will tend to do it better, and a firm's products will be of higher quality. Labour is usually by far an organisation's largest cost, accounting in many cases for over half of the total costs of production.

Personnel problems

Dissatisfaction among employees can lead to significant problems for an organisation. Symptoms of dissatisfaction include:

- High or increasing *labour turnover*, that is a high proportion of workers leaving compared with the past or to similar types of work.
- People leaving after a short time with the firm. This shows that the firm is choosing the wrong type of people or failing to train them properly.
- Workers leaving for jobs of the same or lower status, rather than for promotion.
- Employees leaving soon after completing their training or becoming effective at their jobs. This may be a sign that the firm is not providing enough opportunities for promotion.
- High or rising rates of sickness or absenteeism.
- Petty disputes between workers or with managers.

These problems may be concentrated in particular jobs or departments. This may be due to work being boring or a department being badly managed.

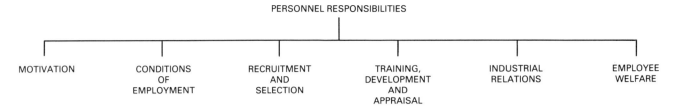

Figure 10.1 Functions of personnel management

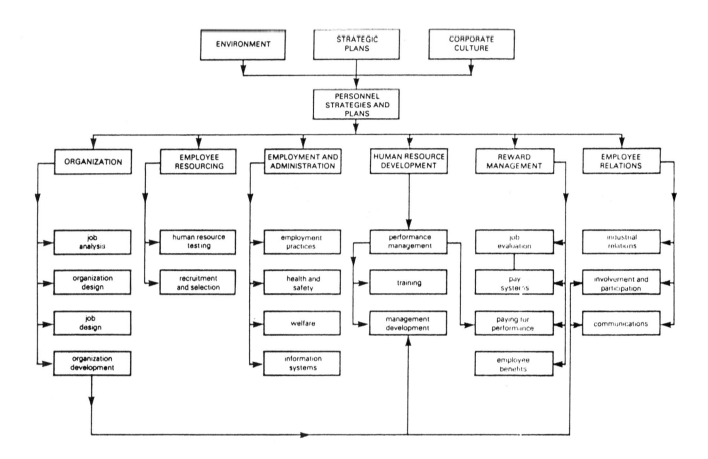

Figure 10.2 Hierarchy of personnel objectives

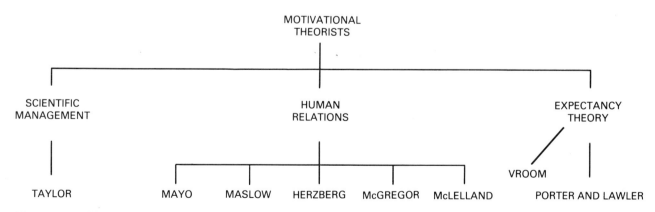

Figure 10.3 Motivational theorists

Motivation

Factors which motivate workers

There are many theories about how firms can motivate their workers to work well. The following are generally thought relevant, although workers may disagree about which are the most important:

- pay and fringe benefits;
- promotion prospects;
- working environment, such as physical surroundings, noise and dirt;
- security of employment;
- status and prestige at work;
- interesting and challenging work;
- personal relationships with other workers;
- style of management;
- hours of work and holidays;
- social life, such as work's outings or office parties;
- good communications within the organisation.

Scientific management

The theory of scientific management is usually associated with the work of F. W. Taylor, who pioneered the application of specialist techniques at the Bethlehem Steel Company in the USA during the late 19th and early 20th centuries. Taylor believed that slack management and lack of understanding of how to organise work led to inefficient production, low profits and low wages for workers.

Taylor started by testing different ways of doing particular jobs, using a stopwatch to time workers. He argued that by establishing the most scientific and efficient method, productivity would be maximised and the worker who met the standard could be rewarded with high wages. He proved that this could be done simply by better organisation.

Taylor's ideas were widely copied and developed into the modern art of work study, partly by Henry Gantt, a colleague of Taylor at Bethlehem Steel. Some of his principles were used by Henry Ford to establish the assembly line for the Model T. However, Taylor's methods were based upon three assumptions which might now be regarded as incorrect:

- workers are only interested in higher wages;
- workers should have no control over how to perform their work;
- employees were considered as isolated individuals, with the 'social context' of work ignored as irrelevant.

Even in the early years of the century, these assumptions were dubious. With an increasingly well-educated workforce and more favourable economic climate, they are now very dated.

The 'human relations' theorists

The 'human relations' school is a general term applied to a variety of thinkers with slightly different ideas, but sharing common assumptions about workers' needs for social contact and personal motivation. They consider people in groups as well as on an individual basis, and usually see wages as a secondary factor to morale in maximising performance.

1. Mayo

Elton Mayo is best known for the famous Hawthorne studies at the Western Electric Company's Hawthorne plant in Chicago. This took place mainly between 1927 and 1932. One of the most famous experiments consisted of putting six female workers in a room by themselves to assemble electrical relays (this was known as the Relay Assembly Test Room).

Various changes were made to working conditions such as length of breaks and the level of light. It was found that even making working conditions worse led to higher productivity because the women formed a close personal group and liked the attention which was paid to them. This led Mayo to conclude that group morale and a sense of personal worth were the most important motivating factors.

2. Maslow

Figure 10.4 Maslow's hierarchy of needs

Abraham Maslow was an American psychologist who put forward the theory in 1943 that human needs consisted of five basic types:

- *physiological*, such as food, sex and oxygen;
- *safety*, such as freedom from danger;
- *social*, that is the need for love and belonging to a group;
- *esteem*, that is to respect oneself (self-esteem) and be respected by others (prestige);
- *self-actualisation* or *self-fulfilment*, for example to develop one's own skills or spiritual well-being.

Maslow argued that these formed a *hierarchy of needs*, in that people had to satisfy one set of needs before they could move up to another. For example a worker paid starvation wages is unlikely to be motivated by praise from managers.

There is considerable argument about whether Maslow's hierarchy really works in the sense of people working their way up through the different needs. However it does help to illustrate the variety of worker needs that must be satisfied if employees are to be motivated.

3. Herzberg

Frederick Herzberg believed that there were two basic groups of factors which were important to workers;

Figure 10.5 Herzberg's motivation and hygiene factors

HYGIENE FACTORS	MOTIVATING FACTORS
Working conditions Pay Job security Status Relationships with other workers Company policy and administration Supervision	Achievement Recognition Responsibility Growth and Development Work itself

"The wants of workers divide into two groups. One group revolves around the need to develop in one's occupation as a source of personal growth. The second group operates as an essential base to the first and is associated with fair treatment in compensation, supervision, working conditions and administrative practices."

(F. W. Herzberg, B. Mausner and B. Snyderman, *The Motivation to Work*, Wiley, New York, 1957)

Herzberg regarded some features of work life as *motivation factors* or *satisfiers* which encouraged personal development and pride, therefore motivating workers to higher performance.

Hygiene factors (also known as *maintenance factors*) were potential *dissatisfiers*. They could not motivate people to work better, but could demotivate people if they were inadequate. For example high wages might not lead to better performance, but workers' performance would suffer if they felt that they were underpaid for their level of skill.

It is noticeable that Herzberg's motivating factors are mainly linked to the actual content of the job, that is what the worker does. Demotivating factors tend to be linked to the environment of the job.

4. McGregor

Douglas McGregor, in *The Human Side of Enterprise* (1960) outlined two opposing views about the psychological characteristics of workers: 'Theory X' and 'Theory Y'.

The Theory X outlook is basically authoritarian, seeing the average worker as someone to be coerced into working harder. This is loosely equivalent to the views of scientific management theorists such as Taylor.

The Theory Y outlook sees the average worker as wanting to work and hold responsibility, given the right conditions and encouragement.

Figure 10.6 'Theory X' and 'Theory Y'

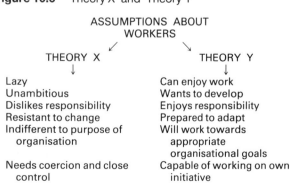

5. McLelland

McLelland classified human needs into three categories: achievement, affiliation (or belonging) and power. One of these is always dominant, although people are affected by all three. This affects individual ability to perform particular jobs and has implications for the training and motivation of particular workers.

McLelland found that high achievers tended to seek responsible and challenging tasks which they felt were achievable. They expected feedback upon whether they had failed or succeeded. They also tended to be less concerned about affiliation (social) needs.

Expectancy theory

This is a branch of theory pioneered by V. H. Vroom in *Work and Motivation* (1964). It argues that to achieve, people must have both ability and motivation. This can be expressed in the simple equation:

$$Performance = Ability \times Motivation$$

Vroom's work was extended by various writers, particularly Porter and Lawler in *Managerial Attitudes and Performance* (1968). They argued that the likelihood of effort leading to reward was vital. They also stressed the importance of the workers' perception of what their role was affected the outcome.

Payment Systems

Time rates

Under *time-rate* payment, a worker is paid a fixed amount per hour, week or month. *Overtime rates* may be paid for work outside the normal hours, such as at night or weekends. Common overtime rates are *time-and-a-half* for nights and *double-time* for weekends or bank holidays. A worker whose normal rate was £5 per hour would be paid £7.50 for time-and-a-half and £10 for double-time.

The advantages of time-rates are that they are easy to calculate and the worker is guaranteed a certain wage providing the hours are worked.

The main disadvantage of time-rates is that the worker gets paid the same amount no matter how much work is done. There is little incentive to work hard.

Piece-rates

Piece-rate or *payment-by-result* systems reward the employee according to the work done. Examples include commission on sales and payments to a bricklayer for the number of bricks laid.

The advantage of piece-rate systems is that they encourage effort by providing higher wages to successful workers.

The disadvantages of piece-rates are that the worker's wage is uncertain, and essential work such as paperwork or cleaning of machines may be ignored if there is no extra payment. Work may be rushed, resulting in poor-quality goods and services. Also many jobs are difficult to measure, for example it would be difficult to assess the work

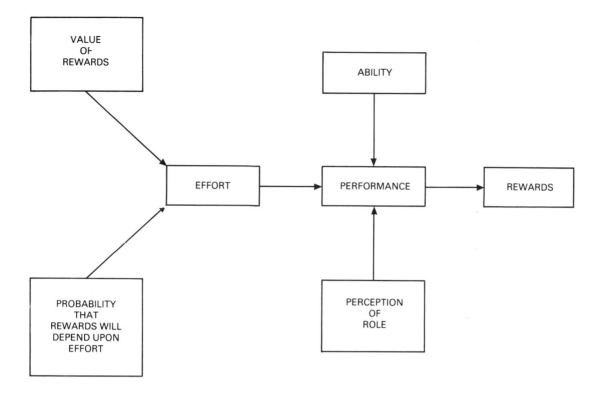

Figure 10.7 Porter and Lawler's expectancy model

done by a teacher or police officer, because so many different tasks are involved.

Because of these disadvantages, very few workers are paid completely by piece-rates.

Incentive schemes

Many employers try to obtain the advantages of time- and piece-rates by paying a basic wage, but giving workers the opportunity to earn extra money by working harder. Typically the incentive will account for up to 25% of the total wage.

1. *Bonuses* are extra payments for workers who reach a set target for production or sales.
2. *Profit-related pay* schemes give workers a share in the company's profits. The Conservative Government has tried to encourage these because of the belief that they make workers more aware of the business's need to make profits.
3. *Merit payments* are given to workers and managers who are believed to have performed exceptionally well. They are sometimes given in the form of *fringe benefits*, for example successful sales representatives may be given cars or exotic holidays.

Fringe benefits

These are given in addition to a salary, and are also called *perks* or *non-monetary benefits*. Common examples include:

1. company cars;
2. discounts on company products;
3. cheap mortgages or personal loans;
4. subsidised canteen and sporting facilities;
5. free or cheap health insurance.

Manpower Planning

The purpose of manpower planning

Manpower planning (sometimes called *human resource planning*) involves forecasting the business's future requirements for different types of workers and the extent to which the supply of workers will be sufficient to meet these needs.

The business's *demand* for labour will depend upon factors such as demand for its products, product range, future market plans, organisational structure, technological change, labour productivity and use of 'bought-in' or subcontracted goods and services.

The *supply* of labour will depend upon factors such as the current level of manpower, labour turnover, competitiveness of wages compared with those offered by other employers, unemployment rates, age structure of current workforce, availability of skilled workers in the industry, and the training policies of the business and its competitors.

Effective manpower planning involves trying to obtain the right *quantity* and *quality* of workers with the skills and experience necessary to enable the firm to operate as efficiently and profitably as possible. It can help management to make crucial decisions about matters such as future recruitment or redundancies, training and development programmes, labour costs, and accommodation requirements such as office or factory space.

Content of a manpower plan

A formal manpower plan would contain details about:

● changes in the number of each type of job;

- implications for recruitment, redeployment or redundancy;
- changes in organisational structure;
- training needs;
- arrangements for communicating plan to employees;
- possible effects upon morale, labour turnover and industrial relations.

The process of manpower planning

For small organisations there may be little or no systematic manpower planning, and many large firms only plan for one or two years ahead, as they feel that their market is not predictable enough to forecast accurately beyond this time-span.

For many businesses, manpower planning is only thought about seriously when there is a foreseeable crisis. For example the fall in the teenage population during the early 1990s has forced many firms to reconsider the attractiveness of their jobs to young workers, and to make plans to attract older workers.

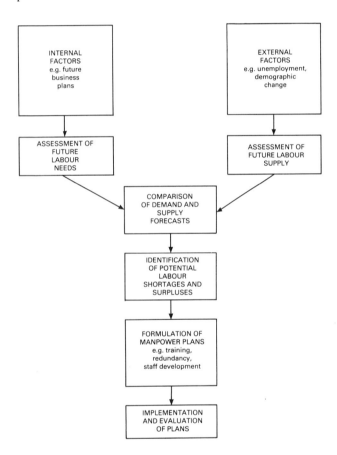

Figure 10.8 The process of manpower planning

Recruitment

Recruitment and selection

Almost all businesses have occasionally to recruit new workers to replace leavers, introduce new skills or take on additional work generated by expansion. Recruitment is

the process of obtaining candidates for a vacancy, whereas selection involves choosing from the candidates recruited.

Figure 10.9 The recruitment and selection process

The job description

The person responsible for recruiting employees should draw up a *job description*. In a small business such as a corner shop the owner may simply decide that he or she wants a part-time assistant 'to serve customers' and not bother to draw up a detailed specification. Larger organisations may set out a formal written job description. In either case certain details will need to be decided in order to attract and interview applicants. These might include as a basic minimum:

- title of job;
- type of work;
- place and hours of work;
- pay and other benefits;
- person to whom the employee will be responsible;
- workers who will be supervised by the successful applicant.

An example of a job description for a hotel reception supervisor is given in Figure 10.10.

Job specification

Having described the duties, the recruiter will have to think about the type of person who will be suitable to fill the post. A *job specification* or *personnel description* may be drawn up. This describes the necessary physical and mental skills and knowledge necessary to do a job successfully.

A job specification may be very simple, such as 'able to carry boxes and count change'. For many jobs it will not be written down and be a rather vague idea in the recruiter's head.

162

Job Title: **Reception Supervisor**
      Victoria Hotel, Chillingsworth

Responsibilities

1. Overall responsibility for supervision of reception area, under the direction of the General Manager.
2. Supervision of staff, including allocation of tasks, drawing up work rotas and basic training and instruction.
3. Dealing with customer enquiries and requests.
4. Completion of records including reservations, payment of bills, requests for services and accounts.
5. Maintaining in self and subordinates a standard of service and dress which reflect the good name of the Company.
6. Attending training courses as and when directed by the General Manager.
7. Being aware of and implementing the Company's Health and Safety procedures.
8. Other duties as may be reasonably required by the General Manager.

Figure 10.10   Job description

1. Physical make-up	–	The receptionist should be presentable to customers, e.g. dress smartly.
2. Attainments	–	Evidence of a good education and supervisory experience would be desirable.
3. General intelligence	–	A reception supervisor would have to think quickly when dealing with hotel guests.
4. Special aptitudes	–	Ability to write in clear English and work with figures would be essential. Knowledge of a foreign language might be useful.
5. Interests	–	An applicant's hobbies may show their ability to work in a team.
6. Disposition	–	The reception supervisor would need to be pleasant to customers and remain calm even when problems occur.
7. Circumstances	–	Night and weekend work would be essential, so the successful applicant would have to be able to work these hours.

Figure 10.11   Job specification

A formal written job specification may be based upon a detailed checklist of skills and personal qualities desired. The most famous is the 'Seven Point Plan' of the National Institute of Industrial Psychology, which lists requirements under seven headings.

Figure 10.11 shows these headings, together with an example of how they might be applied to the job described in Figure 10.10.

The requirements must comply with the law. For example, with certain exceptions, it is illegal to specify qualities which automatically exclude a particular sex or racial group.

Attracting candidates

There are two basic ways of finding applicants.

1. Internal recruitment

The job may be advertised, for example through a staff notice board or bulletin, or even given to a particular person without allowing other staff to apply. There are some advantages to internal recruitment:

- the candidates' strengths and weaknesses are already known;

- the person appointed will be familiar with the work of the organisation and more likely to remain than a complete newcomer;
- internal promotions are good for staff morale;
- it is quicker and cheaper than external recruitment.

The disadvantages are:

- restricted choice, which may lead to unsuitable people being appointed;
- internal promotion can cause jealousy and resentment among people passed over.
- the organisation does not benefit from people with new ideas;
- it is regarded as poor practice in connection with equal opportunity – for example, if a particular ethnic group is not represented in a workforce, internal recruitment will tend to present a barrier to employment for that minority.

2. External recruitment

The advantages and disadvantages of external recruitment are basically the opposite of those of internal selection. Among the possible methods of recruiting people from outside the organisation are:

- *Personal recommendation* from employees, friends and

163

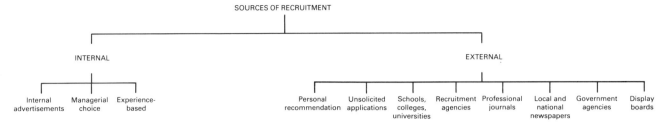

Figure 10.12 Sources of recruitment

business contacts. This is cheap and usually leads to good quality applicants as people will usually only recommend candidates whom they regard as worthwhile. As with internal recruitment, it also limits the field and works against the creation of equal opportunity for minorities not represented within the business.

- *Unsolicited applications*. People often write in to enquire about employment, even where no specific job is available at the time. Some firms keep suitable applications 'on file' until a post becomes available.
- *Schools, colleges and universities*. A firm may have personal contacts with local schools or colleges providing particular types of courses.
- *Recruitment agencies and selection consultants*. There are a large number of these, some general, others specialising in particular types of work. They are often used as a source of casual labour such as temporary secretaries or drivers. A recruitment agency may be involved in drawing up a shortlist of candidates to be selected from by the business.
  For senior management, *executive search* ('head-hunting') may be used. A head-hunter approaches people who are not actively seeking new employment, but who may move if given the right offer.
- *Professional journals*. These are important for specialist workers who may have to be recruited from a wide geographical area. Examples include *Marketing Weekly* and *Economist*.
- *Local and national newspapers*. Local papers will tend to be used for most unskilled and semi-skilled jobs. For professional workers, national papers may be used. Most 'quality' papers such as the *Guardian* and *Independent* have specialist sections on certain days of the week for particular groups of advertisement, such as 'Creative and Media' or 'Computer Appointments'.
- *Government agencies*. These include Job Centres, Careers Service and Professional and Executive Recruitment (PER).
- *Display boards*. Some firms advertise vacancies outside their premises, such as in windows or on special display boards.

Selection

Job advertisements

However the post is advertised, certain details will need to be made known to potential applicants. Some of these will be taken from the job description. Typical information included might be:

- job title;
- description of work involved;
- earnings or salary grade;
- fringe benefits;
- hours of work;
- holidays;
- place of work;
- qualifications or experience needed;
- training and future prospects;
- how to apply for the post.

Some of this information may be omitted, for example to save advertising costs, but the advertisement should be designed so as to contain enough information to attract the right type of person to apply.

Application form

This is the most commonly used means of collecting information about applicants. The information requested will vary, but the basic minimum needed would usually include the following:

- name;
- address and telephone number;
- date of birth;
- education and qualifications;
- work experience;
- personal interests;
- health record, for example details of serious illnesses;
- National Insurance number;
- referees who will provide information about the applicant's character and work record;
- other information showing the applicant's suitability, for example for positions of responsibility it is common to ask how the applicant would organise his or her department if given the job.

Curriculum vitae

A *curriculum vitae* gives similar information to that asked for in an application form, but is set out by the applicant rather than the recruiter. From the company's point of view, there is a problem that essential information may be omitted.

Selection methods

1. *Interviews* are the most commonly-used methods of selection. They are cheap and easy to arrange but have disadvantages:

   - they depend very much upon personal impressions;
   - many good and capable workers suffer from nerves and do badly;
   - interviewers are rarely trained in interview techniques;
   - they do not necessarily give much information about the applicant's ability to do the job.

2. *Aptitude tests* can, if well-designed, provide useful information about applicant's existing abilities and capacity to develop skills in the future. They include tests of general intelligence and of specific skills such as mental arithmetic and typing.
3. *Psychological tests* or *Attitude tests* have to be administered by experts and are therefore expensive. However, the Armed Forces have found them to be the most accurate method of forecasting a recruit's success in the job. They are unlikely to be used as the sole method of selection.
4. *Group selection* is often used for professional jobs and the Forces. Applicants are asked to lead and participate in group exercises such as discussions and practical tasks, often over a period of one or more days. They do provide some insight into a candidate's ability to work and socialise with others, but are essentially a subjective judgement made under artificial conditions.

Induction

Induction is the process of introducing a new worker to the organisation.

Contract of employment

By law, an employee must be given a Contract of Employment within 3 months. This must contain certain basic information:

- employer's name and place of work;
- date employment started;
- title of job;
- rate of pay;
- hours of work;
- holiday entitlement;
- amount of notice to be given by worker or employer;
- procedures for disciplinary matters;
- arrangements for sick pay;
- pension rights.

Some of these items may not be described in detail, but may refer the employee to documents such as national union agreements or pension fund conditions.

Information needed by the new employee

An induction programme, which may take anything from a couple of hours to several months, has three basic purposes:

- to familiarise the new employee with the job and place of work;
- to encourage him or her to become committed to the job and therefore likely to stay;
- to make the employee a useful and efficient part of the organisation as quickly as possible.

For example, a person appointed to a job would want answers to questions such as:

- to whom should I report on the first day?
- where do I take documents such as income tax forms?
- when and where are tea- and lunch-breaks taken?
- where are the toilets?
- whom do I ask for help if I am not sure what to do?
- how do the switchboard, computer and other items of equipment work?
- what authority do I have over other staff, for example can I allow them time off or does someone else do this?

Most of these are very simple questions, and the answers may seem obvious to a person already working in the business. However, not knowing what to do can cause terrible embarrassment to a new employee and may push him or her into leaving very quickly.

Training

The scope of training

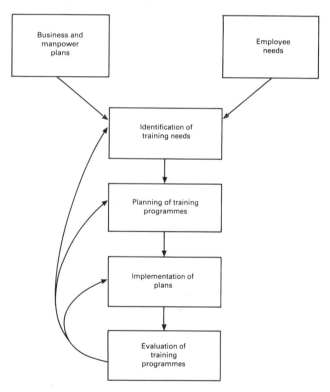

Figure 10.13 The training process

Employees often need training concerned with matters such as:

- the business's organisation work practices;
- use of tools and equipment;
- handling accounts and other records;
- dealing with customers and suppliers;

165

- company products and services;
- health and safety procedures;
- training after or in preparation for promotion.

Development

Development of employees can be distinguished from training by defining it as being concerned with employees' future rather than their present needs. For example an employee might be sent on a course on interviewing of job applicants even though he or she currently has no responsibility for promotion. The aim is to ensure that he or she has the necessary skills when promoted. Development activities also often focus on more general abilities such as teamwork and problem-solving skills.

Types of training

There are two basic types of training:

1. *On-the-job*, with the worker learning as he or she goes along from an experienced fellow-worker, supervisor or trainer. Learning by working alongside a more experienced worker is often referred to as 'sitting by Nellie'.

   On-the-job training may also involve more formal methods such as job instruction, undertaking special projects, using work manuals or specialised computer programs (for example aircraft simulators). Professional employees and trainee managers may be attached to a *mentor*, a senior employee several grades above who may be able to give advice and assistance, particularly on career development.

   The advantages of on-the-job training are:

   - learning can be put into practice immediately;
   - the person teaching may know the job better than a full-time trainer, who cannot be expected to have full up-to-date knowledge of all the jobs involved;
   - trainees often see more relevance to training which occurs in the workplace.

   The disadvantages of on-the-job training are:

   - It is often haphazard. Trainees are simply expected to absorb the job by doing it, and may not be thoroughly or correctly taught techniques and procedures. They may be given repetitive, boring or unpleasant jobs that other workers wish to avoid.

- Many workers are not particularly good at teaching their skills. They may have bad work habits or a narrow approach to the job.
- The trainee's interests may be ignored, especially when workers are under pressure. Trainees may be taken away from training to fill in for other workers or to cope with sudden rushes.
- Untrained workers may make expensive mistakes or be a safety hazard.

2. *Off-the-job* training involves work at home or courses at company training centres, outside training organisations and colleges. Off-the-job training methods include;

   - *Lectures and demonstrations*, which are usually designed to give information or instruction. A large number of trainees can be reached quickly and cheaply. However the value of lectures depends heavily upon the trainer and there is little trainee involvement or practical experience.
   - *Experiential learning* methods such as *simulations*, *role-plays* and *business games* try to involve trainees in practical problems usually based upon those that they will face at work.
   - *Self-study* allows a trainee to work at his or her own pace, using specially designed materials such as manuals, interactive video or computer programs.
   - *External courses* may be put on by colleges or training organisations and range from half-days to two or three years for advanced courses. Many companies use *day release*, with employees being sent to college for one or two days per week. *Block release* involves being away for longer periods such as a few weeks or months.
   - *Secondment* involves an employee being taken away from his or her normal job to undertake a specific project. This may be to another department, plant or company within the group. Alternatively, secondment may be to outside agencies such as community organisations, charities and professional associations. Secondment is expensive, but allows the employee to widen his or her experience.

   The advantages of off-the-job training are:

   - specialist instructors can be used, often with knowledge or experience not available within the company;
   - training can be more concentrated;
   - it is easier to give theoretical instruction;

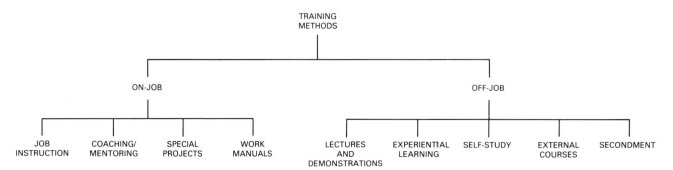

Figure 10.14 Training methods

- there may be a less stressful atmosphere than can be achieved while training on the job.

The disadvantages of off-the-job training are:

- it can be remote from the practicalities of the job – trainees may fail to see the link between the training and their work;
- the training situation may be artificial and too different from that of the workplace;
- specialist trainers may have limited knowledge of current techniques and work practices;
- it is usually more expensive than on-the-job training;
- it takes employees away from 'productive' activity.

Performance Appraisal

Appraisal can be narrowly defined as the process of formally evaluating the performance of an individual in his or her job. This might however be regarded simply as assessment. A broader definition of performance appraisal would include features such as self-appraisal by the employee and the setting of objectives and plans for the future.

The aim of appraisal is to motivate employees to perform better because they are involved in assessing and improving their own progress. Appraisal schemes also attempt to quantify the skills needed for the job and set identifiable goals for the employee to aim at (see *Management by objectives* in Chapter 1).

Most appraisal schemes are based on the completion of an appraisal form. There is usually space for comments by the employee and his or her immediate superior. This is followed by the appraisal interview which includes discussion of past and present performance, employee strengths and weaknesses, future plans for training and career opportunities, and objectives and targets for the next appraisal period (usually a year).

Despite its potential advantages, performance appraisal often fails to meet its objectives for several reasons:

- lack of commitment and understanding of the purpose

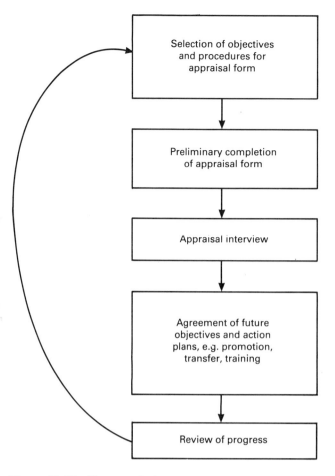

Figure 10.15 The appraisal process

by managers and staff, who may feel that appraisal is a waste of time;
- defensive reactions and mistrust by employees;
- embarrassment or conflict between managers and their subordinates;
- failure to follow up agreements made during the appraisal process.

Worked Examples

Short-answer questions

10.1 In many companies the introduction of new technology may result in a shortage of specialist skills. Give **three** examples of the ways in which the company may cope with this problem.

(AEB)

Answer For example train existing workers, recruit new employees, hire temporary staff as necessary.

10.2 List **two** reasons why an organisation might consider staff training to be important.

(AEB)

Answer For example higher productivity, safety, legal requirements, motivation, new products or processes, long-term development of skills, to cope with change.

10.3 Give **three** possible consequences of unsatisfactory recruitment procedures in a business enterprise.

(AEB)

Answer For example too few applicants, failure to fill vacancies, unsuitable applicants, need to re-advertise vacancies, recruitment more expensive, high absenteeism, high labour turnover, poor-quality workforce, low-quality products, low productivity, high training costs, low morale, employee disputes.

Data-response questions

10.4 Kingston Manufacturers Ltd. has recently appointed a Personnel Manager. This is the first appointment of its kind and is due to an expansion in the workforce at all levels.

One of the first duties of the new Personnel Manager is to consider payment systems for the workforce. At present most employees, whether on the shopfloor or in the offices are paid by time rates (that is, so much per hour), although the rate varies according to the nature of the job. In addition, to remove anomalies, the Personnel Manager is considering the use of Job Evaluation.

(a) What is Job Evaluation? *(2 marks)*
(b) Explain **two** purposes of Job Evaluation. *(4 marks)*
(c) State the factors that you would take into account when evaluating any job known to you. *(6 marks)*
(d) Suggest **three** alternative payment systems that might be introduced. For **each**, suggest **one** advantage and **one** disadvantage. *(6 marks)*
(e) What problems might be encountered in introducing **any** new payment system? *(7 marks)*

Answer (a) Systematic comparison of jobs to establish a rank order for purpose of establishing relative payment levels. Based on skills/training/personal qualities needed for job.

(b) For example:

- provides objective basis for comparing different jobs;
- setting 'fair' rates of pay;
- reduce number of different rates of pay;
- justifying existing wage differentials;
- establishing rates for new or changed jobs.

(c) For example skill level, training, education required, functions of job, such as simple/complex, frequency with which functions are performed, danger, risk, conditions of work, level of concentration, supervisory duties, extent of decision-making.

(d) For example:

piece-rates

- paid according to output;
- advantages; for example based on individual skill/speed, motivation of extra wages;
- disadvantages, for example difficulty of measuring output, work may be rushed, stress on employees.

measured day-work

- employee expected to reach certain output;
- advantages for example gives target to achieve;
- disadvantages, for example target may be less than employee capable of, therefore may reduce output.

profit-sharing

- all employees get % of profits at end of accounting period, on top of basic pay;
- advantage – employees have monetary interest in firm's profitability;
- disadvantages – generally low % of profits, employees have little control over profits.

(e) For example:

- some workers gain while others lose;
- people resent change;
- administrative problems, such as more inspection, more complex wage calculations.

10.5 A company has recently moved from its traditional site in the centre of a town to a newly opened industrial estate on the outskirts of the town. Following the move there has been a sudden increase in the level of labour turnover.

(a) As personnel manager, write a report to the Managing Director, using a suitable format to cover the following areas. *(6 marks)*
   (i) How labour turnover may be calculated. *(2 marks)*
   (ii) Why the company should be concerned about the recent increase in labour turnover. *(7 marks)*
   (iii) Possible reasons for the increase. *(6 marks)*
(b) What steps would you, as personnel manager, need to take to establish clearly the nature of the problem? *(6 marks)*

Answer **(a)** (i)

$$\text{Labour turnover} = \frac{\text{No. of leavers per time period}}{\text{Average no. employed in time period}}$$

(ii) For example:

- cost of recruitment and induction;
- cost of training;
- loss of essential skills/experience;
- disruption to production;
- effect on morale of remaining employees;
- may damage firm's reputation.

(iii) For example:

- transport cost/accessibility;
- difficulties with family arrangements, such as childcare;
- lack of facilities such as shops/cafés;
- may be loss of status by firm.

(b) Establish reasons why people are leaving, for example by 'exit interviews' with leavers, informal enquiries, and meeting with trade unions or other worker representatives, and also check competitors' wages and current recruiting policy, for example are staff being 'poached'?

Essay questions

10.6 Over a period of two years the workforce of a single plant manufacturing business increased from 500 to 2000.

Outline the possible organisational problems presented to management as a result of this growth. Comment briefly on the ways in which these problems may be avoided.

(AEB)

Answer (i) Outline potential problems of such rapid growth, for example:

- more administrative and supervisory costs;
- higher overheads, such as for premises;
- longer chains of command and wider spans of control;
- risk of communication becoming more difficult/formal/slower;
- co-ordination is more difficult;
- larger plants often have higher absenteeism/labour turnover/more industrial action;
- may be difficult to find good-quality recruits in sufficient numbers to cope with growth;
- existing workforce may resent newcomers/larger size of plant;
- workers may want better pay and conditions as their share of increased profits/value of business.

(ii) Explain that some problems are unavoidable and outline possible policies to avoid those that may be preventable, for example participative management, consultation, incentive schemes, internal promotion, profit-sharing, employee share-ownership schemes, senior management should stay accessible to workers and be seen around the plant.

Self-test Questions

Short-answer questions

10.7 Give **three** factors that management might take into consideration when estimating their manpower needs for the coming year.

(AEB)

10.8 List **two** sources of recruitment a firm might use when attempting to fill a vacancy.

(AEB)

10.9 Distinguish between a 'job description' and a 'job specification'.

(AEB)

10.10 Give **two** advantages and **two** disadvantages of appointing senior management from outside the company rather than promoting from within.

(AEB)

10.11 The managing director of an engineering company has asked you as personnel officer to prepare a report in suitable format *(6 marks)* on the training of craft and technician apprentices with particular reference to the following aspects:

(i) the general gains that might be expected from training; *(8 marks)*
(ii) how and where such training should be implemented; *(8 marks)*
(iii) what items of cost need to be included in the company's training budget. *(8 marks)*

(AEB)

10.12 The following information is taken from the Chairman's statement in *W. H. Smith Annual Report 1986*. Study the information and answer the questions below.

Customer Service

I have written before about the importance of service to customers and this includes not only the approach of our staff but the selection of products and the environment provided by the shop itself. For years we have had many own brand and exclusive goods in W. H. Smith shops, and these ranges are being increased and improved, particularly in the selection of our own books. Do It All introduced own brand goods last year and this is just the beginning of an extensive programme. In all this, good product and packaging design is a key factor. The design of our shops is equally important and we have commissioned new concepts for W. H. Smith, Do It All and the specialist book chain. The first of each of these will be opened this autumn and I believe will prove to be popular and commercially sound and therefore the blueprint for each chain over the next few years.

Training

Good training for all our staff is a fundamental ingredient of success and our commitment to it continues and grows. A well-trained staff is our strongest resource.

The Future

Each business in W. H. Smith – whether retail, wholesale or distribution – caters ultimately to the constructive use of spare time and so the Company is especially well positioned for growth.

Analysis of staff

The average number of persons employed by the Group during the 52 weeks ended 31st May 1986 analysed by activity and by hours worked:

	Total	Male	Female
Retailing (Books, stationery, news, recorded music, etc.)	18 522	4 871	13 651
Do it yourself	2 295	1 119	1 176
Wholesaling	4 000	2 868	1 132
Others	893	454	439
	[Europe, Canada, USA and UK]		
Full time	13 294	6 714	6 580
8–29 hrs per week	6 824	1 080	5 744
Less than 8 hrs per week	1 882	561	1 321
	[UK only]		

(a) Make **three** general observations that can be drawn from the data in the table. *(3 marks)*
(b) Explain the term 'own brand' goods and give a reason for their use. *(3 marks)*
(c) State and explain **three** areas in which W. H. Smith considers design to be important. *(6 marks)*
(d) 'A well-trained staff is our strongest resource.'
  (i) Explain why this statement is true for an organisation like W. H. Smith. *(4 marks)*
  (ii) Comment on the knowledge and skills which might be required by a sales assistant in a firm like W. H. Smith. *(4 marks)*

10.13 'Management training is little more than a reward or a mark of approval. It is not a cost-effective contribution to a company's efficiency.' Critically examine this view.

(AEB)

10.14 The head of a school/college will be interviewing a short-list of three candidates for the post of A-level business studies teacher. Candidate A is professionally well qualified, has worked in industry but has no teaching experience. Candidate B is moderately qualified and has two years' successful teaching experience. Candidate C has just qualified as a teacher of business studies. Suggest factors which might influence the head's choice and consider:

(a) how the head might brief himself for the interviews;
(b) the questions he might ask each candidate;
(c) the information he might seek before making his decision. *(25 marks)*

(UCLES)

10.15 Analyse the ways in which selection procedures may contribute to the success of a business enterprise.

(AEB)

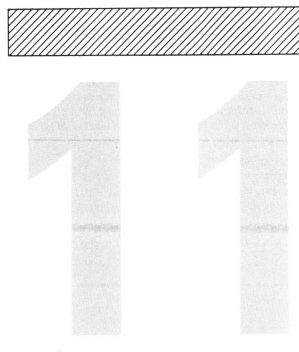

INDUSTRIAL RELATIONS

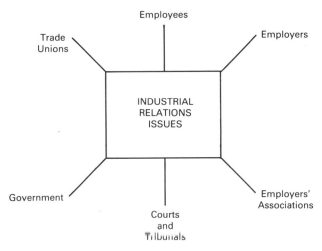

Figure 11.1 Organisations involved in industrial relations

What is Industrial Relations?

Industrial relations (sometimes referred to as *employee relations*) is a general term for the processes by which the managers of an organisation discuss pay and working conditions collectively with its workers and their representatives.

Issues which might be included under this heading include:

- pay and fringe benefits;
- hours of work and holidays;
- health and safety;
- redundancy and dismissal;
- training and promotion of workers;
- disciplinary and grievance procedures.

Industrial relations is sometimes thought of as being concerned with negotiations with trade unions, but in many cases this may not be true. More than half of all workers are non-union members, but they are still concerned with matters such as those described above.

Industrial relations is important to the success of a business. Poor industrial relations can lead to problems such as:

- low productivity;
- interruptions to production such as strikes and other forms of industrial disputes;
- poor quality of goods and services;
- disheartening of employees;
- loss of customers;
- discouragement of potential customers and employees.

For management, good industrial relations is necessary to:

- preserve harmony with the workforce;
- control employee costs;
- avoid disruption of production;
- foster high productivity and quality;
- enable the organisation to cope with change.

Industrial relations is often seen in terms of conflict between employers and employees, but trade unions and

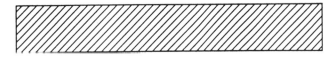

other employee representatives can also gain from stability. Increased productivity, quality and profitability for the business also help to improve job security and wages. Industrial action usually results in workers losing more money than they gain from a settlement.

Trade Unions and Employers' Associations

Trade unions

A trade union is a collection of workers who agree to negotiate with employers as a group of employees rather than individually. This process is called *collective bargaining*. The size of trade unions varies from the Sheffield Wool Shearers Union (17 members) to the Transport & General Workers Union (TGWU) with over a million.

As the list in the previous section shows, trade unions are not concerned just with strikes and negotiating wage rises, but negotiations on a wide variety of issues. Many firms actually encourage union participation because of the advantages it can bring (see Question **11.3**).

Organisation of trade unions

The organisational structure of a typical trade union is illustrated in Figure 11.2.

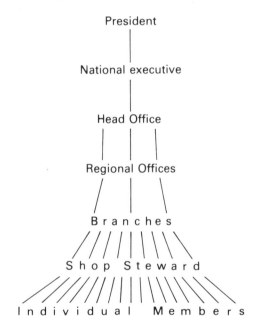

Figure 11.2 Organisation of a typical trade union

Members pay a subscription to the union in return for its services. If a workplace has a *closed shop* agreement, all workers must belong to a particular union. Many firms now have *single-union* agreements, where the firm recognises and negotiates with one particular union. This helps to avoid arguments between unions such as *demarcation disputes*, where unions disagree about whose members should be employed within particular jobs.

Shop stewards are the union's representatives at the

individual workplace. They are elected by the members, and are in daily contact with their fellow workers. The shop steward does not work full-time for the union, but may be given time off from his or her work to carry out union duties. In large factories or offices, there may be several shop stewards who will in turn elect a *convenor*.

The *branch* is usually based upon a local area, although it may consist of members from a single firm. The branch may have a full-time official employed by the union.

Larger unions often have *regional offices* covering a number of branches. For example the TGWU has 11 regions covering the whole of the UK.

The *Head Office* contains the most senior officials, and usually employs specialists such as solicitors and accountants to provide a service to branches.

The *National Executive* is an elected committee, typically of around 40 members representing different areas. Executive members are not usually paid officials of the union.

The *President* or *General Secretary* is responsible for overall co-ordination of the union's activities. By law, senior officials must now be elected by ballot every 5 years.

Types of trade union

Unions are often divided into four types, as shown in Figure 11.3. However, the distinction between each type is not complete. Many unions have merged in recent years and united different types of workers. For example the AEU now has unskilled members.

Trades Union Congress (TUC)

Most unions belong to the Trades Union Congress (TUC), which campaigns on behalf of all workers, and is represented on Government bodies such as the Health and Safety Commission (HSC) and the Advisory, Conciliation and Arbitration Service (ACAS).

TUC policy is decided at the Annual Conference, which is attended by delegates from all unions. The TUC has no power over its member unions, although it is often asked to settle disputes between unions.

Employers' associations

Many industries have employers' associations which represent firms' interests. Like trade unions, employers' associations campaign for their members on issues concerned with industry and employment. For example the Engineering Employers Federation (EEF) negotiates agreements with trade unions, provides advice and assistance to its member firms and represents engineering interests to the Goverment, TUC and the media.

The largest employers' association is the Confederation of British Industry (CBI), which has over 250 000 members, responsible for employing over half of the UK workforce. Some of its activities are similar to those of the EEF, but it represents a wide range of industries. It has recently set up Task Forces to investigate issues relevant to industry such as inner-city development, industry–education links and vocational training. It also conducts research into trading conditions for industry and publishes the monthly *Industrial Trends Survey*.

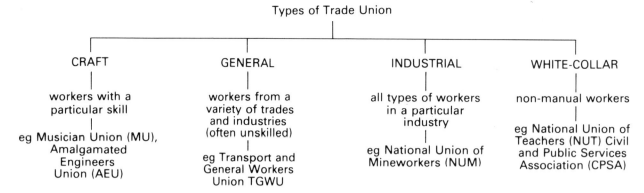

Figure 11.3 Types of trade union

Collective Bargaining

Stages in collective bargaining

Collective bargaining is the process of negotiation between employers and trade unions. Most cases are settled without the need for *industrial action* or *arbitration*, but as Figure 11.4 shows, industrial disputes may go through several stages before agreement is reached.

Types of industrial action

If employers and trade unions cannot reach agreement by talking, either may use industrial action to try to force better terms. Union action may be *official*, which means that the union's full-time officers agree that it should be taken. Sometimes, however, members may take *unofficial* action against their union's advice.

Under the terms of various Acts of Parliament passed during the 1980s, most industrial action now has to be approved by members in a secret ballot. If this is not done, the employer can sue the union for damages caused by the action. In extreme cases a court may *sequestrate* the union's assets, that is hand over financial control of the union to an independent person until it agrees to call off industrial action.

Strikes are the most serious form of union action, with workers refusing to work at all. Members may *picket* their employer's premises by asking fellow workers, customers and suppliers not to go in or out of the workplace.

However, picketing another firm's premises is called *secondary action* and is illegal. Some firms have *no-strike agreements* which prohibit industrial action until certain procedures such as *binding arbitration* have been followed.

Overtime bans are common in certain industries such as transport, postal services and coal-mining, which rely heavily upon overtime to maintain production. By working only the basic hours, workers can create shortages of the good or service.

Sit-ins involve the workers occupying the employer's premises and preventing goods and other items going in or out. They are often used when a firm is planning to close a particular factory or office.

Employer's action may include sacking or suspending workers who are taking industrial action. This is legal as long as all of the workers involved are sacked. Another employer's weapon is a *lock-out* with workers being told to stay at home.

Conciliation, mediation and arbitration

If employers and unions cannot agree, they may ask an independent person or body to *conciliate*, *mediate* or *arbitrate* in the dispute. These three functions are interlinked and are often confused.

Conciliation uses a third party, such as an ACAS or LRA official (see below), to encourage the two parties to reach agreement. The basic rationale is that if the two sides keep talking they will eventually come to an agreement without the need for industrial action. The conciliator does not actually suggest a particular compromise.

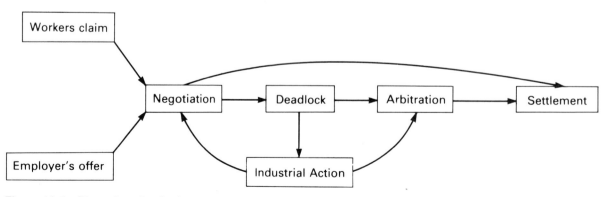

Figure 11.4 Stages in collective bargaining

Mediation involves the third party proposing solutions to problems, which are then considered by the employer and employee representatives.

Arbitration is defined by ACAS as

"... the parties jointly ask a third party to make an award which they undertake to accept"

This definition is often referred to as *binding arbitration*. In many other cases, particularly in public-sector negotiations, one or more parties may refuse to accept the result.

An increasingly common form of binding arbitration is *pendulum arbitration*. The arbitrators cannot simply 'split the difference' between offer and claim, but must decide for one or the other. This is designed to prevent unrealistically low offers by employers and over-ambitious claims by unions.

The main arbitrating agencies in the UK are the Advisory, Conciliation and Arbitration Service (ACAS) in England, Scotland and Wales, and the Labour Relations Agency (LRA) in Northern Ireland. These consist of independent members and representatives of employers and trade unions.

Worked Examples

Short-answer questions

11.1 List three ways in which a government may attempt to influence collective bargaining.

Answer For example:

- legislation;
- as an employer, for example by restricting public sector wage rises;
- negotiating directly with the CBI or the TUC;
- incomes policies;
- exhortation or persuasion, such as tax incentives for profit-related pay;
- through Government agencies such as ACAS, HSC and EOC.

11.2 Define the term 'closed shop'.

Answer Employees must be a member of a particular trade union (or one of a small number) in order to work at a particular job. *Note that* 'all workers must be trade union members' is insufficient, because for example, membership of the National Union of Teachers would not allow a worker to enter a printers' closed shop.

Data-response questions

11.3 Read the article and answer the questions which follow.

UK now has 'more flexible workforce'

The growing emphasis on labour flexibility throughout UK industry, noted by the Advisory, Conciliation and Arbitration Service (ACAS), is again the subject of attention in a newly published ACAS Survey. "Britain," it says, "is developing a more flexible workforce to meet the competitive challenges of the late 1980s and beyond."

If shows that greater use is being made of part-time and temporary employees; patterns of work are changing; increasing flexibility is taking place among skills and crafts, and in payments systems which encourage the acquisition of new skills.

The survey also suggests that many kinds of flexible working practices are becoming widespread, especially in larger organisations, and some forms of flexibility previously associated with the service sector are now being widely adopted in manufacturing industries.

More than one-quarter of the managements surveyed had succeeded in introducing one or more kinds of flexibility in crafts and skills during recent years. One-third had relaxed demarcations to enable production workers to undertake routine maintenance tasks. More than 25 per cent had 'eased' demarcations between craftsmen and manual, technical and clerical skills.

Considerable change was also evident in hours of work. More than one-quarter of respondents had introduced shift working over the previous three years, and 20 per cent planned to increase use of it in the future.

Moves toward more flexible payments systems were also revealed, more than one-fifth of respondents having introduced schemes during the past three years which rewarded the acquisition of new skills.

The survey shows that respondents in manufacturing – hardest hit by the recession – had introduced flexibility primarily to reduce labour costs, to meet fluctuations in demand, and to increase competitiveness.

ACAS warns, however, that the introduction of flexible working practices can mean associated high labour turnover, absenteeism and lack of commitment. Employers should therefore ensure their communications are effective, care is taken with recruitment and selection, and proper induction procedures are in operation. An increase in flexibility also heightens the need for employers to provide adequate retraining facilities.

Source: *Management News*, November 1988

(a) Identify **four** examples of labour flexibility. *(4 marks)*

(b) Comment on ways in which trade unions might respond to management efforts to introduce flexible working. *(10 marks)*

(c) Discuss **two** advantages to the firm of introducing increased labour flexibility. *(6 marks)*

Answer (a) For example:

- more part-time and temporary employees;
- workers change jobs/less demarcation;
- new payment systems, such as bonuses and merit pay;
- changes in working hours, such as flexi-time;
- changes in places of work.

(b) Benefits are, for example:

- more variety of jobs;
- better training;
- learn new skills;
- more valuable in labour market;
- working hours more convenient, such as for parents, commuters, etc.;
- may enjoy jobs more;
- firm more efficient, therefore more secure jobs.

Drawbacks are, for example:

- some workers may lose jobs;
- skills become devalued/outdated;
- reduced legal rights and benefits, such as for part-time and temporary staff;
- reduced trade union power;
- may cause discontent/industrial action.

(c) For example:

- lower labour costs;
- can adjust supply of labour to meet fluctuations in demand, such as seasonal/casual work;
- reduces union power;
- workers more flexible, therefore can switch jobs to cover absences;
- workers more skilled and motivated, therefore higher productivity;
- may be easier to recruit if conditions of work attractive;
- can use machinery premises continuously if necessary.

Essay questions **11.4** Define the term 'free collective bargaining'. Evaluate the advantages and disadvantages of this system to a manufacturing company.

(AEB)

Answer Definition: An employer agrees to negotiate with employees as a group (for example through a trade union) rather than individually.
Advantages are, for example:

- makes consultation and negotiation easier;
- improves communications to and from employees;
- may make changes in working practices easier;
- unions have specialist knowledge and personnel, such as for health and safety;
- may improve worker morale and therefore productivity.

Disadvantages are, for example:

- increased pressure from workforce;
- may lead to higher wages and other costs;
- decisions may be slower/more difficult because of need to consult unions;
- inter-union disputes may occur;
- industrial action more likely;
- unions may resist or block change, for example by restrictive labour practices;
- may have to share information with unions.

11.5 'The main obstacle to change in manufacturing industry in the UK is still multi-unionism, whereby each group of workers is represented by different Trades Unions'. Discuss.

(UCLES)

Answer   (i) Explain the arguments behind the statement, for example:

- difficult and slow to negotiate with different unions – agreements may be accepted by one but not by others;
- often leads to inter-union disputes, for example about demarcation or in order to 'leapfrog' other unions' wage agreements;
- pay scales are more complicated;
- unions often tied to old-fashioned working practices and divisions between skills, therefore difficult to introduce flexible working (see Worked example **11.3**);
- because of union resistance, many firms are unwilling to invest in new equipment for fear of losing their investment.

Because of such problems, some firms have made *single-union agreement* meaning that the employer will recognise only one union for negotiation within a department salary grade or plant. These agreements are usually linked with other arrangements such as *no-strike agreements* and *pendulum arbitration*. No-strike agreements prohibit industrial action until certain procedures such as *binding arbitration* have been followed.

(ii) Explain possible arguments against the statement, for example:

- responsibility for failing to invest rests with management;
- unions have had to protect members' interests;
- managements have been reluctant to allow participation by workers, which encourages a negative attitude.

Self-test Questions

Short-answer questions

11.6   Give **two** sanctions used by trade unions against employers.

11.7   State the main functions of ACAS.

11.8   State **three** reasons in support of employee participation in the decisions of a business enterprise.

(AEB)

11.9   List **three** ways in which a government may attempt to influence collective bargaining.

(AEB)

Data-response question

11.10   A proposed reorganisation of production at your factory would result in the redundancy of 400 employees. As personnel officer, prepare a report in suitable form for the Board of Directors, indicating with brief explanations:

(i)   **four** possible effects of redundancy on the company;
(ii) **four** principles upon which the scheme should be based to preserve good industrial relations;
(iii) any Acts of Parliament known to you which contain provisions relating to redundancy.

(AEB)

Essay questions

11.11   Outline and evaluate the factors which will determine the success of a trade union in negotiating with an employer.

(AEB)

11.12   To what extent have such factors as growing industrial democracy, improved communications and protective legislation changed the role of trade unions in today's business world?

(AEB)

11.13   Differentiate between the role of a foreman and that of a shop steward. Would the qualities required for the effective performance of each role differ significantly?

(UCLES)

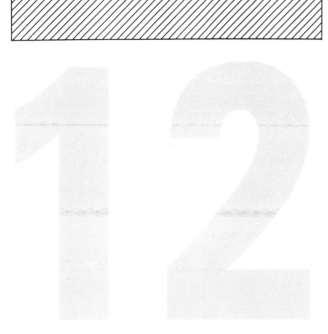

THE ECONOMIC FRAMEWORK

Scarcity and Choice

Any economic system has to solve the problem of *scarcity* of resources. This means that all resources such as land, raw materials, labour and machinery are limited in supply.

Resources are scarce because people have unlimited wants for goods and services. There are not enough resources to satisfy all of these wants.

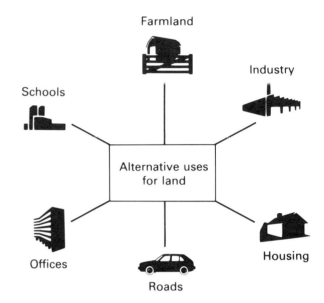

Figure 12.1 Alternative uses of land

For example, a plot of land might be used for any one of a number of purposes, as illustrated in Figure 12.1. However, using it for one of these purposes prevents its use for the others. A decision has to be made about which of the alternative choices is 'best'.

The use which is given up when decisions are made about allocating resources is the *opportunity cost*. For example if a piece of land is used for building a school, the opportunity cost is the alternative use to which it could have been put, such as for offices.

The concept of opportunity cost can be applied to decisions made by a business such as whether to invest in a new factory or take over another firm. Whatever decision is made, the opportunity cost is the next best alternative for which the resources such as capital and management time could have been used.

Any economy, however it is governed, has to make such decisions about how resources are to be used. There are three basic decisions to be made:

1. *What is to be produced?* For example should there be more soldiers and fewer firemen, should houses be built upon farmland in south-east England?
2. *How is it to be produced?* For example should electricity be produced by nuclear rather than coal-fired power stations, should machines be used instead of labour in a particular manufacturing process?
3. *Who gets the goods and services produced?* For example should people have to pay for medical care or be given it by the Government?

Depending upon the particular economy, decisions about production and distribution of goods and services may

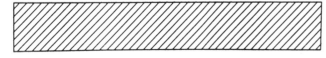

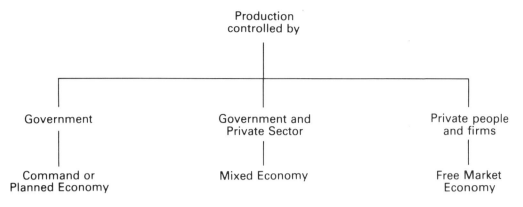

Figure 12.2 Three types of economy

be made by private individuals, the Government, or a combination of the two.

Economies are often divided into three types, which vary according to who makes these decisions. Figure 12.2 illustrates the three types.

This division should only be regarded as a very crude classification, since all economies are in fact mixed economies, with decisions made by both the Government and private individuals or firms. Even in the most rigid communist economies, some choice was left to people about where to work and what to buy. Similarly, all economies have at least some Government intervention.

The Free Market Economy

Free enterprise

In a *free market economy*, decisions about production are made by private individuals and firms. The Government interferes as little as possible in business affairs. Its main purpose is to provide only those services such as defence and the legal structure which are necessary to protect the country's citizens.

The basic principle of the free-market economy is that production is based upon *free enterprise*. Businesses are continually attempting to make as much profit as possible. They can only achieve this by producing goods and services that their customers want, and by producing as cheaply and efficiently as possible.

The role of prices

Prices are the mechanism by which a free-market system works. The price of a good or service depends upon its *demand* (the amount that consumers wish to buy) and its *supply* (the amount that producers are willing to sell). Demand and supply are constantly changing, and this affects prices and amounts produced. This relationship was explained in Chapter 7.

In a free-market economy, the consumer decides what is to be produced by buying goods and services. Businesses which provide goods and services that the consumer wants will be profitable. Those which do not will make losses and eventually go out of business.

Advantages of free market economies

1. Producers have to satisfy the consumer in order to make a profit. The consumer thus has the power to decide what will be produced. This is called *consumer sovereignty*.
2. Free enterprise encourages efficient production because firms must keep their costs low and produce good-quality goods and services. (This is sometimes referred to as the *profit incentive*.)
3. There is as little Government intervention as possible in the economy, which leads to more freedom for people to make their own decisions.

Disadvantages of free market economies

1. The demand for products depends upon people's ability to pay for them. Poorer people may not be able to afford essential goods and services. Resources may be used to produce luxuries for the rich.
2. Some *public goods* such as defence and police services would not be produced.
3. *Merit goods* such as education and health services might not be available to all, which can be harmful to the economy and society.
4. *Monopolies* may occur which are often bad for consumers.
5. Private producers will ignore the bad effects or *external costs* of their activities, such as pollution, if they are allowed complete freedom. They may also fail to take into account any *external benefits* of their activities.

The Planned Economy

Central planning

A *planned* or *command* economy is one where decisions about production are taken by the Government. Planned economies are generally run by Communist Governments, which believe in state control of the economy in order to organise production for everybody's benefit rather than for private profit. The best-known example was the Soviet Union until 1990.

Planning a modern economy is a very complex process. The Government sets out plans for the economy, usually for several years ahead. These plans set prices, wages and targets for production of different goods and services.

To take a simple example, suppose the Government wants to produce a particular number of machines over the next few years. In order to do this it will have to ensure that sufficient labour, steel, machinery and equipment are available to achieve this production. This involves issuing orders for production of steel, coal, machine components and so on.

Taking this a stage further, the coal industry will have to plan for extra production, which will require inputs of labour, machinery and other resources. Every decision about what to produce in turn means that other adjustments have to be made by the central planners. This is a massive task, too big for even the most sophisticated computer.

Advantages of planned economies

1. The Government can plan for the production of essential goods and services. *Public goods* and *merit goods* should be produced in sufficient quantities.
2. Central planners can take into account external costs and benefits which might be ignored by private producers.
3. The Government can aim to make the distribution of income more equal. In practice, however, there is little evidence that this greater equality occurs.

Disadvantages of planned economies

1. Planning a large economy is very complicated, and it is impossible to do without making mistakes. Changes in demand or production problems often lead to shortages and surpluses of basic goods.
2. A large and expensive bureaucracy is needed to make and carry through the Government's plans.
3. Because there is no private profit, there may be little incentive for people and firms to work hard or develop new products. Private farmers in the USSR have been far more productive than the state-owned farms.
4. If prices are fixed in advance, the advantages of the price system as a signal to producers are lost. Prices cannot change to reduce surpluses or cure shortages.

These problems have caused severe difficulties for planned economies such as the Soviet Union and China. During the 1980s, these countries have gradually loosened the Government's control of the economy to allow more private enterprise. In the Soviet Union, this change is called *perestroika* (meaning 'reconstruction').

The Mixed Economy

A *mixed economy* is one in which production is controlled by both the Government and private producers. A good example is the United Kingdom.

As explained above, all economies are mixed economies, since none is completely dominated by private or Government production, but the term is usually applied to countries where there is substantial production by both sectors.

In a mixed economy, production is largely undertaken by private producers, but the government also intervenes in the economy in various ways.

1. The *public sector* (central and local Government and nationalised industries) produces many goods and services, such as education and medical care.
2. The Government influences spending on particular goods and services through its taxation and spending policies, for example heavy taxes on alcohol and cigarettes, tax reliefs on mortgages.
3. The sale of many goods and services is restricted, for example guns are licensed, some products such as drugs or legal advice can only be provided by qualified people.
4. Through social services such as social security, health care and education, the Government attempts to eliminate poverty and guarantee a minimum standard of living to all of its citizens.
5. The Government regulates the economy in various ways, such as by influencing factors like interest rates, investment and the location of industry.
6. Workers are protected by various laws which set maximum hours of work, minimum wages for some jobs, health and safety procedures and workers' rights such as maternity leave and redundancy pay.
7. Consumers are protected by laws such as the Weights and Measures and Trades Descriptions Acts.

Specialisation and Exchange

Modern economies are based upon *specialisation*, with people producing one particular type of good or service, such as being a carpenter or typist.

Mass production, that is producing goods and services in large numbers, depends upon further specialisation, called *division of labour*.

Because people specialise, they do not produce all their daily wants. For example in Britain less than one in thirty workers is involved in producing food. Most people earn money by producing other goods and services and then buy their food.

The process by which people buy and sell products is called *exchange*. In primitive societies this was carried out through *barter*, the exchange of goods without using money.

Because people do not produce all of their own needs, they rely upon other people and firms as consumers and suppliers. This is called *interdependence*.

SPECIALISATION

(people concentrate on production of one good or service, so cannot produce all the products they need)

↓

EXCHANGE

(people buy and sell from each other, e.g. mechanic earns wages by repairing cars and spends money on food, housing, entertainment, etc.)

↓

INTERDEPENDENCE

(people rely on each other as producers and consumers)

Figure 12.3 Specialisation and exchange

External Costs and Benefits

All business activities create *benefits* and *costs*. *External benefits*, sometimes referred to as *social benefits*, are advantages such as employment and income which occur because of business activity. *External* or *social* costs are the problems caused by business such as pollution and traffic congestion.

For example building a new factory on farmland might create the following costs and benefits:

Benefits

- Jobs for workers in the factory.
- Higher income for the area because workers have more money to spend.
- Jobs in local shops and suppliers to the factory.
- Extra tax revenue for the Government.

Costs

- Spoiling of local residents' views.
- Pollution and traffic congestion.
- Loss of output from farmland.
- Lost sales to competitors making the same product.

It is very difficult to estimate the benefits and costs of business activity, especially when trying to forecast what will happen in the future.

For example there were many opposing arguments over the likely effects of building the Channel Tunnel. Jobs will be created for building workers, but may be lost by ferry companies and ports such as Dover and Ramsgate. Travel will be faster, but ships are also getting quicker and cheaper, and the tunnel may not save much time and money. It will be easier to transport goods abroad, but imports may also rise.

Detailed forecasts have been made about these effects, but no-one can predict exactly what will happen. It is also a matter of opinion whether faster travel is worth the sacrifice of ruining parts of the Kent countryside.

The case of the Channel Tunnel illustrates two important points about business activity:

1. It is often difficult to assess the results of any particular policy.
2. Sometimes there is no 'right answer' to business problems, and people will often have differing opinions about what should be done.

Industrial Structure

Production can be classified into *primary*, *secondary* and *tertiary* industries.

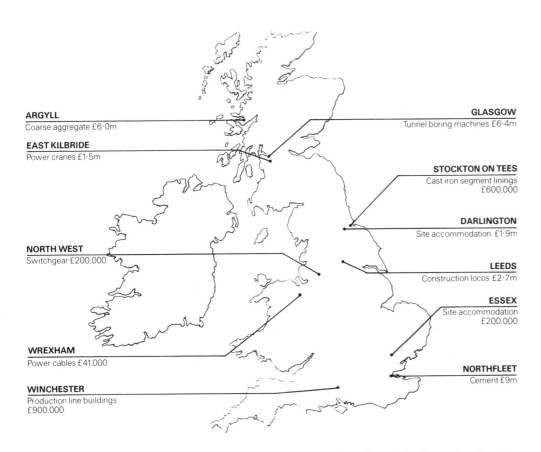

Figure 12.4 The map shows the areas of the country which benefited in the first orders from the construction of the Channel Tunnel

Primary industries

Primary or *extractive* industries are those which produce food and raw materials. They include agriculture, mining, forestry and fishing. Their products are sometimes referred to as *commodities*.

Secondary industries

Secondary or *manufacturing* industries produce goods such as televisions and cars. The construction trades (building and civil engineering) are also included in this category.

Capital or *producer* goods such as machinery, buildings and lorries are used to help produce other goods and services.

Consumer goods are bought for their own sake to satisfy a need. They may be *single-use* goods such as food and washing powder or *durables* such as televisions and furniture.

Tertiary industries

Tertiary industries produce services. These may be *commercial services*, such as banking and retailing, which are used to assist the manufacture and distribution of goods. These are sometimes called the *aids to trade*.

Other services such as education and entertainment are *direct services* which are enjoyed for their own sake. They are sometimes described as *quarternary* production.

The chain of production

Primary, secondary and tertiary industries are the stages in the *chain of production* which is the process by which raw materials reach the consumer as finished goods or services. For example, the chain of production for a wooden table would be as follows:

Primary – a tree is cut down and sawn into planks

↓

Secondary – the wood is shaped into a table

↓

Tertiary – the table is transported and sold by a retailer

Changes in the structure of industry

As an economy becomes more developed, production and employment tend to shift away from primary and secondary production towards the tertiary sector. In the 17th century, over 80% of British workers were employed in agriculture. During the Industrial Revolution in the 17th and 18th centuries, workers moved away from agriculture to manufacturing industry such as textiles.

In the twentieth century, there has been a further shift from manufacturing to service industries such as tourism and banking. Agriculture now provides only 3% of employment, and over 60% of workers are involved in producing services. This type of change is normal for an industrial economy and has also occurred in the USA and Western Europe.

182

The decline in manufacturing industry is called *deindustrialisation*, and has been caused by three factors:

1. New technology has reduced the need for labour in many industries such as car manufacture and coal-mining.
2. Demand for products such as tobacoo and cotton has fallen because of changing tastes and the development of substitutes.
3. Foreign competition has led to lower sales for British firms both in Britain and abroad. Britain now imports more manufactured goods than it exports. In 1950, exports of manufactures were three times as high as imports.

Government Economic Policy

Government spending and taxation

The Government spends about 40% of the national income, amounting to £185 billion in 1988–89.

In economic terms, many of the Government's services are described as *public goods* or *merit goods*.

Public goods such as defence or street-lighting are those which it would be difficult or impossible for private firms to produce at a profit. This is mainly because if they are provided, it is impossible to stop people getting the benefit of them.

For example if the armed forces prevent invasion of a country, all of the country's citizens benefit. If they were asked to pay voluntarily, some would refuse to do so because they are protected anyway. This is known as the *free-rider problem*. Since it would be impossible to make people pay, it would be hard for the firm to make a profit.

Because public goods such as defence and police services are regarded as essential, the Government produces them itself and makes people pay for them through taxes. People are said to become *forced-riders*.

Merit goods such as education and health services can be bought and sold privately, since people who refuse to pay could be excluded from using them. These are services which provide *external benefits* for people other than the person consuming them. For example education produces more productive and adaptable workers, which benefits society as a whole. Although merit goods can be supplied through the market, it is argued that the Government is justified in providing them because they benefit the whole economy.

The Government's revenue comes mainly from taxes. The major taxes used in the UK are as follows:

1. *Income tax* is paid upon wages and other income. In 1990–91 the basic rate was 25%, with a rate of 40% for higher earners. All taxpayers are allowed to earn a minimum amount before they start to pay income tax.
2. *National Insurance* is paid by workers and their employers as a proportion of their wages.
3. *Value Added Tax* (VAT) is the major spending tax in Britain. Certain goods and services such as food, housing and electricity are exempt from VAT. These are usually items upon which lower income groups spend the largest proportion of their income.
4. *Community charge*, better known as *poll tax*, replaced

Chancellor's arithmetic 1990/91 £ bn

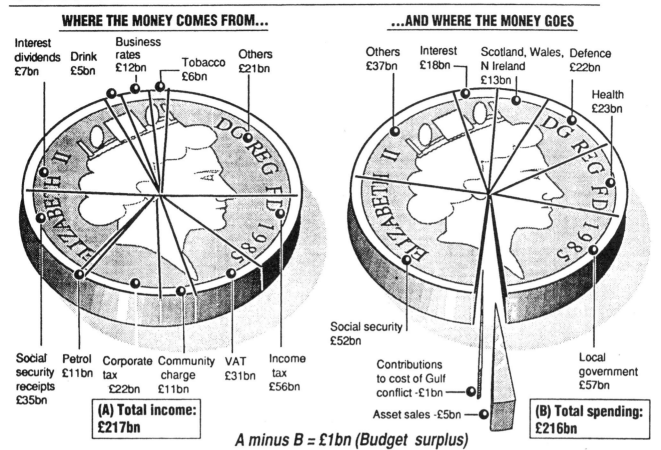

WHERE THE MONEY COMES FROM...

Interest dividends £7bn
Drink £5bn
Business rates £12bn
Tobacco £6bn
Others £21bn

Social security receipts £35bn
Petrol £11bn
Corporate tax £22bn
Community charge £11bn
VAT £31bn
Income tax £56bn

(A) Total income: £217bn

...AND WHERE THE MONEY GOES

Others £37bn
Interest £18bn
Scotland, Wales, N Ireland £13bn
Defence £22bn
Health £23bn

Social security £52bn
Contributions to cost of Gulf conflict -£1bn
Asset sales -£5bn
Local government £57bn

(B) Total spending: £216bn

A minus B = £1bn (Budget surplus)

Source: *The Guardian*, 20 March, 1991

Figure 12.5 Government income and expenditure 1990–91

rates as the major local tax on people in 1990. It is paid as a flat-rate charge by all area residents of an area, with some such as those on low incomes being allowed to pay a reduced rate. Typical examples of these groups include pensioners, the unemployed and students.

5. *Uniform Business Rate* is the tax paid to local authorities by the occupiers of commercial and industrial premises.
6. *Excise duties* are paid upon selected goods and services such as alcohol and tobacco.
7. *Corporation tax* is paid by firms as a percentage of their profits. There is a minimum amount of profit which has to be earned before the tax becomes payable.
8. *Capital taxes* include *capital gains tax*, paid on the profit made from property or other assets such as art or jewellery. *Inheritance tax* is paid when assets are transferred from one person to another.

The Government also obtains revenue from borrowing, interest and profits from past investments, and fees for the use of public services.

Government economic objectives

Although Governments have different political principles and priorities, they all share common objectives and can use similar methods to achieve them. The four basic objectives are as follows.

1. Full employment

In a modern economy it is impossible to achieve 0% unemployment since there will always be people who find it difficult to get jobs, or are 'between jobs'. This is called *frictional* unemployment. *Seasonal* unemployment may occur at certain times of year for workers in industries such as agriculture, tourism and building.

Unemployment may be *structural*, that is the result of the decline of one or more industries such as coal or steel (see the previous section for some causes of structural unemployment). *Cyclical* unemployment occurs when employment throughout the economy is declining because of falling demand (a *recession*). It is also referred to as *demand-deficient* unemployment. The lack of demand may lead to a vicious circle of rising unemployment as illustrated in Figure 12.7.

2. Elimination of inflation

Inflation is regarded by many economists and Government as the most serious economic problem, since it may be the cause of other economic difficulties such as loss of international competitiveness and rising unemployment (see Worked example **12.6**). Although a 2–3% annual rate of price increases might be regarded as 'normal' and not particularly harmful, any rate above this, especially when other countries have lower inflation, is likely to be damaging to the UK economy.

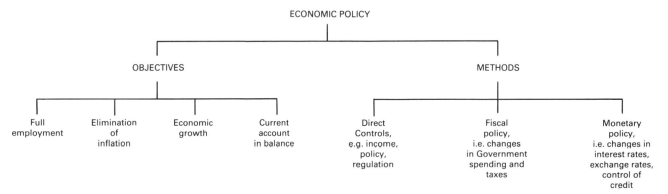

Figure 12.6 Government economic policy

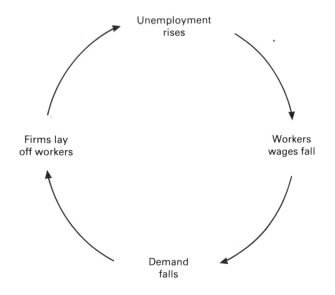

Figure 12.7 The 'vicious circle' of unemployment

The general level of inflation has varied significantly during the past 20 years. There are many arguments about the causes of inflation. These are usually divided into two basic causes; *cost–push* and *demand–pull*.

Cost–push refers to prices rising because of increases in firms' costs, such as wages, expenditure taxes and raw material costs. In order to protect their profit margins when costs rise, firms push their prices up. This may cause workers to demand higher wages, pushing up costs again and leading to a *wage–price spiral* as shown in Figure 12.8.

Demand–pull inflation occurs when demand for goods and services pulls their prices up. It is particularly likely when there is full employment of resources such as labour and land, forcing firms to bid-up wages, rents and other prices to obtain resources. This can be seen in the rapid increase in wages and property prices in south-east England during the late 1980s.

3. Economic growth

Economic growth is an increase in the real national income per head of a country, that is the total income of people, firms and other organisations after allowing for price and population changes. Growth is regarded by most

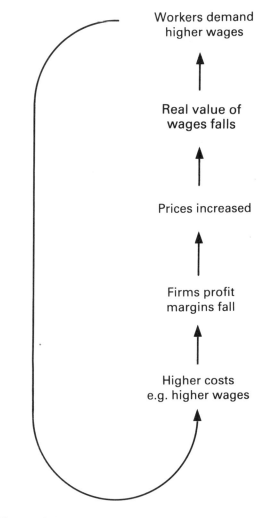

Figure 12.8 The wage–price spiral

economists and politicians as essential for a country's standard of living to improve.

However some people, notably the Green Party and pressure groups such as Friends of the Earth, argue that growth only leads to *external costs* such as pollution, and cannot be sustained indefinitely because it uses up scarce natural resources.

A simple model of how growth occurs can be seen in the circular flow model shown in Figure 12.9, based upon the

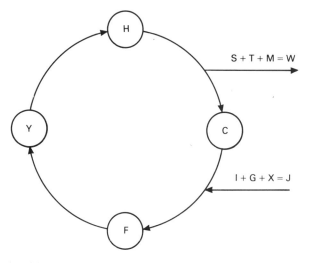

H = Households
F = Firms
C = Consumption (consumer spending on UK goods and services)
Y = National Income
S = Saving
T = Taxes on income (direct taxes)
M = Imports
W = Withdrawals (leakages)
I = Investment
G = Government spending
X = Exports
J = Injections

Figure 12.9 The circular flow of national income

writings of John Maynard Keynes in the 1930s. This is a very simple model in which there are two main groups, households (H) who spend money, and firms (F) who pay this money back to households as wages, rents dividends and other payments.

Households receive income (Y) and spend some of this (C) on British firms' goods and services. The remainder consists of *withdrawals* (W) from the circular flow (savings, taxes and spending on imports) and is not received by British firms. Other things being equal, withdrawals such as these will reduce firms' revenue and therefore also lead to a fall in national income (Y).

As well as consumer spending (C), British firms also receive revenue from *injections* (J) into the flow such as investment, Government spending and export sales. The combination of these four components of demand (C + I + G + X) represents *aggregate demand*, the total demand for goods and services in the economy. Other things being equal, injections will increase firms' revenue and therefore eventually cause a rise in national income.

Looking at the diagram, it can be seen that economic growth (an increase in national income Y) will occur if injections (J) are greater than withdrawals (W). Therefore, for example, if the Government spends more than it receives in taxes national income would rise, all other things being equal. Similarly, a surplus of exports over imports would also cause the economy to grow.

This model does however have some critics. For example it does not include the effects of inflation or changes in population and technology. It can also be argued that growth occurs because of the expertise and imagination of enterprises and the expectation that taking risks may lead to high profits.

4. Current account in balance

Over time, it is important for a country to earn enough from exports to pay for its imports. The analogy can be used of a household which must earn enough to pay for what it spends. Like a household, a country may temporarily finance a deficit by borrowing, but in the long-run its income must at least equal its spending.

Although the Balance of Payments is more complicated than this, continuing current deficits will lead to a declining economy as domestic producers are forced out of business by foreign competition.

There are many possible causes of a current account deficit, such as low productivity, high costs, poor design and marketing of British products and a high exchange rate making exports dearer and imports cheaper.

Methods of economic policy

There are many ways in which the Government can intervene in the economy. Although these often overlap and are used together, they can be classified under three headings.

1. Direct controls

Direct controls involve the Government making specific rules for people and firms to follow. For example the Government may limit wage rises (*incomes policy*) or control prices directly by making firms seek permission to raise them. The Government also regulates industry in many different ways, as outlined in Chapter 13.

Direct controls seem an easy way of controlling an economy, but are often criticised for being unfair or inflexible, thus causing problems. Incomes policy may make it difficult to offer high wages to attract recruits. For example the Government policy of holding down public sector wages during the 1980s led to shortages of teachers, civil servants and other workers.

Similarly, direct controls such as labour or consumer legislation may increase firms' costs, and price control may lower their profits if costs are rising, thus discouraging investment.

2. Fiscal policy

Fiscal policy involves changes in Government spending and taxation in order to influence the decisions of people and firms. It may be *deflationary* (intended to reduce aggregate demand) or *reflationary* (designed to increase aggregate demand). The way in which these policies work is summarised in Figure 12.10.

A deflationary fiscal policy involves increasing taxation and/or reducing Government spending. Increased taxes, particularly on income and profit, reduce the amount which people and firms can spend, therefore reducing aggregate demand. This should keep prices down and also reduces spending on imports. However, it also slows down economic growth and may lead to *demand-deficient unemployment* because of lower demand.

Reflationary fiscal policy involves reducing taxes and/or increasing Government spending. Demand by consumers, firms and the Government will rise, reducing unemployment and stimulating economic growth. However, the increased demand may cause prices to rise and also lead to higher spending on imports.

185

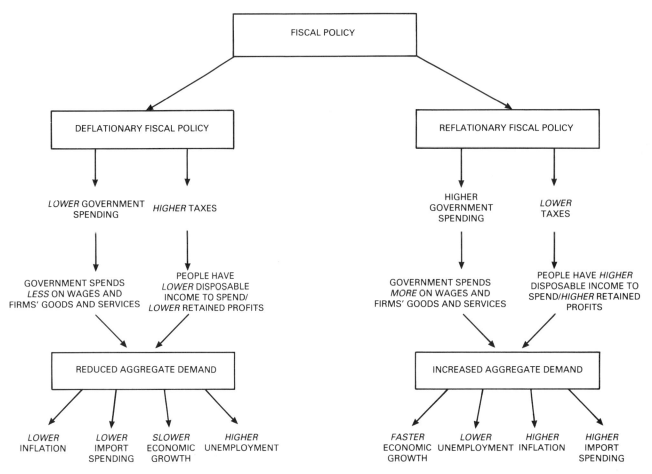

Figure 12.10 Fiscal policy

3. Monetary policy

Monetary policy involves changes in three main economic variables – interest rates, money supply and exchange rates.

Interest rates affect demand by both consumers and firms, since a high proportion of consumer spending and investment is paid for from borrowed money. The Government, as a large borrower and lender in the money markets, can have a large influence upon interest rates.

By increasing interest rates, the Government can reduce demand. However, this policy tends to hit some industries, such as building, cars and consumer durables, more than others. Conversely, lower interest rates will tend to increase demand.

The *money supply* consists mainly of deposits in banks, building societies and other financial institutions. It is largely dependent upon banks' lending, which generates spending and therefore more financial deposits. The Government may influence the volume of lending through various measures such as interest rate changes and direct controls on lending. For example during the 1960s and 1970s, people borrowing to buy cars had to find a minimum deposit and pay the loan back within a minimum period.

One group of economists, known as *monetarists*, believe that excessive growth in the money supply is the main cause of inflation and other economic problems caused by rising prices. They believe that inflation can be cured by restricting the growth of the money supply to the same rate as the growth of the economy.

Exchange rates are vital to exporters and importers, and can be influenced by the Government as explained in the 'Exchange rates' section below. A rise (or *appreciation*) in the exchange rate may be reduced to control inflation by making imports cheaper. However, cheaper imports combined with dearer exports may make UK firms uncompetitive and lead to current account deficits. The most notable case of this process occurred in the early 1980s, when a high exchange rate was largely responsible for a rise of 2 million in the number of unemployed.

The Government may also reduce (*depreciate* or *devalue*) the currency in order to reduce a current account deficit by making imports dearer and exports dearer. However, this may have the effect of increasing inflation, as a large proportion of UK spending is on imports.

International Trade

There are several advantages to allowing *free trade* between countries without restrictions on imports and exports such as *tariffs* and *quotas*.

1. *Countries can obtain goods and services which they cannot produce themselves.* Without international trade, British consumers would be unable to obtain goods and services such as tea, bananas, holidays in Majorca and Australian soap operas.
2. *Countries can specialise.* Because of international

trade, countries can obtain goods and services which they could produce themselves, but which other countries produce more cheaply and efficiently. For example Britain could produce more of its own food, but more land, labour and capital would have to be switched from other industries into agriculture. It is easier to import food and use British resources to produce other goods and services.

3. *International trade makes mass production possible.* International trade allows large-scale production, because firms can sell their products throughout the world. Many products such as aircraft, chemicals and oil are produced more cheaply because they are sold on a world-wide basis. All countries receive the benefits of higher world output and cheaper products because of *economies of scale.*

4. *Competition from abroad encourages efficiency.* If a British firm has foreign competition, it will have to be efficient if it is to stay in business. One of the aims of the European Community is to increase competition across Europe to encourage firms to produce cheaper and better quality products.

5. *Consumers benefit from international trade.* Because of the reasons described above, consumers get a wider choice of goods and services because of the efficiency created by international competition.

6. *Trade between countries leads to international peace and co-operation.* It is often argued that if countries trade with each other, they are less likely to go to war. One of the reasons for establishing the European Community was to encourage international co-operation in order to avoid another World War.

Protectionism

Protectionism means placing restrictions upon free trade between countries. It has two basic aims – to reduce imports and to increase exports.

Methods of protectionism

1. *Tariffs.* Tariffs are taxes upon imports, making them more expensive compared with domestic products. However, they will not reduce spending on imports if demand is price-inelastic.

2. *Quotas.* These are physical limits upon the amount of a good or service which can be imported, for example '*x* tons of tea' or '*x*% of cotton shirt sales'. They may be agreed between Governments and importers, in which case they are called *voluntary export restraints* (VERs). One example was that of Japanese car manufacturers agreeing to limit their sales to 11% of the UK market.

3. *Embargoes.* These are complete bans upon trade with particular countries (sometimes only for certain goods, such as scientific or military equipment). It is usually used for political reasons. Recent examples of UK restrictions were those imposed on trade with South Africa and Iraq.

4. *Subsidies.* Governments sometimes give money to domestic producers to help them compete against foreign firms in the home and export markets.

5. *Exchange controls.* Importers need foreign currency to pay for imports. Governments sometimes limit the amount of currency which can be bought by people and firms. This is usually to prevent the exchange rate of the currency from being reduced by purchases of imports (see the section on 'Exchange rates' below). UK exchange controls were abolished by the Government in 1980, but, are still used by many East European and Third World countries.

6. *Government procurement.* A Government may tell its departments to buy domestically-produced goods and services whenever possible. Within the European Community, all Government contracts above a certain value must now be open to tender by any EC firm.

7. *Special rules and regulations.* Countries may deliberately design regulations about standards for products to make importing more difficult. For example Japan banned imports of European skis on the grounds that Japanese snow is different from European snow.

Reasons for protectionism

1. To cure a Balance of Payments deficit by increasing exports and/or reducing imports.
2. To protect domestic industry and employment.
3. To protect the exchange rate by restricting the supply on the foreign exchange market.

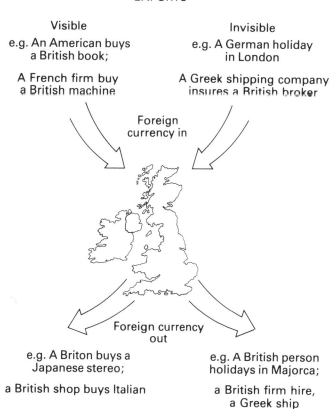

EXPORTS

Visible
e.g. An American buys a British book;

A French firm buy a British machine

Invisible
e.g. A German holiday in London

A Greek shipping company insures a British broker

Foreign currency in

Foreign currency out

e.g. A Briton buys a Japanese stereo;

a British shop buys Italian

Visible

e.g. A British person holidays in Majorca;

a British firm hire, a Greek ship

Invisible

IMPORTS

Figure 12.11 Items in the Balance of Payments (current account)

187

Disadvantages of protectionism

1. It reduces the benefits of *free trade*.
2. If one country puts restrictions upon imports, others may retaliate, so that world trade falls, and all countries suffer. The aim of many international economic institutions such as the General Agreement on Tariffs and Trade (GATT) has been to encourage free trade.
3. The advantages of international specialisation and world-wide markets are lost.
4. Consumers get less choice and higher prices, for example cars and video-recorders would be cheaper if restrictions upon Japanese imports into Europe were removed.
5. Protectionism encourages inefficiency among domestic firms by limiting competition.

The Balance of Payments

Purpose of the Balance of Payments

Visible trade	£ million
Exports	79 422
Less Imports	89 584
Visible Balance	−10 162
Invisible trade	
Exports	80 010
Less Imports	72 352
Invisible Balance	7 658
Current Balance	−2 504

Figure 12.12   UK Balance of Payments (current account)

The Balance of Payments is a record of all transactions between Britain and other countries. These may be payments for goods and services, as recorded in the *current account*, or for investment and other purposes (*capital flows* or *net transactions in assets*).

The Balance of Payments current account

The current account consists of *visible* and *invisible trade*.

1. Visible trade – trade in goods

The *visible balance* (also called the *balance of trade*) is equal to:

Visible exports − Visible imports

Until the 1980s the UK generally exported more manufactured goods than it imported, but this was balanced by large imports of food and raw materials. During the last twenty years, the pattern of visible trade has changed.

Some of the major changes are:

- Food and raw materials have fallen as a proportion of imports, because of an increase in agricultural production and the development of synthetic substitutes for goods such as wool and cotton.
- Britain used to import all of its oil, but is now a net exporter (exports greater than imports) because of the discovery of North Sea oil.
- Britain is no longer a net exporter of manufactured goods.

2. Invisible trade – trade in services

The *invisible balance* is equal to:

Invisible exports − Invisible imports

Generally the UK has had a *surplus* (exports higher than imports) in invisible trade, particularly from insurance and financial services. British people and firms owned foreign assets of £90 billion pounds at the end of 1987, and receive income from these. However in 1990 a deficit was recorded on invisible trade for the first time, and with increasing international competition in financial markets there is no certainty that invisible trade will be in surplus in future years.

3. The current balance

The *current balance* is equal to the *visible balance* plus the *invisible balance*, that is:

(Visible exports − Visible imports)
+ (Invisible exports − Invisible imports)

Since the Second World War, the current balance has been positive (that is exports greater than imports) in about the same number of years as it has been negative.

In the early 1980s, exports were consistently higher than imports, largely because of high earnings from North Sea oil exports. From 1986, as can be seen from Figure 12.13, imports started to exceed exports.

Exchange Rates

How exchange rates are determined

The *exchange rate* of a currency is its value in terms of other currencies. It is in effect the price of the currency to other countries on the foreign exchange market. For example an exchange rate of £1 = \$2 means that a pound sterling will cost a US buyer \$2 (or that a US dollar will cost £0.50 for a UK buyer).

As for any price, exchange rates are determined by demand and supply. The value of sterling therefore depends upon the demand for and supply of pounds on the foreign exchange market.

The demand for sterling depends upon the number of pounds that people, firms and Governments wish to buy. Examples might include German tourists visiting the UK, Japanese firms buying British goods and services, American financial institutions investing in Britain, or the Bank of England buying sterling to support the exchange rate.

The supply of sterling depends upon the quantity of pounds that people, firms and Governments wish to sell in

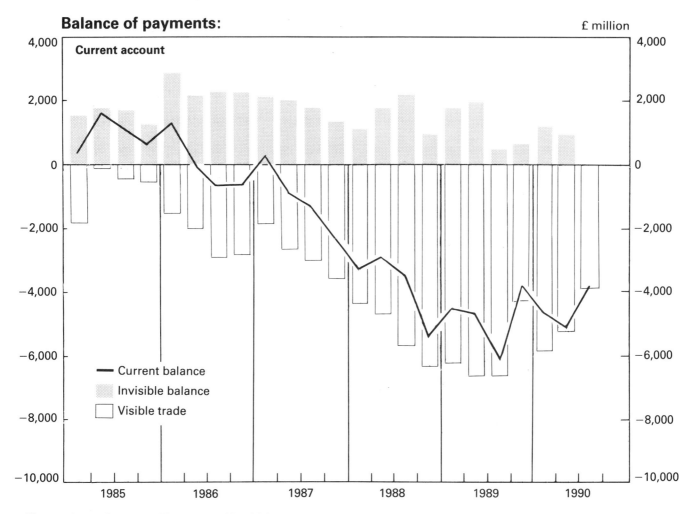

Figure 12.13 Balance of Payments 1985–90 (current account)

order to buy foreign currency. Examples include British tourists buying pesetas to holiday in Majorca, UK firms buying components from Switzerland and the British Government paying for the upkeep of its embassies abroad.

As shown in Figure 12.14, there are four major determinants of the exchange rate.

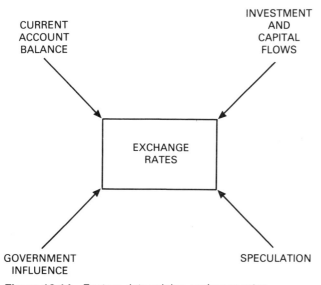

Figure 12.14 Factors determining exchange rates

1. Current account balance

British buyers of imported goods and services generally have to buy foreign currency to pay for them. To do this they supply pounds on the foreign exchange market. Other things being equal, this will put downward pressure on the sterling exchange rate as an increase in supply leads to a fall in price.

At the same time, foreign buyers of British goods and services are buying sterling to pay UK suppliers. This increases the demand for sterling on the foreign exchange market and therefore pushes the exchange rate up.

Putting these two effects together, an increase in the current balance will tend to increase the exchange rate, whereas a decrease in the balance will tend to reduce it. In theory, the current balance should be the main determining factor of exchange rates, since its purpose is to allow trade between countries.

In practice, only about 20% of all currency transactions are for trade purposes, and it is therefore possible for a declining current balance to be accompanied by an increasing exchange rate, for example if high interest rates in the UK attract foreign investors. However, in the long-run the current balance is still a major determinant of the exchange rate.

2. Investment and capital flows

These occur when shares, property or other assets are bought in other countries, or because of movement of bank deposits between countries. For example, there is a large volume of 'hot money' which is moved between countries according to where the best interest rates or other returns can be obtained.

Investment and capital flows are highly sensitive to relative interest rates. For example if UK interest rates are high compared with those of other countries, foreign investors will tend to move their money into British financial institutions, thus pushing up the exchange rate. During the 1980s and early 1990s, British Governments have often increased interest rates in order to maintain or increase the sterling exchange rate.

3. Speculation

Many people and financial institutions buy and sell currencies solely to make profits by gambling on changes in exchange rates. Their activities can often be self-fulfilling prophecies. For example if speculators expect the value of sterling to rise, they will buy pounds. The increased demand will cause the rise in sterling that speculators were expecting.

4. Government influence

British Governments have always been reluctant to allow the exchange rate to change freely, mainly because of the problems caused by rapid fluctuations. They can influence the exchange rate in various ways:

- by buying and selling sterling themselves, using foreign currency reserves – this function is undertaken by the Bank of England;
- through influencing interest rates;
- by Ministerial announcements about Government policy.

The importance of exchange rates

Exchange rates affect businesses by altering the relative prices of exports and imports. For example suppose a UK manufacturer is selling a small machine to the USA and wants to receive £1000.

If £1 = $2, the US price will be $2000. This is because the US buyer will have to supply $2000 to obtain £1000 for payment to the UK firms.

If the exchange rate rises to £1 = $3, the US buyer will need $3000 to obtain £1000. A rise in the sterling exchange rate has led to an increase in the price of British exports.

With imports, the opposite occurs. For example at a rate of £1 = $2, a machine with a USA price of $3000 will cost a UK buyer £1500. If the sterling exchange rate rises to £1 = $3, the UK buyer will only need £1000. The rising exchange rate has made imports cheaper.

These are very simplified examples, and assume that importers and exporters do not alter their prices to allow for exchange rate changes. However, in simple terms the effect of exchange rate changes can be summarised as follows:

- a RISE in the exchange rate will
    make exports DEARER
    and imports CHEAPER;
- a FALL in the exchange rate will
    make exports CHEAPER
    and imports DEARER.

The effect of a change in the exchange rate, however, needs to take account of the elasticities of demand for exports and imports. Although a rise in the value of sterling will make exports dearer, and should therefore reduce the VOLUME of exports, the VALUE of exports may actually rise if demand for British products is inelastic.

Similarly, if UK demand for imports was inelastic, a rise in the exchange rate would increase the VOLUME of imports but reduce their VALUE. The UK would be buying larger quantities of imports but paying less for them.

As well as the actual level of exchange rates, firms are also affected by the way in which they change. In particular, large fluctuations in exchange rates make it difficult for importers and exporters to plan costings and prices, and may cause similar fluctuations in demand.

For example many fuels and raw materials are priced in dollars on the international markets. A fall in the value of the pound against the US dollar will therefore increase the costs of UK firms such as airlines and petrol retailers. Unanticipated changes can cause significant disruptions to such firms' planning.

The problems caused by fluctuating exchange rates have led Governments to attempt to stabilise currency values in various ways. They often co-operate with other countries in this process by supporting each others' currencies. The European Community's Exchange Rate Mechanism (ERM) is one scheme which attempts to keep members' currencies within certain levels. In October 1990, the UK Government promised to maintain the exchange rate of the pound between certain values, for example between DM2.77 and DM3.13.

Difficulties of Exporting

Firms trying to sell abroad face special difficulties which do not occur when selling in Britain:

1. *Language.* Documents, advertising and trade names may have to be translated into other languages.
2. *Information and distribution* It may be difficult to obtain information about how to sell products abroad, or to arrange sales agents and transport. Delivery may also be more complicated and expensive than for home trade.
3. *Risk of non-payment.* The risk of bad debts is much higher in many other countries, especially those which are politically unstable. The Export Credits Guarantee Department (ECGD) helps exporters by insuring against credit risks (see Chapter 13).
4. *Laws and regulations.* Most exporters have to deal with different technical and legal rules in other countries, such as left-hand drive and safety regulations for car manufacturers. These are sometimes designed specifically to restrict imports. Part of the procedures for implementing the Single European Market is to develop identical standards throughout the EC.
5. *Currency changes.* The value of sterling may change, affecting both costs and income from exports. A rise in the value of the pound against the dollar, for example, would make British goods and services more expensive for foreign buyers.

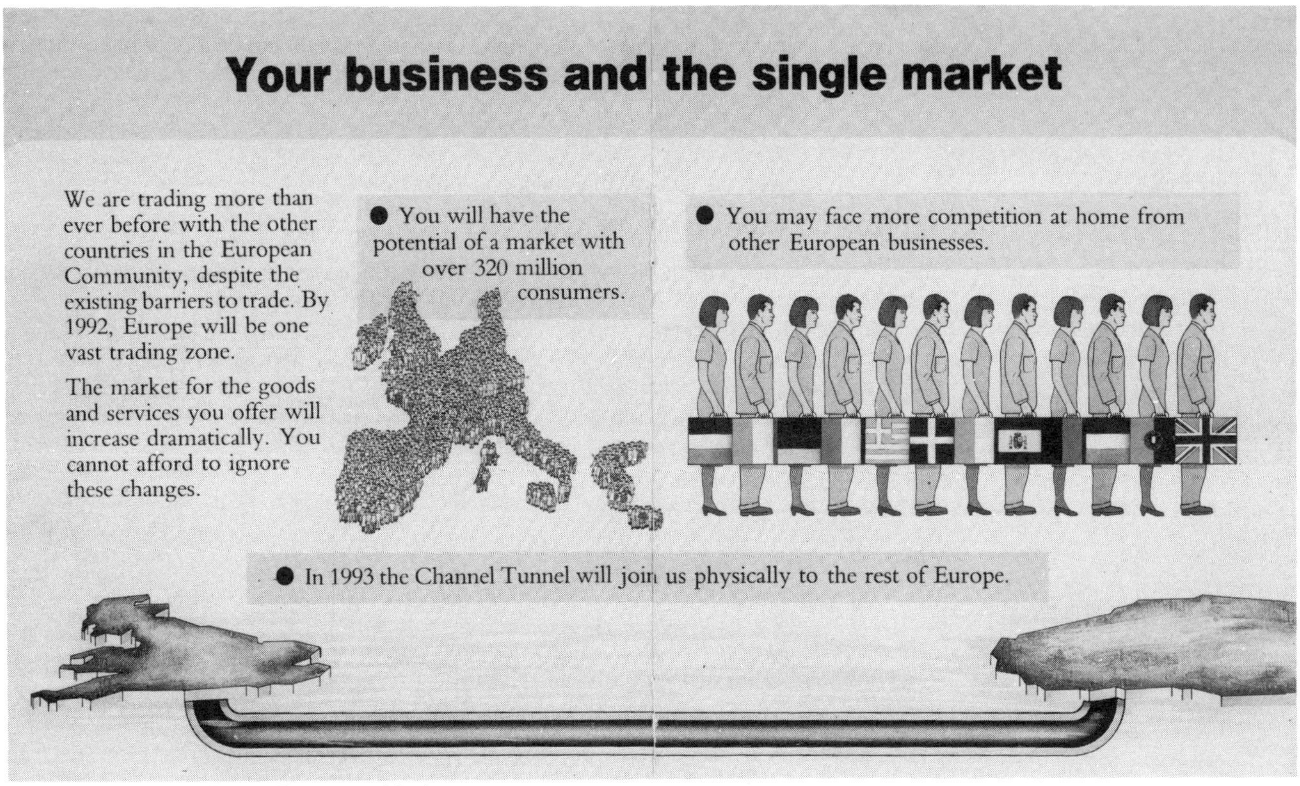

Your business and the single market

We are trading more than ever before with the other countries in the European Community, despite the existing barriers to trade. By 1992, Europe will be one vast trading zone.

The market for the goods and services you offer will increase dramatically. You cannot afford to ignore these changes.

● You will have the potential of a market with over 320 million consumers.

● You may face more competition at home from other European businesses.

● In 1993 the Channel Tunnel will join us physically to the rest of Europe.

Figure 12.15 The Single European Market

6. *Tastes and habits.* These can vary considerably between countries. For example Rowntree Mackintosh had difficulty when selling Kit-Kat in Europe, because it was less suitable with mineral water or wine than with tea, its traditional UK accompaniment.

Firms can obtain help from a variety of Government and private sources to overcome these difficulties.

The European Community (EC)

The European Community (EC) is an organisation of 12 countries with 320 million people. The 12 are responsible for 20% of world trade. It is often known as the 'Common Market', because one of its main aims is to have free trade and movement of workers and capital between its members. In 1986 the twelve member countries signed the Single European Act, which is designed to remove all trade restrictions between member states.

Worked Examples

Short-answer questions

12.1 List three ways in which a Government may seek to encourage investment in manufacturing industry.

(AEB)

Answer For example lower interest rates, cut taxes, subsidies, regional policy, build infrastructure, nationalisation, privatisation, protectionism, higher Government spending.

12.2 The value of the pound to the US dollar falls from £1 = $2 to £1 = $5. Why might a UK exporter of goods to America decide not to reduce the price of his goods on the American market?

(AEB)

Answer For example to preserve profit margins (before, a good costing $3 in the USA would be worth £1.50 to exporter; after change, would be worth £6). His decision depends upon the price elasticity of demand. If it is inelastic, cutting the price will simply reduce revenue.

12.3 The Government increases tariffs on a range of goods. Explain why demand for these imported goods may not decline.

(AEB)

191

Answer   For example no domestically-produced alternative, consumer taste/brand loyalty, foreign goods of higher quality/prestige, inelastic demand, exchange rates rises at same time, imports still cheaper, importers pay tariff themselves.

Data-response questions

12.4   Read the article and answer the questions which follow.

TOURISM PERFORMANCE IN 1986

The United Kingdom attracts visitors from all over the world. Last year 13.8 million came, 60% from Western Europe, 21% from North America and the rest mainly from the Far East and Australia. Visits from Western Europe increased by 5% over 1985 whilst due to well published but essentially short-term fears those from North America fell by 24%, with the drop largely concentrated during the summer months. But our broad market base meant that overall, visits fell by only 4%, and the picture on spending was even more encouraging. Many of our European competitors fared worse. Recent trends indicate continued long-term growth.

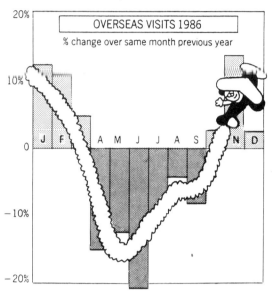

After the sharp fall in numbers of overseas visitors early in the year, there was a strong recovery in the last quarter making 1986 the second highest year on record. December visits from North America were 10% above 1985 – which, together with the high level of forward bookings, promises well for 1987.

Source: 'A Bumper Year for Tourism', *Action for Jobs*, Department of Employment, 1987

(a) Explain why the data in the diagram on 'Overseas Visits 1986' is presented in two different ways. *(2 marks)*

(b) Explain why a 'high level of forward bookings' would benefit businesses involved in tourism. *(2 marks)*

(c) Within which category would earnings from foreign tourism appear in the Balance of Payments Current Account? *(2 marks)*

(d) State and explain **three** positive effects that 'continued long-term growth' in overseas visitors is likely to have on United Kingdom industry. *(9 marks)*

(e) Explain how a rise in the value of the £, via its effects on foreign tourists in the United Kingdom and United Kingdom tourists abroad, would affect the tourist industry in the United Kingdom. *(10 marks)*

Answer   (a) Line shows general trend, simplifies data, more attractive, may be intended to mislead by hiding sharp drop in September.
Bar-chart shows exact information.

(b) For example:

- know that will have certain level of revenue;
- safer to invest, for example plan expansion of facilities;
- better cash flow.

(c) Invisible exports.

(d) For example:

- higher revenue and profit;
- increased employment in tourist industries;
- higher spending throughout economy as knock-on effect of increased tourism;
- tourist regions benefit from extra trade;
- external costs, such as congestion and litter.

(e) For example:

- Exchange rate of £ rises, therefore imports cheaper for UK, exports dearer. Therefore more UK tourists should go abroad, fewer foreign tourists will come to Britain.
- Lower tourist spending by both UK and foreign tourists will lead to lower profits and employment for UK tourist industry.

- Some types of tourism will be hit harder than others, for example seaside resorts are likely to suffer more than day-trip destinations.
- Depends upon price elasticity of demand for tourism, that is if demand for tourism is inelastic, UK tourist spending abroad will fall, foreign spending in UK will rise, therefore UK tourist industry benefits.
- Exchange rate change may not be large enough significantly to affect people's holiday plans.
- Other factors may be stronger than exchange rate change, such as rising income and weather.

Essay questions   **12.5** From 1992 there will be A 'Single European Market'. Discuss the likely implications for UK firms.

(AEB)

Answer (i) Explain what is meant by the Single Market, that is freedom of movement throughout the European Community (EC) for goods and services, labour and capital. For example, by 1992 it should be possible for an EC citizen to work anywhere in the twelve countries, and for any good which can be sold legally in one country to be sold in any of the others.
   (ii) Possible benefits include:

- larger market for UK firms;
- less bureaucracy and administration for export orders;
- products accepted as legal in the UK can be sold anywhere in the EC;
- ancillary services such as banking and insurance will be more efficiently organised.

Possible difficulties include:

- increased competition from abroad;
- products will have to meet EC standards which may involve redesign or better quality design;
- adapting to foreign tastes and language differences.

12.6 **(a)** Briefly explain how you would measure the rate of inflation. *(5 marks)*
(b) Discuss the likely consequences for your company, a UK-based washing machine manufacturer, of a significant increase in the rate of inflation. *(12 marks)*
(c) What policy measures might you expect a company retailing your products to adapt in reaction to this change? *(8 marks)*

(UCLES)

Answer **(a)** Describe the retail price index, that is weighted index with a base year. Weights represent the proportion of consumer expenditure on a good or service. Index numbers represent the price of a product as a percentage of its price in the base year. For example an index of 120 shows that prices have risen 20% since the base year.

(b) Inflation can have various effects, for example:

- may lead to higher costs of wages and materials;
- makes planning more difficult because of uncertainty about future prices;
- if inflation is higher in UK than other countries, the firm may be uncompetitive with foreign manufacturers both in UK and export markets;
- Government policies to reduce inflation often involve depressing demand through measures such as higher taxes and interest rates;
- because of above factors, firm may be in 'double squeeze' because costs are rising but there is pressure from customers to hold prices down.

(c) Various possibilities might be described, for example:

- retailer will be worried about trying to sell to consumers at higher prices, so may try to hold down price it pays to retailer;
- may look for cheaper machines abroad;
- may want longer credit terms since value of money falls and interest rates may be higher, therefore it is dearer to pay for and hold stocks;
- may want guaranteed prices agreed in advance.

12.7 Examine how an enterprise might alter its plans if a prolonged period of heavy unemployment is predicted.

(AEB)

Answer (i) Explain the major likely effect of prolonged unemployment, that is reduced incomes and lower demand for most goods and services.
   (ii) Use the concept of *income elasticity of demand* to demonstrate that demand for some products will fall more than others. For example demand for products such as holidays, cars and consumer durables will fall more than demand for food, basic household goods and fuel.
   (iii) Outline possible policies for the firm, for example:

- move 'downmarket' to cheaper products, but this will cause problems such as devalued image and lower profit margins;

193

- move 'upmarket' because higher income groups are less likely to be affected by unemployment;
- may change 'product mix', for example supermarkets switch shelf-space from non-food to food;
- attempt to increase exports;
- cut back by reducing overheads, shedding labour, etc.

   (iv) Mention possible benefits, such as lower wages, easier recruitment and retention of staff.

Self-test Questions

Short-answer questions

12.8   Explain the term 'opportunity cost'.

(AEB)

12.9   State and explain one effect of an increase in interest rates on a business organisation.

(AEB)

12.10   Indicate two ways in which a high level of unemployment might affect industry.

(AEB)

Data-response questions

12.11   Read the two extracts and answer the questions which follow.

"A recent study by the Economist Intelligence Unit uncovered estimates suggesting that counter trade accounts for 40% of world trade."

(Adapted from *The Economist*, October 5th, 1985.)

Pakistan selects companies for counter trade project
BY JOHN ELLIOTT IN ISLAMABAD

THREE international trading companies have been chosen by Pakistan to launch the country into its first official programme of counter trading, which the Government hopes will boost its flagging exports by $500m (£350m) in the coming year.

The companies chosen from a list of about 50 applicants, are Sukab of Sweden and Marco of Switzerland which have each agreed to do $200m of export business and Mitsubishi of Japan which is to do $100m. A further batch of agreements for another $500m might follow within a year, taking the total of counter trading business to $1bn.

Islamabad is apprehensive about the possible disadvantages of counter trading, and this has held up a final decision on the plan which is awaiting the go-ahead from President Zia ul Haq and Prime Minister Muhammad Khan Junejo.

Counter trade is being tried because the Government can think of no other way to improve its exports which last year totalled only $2.4bn, far short of a target of $3.1bn. This result is unlikely to be improved much this year, according to present trends.

The country's trade imbalance is more than $3bn a year against imports of $6bn. The overall position has been worsened during the past three years by a sharp decline in remittances from Pakistanis working abroad.

Pakistan has been experiencing problems exporting its major surpluses of cotton amounting to about its annual crop of 5.5m–6m bales, as well as products from its new steel mill in Karachi and leather hides and manufactured products. It also has a $190m surplus of carpets, exports of which have suffered a 19 per cent decline this year

In all these areas it has been hit by falling international prices, international protectionism and lack of Pakistani exporting expertise.

So it has decided to try to persuade countries in the Middle East, where it buys oil and other countries such as Sri Lanka, Malaysia and Japan, where it buys tea, edible oils and engineering products, to match these imports with counter trade purchases.

Individual Pakistan companies have traded by barter for several years. The trade has involved eight East European companies, Sukab of Sweden and Kemira of Finland. It amounts to about $300m a year.

(*Financial Times*, November 7th, 1985)

You are employed as a Sales Director of a multinational trading company. Write a report to the Managing Director of your company using a suitable format *(6 marks)* to cover the following areas:

(a)   What is meant by 'counter trade' as used in the text.   *(3 marks)*

(b)   Explain why the growth of countertrade might be important to your company.   *(2 marks)*

(c) What points the company should take into consideration before it embarks upon counter-trading deals. *(9 marks)*

Essay questions

12.12 What would be the consequences for industry of the Chancellor of the Exchequer increasing the rates of expenditure taxes?

(UCLES)

12.13 **(a)** What do you understand by the phrases 'market share'; 'import penetration'; 'cross-elasticity of demand'? *(5 marks)*
(b) How might a UK-based firm attempt to counteract the problem of increasing foreign competition? (If you wish, you may choose to confine your answer to a specific industry.) *(20 marks)*

(UCLES)

12.14 'Most bulk chemical products are priced in US dollars' (*Financial Times*).
Discuss the problems likely to be encountered by a British company involved in the chemical markets at home and abroad.

(UCLES)

12.15 Describe and discuss the problems experienced by a business trading both at home and abroad as the result of a depreciation in the external exchange rate.

(AEB)

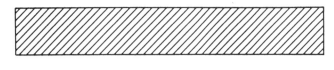

External Influences on Business

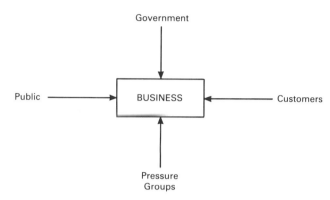

Figure 13.1 External influences on business

THE EXTERNAL ENVIRONMENT OF BUSINESS

As well as internal influences such as workers and owners, the managers of a business are subject to the influence of outsiders such as the general public, pressure groups and outside agencies. These groups place differing demands upon the firm.

Government Assistance to Business

Advice

Firms can obtain advice from several Government Departments. The most important is the Department of Trade and Industry, whose *Enterprise Initiative*, announced in 1988, pays part of the cost of advice and consultancy for marketing, design, quality control, manufacturing technology, business planning, financial and information systems.

Information

The Government publishes vast amounts of information for firms, particularly in *Official Statistics*.

Regional assistance

Firms creating jobs in the Assisted Areas can obtain grants and tax reliefs. Assisted Areas are mostly areas of high unemployment where traditional industries such as coal and steel have declined.

Help for small firms

The *Small Firms Service* provides free information and advice to new and expanding small businesses.

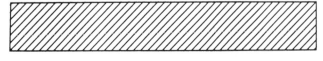

Just what your business needs.
Someone to pull your products apart.

Your products are selling nicely enough. So it's probably best not to make too many changes, right?

Wrong. If you want to stay ahead of the game, you have to make the running.

And that often involves taking a long, hard look at your products, to see if there's room for improvement.

And if you think that's a job for an expert, you're right.

It's a job for a product designer.

Contrary to popular opinion, designers do more than just make products look better.

Instead, they look for better ways to make products. Or ways to make them better products.

They look for better materials to make them from. Or techniques to make them cheaper. Or even, just occasionally, more expensive.

Which is all very well, but what if your business is too small for you to afford a designer of your own?

Coincidentally enough, that's where DTI can help.

Take the Design Initiative, and DTI will pay for up to two thirds of a designer's fee for up to 15 days.

A designer with skills and experience relevant to your product field.

The Design Initiative is open to manufacturing and service companies that employ fewer than 500 people.

If you'd like to find out how to improve your products before your competitors do, cut the coupon or phone free on 0800 500 200.

Post to: Enterprise Initiative, FREEPOST BS3333, Bristol BS1 6GZ. ☎ Or call free on **0800 500 200.**

Name _____ Position _____

Name of Firm _____ **dti**
                                    the department for Enterprise

Address _____

Postcode _____ Telephone _____ No. of employees ____

Is your business primarily involved in:

Construction ☐ Manufacturing ☐ Service ☐

the
Design
initiative

Figure 13.2 Government advice for firms

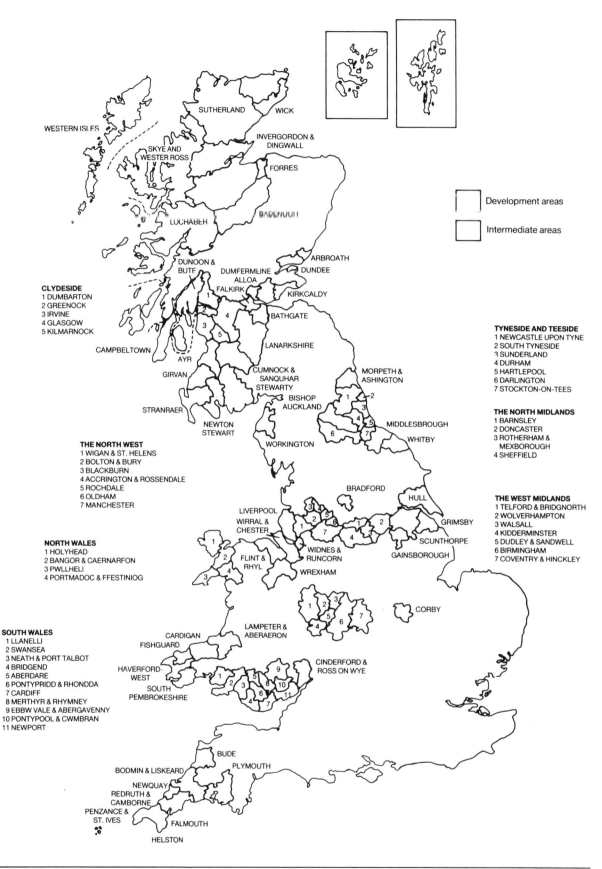

WESTERN ISLES

SUTHERLAND
WICK

INVERGORDON &
DINGWALL

SKYE AND
WESTER ROSS

FORRES

BADENOCH

LOCHABER

ARBROATH

DUNOON &
BUTE
DUMFERMLINE
ALLOA
FALKIRK
DUNDEE

KIRKCALDY

CLYDESIDE
1 DUMBARTON
2 GREENOCK
3 IRVINE
4 GLASGOW
5 KILMARNOCK

BATHGATE

LANARKSHIRE

CAMPBELTOWN

AYR

GIRVAN

CUMNOCK &
SANQUHAR
STEWARTY

MORPETH &
ASHINGTON

BISHOP
AUCKLAND

STRANRAER

MIDDLESBROUGH

TYNESIDE AND TEESIDE
1 NEWCASTLE UPON TYNE
2 SOUTH TYNESIDE
3 SUNDERLAND
4 DURHAM
5 HARTLEPOOL
6 DARLINGTON
7 STOCKTON-ON-TEES

WHITBY

NEWTON
STEWART

WORKINGTON

THE NORTH MIDLANDS
1 BARNSLEY
2 DONCASTER
3 ROTHERHAM &
  MEXBOROUGH
4 SHEFFIELD

THE NORTH WEST
1 WIGAN & ST. HELENS
2 BOLTON & BURY
3 BLACKBURN
4 ACCRINGTON & ROSSENDALE
5 ROCHDALE
6 OLDHAM
7 MANCHESTER

BRADFORD

HULL

LIVERPOOL
WIRRAL &
CHESTER

GRIMSBY

SCUNTHORPE

THE WEST MIDLANDS
1 TELFORD & BRIDGNORTH
2 WOLVERHAMPTON
3 WALSALL
4 KIDDERMINSTER
5 DUDLEY & SANDWELL
6 BIRMINGHAM
7 COVENTRY & HINCKLEY

NORTH WALES
1 HOLYHEAD
2 BANGOR & CAERNARFON
3 PWLLHELI
4 PORTMADOC & FFESTINIOG

WIDNES &
RUNCORN

GAINSBOROUGH

FLINT &
RHYL

WREXHAM

CORBY

LAMPETER &
ABERAERON

SOUTH WALES
1 LLANELLI
2 SWANSEA
3 NEATH & PORT TALBOT
4 BRIDGEND
5 ABERDARE
6 PONTYPRIDD & RHONDDA
7 CARDIFF
8 MERTHYR & RHYMNEY
9 EBBW VALE & ABERGAVENNY
10 PONTYPOOL & CWMBRAN
11 NEWPORT

CARDIGAN

FISHGUARD

HAVERFORD-
WEST

SOUTH
PEMBROKESHIRE

CINDERFORD &
ROSS ON WYE

Development areas

Intermediate areas

BUDE
PLYMOUTH

BODMIN & LISKEARD

NEWQUAY
REDRUTH &
CAMBORNE
PENZANCE &
ST. IVES
FALMOUTH

HELSTON

1 As defined by the Department of Trade and Industry at 29 November 1984.

Source: *Department of Trade and Industry.*

Figure 13.3 Assisted Areas

The *Business Expansion Scheme* gives tax relief to people investing in small businesses. In 1990 it allowed an investor to claim tax relief on purchases of equity of up to £40 000, for example a top-rate taxpayer could save £16 000 in tax (40% of £40 000). The capital must be left in the business for at least 5 years.

HOW TO TRAIN YOUR SMALL BUSINESS INTO A GROWING CONCERN.

There are many ways of growing your business. You can invest in new machinery. You can improve your marketing. You can even relocate to better premises.

You can do all this but you will still only be as good as your people.

The real key to developing a small business is to grow the people in it.

A planned training programme unlocks their potential and makes your business grow at the same time.

Your local Training and Enterprise Council is there to help you with precisely this kind of programme.

Call the number below and watch your business blossom.

TECs UNLOCK POTENTIAL

TEC

Make the most of your company's future, call
0800 444 246.

Figure 13.4   Government help for small firms

The *Loan Guarantee Scheme* guarantees bank loans to small firms. This is designed to encourage banks to lend more to small firms.

The *Enterprise Allowance Scheme* pays unemployed people an allowance to set up in business.

Local Enterprise Agencies have been established for certain areas to advise local firms.

Export aid

The Department of Trade and Industry provides assistance for exporters, mainly through the *British Overseas Trade Board* (BOTB):

1. information and advice upon foreign markets;
2. introductions to business contacts and distributing agents;
3. specialist library of statistics and intelligence;
4. export market research;
5. technical advice about foreign standards;
6. advice on preparing documents;
7. trade missions and special promotions in other countries.

The Export Credits Guarantee Department (ECGD), a Government Department, arranges insurance for exporters against the risk of not being paid by their customers for reasons such as:

- bankruptcy or refusal to pay;
- failure to pay within six months;
- wars or political difficulties preventing trade;
- a foreign Government preventing payments abroad, for example through exchange controls;
- cancellation of orders.

Figure 13.5 Export Credits Guarantee Department (ECGD)

Government Regulation of Business

Many laws affect the activities of businesses, particularly in three areas:

1. consumer law;
2. employment law;
3. competition law.

Consumer law

1. Sale of Goods Act 1979

This replaced and combined the Sale of Goods Act 1893 and the Supply of Goods (Implied Terms) Act 1973. All goods must be:

- *'of merchantable quality'*, that is capable of doing what would be expected in normal use, and last for a reasonable length of time;
- *'as described'*, that is must be what they are said to be – for example a 'solid gold' ring must not be made of some other metal;
- *'fit for the purpose'*, that is if a seller gives incorrect advice, he or she can be held responsible – for example wallpaper described as suitable for a bathroom should be resistant to water.

The provisions about 'implied terms' make it illegal for a seller to attempt to take away the consumer's legal rights. Before they were made illegal, some sellers tried to include *exclusion clauses* or notices such as 'no refunds' or 'no guarantees'. If the buyer is given extra rights such as 'your money back if not satisfied', the seller must point out that 'statutory rights are not affected'.

2. Unfair Contract Terms Act 1977

Sellers of services cannot use exclusion clauses to take away customers' statutory rights. For example a launderette notice saying 'we accept no responsibility for damage however caused' would be illegal.

3. Supply of Goods and Services Act

This applies to services such as meals out and home improvements. The supplier must provide a reasonable standard of work within a reasonable time and at a reasonable price (assuming that the time and price are not agreed in advance).

4. Trade Descriptions Act 1968

It is a criminal offence to tell lies about a good or service such as the size, weight, materials and methods used.

5. Unsolicited Goods and Services Act 1971

Consumers who are sent goods that they have not requested can give the sender notice to collect the goods, and keep them if they are not collected within 30 days. If the consumer does not inform the company, they become his or her property if the sender does not collect them within six months.

6. The Weights and Measures Act 1979

This is one of a series of Weights and Measures Acts which make it an offence to give 'short weight' or 'short measure', even by accident. Equipment such as scales or petrol pumps must also be tested and approved by the Trading Standards Department.

7. Consumer Protection Act 1987

This gives the Government the power to prevent the sale of unsafe goods and make rules about products. Manufacturers are also responsible for damage or injury covered by defective products (not including food) unless they can prove that the danger could not have been foreseen.

8. Consumer Credit Act 1974

A business which offers credit to customers must be registered as a licensed credit broker. The Annual Percentage Rate of interest (APR) must be shown on all advertisements and documents. The provider of credit is also jointly responsible with the supplier for faulty goods or services for transactions between £50 and £30 000 (with some exceptions).

9. Food and Drugs Act

This sets rules about the sale and serving of food in shops and catering premises.

10. Fair Trading Act 1973

This established the Office of Fair Trading (OFT), a Government agency, to protect consumers against unfair practices by firms. The OFT's functions include:

- publishing leaflets to help people to know their rights;
- encouraging trade organisations to prepare voluntary *codes of practice* for dealing with customers;
- suggesting new consumer laws and regulations;
- prosecuting traders who break the law;
- issuing licences under the Consumer Credit Act;
- recommending to the Monopolies and Mergers Commission that certain firms or markets should be investigated.

Most consumer legislation is enforced by local councils, particularly by the *Trading Standards* or *Consumer Protection Department* and the *Environmental Health Department*.

The Trading Standards Department enforces laws such as the Weights and Measures Act. Trading standards officers carry out tests and surveys to check that traders are giving full weight and full measure, investigate complaints from the public traders and often run Consumer Advice Centres.

Environmental Health Departments' responsibilities include checking that food is sold and served in clean and hygienic conditions. They inspect shops, cafés and restaurants, and prosecute traders who break food regulations.

Employment law

1. Health and Safety at Work Act 1974

Employers must take all reasonable care to ensure the

West Yorkshire Trading Standards Service

AT YOUR SERVICE IN **BRADFORD** Metropolitan District

The West Yorkshire Trading Standards Service is operated by a Joint Committee of the Metropolitan Districts of Bradford, Calderdale, Kirklees, Leeds and Wakefield.

STANDARDS...

OF QUANTITY The accuracy of all weighing and measuring equipment is a basic requirement of FAIR TRADING. All equipment is tested before and during its use. All packages of food and non-food goods are tested to ensure they contain the correct quantity.

OF QUALITY We have a right to know what goes into food. The Service samples food in shops and at manufacturers for testing by the Public Analyst. The law requires that food is accurately described and labelled to help us choose what we want to buy.

OF SAFETY Consumers have a right to safe products – electrically safe, safe for children to play with, safe to use. The Service inspects and tests goods made at home and abroad to improve safety standards. Action is taken when unsafe products are discovered.

OF FAIR TRADING Goods and services must be described accurately. Price comparisons must be truthful. Checks are carried out on the accuracy and truth of trade descriptions, e.g. used car mileages, counterfeit goods, holidays, textile products, bargain offers and credit advertisements.

OF SERVICE Contact the Service for help with consumer problems. Advice is also available to traders to enable them to comply with trading laws, labelling, and other areas of concern.

DO YOU GET A FAIR DEAL?

There are laws relating to consumer purchases. If you are dissatisfied with any one, the Trading Standards Service may be able to help you. Complaints about weight or measure, prices, faulty goods, misdescriptions, unsafe goods and non-delivery are among those received every day.

SAFETY OF GOODS

How often have you heard the expression "You can't be too careful"? The Trading Standards Service tests toys, electrical goods, nightwear, heating appliances, used car tyres, etc. It also takes action when unsafe products which are not covered by the legal rules are found. Our vigilance is your safeguard but, if you are concerned about the safety of any product, we'd like to know.

WHO CHECKS FOR CORRECT WEIGHT?

How do you know that you receive correct weight or measure? Do you always get the petrol you pay for at the advertised price? The Service checks on these things for you. We do not take things for granted – so you can!

DESCRIPTIONS & LABELLING

Do you believe low-mileage used cars are good value for money? Is it worth paying extra for an all-wool British sweater? Checks on descriptions of cars and textiles increase consumer confidence and promote fair trading.

 **OVERLOADED LORRIES**

It costs millions of pounds to repair road damage caused by overloaded lorries. Then there is the hidden damage to sewers and gas and electricity mains. In some cases overloading can lead to a reduction in safety, and, with the help of the police, the Trading Standards Service aims to check 10,000 lorries travelling through West Yorkshire each year.

Figure 13.6 Functions of Trading Standards Departments

safety of their employees. Employees also have a duty to co-operate with the employer to ensure the safety of all workers. Employers with 5 or more staff must have a written statement of their health and safety policy.

Figure 13.7 Health and safety hazards

2. Employment Protection Act 1978

This gives employees rights such as compensation for unfair dismissal and entitlement to return to their jobs after having a baby.

3. Sex Discrimination Acts 1975, 1986

These make it illegal to discriminate against a person because of his or her sex, such as advertising a job as 'for women only'. Certain exceptions are allowed, for example domestic servants or changing-room attendants.

4. Equal Pay Act 1970

Women must not be paid a lower rate than men employed in the same job or work of 'equivalent value' where all employees are of one sex. For example a canteen supervisor in a shipyard convinced a court that her work was as skilled as an engineering foreman who received higher wages.

5. Race Relations Act 1976

It is illegal to discriminate against a person because of their race, for example by refusing to employ Asian or Irish workers. This may include indirect discrimination, for example insisting on women workers wearing skirts might be regarded as discrimination unless the job obviously required such clothes.

Competition Law

The Government tries to ensure competition between firms by various means:

1. Investigating mergers which might restrict competition. This is recommended by the Office of Fair Trading (see above). The investigation is carried out by the Monopolies and Mergers Commission, which is appointed by

British Coal under fire from MMC

Patrick Donovan
Industrial Correspondent

BRITISH Coal was yesterday accused of investing millions of pounds in a mine which it knew was not commercially viable in a report by the Monopolies and Mergers Commission which calls for the company's finances to be rigidly controlled.

In a stinging indictment of the loss-making privatisation target's financial affairs and the quality of its management, the MMC recommended yesterday that British Coal should be forced to "commit itself firmly to specific quantified financial objectives for the next five years".

The findings will add weight to the Government's plans to sell off the industry if it returns to power in the next election.

The MMC added: "All investment projects and the investment programme as a whole should be related to these targets."

It singled out for specific criticism British Coal's decision to develop the new Asfordby mine. This project had never "been demonstrably viable according to British Coal's investment criteria", the MMC report said.

The report said that the company "should take a more positive view of the opportunities which existed to influence vital aspects of its business future.

"British Coal should update and run its forecasting models more frequently and should incorporate the UK coal market into its world model. It should use its models to consider the effect on the industry of a wider range of possible developments."

More attention should be given to looking at "exchange rate movements, competition from alternative fuels and possible rapid growth in world trade in coal", the report said.

The findings, however, concluded that the company was "not operating against the public interest" and commended its efforts to introduce flexible working hours.

Figure 13.8 Competition law in practice

the Secretary of State for Trade and Industry. In some cases mergers are prohibited, for example the Kingfisher group (owners of Woolworth, Comet and B&Q) were prevented from taking over Dixons in 1990.

2. Preventing 'unfair practices' such as price-fixing between firms, which restrict competition (see Figure 13.8).

3. Regulating privatised firms through regulatory agencies such as *Oftel* and *Ofgas*, which supervise the telecommunications and gas industries. For example British Telecom has been made to keep its price rises to prescribed limits.

4. Through European Community law, which regulates competition between EC countries. One example is the directive to car companies to charge not more than 12% difference in the pre-tax price of cars in different countries. The EC can also investigate large-scale mergers of firms in two or more EC countries and disallow Government subsidies to firms such as some of those given by the British Government when selling the Rover Group to British Aerospace.

Consumer Organisations

As well as Government agencies and local council departments there are many private or semi-private organisations which exist to protect consumers and represent their interests. Some of these are fully independent, whereas others are partly or wholly funded by the Government or

PUBLIC INTEREST

Water p494

Whether a meter might save you money.
And why our water is below scratch

Consumer safety p540

Tightening up the law on unsafe products
– we campaign for changes

ABOUT THE HOUSE

Telephones p498

Best Buy home phones

Typing at home p524

Electronic typewriters, word processors
and printers

Filter coffee makers p532

Several recommended from our tests

LEISURE

Zoom lenses p503

On test: wide-angle-to-semi-telephoto
camera lenses

**House swapping
for holidays** p511

California to Clapham – and very cheerful

Stereo systems p534

Sets worth buying for £300 or less, with
or without CD

MONEY

**Where to keep
your savings** p506

Best Buy building society accounts, and
other rewarding homes for your money

Money facts p510

Facts to help borrowers and investors

A typical issue of *Which?*

CONTENTS

Inside Story p491

Credit cards; phone calls; safety
warnings; car imports; the NHS; and a
new instant picture camera

Annual Report p537

CA's successes and achievements: April
1985 to March 1986

Figure 13.9 A typical issue of *Which?*

by the industry concerned. Some of the major groups are as follows.

1. Citizens Advice Bureau (CAB)

The CAB is an independent organisation which receives some grants from the Government, but relies upon unpaid volunteers for much of its work. It has offices in most towns which help with many types of consumer problems.

2. Consumers Association

The Consumers Association campaigns for consumers. It is most famous for its *Which?* magazine, which tests and surveys goods and services. The contents of a typical issue are shown in Figure 13.9.

3. Nationalised Industry Consumer Councils

Each nationalised industry has a Users' Council which represents the interests of consumers. For example the Electricity Consumers' Council has investigated issues such as prices, methods of bill-paying and procedures for disconnecting non-paying customers.

4. British Standards Institution (BSI)

The British Standards Institution sets standards for a massive range of goods and services. It is best known for its 'Kitemark' and other safety markings, which show that a good is claimed to conform to British Standards. Figure 13.11 shows how British Standards apply to the construction industry. The BSI has also been involved in setting European Community standards which are to apply under the Single European Act.

5. National Consumer Council

The National Consumer Council is appointed by the Government to campaign on behalf of consumers. It regularly publishes reports on matters of consumer interest such as housing problems, hospital waiting lists and pension arrangements.

6. The Advertising Standards Authority (ASA)

The Advertising Standards Authority (ASA) is an independent body financed by the advertising industry. It is responsible for supervising almost all advertising in the

Transport Users Consultative Committee

Complaints
or
comments
about
rail travel

Waiting Ro...

Class Ticket type
STD RETURN

From MEMPHIS CENT
To LONDON BR
↦ British Rail

Adult
ONE
Number
41651

Date
17 FEB 00

Valid
TICKET MONTH

Route

What to do....

Passenger representation.....

Locally:

Your local TUCC is keeping watch on:

Punctuality

Timetable changes

Overcrowding

Cleanliness

Quality and design of coaches

Ticketing – purchase and inspection

Station information and facilities

Nationally:

The London-based **Central Transport Consultative Committee** co-ordinates the work of the regional TUCCs and deals with issues affecting rail users nationally. *It liaises with British Rail headquarters and with Government.* Its members include the Chairmen of the TUCCs.

Consumer protection.....

Transport Users Consultative Committees – INDEPENDENT RAIL USERS WATCHDOGS

There are *8 TUCCs* set up by Parliament to protect rail users' interests in *England, Scotland and Wales.*

They take up complaints when further help is needed.

They meet regularly with British Rail to discuss policy and service issues affecting rail users in their areas. *They put over the passenger's viewpoint.*

They have the power to recommend changes in BR practice both locally and, through the Central Committee, on a national scale.

TUCCs have a special responsibility to consider passengers' objections to any plans by BR to close a station or line. They have to report to the Government on any hardship that closure could cause and may suggest ways of alleviating this.

TUCC members represent a wide cross-section of rail users – including commuters, business travellers, pensioners and disabled people.

Figure 13.10 A local Nationalised Industry Consumer Council

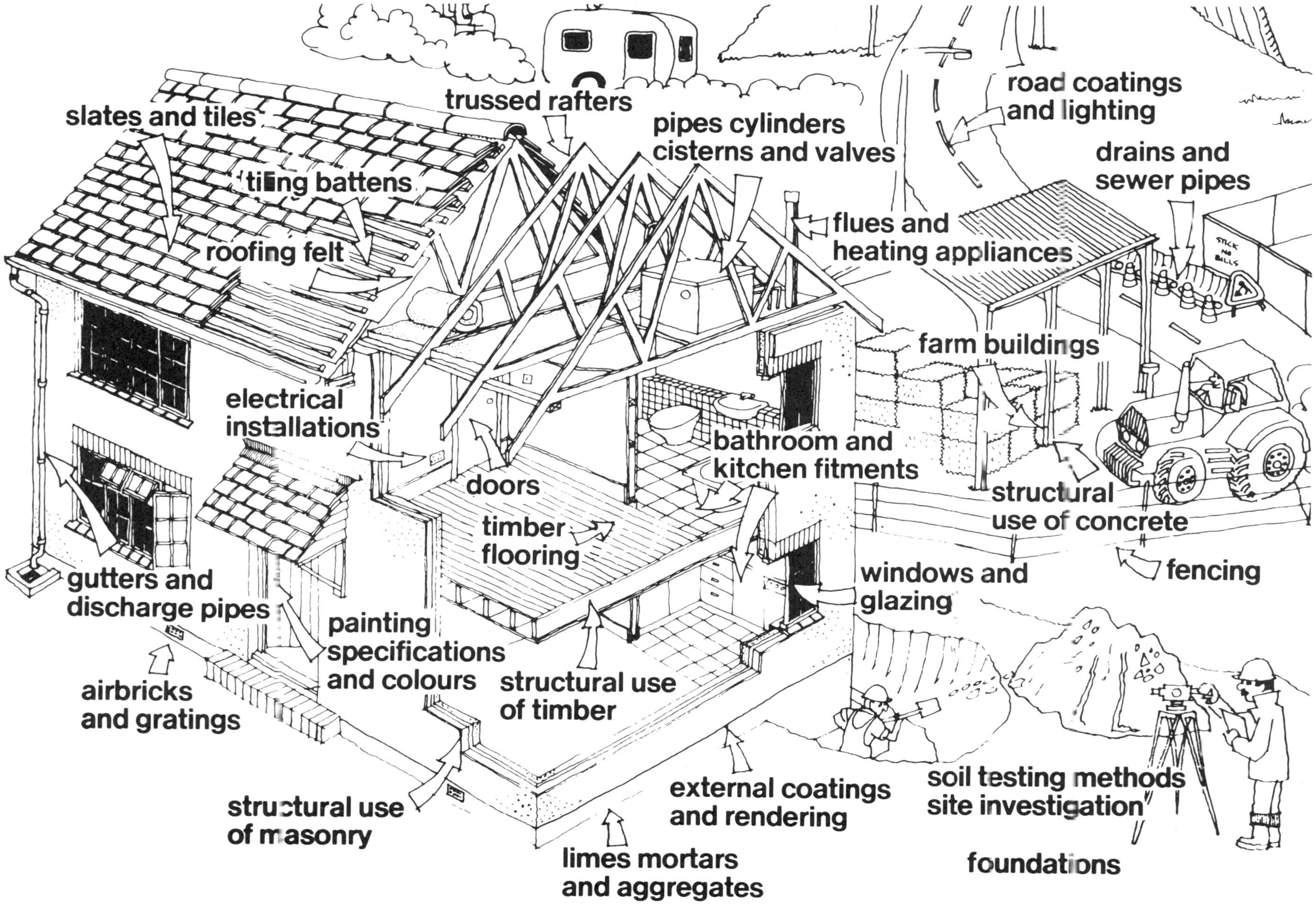

Figure 13.11 British Standards in construction

slates and tiles

tiling battens

roofing felt

trussed rafters

pipes cylinders cisterns and valves

road coatings and lighting

drains and sewer pipes

flues and heating appliances

farm buildings

structural use of concrete

fencing

windows and glazing

bathroom and kitchen fitments

electrical installations

gutters and discharge pipes

airbricks and gratings

doors

timber flooring

painting specifications and colours

structural use of timber

structural use of masonry

external coatings and rendering

limes mortars and aggregates

soil testing methods site investigation

foundations

Section C.I Advertisements containing health claims

CURE

51 No advertisement should employ words, phrases or illustrations which claim or imply the cure of any ailment, illness or disease, as distinct from the relief of its symptoms.

APPEALS TO FEAR, AND EXPLOITATION OF CREDULITY

5.4 No advertisement should cause those who see it unwarranted anxiety lest they are suffering (or may, without responding to the advertiser's offer, suffer) from any disease or condition of ill health, or suggest that consumption or use of the advertised product is necessary for the maintenance of physical or mental capacities, whether by people in general or by any particular group.

Section C.IV Slimming

WEIGHT LOSS

21 The only way for a person in otherwise normal health to lose weight, other than temporarily, is by taking in less energy (calories) than the body is using, i.e. burning up the excess fat the body has stored. A diet is the main self-treatment for achieving a reduction in this excess fat. Diet plans, and aids to dieting of the kinds dealt with below, are therefore the only products which may be offered in advertisements as capable of effecting any loss in weight. Claims that weight loss or slimming can be achieved wholly by other means are not acceptable in advertisements addressed to the general public.

Section C.VI Mail order and direct response advertising

FULFILMENT OF THE ORDER

101 All mail order advertisements should indicate the period within which the advertiser undertakes to fulfil orders, or, when appropriate, provide services. Except in the circumstances noted below, or any others in which CAP is satisfied that it would be unreasonable, the period should not be greater than 28 days from receipt of order.

Section C.VII Advertising of financial services and products

12 All advertisements within the scope of this section should be prepared with care and with the conscious aim of ensuring that members of the public fully grasp the nature of any commitment into which they may enter as a result of responding to an advertisement. Advertisers should take into account that the complexities of finance may well be beyond many of those to whom the opportunity they offer will appeal and that therefore they bear a direct responsibility to ensure that in no sense do their advertisements take advantage of inexperience or credulity.

Section C.VIII Advertisements offering employment and business opportunities

51 Advertisements for SCHEMES IN WHICH A PERSON IS INVITED TO MAKE ARTICLES AT HOME should

– contain an adequate description of the work to be done;

– make clear whether the home-worker is to be employed by the advertiser, or will be self-employed; and

– whenever possible, indicate what level of earnings may realistically be expected. If, as when a scheme is in its infancy, no reliable forecast of earnings can be made, no claim as to earnings attainable should be attempted.

Section C.X Children

GENERAL

11 Direct appeals or exhortations to buy should not be made to children unless the product advertised is one likely to be of interest to them and one which they could reasonably be expected to afford for themselves.

13 No advertisement should cause children to believe that they will be inferior to other children, or unpopular with them, if they do not buy a particular product, or have it bought for them.

Section C.XII Advertisements for Alcoholic Drinks

RULES

51 Advertisements should be SOCIALLY RESPONSIBLE and should not encourage excessive drinking. In particular, they should not exploit the young, the immature, or those with mental or social incapacities.

5.21 Advertisements should not be directed at PEOPLE UNDER EIGHTEEN whether by selection of the medium or context in which they appear, or by reason of their content or style of presentation.

5.2.4 PEOPLE SHOWN DRINKING in advertisements should always clearly be adults; and to ensure that this is the impression created, advertisers should not engage as models people under twenty-five, or people who look as though they may be under twenty-five, if these people are to be shown in any advertisement either drinking or about to drink.

5.7 Advertisements should not depict *activities or locations* in connection with which the consumption of any drink whatever would be unsafe or unwise. Particular care requires to be taken with advertisements which depict powered vehicles of any kind and especially motor cars.

Appendix 1. Advertising of cigarettes, of the components of manufactured cigarettes and of hand-rolling tobacco

11 (part) The Cigarette Code is the outcome of discussions between the Department of Health and Social Security (on behalf of the UK Health Departments), the manufacturers and importers of cigarettes (as represented by the Tobacco Advisory Council and the Imported Tobacco Products Advisory Council) and the Advertising Standards Authority.

1.9 The essence of the Code is that advertisements should not seek to encourage people, particularly the young, to start smoking or, if they are already, smokers, to increase their level of smoking, or to smoke to excess, and should not exploit those who are especially vulnerable, in particular young people and those who suffer from any physical, mental or social handicap.

THE ESSENCE OF THE CODE
The Code is applied in the spirit as well as in the letter.

Figure 13.12 Extracts from the *British Code of Advertising Practice*

UK (except for television and radio).

The ASA's slogan is that all advertising must be 'legal, decent, honest and truthful'. Its *British Code of Advertising Practice* sets rules for all advertisers to follow (see Figure 13.12).

The ASA monitors advertisements and sales promotions, and receives around 10 000 public complaints every year. If an advertisement or sales promotion breaks its rules, the ASA will ask the advertiser to change or discontinue it.

7. The Independent Television Commission (ITC)

The ITC is responsible for controlling television advertising. All TV adverts must be approved before they can be broadcast. About a third are rejected or changed. Radio advertising is now controlled by the Radio Authority.

The conditions for television and radio advertising are very similar to those set by the Advertising Standards Authority (see above) but there are some extra rules. Some products, such as cigarettes, cannot be advertised and some can only be advertised late at night.

Pressure Groups

Pressure groups are organisations which seek to influence the decisions of business and Government. Many are large formal organisations such as the Consumers Association or Greenpeace. However, a group of local residents campaigning about noise or nuisance from a factory is also a pressure group.

Pressure groups can have a large influence upon the activities of firms. In recent years, for example, environmental pressure groups have caused companies to change their policies upon matters such as the use of CFCs in aerosols, supplying unleaded petrol and controlling exhaust fumes from cars.

Business and Change

Businesses have to cope with constant change in society and the economy. These changes are illustrated throughout this book, but important recent changes include:

1. *Economic*, for example increased levels of unemployment and inflation affecting the demand for products and the cost of inputs. British firms have also faced increasing competition from abroad in both the UK and export markets. This trend is likely to continue in the future because of factors such as the Single European Market and the emergence of the newly industrialised countries such as Singapore, Korea and Taiwan.

    Economic changes also create opportunities. For example rising incomes and more leisure time in recent years have led to increases in demand for many services such as sporting facilities and travel.
2. *Demographic changes* such as the growth in the number of over-65s have created new markets for products such

Figure 13.13 Greenpeace – a pressure group

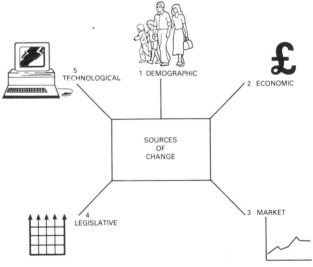

Figure 13.14 Sources of business change

as private nursing homes and sheltered accommodation. The fall in the number of teenagers during the 1990s will make it difficult for employers such as hospitals and building firms to recruit new workers, and affect the sales of products bought by teenagers.

Today

NEWSPAPER OF THE YEAR

WEDNESDAY, NOVEMBER 29 1989

SAFEWAY BAN ON CRUELTY

by **CATHY GUNN**
and **SIMON TRUMP**

GREEN supermarket Safeway has become the first major grocery chain to ban products tested on animals.

Its stand follows a TODAY exposure of the cruel experiments.

The company, which has 275 stores and a turnover of £3 billion, has targetted suppliers of everything except food.

Firms making products like cosmetics, detergents and household cleaners must give a written guarantee that they do not test on animals.

If they fail to do so by Christmas they will be black-listed.

Beauty

The move brought praise from animal rights campaigners for both Safeway and TODAY.

Safeway's environment director Tony Coombes said: "As a company we do not test any of our beauty products and non food items on animals. Testing on animals is both unnecessary and cruel."

He said the company already seeks and checks verbal assurances from suppliers. Now it wants cast-iron guarantees.

Figure 13.15 Example of social pressure on a business

3. *Legislation* may force a business to make changes such as avoiding discrimination against women or changing products to meet new safety standards. Government legislation on pollution and other environmental issues will force firms to change their products and production methods in the next few years. For example waste disposal is likely to be more restricted and cars will have to be made with reduced emission levels.

4. *Social changes and changing tastes* mean that the firms must always be prepared to adapt their goods and services. For example food manufacturers now have to make 'additive-free' and 'environmentally friendly' products to keep their customers. Factors such as more women working affect a firm's attitude to its workers, for example through increasing opportunities for part-time work.

5. *New technology* has created products which were unknown only a few years ago, and opportunities for service industries such as video-rental and computer programming. It has also led to rapid changes in production methods, which may change the way in which people work or remove the need for their skills. For example traditional printing skills have been made outdated by computerised printers.

Worked Examples

Short-answer question

13.1 List two groups to whom a firm has some responsibility.

(AEB)

Answer For example owners/shareholders, workers, customers, suppliers, Government bodies, general public.

Data-response questions

13.2 In February 1986 the Greater London Council introduced a policy to control the movement of heavy lorries in the Greater London area.

Greater London Council scheme

(i) Lorries over $16\frac{1}{2}$ tonnes banned from 9.00 p.m. to 7.00 a.m. every weekday.
(ii) The ban operates all day at weekends.
(iii) Companies wishing to use heavy lorries during banned hours are required to fit 'hush kits'. Heavy lorries without such kits require a permit to enter the area.

(a) What reasons might the GLC have had for introducing these regulations? *(6 marks)*
(b) Briefly state the arguments which firms might make publicly against the introduction of these regulations. *(12 marks)*
(c) The 'hush kits' have been readily available for some time. Why have very few firms fitted them to their lorries? *(2 marks)*

Answer **(a)** For example reduced noise nuisance for residents, save wear on roads, fewer accidents, reduced congestion, less damage to buildings.

(b) For example higher transport costs such as fuel and wages, leading to higher prices of goods, slower deliveries, falling profits, loss of lorry drivers' jobs, may be switched to more lorries of less than $16\frac{1}{2}$ tonnes therefore more rather than less noise, lorry-owners already pay taxes for use of roads so ban is unfair.

(c) For example no need to bother, added expense, noise cost is external to firm so not prepared to pay for it.

Essay questions

13.3 There are a number of groups and parties with an interest in the activities of a business. What are these groups, what are their objectives and how might a business respond to them?

(AEB)

Answer **(i)** List the groups who might have an interest in the activities of a business, together with some explanation of their objectives, that is what they expect from the business, for example:

- owners (profits, security of investment);
- workers (pay, good working conditions, job satisfaction, safe workplace);
- customers (good-quality safe products, service);
- suppliers (continuity of business, regular payments);
- lenders (return on loans, adequate liquidity);
- local community (safe clean production, employment);
- Government (taxes, compliance with legal requirements);
- competitors (fair and ethical competition).

(ii) Explain that there may be conflict between the objectives of the business's owners and other groups. Illustrate with examples, such as higher wages for workers may reduce profits, legal requirements such as consumer and environmental laws may increase costs.

(iii) Explain that the owners' objectives may be reconciled with those of other groups, for example good working conditions may motivate workers to increase productivity, high-quality products may be more profitable.

(iv) Outline the ways in which a business may resolve conflict and co-operate with interested parties, such as negotiation, outright conflict, meetings, public relations, support for community projects, political lobbying, voluntary codes of practice, for example on quality of goods and services.

13.4 Change is a critical element in an organisation's ability to survive and grow. Why, then, is change often resisted and how might the process of change be eased?

(AEB)

Answer **(i)** Explain some of the basic sources of change, such as demography, economic and social changes, new technology, legislation.

(ii) Explain the basic nature of change, which is predictable only in vague outline and not in detail. It may be unexpected and result in very rapid changes. Relate this to the first part of the question by explaining that if the organisation fails to recognise change and adapt its policies it will be unsuccessful and may go out of business. Give examples of organisations which have failed to cope with change, such as UK car and motorcycle manufacturers.

(iii) Analyse the second statement, explaining that people may resent and resist change for various reasons, such as apathy, fear of losing jobs, skills or status, inconvenience, memory of past disruptions, unwillingness to retrain, laziness, uncertainty, fear of making mistakes in unfamiliar situations.

(iv) Outline the ways in which an organisation might attempt to make the process of change easier and less disruptive to employees and production, for example consultation and negotiation, retraining, explanation of policies designed to cope with change, working parties, avoidance of pay cuts, demotions or increased workloads, incentive schemes for new working arrangements.

13.5 Discuss how economic and other constraints might influence the exploration and development policy of an oil company.

(UCLES)

Answer **(i)** Outline the basic economic factor affecting an oil company's exploration and development decision, that is the return should justify the cost of investment. Explain briefly that quantitative investment appraisal methods such as discounted cash flow may be used to make this decision.

(ii) Explain the factors which affect the return on investment, such as interest rates, availability of capital, opportunity cost as measured by return on alternative investments, discount factors used, present and expected future price of oil, risk of failure, political events such as Middle East wars, Government policy, for example of self-sufficiency in oil, taxes, state of competition in the market, owners' confidence in the future, prices of alternative energy sources.

(iii) Explain 'non-financial' constraints, such as environmental pressure, Government policy, political instability in some oil-producing areas. These may prevent or act as a deterrent to otherwise potentially profitable investment.

Self-test Questions

Short-answer questions

13.6 Name two pressure groups whose activities may affect business decision making.

(AEB)

13.7 Apart from fiscal and monetary policies the Government also attempts to influence the behaviour of the private sector by direct controls. Give **three** different examples of measures employed by Governments in the past fifteen years.

(AEB)

Essay questions

13.8 Outline the main aspects of consumer protection provided by the law and discuss the consequences of such protection for the consumer.

(AEB)

13.9 (a) 'British industry has failed to react to change.' What have been the consequences of this? *(10 marks)*
(b) Discuss ways in which creativity might be encouraged and effectively harnessed in business. *(15 marks)*

(UCLES)

13.10 A company's production processes are regarded by a pressure group as polluting the environment. Discuss how the company might be affected by the actions of the pressure group in this situation.

(AEB)

COURSEWORK 14

Why Do Coursework?

Examination coursework is part of some A-Level Business Studies syllabuses for several reasons:

- it allows you to investigate a topic at length;
- the pressure of the exam room is removed;
- it encourages you to work with others;
- approached properly, it can be great fun and motivate you to produce good work;
- it develops skills such as interpretation of data which are tested in written examination papers.

Coursework Requirements

A-Level syllabuses which include coursework describe the way it must be undertaken and marked. Each syllabus has its own requirements about matters such as subject content, number and length of assignments.

As with written examinations, A-Level coursework assignments are marked according to the coursework mark schemes given in the syllabus. To get good marks, your assignment must show that you can use the skills specified in the scheme for your syllabus.

This point can be illustrated by looking at the mark scheme for the ULSEB A-Level Business Studies syllabus (in Figure 14.1). This shows how the marks for coursework are awarded.

Each syllabus has a different mark scheme, but the skills that examiners are looking for are similar in all A-Level Business Studies syllabuses. You will need to look at the scheme for your particular syllabus. It may be difficult to follow, so you might have to ask your teacher to explain some points.

Getting Ideas for Coursework

Your coursework assignments may be set by the Examining Group or your teacher. However, if you do have some choice, there are several ways of generating ideas for coursework.

Notes and books

Go through your notes and any books you have used or can find in the library. Make a list of any topics that you have found interesting, and try to form at least one question or hypothesis for each one.

Do not limit yourself to work that you have done in Business Studies. You may have been interested in topics in another subject which could be investigated from a business point of view.

Interests and hobbies

Most people have a particular interest in a sport or hobby.

	maximum marks
1. Aims and Purpose of the project.	10
2. Application of terminology, conventions, principles, facts and techniques of presentation appropriate to the project chosen.	20
3. Clarity of presentation, planning and logical sequence.	20
4. Analysis of the information being presented.	20
5. Content and comment.	15
6. Judgement and conlusions.	15
Total	100

Assessment Criteria

1. *Aims and Purpose of the Project*
   (maximum of 10 marks)
   - 1–3 Has little or no understanding of the aims and purpose.
   - 4–6 Has some understanding of the aims and purpose of the project.
   - 7–10 Has clear understanding of the aims and purpose of the project within the assessment framework for this area.

2. *Application of terminology, conventions, principles, facts and techniques of presentation appropriate to the project chosen.*
   (maximum of 20 marks)
   - 1–5 Has made little use of terminology, facts, techniques, data and conventions.
   - 6–10 Has made limited use of terminology, facts, techniques, data and conventions.
   - 11–15 Has made adequate use of terminology, facts, techniques, data and conventions where appropriate.
   - 16–20 Has made full use of terminology, facts, techniques, data and conventions where appropriate.

3. *Clarity of Presentation, Planning and Logical Sequence*
   (maximum of 20 marks)
   - 1–5 Presentation is untidy. Illustrative material is absent or inappropriate. Sources of information are not given.
   - 6–10 The account is weak, lacking in clarity and rambling. Inadequate use of illustrative material. Sources of information are incomplete or absent.
   - 11–15 The account is reasonably well presented. However, illustrative material is not used to full effect. Sources of information are incompletely acknowledged.
   - 16–20 Has set out text clearly and concisely. Graphs, diagrams and other illustrations used to maximum effect and in appropriate manner. Sources of information clearly indicated.

Analysis of the Information being Presented
(maximum of 20 marks)
- 1–5 Has made little attempt to analysis and shows little appreciation of the limitations of the information.
- 6–10 Has made limited use of information, not always in an appropriate manner. The limitations are not generally realised and, little or no use is made of statistical method.
- 11–15 Has made adequate use of the information but limitations are not always appreciated.
- 16–20 Has made full use of the information in a suitable way. Limitations of the information are clearly identified, with full use of statistical techniques where appropriate to assist analysis.

Content and Comment (maximum of 15 marks)
- 1–5 Has provided limited understanding of the objectives of the project and has failed to give a balanced account. Little evidence of background reading or use of relevant syllabus topics.
- 6–10 Has provided some understanding of the objectives of the project but the project lacks balance. There is some evidence of background reading and use of related topics.
- 11–15 Has provided clear understanding of the objectives of the project and gives a balanced account of the issue(s) involved. Has provided evidence of substantial background reading and use of related topics.

Judgement and Conclusions (maximum of 15 marks)
- 1–5 Limited judgements and deductions and assessment of the information collected is weak.
- 6–10 Fair, rational deductions regarding the topic chosen and the issues raised.
- 11–15 Has made logical deductions based on the information and data considered. Has given comprehensive judgements related to the case presented and issues raised.

Figure 14.1 ULSEB coursework mark scheme

In pursuing this interest they will usually buy goods and services from firms or other organisations. You could study a firm or industry which is involved with your interest, as long as you remember that you are undertaking a Business Studies assignment. For example, you may be fascinated by different computer operating systems, but the examiner will only be interested in the details of MS/DOS and CPM if there is some commercial relevance to the difference.

Newspapers and magazines

You may be able to find ideas from newspapers and magazines. If you find an article that interests you, you could try to find out more about the particular issue. If it is controversial there will be plenty of people and organisations with something to say about it. Local newspapers are usually a good source.

Mini-enterprises

Many students are involved in running 'mini-companies', for example under the Young Enterprise scheme. This type of activity could be used as the basis for an assignment if it is carefully planned. You could focus upon a particular theme such as:

- how the product was chosen;
- the methods of market research;
- costing and pricing;
- the organisation of production.

Work experience

You may have a part-time job or the chance of a placement on a work experience scheme. You could use this opportunity to investigate an issue at your place of work such as health and safety or the marketing of the firm's products.

Choosing a Title

Your assignment should be regarded as an *investigation* into a business problem or issue. As can be seen from the example given above, a large proportion of the marks awarded are for stating the aim of the assignment, collecting relevant data and drawing conclusions which are directly related to the aim of the information. If your assignment does not have a specific aim, you will lose a high proportion of the marks before you even start.

The best way of avoiding this problem is to phrase your assignment aim as either a *question* or a *hypothesis*.

An example of a *question* that might be investigated is:

What is the fastest-growing industry in this area?

If your title is a question, you will need to answer it. This example would involve looking at what is meant by 'fastest-growing' – for example does it mean growth of output, employment, profit, etc.? You would then need to look for information to answer the question.

A *hypothesis* is a statement about an issue which can be tested by collecting and using information. An example of a hypothesis which might be investigated is:

Private contractors are more efficient than local authorities at providing refuse collection services

If you decided to test this hypothesis you would need to consider what is meant by 'efficient' – does it mean cheap, best quality of service, use of labour, etc.? You could obtain information and opinions from a variety of sources such as trade unions, firms, local councillors and the public.

Examples of possible titles are given in Figure 14.2.

UCLES Modular A/AS

1. How can AC Bank improve their position in the ever-increasing market of financial services?

2. How should the education and training department of A.N. Other re-organise its activities in order to meet the demands of a newly discovered market?

3. Should XYZ publishing purchase ABC magazine?

4. What are the main causes of differences arising between accounts in its subsidiary and payments made by the Parent Company? What can be done to reduce the number of items in dispute?

5. How can Z Bank maximise products and services sold to present personal sector customers?

6. How can the processing of everyday information at ABC Town Council be improved?

7. How effective has been the present Equal Opportunities policy of XYZ Hospital and how might it be improved?

8. How can the customer awareness of the FGH store be improved?

ULSEB 'A'

The impact and "cost" implications of pollution in the countryside.
U.K. Industrial Disputes – a statistical assessment and comparison.
The case for Britain to join the European Monetary System.

An assessment of the impact of recent changes in the legislative framework surrounding the financial service sector of the U.K. economy.

Figure 14.2 Examples of coursework titles

What Information is Needed?

In deciding upon the data that you wish to collect, the most crucial thing to remember is that it should be *relevant* to your title. The most common problem of examination coursework in Business Studies is that too many assignments are simply 'scrapbooks' of mostly irrelevant information.

For example it is fairly easy to collect lots of material about a large company such as Tesco or ICI. Many students simply rewrite or 'cut and paste' the glossy brochures sent out by these companies, without explaining why they are including them or why they are relevant to their assignment.

This type of assignment gains very low marks. Unless a piece of information is directly relevant to the aim of the assignment, it should not be included. One way of ensuring that data is relevant is always to make a point of explaining why it is included, for example:

"The tables show that labour turnover and absenteeism at Garrett's Ltd fell sharply over the last few months. This may be a sign that the management's efforts to improve morale were successful."

Before deciding to look for or include any piece of information in your assignment, ask yourself questions such as:

- Why is this relevant to my assignment?
- What does it prove?
- Is there any connection between this piece of data and other information I have collected?
- Am I including it because it looks pretty or helps to make the assignment look bigger?

Irrelevant information is regarded by examiners as 'padding' and does not gain marks. If you answer the questions honestly you will produce a better assignment and save yourself a lot of wasted time. You will have to learn to be ruthless in discarding data, however interesting or pretty it may look, which does not further the aim of your assignment.

One way of sorting out what information is needed is to ask questions about the subject matter of the assignment. You can then decide which questions need to be answered, and work out how to go about it.

Sources of Information

There are several different methods of collecting information. You should not attempt to use them all – be selective and choose the most appropriate.

Questionnaires

These should only be used where strictly necessary, as they are time-consuming and the answers given are often inaccurate (for example Government surveys show that people admit to smoking only half of the amount of tobacco that they actually buy).

If questionnaires are used:

- ensure that all of the questions provide necessary information;
- stick to a small number of questions;
- avoid too personal questions, such as asking strangers their age or income;
- be polite;
- do not pester people who are obviously too busy to answer your questions;
- do not try to 'lead' people, such as saying 'the wages for nurses are too low, aren't they?';
- choose a suitable 'sample', for example if enquiring about tastes in food include people of different ages and sex;
- be wary of 'postal' surveys or giving people questionnaires to take away for completion – you may get a lot of non-replies.

Interviews

Personal interviews allow more detailed answers than questionnaires. They are particularly useful for:

- interviewing somebody with specialist knowledge and experience;
- examining opinions or attitudes in more detail;
- being flexible about the questions which are asked;
- providing a more relaxed atmosphere – people are likely to tell you more.

If you interview people, you will be taking up their time (and your own) so make sure that the interview is worthwhile. To do this you should:

- Decide upon the type of person or persons that you need to interview.
- If you need to talk to people whom you do not know, write or phone politely. Explain what you are doing, why you wish to interview them and how long the interview is likely to take.
- Plan the interview carefully, writing down the questions you wish to ask (be prepared to change these if necessary).
- Turn up on time, but do not be surprised if your interviewee keeps you waiting.
- Thank your interviewee for their help. Follow this up with a written thank-you later.
- Write up your interview notes as soon as possible.
- Decide which parts of the interview are relevant.
- If you use a direct quote make sure that it is accurate and written in speech marks.

Visits to firms

Visits to firms and other organisations have the same benefits as personal interviews, and similar rules apply. If you are allowed to roam about the building, be careful. Do not get in the way of people or machinery, and do not disturb people while they are in the middle of lifting boxes or counting figures.

Letters

It is sometimes possible to obtain information by writing to people or firms. Do not be disappointed, however, if you receive no reply or a letter which simply includes glossy brochures which are irrelevant.

Letters should be short, simple and to the point, typed or neatly written on blank white A4 paper and set out in the correct business manner. You should also ask your teacher or lecturer to check the letter before you send it.

Tests and experiments

Depending upon your assignment, tests or experiments may be useful. For example if you are studying market research or running a mini-company, you might carry out 'blind-tastings' to find out if people can distinguish between 'own-brand' and 'brand-name' products.

Observation

Observation means looking and listening very carefully, such as watching people at work, a manufacturing process or shoppers in a supermarket. You might also be a 'participant observer', for example using a work experience placement to see what it is like to work in a particular firm.

If you intend to use observation as a research method, think about:

- what you are trying to observe;
- whether people will know that you are watching them (people may be hostile if they think you are 'spying' on them);
- whether you will take notes as you go along.

Newspapers and magazines

Newspapers and magazines can be very useful. Some such as the *Times* and the *Economist* have indexes of articles, which should be available together with back numbers in a good Reference Library. If you are investigating a particular industry there may be a 'trade journal' which will be helpful. A local newspaper may allow you to consult its cuttings files.

Articles can also be used as 'leads'. The names of people or organisations mentioned should be circled and considered as sources of information.

Television and radio

If your assignment concerns an issue which is currently in the news, you may be able to use TV or radio programmes to obtain information. This will mean paying attention to programmes such as 'Panorama' and 'Newsnight' rather than 'Neighbours' or Radio One. It is advisable to check through the *Radio Times* and *TV Times* for details.

If possible, record a programme so that you can check on details or listen to arguments at your own pace. Your school or college may also have recordings which are relevant to your topic.

Books

Although one of the aims of Business Studies coursework is to get away from textbook theories, books can be useful for providing background information, explaining terms and providing facts and figures.

To help find relevant books:

- Look in your own textbooks.
- Ask your teacher.
- Try the school or college library.
- Go to the Central Reference Library for your area.
- Find out the Dewey Decimal number for the subject area. The librarian will look this up for you if you ask nicely. You can also check the shelves and catalogue for suitable books.

Reference sources

Reference and statistical books are published by the Government and other organisations. If you are studying an industry you should be able to find information on matters such as employment, sales, foreign trade and prices.

If you use reference sources, be careful to explain why they are important. You may find them difficult to interpret, so be prepared to ask for help. Remember also that the information may be 'biased' or unreliable.

People

People you know can be the most useful resource of all. Be ready to consult your teacher and anybody else. Even your ignorant out-of-touch parents may know more than you think, or know where to look for information.

Writing the Assignment

If you have planned and researched your assignment thoroughly, the actual writing should be easy. The best assignments will be a good interesting read. This will happen if you:

- list the contents of your assignment, for example Introduction, Methods of research, Section titles, Conclusion, Acknowledgements;
- start by explaining the aim of the assignment, that is what you wanted to find out;
- explain how you decided upon your research methods;
- use original material and explain why it is important;
- label all diagrams and figures and say why they are included;
- use different ways of showing information, such as graphs, pie-charts, pictures, maps, etc.
- ruthlessly discard irrelevant data – your assignment should not be a 'scrapbook';
- point out possible 'bias' or inaccuracy in your information, for example by pointing out data which may be based upon opinion rather than fact;
- present your assignment logically and attractively with clear sections and headings;
- put quoted material in inverted commas and write down the source (copying material without acknowledgement could be classed as 'cheating');
- give the names of people who have helped (you will probably be expected to do this on an official form);
- use business terms and ideas where relevant;
- give conclusions and recommendations justified by the data you have collected;
- stick to any format and number of words specified in the syllabus

INDEX

absenteeism 157
absorption pricing 124–5
acid test ratio 70
accounting 63
ACORN system 108, 119–20, 130
advertising 127–9, 137, 142
    agents 132
    control of 204, 207–8
Advertising Standards Authority (ASA)
    204, 207–8
Advisory, Arbitration and Conciliation
    Service (ACAS) 173–5
Ansoff matrix 121
application forms 164
appraisal see performance appraisal
aptitude tests 165
arbitration 174–6
Articles of Association 19, 23
assembly line 84–5
assets 66
Assisted Areas 196, 198
authority 146–7, 150–2, 155
average rate of return (ARR) 46–7

balance of payments 185–90
balance of trade 188
balance sheet 61, 65–6, 71
bar charts 31–2
barter 180
batch production 84
'big bang' 56
bonuses 16, 51
borrowing 54–5, 56–9, 68–9, see also
    gearing
brand names 66, 122, 126
break even analysis 71, 73–5
British Overseas Trade Board (BOTB)
    200
British Standards Institution 206–7
Business Expansion Scheme (BES) 198
business names 16, 22

capital
    employed 5, 65, 70
    fixed 66
    return on capital employed (ROCE)
        70, 119
    working 9, 52, 65, 68–9, 92, 119
capital goods 100
capital taxes 183
'cash cows' 121, 123
cash-flow 68–9, 77
centralisation 85, 151–2
Certificate of Incorporation 19
Certificate of Trading 19, 23
chain of command 150–1
change 208–11
channel of distribution see place under
    marketing mix
choice 178–9
closed shop 173
collective bargaining 174–7
command economy 178–80
Common Market see European
    Community (EC)

communication 10, 90, 152–5
Community Charge (poll tax) 182–3
companies
    registration of 19
    types of 2, 16–27
Companies Acts 15, 17, 19
competition law 203
computers see information technology
    (IT)
conciliation 35, 174
Confederation of British Industry (CBI)
    173
conglomerates 6, 8
consortia 54
Consumer Credit Act 201
consumer goods 100, 111, 113–14, 193
consumer law 201
consumer organisations 203–8
Consumer Protection Act 201
Consumers Association 204
contract of employment 165
contracting out 9, 22
contribution 75–7, 125, 137–8
Co-operative Development Agency
    (CDA) 19
Co-operative Retail Society (CRS) 20–1
Co-operative Wholesale Society (CWS)
    20
Co-operatives 2–3, 19–21, 26
corporation tax 50, 183
cost centre 76
cost of sales 67–8
costs
    average 64–5, 124–5
    direct 63
    fixed 63–4, 124–5
    indirect 63
    semi-variable 64
    total 124–5
    unit see average under costs
    variable 63–4
coursework 212–16
creaming 125
credit factoring see factoring
creditors 66
cross-elasticity see elasticity of demand
curriculum vitae 164

data 28–33, 108, 192
data processing 90
database 90, 108
debentures 54
decentralisation 151–2
decision trees 33–5, 41
decision-making 28
deindustrialisation 182
deintegration 9, 52–3
delegation 146–7, 150, 155
demand 101–3, 105–7
demerger 9–10, 53
denationalisation 22
depreciation 63, 66, 72–3, 77
deregulation 22
design 90–1, 94, 139

desk research 108
Development Areas 93
direct mail 130–2
direct response advertising 130
directors 12, 23, 150
discounted cash-flow 46–7, 60
diseconomies of scale 7
dissatisfiers 160
distributed profits see dividends
divestment 9, 52–3
dividends
    cover 71
    per share 70
    yield 71
division of labour 5, 84–5, 180
durable goods see consumer goods

earliest start time 36–9
earnings per share 70–1
economic growth 184–6
economies, types of 178–80
economies of scale 5–8, 13, 64
EFTPOS 90
elasticity of demand
    cross 107, 113
    income 100–1, 106, 113, 193–4
    price 105–6, 111, 113
electronic mail 130, 154
embargo 187
employee appraisal see performance
    appraisal
employers' associations 173
Employment Protection Act 203
Enterprise Agencies 200
Enterprise Allowance Scheme 200
environment and business 3, 7, 184,
    208–11
Environmental Health Department 201
Equal Pay Act 203
European Community (EC) 105, 187,
    190–1, 203
exchange controls 187
exchange rates 113, 186–93
excise duties 183
exhibitions 130
expectancy theory 160–1
Export Credit Guarantee Scheme
    (ECGD) 190
exports
    assistance for exporters 190, 200
    in balance of payments accounts 200
    difficulties of exporting 138–41, 190
external benefits 181–2
external costs 181–2, 184, 192
external economies of scale 5–7
external finance 25

facsimile transmission (fax) 154
factoring 52, 54–5, 59
Fair Trading Act 201
field research 108
finance for business
    external 54, 61
    internal 52–3, 61
finance houses 54

fixed assets 66
flow production 83–4
Food and Drugs Act 201
franchising 11–12, 134
free market economy *see* market economy
fringe benefits 161
full-cost pricing 124–5
funds-flow statement 66, 76

Gantt, H. 159
gearing 9, 70–1
General Agreement on Tariffs and Trade (GATT) 188
General Reserve 52, 66
goodwill 66, 71
Government
  assistance to business 56, 93–4, 164
  economic policy 182–94
  finance 182–3
  influence on business 2, 11–12, 15–16, 23, 88–9, 103–5, 111–13, 141, 173, 175, 179–80, 182–8, 190, 200–1
  ownership of business 2, 16, 21–7
graphs 30–1
gross profit margin 70
growth of organisations 7–10, 169

Hawthorne experiments 159
Health and Safety at Work Act 201, 203
Herzberg, F. 159–60
hierarchy 10
hierarchy of needs 159
histogram 31, 33
holding company 23
'human relations school' 159–60
hygiene factors 160

income elasticity of demand *see* elasticity of demand
income tax 182
incomes policy 185
incorporation 12, 15
imports, restriction of *see* protectionism
Independent Television Commission (ITC) 208
index numbers 33, 40, 45–6
indirect costs 63
induction of employees 165
industrial action 174
industrial inertia 88
industrial relations 172–7
industrial structure 181–2
inflation 29, 183–6, 193, 208
information 28–33
information technology (IT) 88–92, 95, 209
Inheritance Tax 183
intangible assets 66
integration 8–9
interdependence 180
interest cover 70–1
interest rates 6, 60–1, 70, 76, 103, 106, 113, 184, 186, 190–1
internal data 108
internal organisation of business 146–52
international trade 186–94
interviews
  job 165
  market research 111
investment appraisal 42–7
investor ratios 69–71
invisible trade 187–8
issuing house 59

job description 162–3
job evaluation 168
job production 82
job specification 162–3
joint demand 102
joint stock companies 15
joint ventures 9, 121
'just-in-time' production 92

Labour Relations Agency 174–5
labour turnover 157, 168–9

leasing 54, 60–1
liabilities 66
limited companies *see* joint stock companies
limited liability 12, 15–19
'line and staff' management 154
liquidity 69–71, 77
Loan Guarantee Scheme 200
loans *see* borrowing
location of industry 87–9, 93
lock-out 174
loss-leading 126

McClelland, D. 160
McGregor, D. 160
mail order 130
maintenance factors 160
management, functions of 1, 146–52, 155
management buyouts 9, 26–7
management by objectives 4
manuals 154
market capitalisation 5
market demand 101–3, 111–14, 193–4
market economy 179
market price 104–5
market research 107–11, 113
market share 2, 8, 123
market supply 103–4
marketing 1, 95, 98–142
marketing mix 98, 116–17, 141–2
  place 116, 132–6, 141
  price 116, 124–6, 140–2
  product 116–24, 141
  promotion 116, 126–35, 141
markets
  consumer 99–100
  industrial 99–100
Maslow, A. 159
mass production 83–5, 180
mature markets 123–4, 126
Mayo, E. 159
measured day-work 168
mediation 174–5
memoranda (memos) 154
Memorandum of Association 19, 23, 61
merchant banks 59
mergers 7–10, 23
merit goods 182
merit pay 161
microfilm 154
mixed economy 179–80
monopolies
  control of 203
  natural 21
  statutory 22
Monopolies and Mergers Commission 23, 203
motivating factors 160
motivation of employees 86, 147, 159–61
multinational companies 6–7, 11

National Consumer Council 204
National Insurance 182
nationalisation 21–7, 135, 203–5
nationalised industry consumer councils 204–5
net present value (NPV) 44–5
net worth 65
network analysis 35–9, 41
niche marketing 119
nodes 35–9, 41
non-price competition 126, 137

objectives of business 1–4, 210
observation 111
offer-for-sale 59
Office of Fair Trading (OFT) 201, 203
Official Statistics 108
operational research (OR) 38
opportunity cost 119, 178–9
ordinary shares *see* shares
organisation 146–52
organisation charts 147–50
overdraft 54
overheads 63

overtime pay 160
owner's capital *see* General Reserve

partnerships 16–17, 27
pay 160–1, 168
payback 42–3
payment-by-results (PBR) 160–1
pendulum arbitration 175
perestroika 180
performance appraisal 4, 167
personal selling 132
picketing 174
piece rates 160–1, 168
placing of shares 59
planned economy 179–80
planning 146–7
poll tax *see* Community Charge
population 102–3, 208
preference shares 54, 56
premium pricing 125–6
pressure groups 208, 211
price discrimination 137, 141–2
price elasticity *see* elasticity of demand
price leadership 122
price-taking 126
pricing policies 124–6, 140–2
primary industry 182
private limited company 17, 23, 54
privatisation 2–7
probability 33–5, 41–2
product
  development 122–3
  life-cycle 121–4, 139
  mix 118–19, 121, 194
production 1, 82–95, 114
productivity 24–5
profit
  calculation of 65
  gross 68
  importance of 2
  incentive 2, 77
  maximisation 2, 77
  net 68
  retained 52
profit and loss account 67–8
profit sharing 161, 168
profitability 5, 69–70, 95, 119
progress-chasing 85
project and evaluation review technique (PERT) 35–9
promotion 126–35
protectionism 186–8
psychological tests 165
public corporations 21–2, 23–7
public goods 182
public limited companies (PLCs) 2–3, 7, 18–19, 23, 54, 56, 58–60
public relations (PR) 126, 132, 134–5
purchases 67
purchasing 85

qualitative data 108
quality circles 86
quality control 85–6
quantitative data 108
questionnaires 108, 110, 215
quick ratio *see* acid test ratio
quota sampling 108
quotas, import 187

Race Relations Act 203
random sampling 108
ratio analysis 69–71, 76–7
real income 101–2
real wages 111
recruitment 162–4, 167–9
regional policy 88, 93, 196
Registrar of Companies 19
registration of companies 19
research and development (R&D) 86–7, 90, 140
responsibility of business 12, 209–10
retail price index 29, 45–6, 193
retained profit 52
return on capital employed (ROCE) 70, 119

revenue 65
rights issue 59
robots 90–2

Sale of Goods Act 201
sales 132
sales promotions 128–30
samples 29, 108
satisficing 3
scarcity 178
seasonal demand 103
secondary data 108
secondary industry 182
secondment 166
selection of employees 164–5
service industries 182
Sex Discrimination Acts 203
share prospectus 58
shareholders 12, 18, 150
shares
  buying and selling 56–9
  fully paid-up 15
  new issues 58–9, 61
  nominal value 59
  types of 54–6
shop steward 173
simultaneous activities 35
Single European Market 191, 193, 208
single-union agreements 173
size of business 4–5, 12–13
skimming 121, 125
small firms 7, 13–14, 196
Small Firms Service 196
social benefits 181, 210
social costs 181, 210
sole trader 16

span of control 10, 150–1
specialisation 180, *see also* division of labour
sponsorship 132
'staff' 154
Statement of Source and Application of Funds *see* funds-flow statement
Statutory Declaration 19, 23
stock control 92, 94, 96
Stock Exchange 5, 9, 15, 23, 54, 56–7, 59
Stock Exchange Automated Quotation System (SEAQ) 56–7, 154
stock turnover 69
stocks 52, 94
strikes 174
structure of industry 181–3
subsidies 104
supply 103–5
Supply of Goods and Services Act 201
surveys 108
synergy 9

tables 30
takeovers *see* mergers
tariffs 187, 191–2
taxes 103–4, 111–13, 182–7, 191, 193
Taylor, F. W. 159
telephone marketing 130
teletext 154
Telex 154
tender, for shares 59
tertiary industry 182
test marketing 111
Theory X and Theory Y 160
Third Market 56

time rates 160
time-series graphs 31
trade associations 108
trade journals 108
trade unions 173–5
Trades Descriptions Act 201–2
Trades Union Congress (TUC) 173
Trading Standards Department 201–2
training 165–7, 199
Training and Enterprise Councils (TECs) 199
turnover 4, 67

ultra vires 23
undistributed profit 52
unemployment 183–6, 193–6, 208
Unfair Contract Terms Act 201
Uniform Business Rate 183
unions *see* trade unions
unlimited liability 15–17
Unlisted Securities Market (USM) 56
Unsolicited Goods and Services Act 201

Value Added Tax (VAT) 182
visible trade 187–8
voluntary export restraints (VERs) 187
Vroom, V. 160

wages *see* pay
Weights and Measures Act 201
Which? 204
wholesalers 136
word processing 90
working capital 9, 52, 65, 68–9, 92, 119